P9-DVV-565

The
BUCCANEERS
of AMERICA

S.^r HEN: MORGAN

The
BUCCANEERS
of AMERICA

A true account of the most remarkable assaults
committed of late years upon the coasts of the
West Indies by the Buccaneers of Jamaica and
Tortuga (both English and French)

BY

JOHN ESQUEMELING
One of the Buccaneers who was present at those tragedies

CONTAINING ALSO BASIL RINGROSE'S ACCOUNT OF
THE DANGEROUS VOYAGE AND BOLD ASSAULTS
OF CAPTAIN BARTHOLOMEW SHARP AND OTHERS

With a new Introduction by
PERCY G. ADAMS
Louisiana State University

DOVER PUBLICATIONS, INC.
NEW YORK

Copyright © 1967 by Dover Publications, Inc.
All rights reserved under Pan American and
International Copyright Conventions.

Published in Canada by General Publishing Company, Ltd., 30 Lesmill Road, Don Mills, Toronto,
Ontario.
Published in the United Kingdom by Constable
and Company, Ltd., 10 Orange Street, London WC 2.

This Dover edition, first published in 1967, is an
unabridged and unaltered republication of the work
first published by Swan Sonnenschein & Co. in 1893.
It contains a new introduction by Percy G. Adams.

Library of Congress Catalog Card Number: 66-30381

Manufactured in the United States of America
Dover Publications, Inc.
180 Varick Street
New York, N.Y. 10014

INTRODUCTION TO THE DOVER EDITION.

THE great historians of piracy, such as Philip Gosse, agree that *The Buccaneers of America* is the "chief source of information about the life of the buccaneers. It might well be described as the Handbook of Buccaneering." In fact, only one other among all the many accounts of plunder at sea has been so widely read or so broadly influential, and that is *A General History of the Robberies and Murders of the Most Notorious Pirates*. Said to have been written by Captain Charles Johnson, but almost surely the work of the prolific Daniel Defoe, this volume tells the gruesome but fascinating stories of those pirates, largely of the early eighteenth century, who attacked the ships of all nations promiscuously. *The Buccaneers of America* recounts an earlier story, that of the English, French, Dutch, and Portuguese seamen who in the late seventeenth century plundered Spanish shipping at sea and raided Spanish settlements in the New World.

But in spite of their reputation and their fascinating contents these two volumes tell only part of the intriguing tale of sailing robbers. The ancient Phoenicians, for example, were often not scrupulous about whom they attacked. In 78 B.C., Julius Caesar was captured by pirates in a famous adventure; after paying a ransom and gaining his freedom, he landed at the nearest port, borrowed four war galleys and five hundred soldiers, and returned to capture the pirates, sink their ships, and retrieve the fifty talents he had given for his freedom. When the fall of Rome in the fifth century caused trade to subside for a thousand years, piracy also became less profitable until the Crusades revived both commerce and the sailing robbers who preyed on it. Among the most notorious of these were the Barbary corsairs of the Mediterranean, who became so powerful that several

European nations combined in an unsuccessful attempt to destroy them in 1390. On the other side of Europe the Hanseatic League, begun in 1241 by Hamburg and Lübeck, was somewhat more fortunate in its defense against the bold Vikings of the north, and on the nearby British coast the League of Cinque Ports was organized to suppress Channel piracy in the fourteenth century.

With the discovery of the Western Hemisphere, geographical knowledge was extended, ships were forced to grow larger and sail faster, commerce increased in every part of the world, and piracy prospered even more. Equipped with commissions from the Sultan of Turkey, the notorious red-bearded Moorish brothers Barbarossa captured Papal treasure ships on the Mediterranean, fought off entire navies, and kept Christian nations paying tribute. Their "religious"—but undeclared— war foreshadowed one even more notorious and longer lasting, begun when Roman Catholic Spain tried to force the trading world, especially Protestant England and Holland, to honor its claim to the newly discovered continents, a claim based not just on Columbus's voyage but even more on the Papal decree of 1494 that divided half the earth between the two Iberian neighbors. During the reign of Elizabeth great pirate "combines" grew up in the ports of Britain which sent out commissioned ships to raid Spanish commerce, a successful captain and crew normally receiving one-fifth of the loot, the rest going to merchant financiers ashore, such as Sir John Killigrew, relative of Queen Elizabeth's minister Lord Burleigh. It was a most lucrative business that elicited from the ambassadors of Spanish King Philip angry threats that occasionally forced the Queen to punish certain captains. Among the best-known English sailors of the time tried for piracy and exonerated, usually with properly placed bribes, were William Hawkins and Sir Richard Grenville. After Holland fell to Philip, who was exacting vengeance for what he termed Dutch piracy, only the width of the English Channel kept the power of Spain from overrunning Britain in reprisal for the deeds of its sailors.

It was this sixteenth century which saw the might of Spain spread amazingly through North and South America and over the Pacific. The craftsmanship of its colonists and, especially, the mines it dug with Indian slaves produced a wealth that poured into the coffers of Philip and his merchants at home and then out again to support the great armies and navies he commanded. From Valdivia on the lower Pacific coast of South America to Acapulco in northern Mexico, goods and ores were sailed to Panama, transported across the Isthmus on the backs of heavily guarded Indians, and reloaded aboard ships that hurried off to join others from the Caribbean Islands and Mexico in forming the great flotillas that periodically left for Cadiz surrounded by Spanish warships. On the Pacific side of the Western Hemisphere other treasure-laden vessels made the yearly round trip between the Philippines and Acapulco; normally only one or two in number, they sailed without guard because of the relative security afforded by the distance from European ships and by the size of the Pacific Ocean. These were the rich Manila Galleons, the very mention of which made Protestant palms itch.

And it was this vast trade activity, spread out over so many parts of the world, that aroused the greed of the Dutch and English merchant combines operating with the tacit consent of their rulers. In the 1570s British sea dogs such as Hawkins and Drake made daring raids in the Caribbean, and then in 1580 Drake completed one of the most amazing and successful voyages of harassment ever undertaken by a captain whose country was not at war. He sailed without warning through the Strait of Magellan, sacked unprotected and unsuspecting towns on the Peruvian coast, captured ships whose shocked crews offered little opposition, took the first Manila Galleon ever taken from the Spanish, and returned home across the Pacific and around Africa. There the Queen accepted some of his wealth and knighted him in a ceremony aboard his by now famous *Golden Hind*, thereby condoning an exploit that for over one hundred years would be the great model for other daring and clever sea captains.

After such a dramatic success and with the defeat of the Armada, Spain was even less able to protect itself against the Protestant privateers. Dutch fleets like those of Le Maire and Schouten circumnavigated the globe, trading and plundering in the wake of the *Golden Hind*. In Jacobean times British sailors, lacking a strong navy to join, continued on their separate piratical ways. Captain Peter Easton raided the Spanish so successfully that he was able to retire to a life of luxury at Villefranche. Sir Henry Mainwaring, with a commission from the Lord High Admiral, recruited sailors at Newfoundland and pursued Spanish shipping all over the Atlantic before being called home to receive a pardon, be made a gentleman of the King's bed-chamber, and write *Of the Beginnings, Practices, and Suppression of Pirates*, an important inside exposé of privateering and piracy that has never been published.

Toward the middle of the seventeenth century, Spain felt another kind of threat. Tortuga, one of her islands in the Caribbean, began to attract a motley group of settlers—French, Dutch, English, and Portuguese—bondsmen from Jamaica's sugar plantations, escaped indentured servants, runaway slaves, dissatisfied sailors, and logwood cutters from the Bay of Campeachy in Mexico. Unhappy with these uninvited guests, Spanish authorities drove them away to Hispaniola. But when Spain made no effort to keep Tortuga, the evicted settlers returned. There they existed partly by hunting, cooking their game on wooden grills which the Carib Indians called "boucans," a term taken over by the French in *viande boucanée*, a kind of dried meat that could be preserved for long periods of time. When Spanish opposition continued, the hunters, or *boucaniers*, of Tortuga banded together, stole boats from their enemies, and returned the oppression, more for plunder perhaps than for revenge. A half-century of buccaneering had begun. It is the history of this half-century that is told, and told best, in *The Buccaneers of America*, written by Alexander Olivier Exquemelin (or Oexmelin; anglicized in the first English edition of this work as John Esquemeling) and Basil Ringrose, two adventurers who helped make the history they wrote about. Since their intriguing story tells itself, only a very few additional facts need be known in order that their accounts may be read in perspective.

Because so many of the Caribbean buccaneers were from France, that country sent out a governor to Tortuga, one who was always willing to give letters of marque authorizing expeditions against the Spanish. In fact, William Dampier, whose travel books made him one of the most respected of buccaneers, has told us that a captain often received blank commissions from the French governor with the understanding that they could be handed out to any friends who might need them. Provided only with such commissions and their small arms, with which they were deadly shots, bands of buccaneers would slip out in row boats, surprise a large Spanish brigantine, shoot its cannoneers, clamber aboard, take possession, and set out "on account." The buccaneer crews were very democratic, electing or deposing a captain at will, abiding by the economic rule of "no prey, no pay," and establishing a system of rewards that gave special consideration to the surgeons who accompanied them and to men injured while on raids. These customs continued through the great days of buccaneering and on into the eighteenth century and the time of pirates like William Kidd and Edward Teach (Blackbeard). In May, 1686, for example, Raveneau de Lussan, one of the most famous of buccaneers, gave this explanation of the fair dealing to be expected in South-Sea adventures:

> next Day our Chirurgeons had Orders to give in an Account of those among the Wounded, who were crippled, to the End we might make them Satisfaction before we divided. They told us we had four Men crippled, and six hurt, to which we gave six hundred Pieces of Eight a Man, and a thousand to those that were crippled, as it was our constant Custom in those Seas.*

Among the earliest of the buccaneer leaders was a Frenchman named Pierre le Grand, who ordered his little boat sunk before boarding the enemy, a stratagem very successful in forcing a fight to the finish because it cut off any escape route for his companions. As buccaneering became more profitable the men became more daring and more systematic. Another Frenchman, Jean David Nau, who called himself L'Ollonois, was the first to organize the crews of several ships into one big raiding group. With a fleet of eight vessels and four hundred men he attacked towns on the Atlantic side of Spanish America, sometimes marching for great distances overland, and coming away with incredible plunder after committing sometimes unbelievable deeds of violence and cruelty. The careers of both these buccaneers were given in detail by Esquemeling.

* Raveneau de Lussan, *Journal of a Voyage to the South Seas* (London, 1741), II, p. 223.

But his chief hero, or villain, was the greatest of all such organizers, Henry Morgan. Elected by the buccaneers themselves, after his uncle had been killed leading them unsuccessfully against the Spanish, Henry Morgan, carrying a commission from the Governor of British Jamaica and commanding a dozen ships and seven hundred men, captured Puerto del Principe, the second largest city in Cuba. In the next year, 1668, by marching his men across land to attack the forts from the rear, he took Porto Bello in the most famous of many buccaneering raids on that Central American town. Then he remained a month to loot, burn, and rape the town and defeat a large Spanish rescue force. Three years later, after leading another expedition across the Isthmus to sack cities on the Pacific side, he returned to Jamaica a hero, even though he had apparently sailed away with most of the plunder in his own ship. When England decided to appease Spain, as it had sometimes done in the days of Elizabeth and her privateers, both Morgan and Governor Modyford were called to London. There Modyford was kept in luxury in the tower and Morgan was idolized as a hero in the tradition of Alexander. Shortly he was back in Jamaica as Deputy Governor Sir Henry Morgan ruthlessly stamping out the "piracy" that had shortly before been called buccaneering or privateering.

In 1684, while Morgan was again being acclaimed in London, the first English edition of Esquemeling's book was published there. A translation of a Spanish translation of the original (1678) Dutch work entitled *De Americaeneche Zee Roovers, The Buccaneers of America* told much of the history of buccaneering to that date, including eye-witness accounts of such incidents as the bloody rape of Porto Bello. It also made statements that aroused the spleen of the hero Morgan, who according to the *London Gazette* successfully sued the British publisher of Esquemeling's book for "many False, Scandalous and Malicious Reflections" on his life.

The author of the much translated book was a Frenchman*
from Honfleur, near Le Havre, who had gone out to the West

---

* See Philip Gosse, *The History of Piracy* (New York, 1934), pp. 146–47, whose information seems to settle the much debated question of the nationality of Esquemeling.

Indies as a boy apprentice. Eventually sold to a barber-surgeon, he learned his master's trade well enough to serve almost ten years with the buccaneers as surgeon on some of their bloodiest expeditions, apparently keeping a journal when he was not amputating limbs, cauterizing wounds, or mixing salves. No one knows how much of Porto Bello's treasure he himself carried back to Europe, although it was well known that the surgeon's share was always second in size only to that of the captain in whose crew he served. At any rate, the medical experience he gained with the buccaneers was such that within a year after publishing his book in Amsterdam he passed the state examination for surgeon in that city.

While Esquemeling's book was being translated into all the languages of western Europe and making him famous, buccaneering underwent a new period of success in the 1680s and 1690s under such French leaders as Raveneau de Lussan and the Sieur de Montauban and under such British captains as John Coxon, Richard Sawkins, Peter Harris, and Bartholomew Sharp. But now the greatest exploits were on the Pacific side of America. In 1680 Sharp and Coxon conducted another sack of Porto Bello and then marched their men across Darien, reinforced by other pirate crews and assisted by native Mosquito Indians. On the Pacific coast, hot and quarrelsome, the buccaneers manned canoes, captured Spanish boats—then several small men-of-war, then one large man-of-war—and went on to sack Panama City and other ports before breaking up into a number of small expeditions that led some of the captains across the Pacific and others all over the Atlantic.

The march of Sharp and Coxon across Central America was destined to be made famous because on it at least five journals were kept and later published. One is the account of Lionel Wafer, also a surgeon, whose description of the natives and of the flora and fauna of Panama is still considered the best of his century. Another of the journals is that of William Dampier,* who was to circumnavigate the globe three times and become perhaps the most honored of all travel writers. Still another of the journals was kept by Basil Ringrose, who remained with

---

* Published in 1698 as part of *A New Voyage round the World*. To be reprinted by Dover Publications, Inc., in 1967.

Captain Sharp while Dampier and Wafer went with other commanders. The author of this journal landed in England in 1682, and in 1685 the publisher of Esquemeling's *Buccaneers of America* added a second volume described thus:

> Bucaniers of America. The second volume Containing the Dangerous Voyage and Bold Attempts of Captain Bartholomew Sharp, and others; performed upon the Coasts of the South Sea, for the Space of two years, etc. From the Original Journal of the said Voyage. Written by Mr. Basil Ringrose, Gentleman who was all along present at these transactions.

Since its first issuance this account has traditionally been bound with that of Esquemeling, the two together being called *The Buccaneers of America*.

Of Basil Ringrose's life nothing is known before 1680, when he joined the buccaneer fleet at Jamaica in time for the raid on Porto Bello and the famous crossing of the Isthmus of Panama. He accompanied Captain Sharp to London in 1682, and three years later his journal was published. Before he could profit from the fame and income derived from his writing, however, he departed for the South Seas on the *Cygnet* as one of the group of merchants backing that ship's expedition to rob the Spanish. Reported to be a man of great physical strength and courage, he was among the fifty men from the *Cygnet* who in February of 1686 were ambushed by the Spaniards and killed near the little town of Compostela in Mexico. William Dampier described the ambush in some detail in *A New Voyage round the World*, calling Ringrose "my Ingenious Friend" and always speaking with respect of his journal. A few of the pages of that journal, which Dampier knew so well, were not exactly as Ringrose had written them, however. It has been shown, for example, that certain passages in the original manuscript, now in the British Museum, were tampered with in order that Captain Sharp might be made a more attractive figure in the published version. Either Sharp or his friend William Hacke, both of whom were in London at the time of publication, could have made the changes. But such tamperings were few and Ringrose's journal is a worthy sequel to the history of Esquemeling.

As one might expect, the two parts are different in style and structure. Esquemeling's is a history covering a quarter of a century of buccaneering, with few references to his own exploits until he has told in some fifteen detailed chapters the stories of famous robber captains from Pierre le Grand to Henry Morgan. On the other hand, Basil Ringrose faithfully kept a day-by-day journal of adventures he participated in. Similarly Esquemeling included history of the islands of Tortuga and Hispaniola, while Ringrose cared little for the history of places he visited, concentrating on giving an on-the-spot report.

Furthermore, Esquemeling's portion has a number of long descriptions of plants and animals, of tobacco growing and curing, of the buccaneers as meat hunters; his fourth chapter, for example, is called "On the Fruits, Trees, and Animals of Hispaniola." Although Ringrose was careful to tell what his companions ate, what fish they caught, and what animals they killed, he never stopped for careful descriptions of flora or fauna, even though he went further in recording winds, tides, and compass variations.

Esquemeling gave all the bloody details of L'Ollonois's career and pictured Morgan as a lustful tyrant who forced his attentions on women prisoners. Ringrose included the blood from many battles but pictured his comrades as humane in handling prisoners and as gentlemen where women were concerned. Not that Captain Sharp's men had no eye for the ladies. Once Ringrose recorded, after a Spanish treasure ship and its passengers were taken, "In this Vessel I saw the beautifullest Women that ever I saw in the South-Sea." But these and other captured women were always released untouched by the English buccaneers under Captain Sharp.

Finally, Esquemeling's history is consistently more attractive reading: It has no dull spots. But while the last part of Ringrose's journal, that part which recounts the voyage around Cape Horn and back to the West Indies, is sometimes simply a kind of log of latitudes, winds, and weather, his journal rises to greater heights because he dramatized more of what he himself saw. For example, in nineteen days in the month of July he participated in the taking of three Spanish ships. The first one, the *San Pedro*, had been captured and freed by the same men a year before, but this time it was loaded with treasure—234 pieces of eight per buccaneer. The second ship, a small one, was searched, found empty, and sent away. The third, the *Rosario*, provided six hundred jars of wine and brandy as well as "ninety-four Pieces of Eight a Man." Luckily one does not have to choose between the more impersonal account of Dr. Esquemeling and the more vivid reporting of the fighter Basil Ringrose. We have them both.

But it is not just the blood and battle and booty that make this volume a classic in the history of piracy, privateering, and buccaneering. Esquemeling and Ringrose left their imprint on travel literature as a type and, consequently, on all literature for more than a century. By them more than by anyone else, William Dampier was taught how to write a travel book that would be informative as well as entertaining. From Esquemeling he learned to gather stories and legends in the lands he visited and to take careful notes so that he could describe plants, animals, places, and people. From his companion and friend Ringrose he learned to keep a detailed journal, to be exact about tides, winds, harbors, currents, to provide eye-witness accounts of raids and sea fights. From both he learned to be objective and exact, to be an aid to the Royal Society in its scheme of promoting science, to write clear and simple prose. And from both he learned to mix the personal with the objective, to avoid long sections of history or description that might grow dull, to provide pictures and drawings. Nor was William Dampier to be the most important writer inspired by Esquemeling and Ringrose. Through him their influence would be delivered to Daniel Defoe and to Jonathan Swift, the greatest of all authors of pseudo-travels in English. In short, at the very beginning of the modern age of science and of realism in literature, Esquemeling and Ringrose became a source for scientists at home who used their facts and an inspiration to travelers and novelists who discovered from them the pleasures of keen observation and the profit in money and prestige that might derive from a successful travel journal, whether real or fictional. *The Buccaneers of America* is as important as it is fascinating.

PERCY G. ADAMS

Knoxville, Tennessee
June, 1966

For Further Reading

Dampier, William. *A New Voyage round the World*. London, 1697. To be reprinted by Dover Publications, Inc., New York, in 1967.

Gerhard, Peter. *Pirates on the West Coast of New Spain, 1575–1742*. Glendale, California, 1960.

Gosse, Philip. *The History of Piracy*. New York, 1932.

Gosse, Philip. *The Pirates' Who's Who*. Boston, 1924.

Hacke, William. *A Collection of Original Voyages*. London, 1699.

Kemp, P., and C. Lloyd. *The Brethren of the Coast*. London, 1960.

Lindsay, Philip. *The Great Buccaneer, Being the Life, Death and Extraordinary Adventures of Sir Henry Morgan, Buccaneer and Lieutenant Governor of Jamaica*. New York [1951].

Raveneau de Lussan. *Journal du voyage fait à la Mer du Sud*. Paris, 1689. Eng. trans. by M. E. Wilbur, Cleveland, 1930.

Snow, Edward Rowe. *Pirates and Buccaneers of the Atlantic Coast*. Boston, [1944].

Villestreux, Général de la. *Les Flibustiers aux Antilles*. Paris, 1930.

Woodbury, George. *The Great Days of Piracy in the West Indies*. New York, [1951].

CONTENTS

PAGE

INTRODUCTION TO THE 1893 EDITION xxi
THE TRANSLATOR TO THE READER xlv

CHAPTER   *PART I.*

I. The Author sets forth towards the Western Islands, in the Service of the
West India Company of France. They meet with an English frigate,
and arrive at the Island of Tortuga 1

II. Description of the Island of Tortuga: of the fruits and plants there growing : how the French settled there, at two several times, and cast out
the Spaniards, first masters thereof. The Author of this book was twice
sold in the said Island. 6

III. Description of the great and famous Island of Hispaniola . . . 16

IV. Of the Fruits, Trees and Animals that are found at Hispaniola . . 21

V. Of all sorts of quadruped Animals and Birds that are found in this island.
As also a relation of the French Buccaneers 34

VI. Of the Origin of the most famous Pirates of the coasts of America. A
notable exploit of Pierre le Grand 53

VII. After what manner the Pirates arm their vessels, and how they regulate
their voyages 58

PART II.

I. Origin of Francis L'Ollonais, and beginning of his robberies . . . 79

II. L'Ollonais equips a fleet to land upon the Spanish islands of America, with
intent to rob, sack and burn whatever he met 84

III. L'Ollonais makes new preparations to take the city of St. James de Leon;
as also that of Nicaragua, where he miserably perishes . . . 101

IV. Of the Origin and Descent of Captain Henry Morgan—his Exploits and
a continuation of the most remarkable actions of his life . . . 120

V. Some account of the Island of Cuba. Captain Morgan attempts to preserve
the Isle of St. Catharine as a refuge and nest to Pirates; but fails of his
designs. He arrives at and takes the village of El Puerto del Principe 130

VI. Captain Morgan resolveth to attack and plunder the city of Porto Bello.
To this effect he equips a fleet, and with little expense and small forces,
takes the said place 140

VII. Captain Morgan taketh the city of Maracaibo, on the coast of New Venezuela. Piracies committed in those Seas. Ruin of three Spanish ships,
that were set forth to hinder the robberies of the Pirates . . . 150

PART III.

I. Captain Morgan goes to the Isle of Hispaniola to equip a new fleet, with
intent to pillage again upon the coasts of the West Indies . . . 183

II. What happened in the river De la Hacha 186

III. Captain Morgan leaves the Island of Hispaniola, and goes to that of St.
Catharine, which he takes 191

IV. Captain Morgan takes the Castle of Chagre, with four hundred men sent
for this purpose from the Isle of St. Catharine 198

V. Captain Morgan departs from the Castle of Chagre, at the head of one
thousand two hundred men, with design to take the city of Panama . 206

VI. Captain Morgan sends several canoes and boats to the South Sea. He
sets fire to the city of Panama. Robberies and cruelties committed
there by the Pirates till their return to the Castle of Chagre . . 223

VII. Of a voyage made by the Author, along the coasts of Costa Rica, at his
return towards Jamaica. What happened most remarkable in the said
voyage. Some observations made by him at that time . . . 239

VIII. The Author departs towards the Cape of Gracias à Dios. Of the Commerce which here the Pirates exercise with the Indians. His arrival
at the Island De los Pinos ; and finally, his return to Jamaica . . 249

IX. The Relation of the shipwreck, which Monsieur Bertram Ogeron,
Governor of the Isle of Tortuga, suffered near the Isles of Guadanillas.
How both he and his companions fell into the hands of the Spaniards.
By what arts he escaped their hands, and preserved his life. The
enterprise which he undertook against Porto Rico, to deliver his people.
The unfortunate success of that design 259

CHAPTER   PAGE

X. A relation of what encounters lately happened at the Islands of Cayana
and Tobago, between the Count de Estres, Admiral of France, in
America, and the Heer Jacob Binkes, Vice-Admiral of the United
Provinces, in the same parts 267

PART IV.

I. Captain Coxon, Sawkins, Sharp and others set forth in a fleet towards
the province of Darien, upon the continent of America. Their designs
to pillage and plunder in those parts. Number of their ships, and
strength of their forces by sea and land 275

II. They march towards the town of Santa Maria with design to take it.
The Indian King of Darien meets them by the way. Difficulties of
this march, with other occurrences till they arrive at the place . . 279

III. They take the town of Santa Maria with no loss of men, and but small
booty of what they fought for. Description of the place, country and
river adjacent. They resolve to go and plunder for the second time
the city of Panama 285

IV. The Buccaneers leave the town of Santa Maria, and proceed by sea to
take Panama. Extreme difficulties, with sundry accidents and dangers
of that voyage 289

V. Shipwreck of Mr. Ringrose, the author of this narrative. He is taken by
the Spaniards and miraculously by them preserved. Several other
accidents and disasters which befel him after the loss of his companions
till he found them again. Description of the Gulf of Vallona . . 293

VI. The Buccaneers prosecute their voyage, till they come within sight of
Panama. They take several barks and prisoners by the way. Are
descried by the Spaniards before their arrival. They order the Indians
to kill the prisoners 300

VII. They arrive within sight of Panama. Are encountered by three small
men-of-war. They fight them with only sixty-eight men, and utterly
defeat them, taking two of the said vessels. Description of that bloody
fight. They take several ships at the Isle of Perico before Panama . 304

VIII. Description of the state and condition of Panama, and the parts adjacent.
What vessels they took while they blocked up the said Port. Captain
Coxon with seventy more returns home. Sawkins is chosen in chief . 311

IX. Captain Sawkins, chief commander of the Buccaneers, is killed before
Puebla Nueva. They are repulsed from the said place. Captain
Sharp chosen to be their leader. Many more of their company leave
them and return home overland 318

X. They depart from the Island of Cayboa to the Island of Gorgona, where
they careen their vessels. Description of this Isle. They resolve to
go and plunder Arica, leaving their design of Guayaquil . . . 323

XI. The Buccaneers depart from the Isle of Gorgona, with design to plunder
Arica. They lose one another by the way. They touch at the Isle of
Plate, or Drake's Isle, where they meet again. Description of this
Isle. Some memoirs of Sir Francis Drake. An account of this
voyage, and the coasts all along. They sail as far in a fortnight, as the
Spaniards usually do in three months 331

XII. Captain Sharp and his company depart from the Isle of Plate, in prosecution of their voyage towards Arica. They take two Spanish vessels
by the way, and learn intelligence from the enemy. Eight of their
company destroyed at the Isle of Gallo. Tediousness of this voyage,
and great hardships they endured. Description of the coast all along,
and their sailings 342

XIII. A continuation of their long and tedious voyage to Arica, with a description of the coasts and sailings thereunto. Great hardship they endured
for want of water and other provisions. They are descried at Arica,
and dare not land there; the country being all in arms before them.
They retire from thence, and go to Puerto de Hilo, close by Arica.
Here they land, take the town with little or no loss on their side, refresh
themselves with provisions; but in the end are cheated by the Spaniards,
and forced shamefully to retreat from thence 358

XIV. The Buccaneers depart from the Port of Hilo, and sail to that of Coquimbo. They are descried before their arrival. Notwithstanding
they land: are encountered by the Spaniards, and put them to flight.
They take, plunder, and fire the City of la Serena. A description

| CHAPTER | | PAGE |

thereof. A Stratagem of the Spaniards in endeavouring to fire their ship, discovered and prevented. They are deceived again by the Spaniards, and forced to retire from Coquimbo, without any ransom for the City, or considerable pillage. They release several of their chief Prisoners 375

XV. The Buccaneers depart from Coquimbo for the Isle of Juan Fernandez. An exact account of this voyage. Misery they endure, and great dangers they escape very narrowly there. They mutiny among themselves, and choose Watling to be their chief commander. Description of the island. Three Spanish men-of-war meet with the buccaneers, at the said island ; but these outbrave them on the one side, and give them the slip on the other 388

XVI. The Buccaneers depart from the Isle of Juan Fernandez to that of Iquique. Here they take several prisoners, and learn intelligence of the posture of affairs at Arica. Cruelty committed upon one of the said prisoners, who had rightly informed them. They attempt Arica the second time, and take the town, but are beaten out of it again before they could plunder, with great loss of men, many of them being killed, wounded, and made prisoners. Captain Watling, their chief Commander, is killed in this attack, and Captain Sharp presently chosen again, who leads them off, and through mountains of difficulties, makes a bold retreat to the ship 403

XVII. A description of the Bay of Arica. They sail hence to the Port of Guasco, where they get provisions. A draft of the said port. They land again at Hilo to revenge the former affronts, and take what they could find 414

XVIII. They depart from the Port of Hilo to the Gulf of Nicoya, where they take down their decks and mend the sailing of their ship. Fortyseven of their companions leave them, and go home over land. A description of the Gulf of Nicoya. They take two barks and some prisoners there. Several other remarks belonging to this voyage . 424

XIX. They depart from the Gulf of Nicoya to Golfo Dulce, where they careen their vessel. An account of their sailings along the coast. Also a description of Golfo Dulce. The Spaniards force the Indians of Darien to a peace, by a stratagem contrived in the name of the English 434

XX. They depart from Golfo Dulce, to go and cruise under the Equinoctial. Here they take a rich Spanish vessel with 37,000 Pieces of Eight, besides plate and other goods. They take also a Packet-boat bound from Panama to Lima. An account of their sailings and the coasts along 442

XXI. They take another Spanish ship richly laden under the Equinoctial. They make several dividends of their booty among themselves. They arrive at the Isle of Plate, where they are in danger of being all massacred by their slaves and prisoners. Their departure thence for the port and bay of Paita, with design to plunder the said place . 448

XXII. They arrive at Paita, where they are disappointed of their expectations, as not daring to land, seeing all the country alarmed before them. They bear away for the Strait of Magellan. Description of the bay and port of Paita, and Colan. An account of their Sailings towards the Strait afore-mentioned 454

XXIII. The Buccaneers arrive at a place incognito, to which they give the name of the Duke of York's Islands. A description of the said islands, and of the gulf, or lagoon, wherein they lie, so far as it was searched. They remain there many days by stress of weather, not without great danger of being lost. An account of some other remarkable things that happened there 465

XXIV. They depart from the English Gulf in quest of the Straits of Magellan, which they cannot find. They return home by an unknown way, never navigated before 476

XXV. The Buccaneers continue their navigation, without seeing any land, till they arrive at the Caribbean Islands in the West Indies. They give away their ship to some of their companions that were poor and disperse for several countries. The author of this Journal arrives in England 489

INDEX 501

LIST OF PLATES.

SIR HENRY MORGAN . . . . *to face Title page*

BARTHOLOMEW PORTUGUES . . . . . . *to face page* 65

ROCK BRASILIANO . . . . „ 69

FRANCIS LOLONOIS 79

THE CRUELTY OF LOLONOIS . . . . . . „ 104

THE TOWN OF PUERTO DEL PRINCIPE TAKEN AND SACKED „ 155

THE SPANISH ARMADA DESTROYED BY CAPTAINE MORGAN „ 171

MAP OF THE SOUTH SEA AND COASTS OF AMERICA 274

INTRODUCTION TO THE 1893 EDITION.

THE term Buccaneer, in French Boucanier, is usually applied to certain pirates who during the seventeenth century committed great ravages upon the Spanish settlements in the West Indies, the adjacent main land, and the coast of Chili and Peru, and whose exploits it will be our province to describe in the following pages. Such term was, however, more accurately applied to a body of cattle hunters of all nations, but mainly French, who pursued their avocations in the forests of the Western and North Western districts of the Island of Hispaniola —circumstances to be described hereafter caused these hunters to combine the trade in cattle with that of piracy, and the name, in consequence, lost its first significance of hunter and acquired its modern and better known one of pirate.

Our readers living in the present age of highly organized communications with all parts of the globe, cannot sufficiently realize the magnitude of the task undertaken by the first explorers and colonisers of the New Continent, still less the extraordinary rapidity with which the work of exploration and colonisation was carried on by the Spanish and Portuguese, upon means that to us would appear ludicrously inadequate to the enormous extent of the newly discovered territories. Scant justice has been done by posterity to the enthusiastic energy and perseverance of the natives of the Iberian peninsula, who during the first half of the sixteenth century, at least fifty years in advance of any other European nation, established their rule over the West India Islands, Central and South America, subdued the great and powerful empires of Mexico and Peru, and filled the conquered territories with numerous and flourishing settlements, extending from Florida to the River Plate on the one side, and from California to Chili on the other. Nor does the enormous emigration consequent on the conquests and occupation the less appeal to the imagination, when we come to consider that it took place simultaneously with large discoveries and settlements in the East Indies, and with prolonged warfare upon a very large scale against the principal nations of Europe. Rapid and striking as was the success of the Spanish and Portuguese conquerors and colonists, it has in the long run proved to be ephemeral, and other nations, who entered the field many years later with inferior advantages in soil and climate, have achieved greater and more enduring results, as must be manifest upon a comparison of the United States and Canada with the Central and South American Republics. This failure, apart from religious and racial causes, must be attributed to the commercial policy (conspicuous for its selfishness in an age of extreme selfishness) adopted by the mother country, Spain, in its relations with its colonies. Even at the present day much useful experience may be gained by the colonial ministers of the greatest powers from a study of a fiscal system specially constructed to protect the interests of a few merchants at the expense and in disregard of the expressed wishes of the colonists.

Soon after the discovery of America, with a view to settle disputes between Spain and Portugal as to their title to the newly found regions, Pope Alexander the Sixth issued his famous donation by which he gave to Spain the whole of America, except the Brazils, which was assigned to Portugal, and under which the Kings of Spain claimed to exclude not merely foreigners but also their own subjects not Spanish from access to the American continent and islands, and for a time practically succeeded in preventing all other nations from trading or even landing in the New World. This exclusion could not however be kept up, and we find traders from the Netherlands and England visiting the islands at a very early period, followed by Hawkins, Drake, and others in their capacity of slavers and merchant adventurers, the French appearing later still. It stands to reason that the foreign traders would not have undertaken voyages so long and hazardous without considerable encouragement from the colonists, who, dependent otherwise on the fleets annually despatched to Europe, found no doubt their advantage in evading the fiscal regulations of their own government, to obtain not merely European goods at low prices, but also what was to them of paramount importance, a supply of labour in the shape of negro slaves from Africa.

To put down the foreign traders or interlopers the Spanish government employed armed revenue cruisers, or *guarda costas*, and were accustomed to instruct their officers to destroy every strange ship they met with, and to take no prisoners ; and in the case of foreign settlements on unoccupied lands, soldiers were sent to destroy the buildings and plantations and massacre the inhabitants. Harsh measures like these produced their natural effect, and in no long time the interlopers learnt to meet force by force, to combine for mutual defence, and to treat every Spaniard as an enemy. Not unnaturally the foreign seamen, traders and colonists drifted into a state of perpetual warfare with the various local governments, and in comparatively a short time the marine carrying trade between the various colonies, excepting the annual fleets, which were usually strongly manned and heavily armed, was either annihilated or passed into the hands of the foreign interlopers.

To applications addressed to the various European princes for redress of injuries committed by their subjects in American waters, the usual answer was to the effect

that the King of Spain was at liberty to proceed as he
pleased against all persons acting without their commission.   Elizabeth of England, with greater frankness,
replied that the Spaniards themselves were to blame for
the depredations complained of, which were brought on
solely by their own severe and unjust dealing.   She did
not understand why her subjects should be debarred
from traffic in America, nor would she acknowledge titles
given by the Bishop of Rome to lands of which Spain
was not in actual possession.   This unsatisfactory state
of affairs (further aggravated by religious differences)
lasted from the early visits of Hawkins, Drake, and
others, to the end of the Thirty Years' War, during which
period the interlopers were continually reinforced, first by
the buccaneers proper from Hispaniola, and secondly by
corsairs of all nations serving under the Protestant flag,
such as the *Gueux de la Mer*, or sea beggars, from the
revolted Netherlands, French Huguenots, etc.

The island of Hispaniola, or Hayti, was described by
the original discoverers in glowing terms, as being of
great beauty and fertility, and containing a population of
at least a million, but twenty years of Spanish government (so miscalled) reduced the aboriginal inhabitants to
less than sixty thousand in number, and the land (beyond
the limits of a few small towns and scattered plantations)
to a state of primeval forest tenanted only by wild cattle
and a few wandering Indian hunters.   The foreign traders
soon began to appreciate the attractions offered by the
seclusion of these districts, and by the facility of victualling and obtaining wood and water.   Among other
articles of food supplied by the Indians, beef and pork
cured by the *boucan* process obtained a high repute,
and many of the sailors finding it to their interest to
adopt the hunters' life, a large trade in *boucaned* meat soon
sprang up.   The charm of the wild life attracted to the
region increasing numbers of Europeans, who pursued
indifferently the trade of hunters and corsairs.   Many

also became planters, and the latter (among whom the French element predominated) spread over the western portion of the island. Eventually this district became entirely French, and for a long time was the most flourishing colonial possession of the crown of France, its prosperity lasting until the Revolution of 1789, when the negro inhabitants, under Toussaint L'Ouverture, revolted, and having massacred or expelled the whites, established a republic ; this gave way to an empire, and again to a republic ; finally the French and Spanish negroes each established republican governments of their own, which have lasted down to the present day.

A few words will not be here out of place by way of description of the manners and customs of the buccaneers, and of illustration of the simple yet effective means by which they organized victory over a nation which at that period enjoyed the highest military reputation.

The term buccaneer is the English version of the French word *boucanier* (*i.e.*, one who cures meat by the *boucan* process). It is curious that the English pirates should have adopted the term from their French comrades and made it their own, while the latter simultaneously took the title of Flibustier, which is the English word " freebooter" pronounced in the French manner. Another and very common appellation by which they were known was Brethren of the Coast, and by these rude warriors of all races, who were accustomed to work together irrespective of nationality, this last title was deemed peculiarly appropriate and expressive.

For the pursuit of the wild oxen and swine that pastured in the Haytian forests the hunters used to form parties of five or six in number, each member provided with musket, bullet-bag, powder-horn, and knife, and dressed in garments made out of the skin, and stained with the blood of the slain animals ; horses were never used, the tangled nature of the country rendering a pursuit on foot more practicable. The flesh, when obtained,

was cut into long strips (sometimes salted, when required
for a long voyage). The special feature of the process
consisted in laying the meat upon boucans or barbecues
(*i.e.*, gratings constructed of green sticks), and exposing
it to the smoke of wood, fed with the fat, bones and
offal of the carcass, and the trimmings of the hide. By
this means a very appetising flavour was imparted to
the flesh, which, when cured, was usually of a bright red
colour, and kept good for a long time. Pork was generally considered the best of the boucaned meats, except by
the savage Caribs of the Lesser Antilles, to whom the
barbecued flesh of an enemy was thought to be the food
most grateful to a warrior. The charqui or jerked beef,
so frequently alluded to in contemporary accounts, was
prepared by cutting the meat into strips and drying it in
the sun—this process being better suited to a dry climate
was chiefly made use of in Peru, Chili, and the River
Plate.

Analogous in their habits to the buccaneers of Hispaniola were the logwood cutters and cattle hunters in
the peninsula of Yucatan or Honduras. Like them they
were used to vary the monotony of timber-felling and
bullock-driving by an occasional foray upon the Spanish
settlements in the immediate neighbourhood. It must,
however, in justice to the logwood cutters be admitted
that they were not the original aggressors, but for the
molestation inflicted upon them by the Spanish forces
they would have been content to pursue their avocation
in obscurity and peace. The colony of British Honduras
was founded by their descendants, who still carry on the
trade in logwood and mahogany. It would be unjust to
omit allusion to the Mosquito Indians, the attached friends
and allies of the buccaneers, who, from their strong affection to the English, their knowledge of pilotage, and
their extraordinary dexterity in the arts of the fisherman,
particularly in the use of the fish spear, were almost indispensable members of every expedition to the South

Sea. Their chief Cacique usually received a kind of investiture from the governors of Jamaica, and numerous English planters settled among them, mostly in the neighbourhood of Blewfields. The territory has for some time past been absorbed into the adjacent republic of Honduras.

Previous to embarking upon an expedition it was the universal custom of these freebooters to hold a preliminary meeting to determine the object of attack, to raise funds, to elect officers, and generally to discuss all minor details. The next step was to draw up articles of association for signature by the adventurers, binding them to contribute a fixed minimum sum to the common fund, to observe due order and discipline, and to allot the spoil in the manner pointed out in the articles. A certain number of shares, from two to eight according to rank, was assigned to each officer, and one to each adventurer, but before apportioning the plunder among individuals preferential shares were almost invariably set aside as compensation for wounds, and losses of eyes and limbs ; the representatives of the slain were not forgotten, and generally received the share that the adventurer would have taken if he had survived. It was not an uncommon practice for two buccaneers to swear brotherhood, to stand by each other during life, and each to make the other his heir, and these curious partnerships once entered into were observed with a fidelity almost touching. Rewards were also given to the first man who sighted the chase, to the first who boarded an enemy, and for other services of distinction.

Great honesty and integrity usually characterized their dealings with each other, and with the Indians with whom they were frequently brought into contact ; to their prisoners also they behaved with much greater humanity than was usual at the period, and from their considerate treatment of Indians and captives they frequently derived much information and advantage in war.

To this rule, however, a few marked exceptions, such as Montbars and L'Ollonais, must be made, and it must also be admitted that towards the end of their career a great change for the worse took place in this respect, the ferocity and bad faith characteristic of the vulgar pirate becoming painfully conspicuous. The earlier free-booters were content to wage war against Spain only, but their successors evinced no such nice discrimination, and impartially plundered and burnt the ships of all nations whenever a favourable opportunity occurred.

Offensive operations were carried on for the most part in the following manner. In the early days of bucca-neering notice of an intended expedition, naming a ren-dezvous, would be sent to the principal resorts of the pirates, and if the suggested commanders were popular the summons would be freely responded to. The usual place of meeting was the west end of the island of Tortuga, off the northern coast of Hayti, but after the capture of Jamaica in 1654 by Cromwell's forces, the English pirates generally made that island their centre, while the French remained constant to Tortuga, their old place of resort. Nor were the Dutch, French, and English colonies in the West Indies afflicted with many scruples as to the propriety of allowing filibusters to build, fit out, and repair in their ports armed vessels intended to cruise against their Spanish neighbours, with whom their respective mother countries were nominally at peace. The traders and planters of Mar-tinique, Curacoa, St. Kitts, Barbados, and especially Jamaica, greatly encouraged the trade, on account of the large profits made on the purchase of plunder from the pirates and the prodigality with which the successful adventurers scattered their hardly won spoils—to such cause doubtless was owing much of the early prosperity of these colonies. In many cases even the precise and pious New Englanders did not disdain to participate in the gains of the atrocious Blackbeard and his associates, who flourished in the first quarter of the eighteenth century.

But to return to the early days of buccaneering, when the aspirations of the pirates were more modest, and captains were content to start in business in a very humble way. The mode of procedure was—*mutatis mutandis*—nearly always the same, irrespective of the numbers engaged. A party, varying in number from twenty to fifty men, would meet to discuss ways and means, to sign agreements, and to choose officers; this done, they would put to sea in canoes or small vessels, and cruise on the usual trade routes. If fortunate enough to discover a Spanish vessel, the pirates were not likely to be deterred from the attack by any disparity in force, however great, apparently trusting by superior seamanship and discipline to place themselves at least on an equality with the enemy. Their first approach was generally made with great judgment, their tiny craft being so steered as to avoid the direct fire of the heavy artillery, while their picked marksmen attempted to strike down the helmsman first, and next the men attending to the sails. This effected, they would get under the stern, or other part of the ship where the guns could not be sufficiently depressed to reach them, the crew of one of the boats would proceed to wedge up the rudder, while the others would keep up a fire of musketry directed at the portholes and bulwarks, so accurately aimed as to prevent any of the Spanish crew from showing themselves.[1]

When the guns had been thus silenced, and the crew

---

[1] It will be within the memory of our readers that during the Crimean War the forts at Bomarsund, in the Baltic, were captured chiefly through their guns being silenced by the sharp shooters of the Allies. At the siege of Sebastopol also, the Russian riflemen so annoyed the advanced batteries of the besiegers by firing into the embrasures, that strong rope screens filling up the whole of the embrasure and closely surrounding the muzzle of the gun (which would otherwise have been quickly silenced by the rifle fire), had to be devised, and were employed on both sides during the remainder of the siege.

forced to seek shelter, the assailants would board from
several quarters at once ; the deck once reached, their
personal dexterity in the use of their weapons, and their
activity and courage were so marked that they rarely failed
to overpower their opponents.   A very good example of
their mode of fighting may be found in the action off
Panama, between the buccaneer flotilla of Captain Sawkins and the Spanish squadron, described in chapter 7 of
the last part of the present work.   The prisoners, except
officers and others whose means enabled them to pay a
ransom, were either put ashore or set adrift in one of the
captured craft otherwise useless to the captors, and left to
find their way to the land.   The prizes, if adapted for
the purpose, were often manned and armed for a further
cruise.   Vessels of large size were seldom used—those
employed rarely carried more than four to six small guns,
although ships of thirty to forty guns are occasionally
mentioned as taking part in the larger expeditions.   On
or previous to the return to port a general meeting of the
adventurers would be held, and the spoil duly divided ; if
the voyage happened to be a long one dividends were
frequently declared after the capture of each considerable
prize.   Large amounts, £700, £800, or £1,000, were
frequently realized even by the common seamen, only to
be rapidly dissipated in gambling and debauchery.   Their
money spent the buccaneers would either take to the
woods or go upon a fresh cruise, as their inclination
prompted.   A popular and successful captain had only
to announce his intention to fit out a squadron to attract
any number of followers ; and in the latter part of their
career, when all the smaller craft had been driven from
the sea, and the Spaniards never dared to put to sea
except in large and well armed fleets, the large towns
situated even at a considerable distance from the coast
became the object of attack, and expeditions comprising
thirty or forty ships, conveying from one to two thousand
men, were not at all unusual.   The varied training of

this mixed body of soldiers, sailors, lumberers, etc., produced in them great skill in the use of arms, and
immense strength and agility, together with an extraordinary power of enduring hunger, thirst and exposure ;
while the rude sense of honour and integrity, and the
obedience to discipline which so long distinguished them,
enabled them to live together in brotherly harmony, and
carry on with nearly uniform success their eternal warfare
against the common enemy—the Spaniard. For many
years, and indeed up to the very last, they were constantly victorious by sea and land, and their organization
broke down in the end from internal dissension, arising
from the following causes :—

Firstly and chiefly from the fact that Spain, instead of
being confronted, as heretofore, by the protestant nations,
now found it to her interest to seek alliance against the
increasing influence of France under Louis XIV. among
the northern powers. Hence the treaty of peace with
England in 1670, already alluded to, which, however,
had but little effect at the time.

The various quarrels between French, English, and
Dutch, were an additional cause of disintegration the
final blow being probably given by the accession of a
Bourbon to the throne of Spain in 1700. By this time
the greater part of the freebooters had ranged themselves under the flags of their respective nationalities,
had settled down as planters or returned to Europe,
while the residuum became ordinary pirates, preying
upon the trade of all nations alike.

Secondly, from the decay of the strong spirit of religious
antagonism which all the protestant nations (from whom
the buccaneer community received at least nine-tenths
of their recruits) bore to Spain. Spain was Antichrist,
the Bulwark of the Inquisition, the enemy of Freedom,
in short the embodiment of religious and political
tyranny to the descendants of Hollanders oppressed by
Alva, of Huguenots who had battled with the League,

and of English to whom the memory of the great struggle with Philip II. was a source of national pride.

This spirit was emphasized in the minds of all protestant nations by the great struggle of the Thirty years' war, still in progress in the first part of the century and exemplified in the religious and law-abiding habits, almost universal among the brethren in early days, and in some crews existing almost to the last.[1]

A third cause of antagonism was the fiscal tyranny already spoken of. Had a more enlightened commercial policy been adopted towards protestant traders and colonists, it is not unlikely that the tide of emigration might have been turned from the inhospitable districts of New England and the Canadas to the more genial districts on the coast of the Gulf of Mexico, extending from Texas to Florida. It would be here out of place to speculate as to what would have been the position of the United States under such altered circumstances, but their development would probably have been considerably affected.

It now becomes necessary to give a short summary of the principal incidents of the history of the buccaneers, founded chiefly upon the narratives of Esquemeling and Ringrose, but also including circumstances unknown to or omitted by these writers, in order that the reader may have a complete account of the epoch before him.

For the present purpose it will be sufficient to commence with the year 1625, by which time the organization or confederacy of the brethren had probably assumed the shape which it maintained until the close, and to take as a starting point the joint settlement of the Island of St. Christopher, or St. Kitts, by the English and French.[2]

---

[1] Divine service was by the English nearly always celebrated each Sunday at least, and rules prohibiting profane language, gaming, etc., were frequently included in the articles signed by the adventurers.

[2] The island of St. Kitts (to make use of its popular designation) was at this time covered by forests, which have since disappeared, and inhabited by Caribs, a race who then extended from the coast of Caraccas

In consequence of the increasing importance of the trade carried on by the interlopers in the West Indies, England and France agreed to plant each a colony side by side, and the island of St. Kitts being chosen for the purpose, in 1625 the colonists landed and divided the territory between them. The two colonies, in spite of occasional disputes, were very successful, and the English also took possession of the adjacent Island of Nevis.

In 1629, however, a large fleet from Spain, without warning or provocation, attacked and totally dispersed the colonists, and then proceeded on their voyage to the Brazils. The fugitives soon returned, the English for the most part settling in Nevis; a few of the French reoccupied their old settlements in St. Kitts, but the greater portion of the dispossessed planters in 1630 removed to Tortuga, an island on the north coast of Hispaniola, and not far from the *boucan* establishments already existing. Here they seem to have enjoyed considerable prosperity, so much so as to induce the Governor-General of the French West Indies, who had been previously stationed in St. Kitts, to transfer in 1634 his seat of government to Tortuga. In 1638 the Spaniards attacked Tortuga, and temporarily expelled the inhabitants, who, however, very shortly recaptured the place, and the French party so improved their position as to be strong enough to expel their English allies in 1641. These latter maintained a precarious existence partly among the buccaneer settlements on the main island, and partly by piracy, until the capture of Jamaica by Penn in 1654, and Venables (in which the English freebooters took part and greatly distinguished themselves), provided them with a new settlement and base of operations; the western part of

over the whole of the Lesser Antilles. A few are still to be found in the island of Grenada, but the largest body of representatives of the nation are now dwelling in the island of Dominica; to the inaccessible mountains and tangled forests of which they owe their preservation. They number at present about 300, are steadily dwindling away, and another generation will probably see them everywhere extinct.

Hispaniola being then wholly abandoned to the French. Tortuga was again captured by the Spaniards in 1654, and remained in their possession for six years, after which it was finally recovered by the French.

During the period between 1625 and 1655 constant maritime warfare had been carried on, and as an almost necessary consequence the commerce of the Spanish colonies with each other and with the mother country dwindled down almost to nothing, and the piratical community, deprived of the plunder of the local mercantile marine was obliged, in sheer necessity, to turn their arms against the large towns on shore, New Segovia, in Honduras, being the first victim, in 1654.

Among numerous smaller exploits which it is not here necessary to describe, must be especially noted that of Pierre le Grand (perhaps deservedly so named) who, with a small boat containing twenty-eight men, was skilful and fortunate enough to capture the Spanish Vice Admiral himself, and his galleon ; that of Alexandre, who, with means equally inadequate, also took a large man-of-war ; of Montbars, surnamed the Exterminator; of Bartholomew Portuguez, Michael le Basque and Roche Brasiliano; of Lewis Scot, who took and pillaged the city of Campeche ; of John Davis, who plundered Nicaragua, and especially of Van Horn, Granmont and De Graaf, who in 1683 sacked the town of Vera Cruz and carried away an immense booty.

In 1664, Mansveldt, perhaps the ablest of all the pirate chiefs, formed a project of founding an independent buccaneer settlement with a government and flag of its own,[1] at Santa Katalina, or Old Providence (so

---

[1] This is by no means the only instance of an attempt to found a piratical state. The sea rovers who infested the Indian Ocean in the early part of the eighteenth century often possessed large establishments on the coast of Madagascar, and were very successful in conciliating and governing the natives. Several small states, administered directly and indirectly by pirates, were established on that island, but no attempt at confederation was made, and none lasted beyond the lives of their

named to distinguish it from New Providence in the
Bahamas, a place noted as the resort, in the seventeenth
and eighteenth centuries of pirates and in the nineteenth
of blockade runners), but his death and the pronounced
opposition of the Governor of Jamaica, deterred his
successor Morgan from pursuing the subject further.
It may indeed be doubted whether Morgan, although
equally eminent as a leader, was possessed of abilities to
comprehend, much less to carry out, what to him would
have seemed plans of colonisation of a visionary character which did not appeal to his self interest.   To go out
of his way to establish a new base of operation was to
him a waste of time.   Jamaica was a place which fully
suited his convenience for purpose of refitting and of
disposing of his plunder, and that was all he cared
about.[1]   Under the leadership of Morgan the buccaneers
reached the zenith of their reputation.   Never had their
plundering raids been organized on a larger scale or with
more success.   Even in Mansvelt's time many of the
largest towns only escaped destruction by the payment
of heavy blackmail to the freebooters, and the new
commander apparently had only to march against the
remaining colonies successively in order to extinguish
them.

Morgan's first independent enterprise of any importance after the death of Mansvelt was the capture and
sack of the town of Puerto del Principe, in Cuba; he next
surprised and took the city of Porto Bello on the mainland.   He then proceeded to attack the unfortunate
towns of Maracaibo and Gibraltar, which had been
not long before plundered by L'Ollonais.   They were

---

founders.   Given, however, a leader capable of uniting the various
chiefs under one rule, and a colony equal to Java might have been
created with ease.

[1] Jamaica was the resort of the English freebooters until their ex-
tinction at the end of the century.   The pirates of the next generation
under Teach and others made the town of New Providence in the
Bahamas their principal base of operations.

taken for the second time by Michael le Basque, while Morgan was engaged at Puerto del Principe. This last raid did not however save them from Morgan, who for the third time harried these wretched cities. In order to wring from the inhabitants their last coins he remained so long in possession as to enable the Spaniards to send a strongly armed squadron to occupy the mouth of the Lake of Maracaibo, to prevent his retreat. The skilful manner in which he totally destroyed the Spanish ships, and evaded the forts at the entrance, gained him great credit, and was said to have caused the Spanish court to make very strong applications for redress to England. Upon the conclusion of a treaty of peace in 1670,[1] between the two nations, which confirmed England in her possessions in the West Indies, but forbade her subjects to trade to any Spanish port without a license ; a proclamation was issued in pursuance of such arrangement which greatly exasperated the freebooting community and the direct result of which was the assemblage of the largest fleet ever brought together by the buccaneers, amounting to 37 ships of all sizes, manned by more than 2,000 pirates. They met in December, 1670, at Cape Tiburon, and held a council to decide whether their forces should be directed upon Carthagena, Vera Cruz, or Panama. The last was chosen, as being the richest, and Morgan was elected Admiral ; and the island of Santa Katalina, or Old Providence, was, after a feigned resistance, occupied as a base of operations. A detachment was next despatched against Fort San Lorenzo at the mouth of the Chagre river, which was taken after a most gallant defence by the Spanish garrison. Having securely garrisoned Old Providence and the Chagre forts, the main body, then

---

[1] It may be here noted that the existence of a continual war between Spaniards and English is virtually admitted in the treaty ; which indeed practically condones the offences of the buccaneers antecedent to the date thereof.

numbering about 1,200 men, marched across the isthmus, and after nine days of severe hardship, in consequence of the enemy having laid waste the country over which they were obliged to advance, came in sight of Panama. Another day of severe fighting against a force of 2,500 men, which was defeated and put to flight, gave them possession of the coveted city. A large number of the pirates were strongly disposed to pursue their advantage against Peru, which lay temptingly open and almost defenceless before them. Morgan, however, was able to induce his companions to forego any further enterprise in the South Sea, and (after a stay of about three weeks) to evacuate Panama and return across the isthmus. The amount of spoil obtained being very unsatisfactory, he was, with some justice, suspected of embezzling a large part of the booty, and his consequent unpopularity led to his abandoning his comrades and accepting the post of Lieutenant Governor of Jamaica. He was subsequently knighted and made Governor of the Island, in which capacity he showed considerable energy in suppressing piracy. His secession from the buccaneer community just when there was no other leader of capacity to succeed him was a severe blow to their cause. From this time forth the harmony, which up to this time had prevailed between the various nations hitherto united against the Spaniards, was much weakened, and an increasing disposition among individuals to identify themselves with the disputes of their several mother countries took its place. From this point the account of the various occurrences on the Atlantic side of the Isthmus will be carried on to its close, and the narrative of the proceedings of the freebooters in the South Sea reserved for the conclusion.

About 1673 the French buccaneers took part (as privateers under their national flag in the war between France and Holland) in two unsuccessful expeditions against the Dutch Island of Curaçoa ; soon after the latter of which, Puerto del Principe, in Cuba, and the ever unfortunate towns of Maracaibo and Gibraltar, were again pillaged.

In 1679 the Spaniards almost exterminated the French settlers at Samana, in Hispaniola, and in the same year Porto Bello was again plundered. In 1683, a body of 1,200 French pirates took Vera Cruz by stratagem, and carried off an immense spoil. In 1684 negotiations to induce the French flibustiers, then about 3,000 in number, to settle in Hispaniola were entered into, but met with only moderate success. In 1686, Grammont and De Graaf plundered and burnt Campeche. The former of these two chiefs put to sea on a fresh expedition soon afterwards, but was never again heard of, the latter entered the service of France, and became in his way as useful as Morgan in putting down his former companions. In 1688, the English settlers were driven out of St. Kitts by the French. War, however, broke out between France and Spain. England soon afterwards joined the latter, and the buccaneers ranged themselves under the flags of their respective countries. St. Kitts was retaken in the following year, and the remaining French colonists expelled.

Almost the last enterprise in which the buccaneers, as such, were engaged, was directed against Carthagena by the governor of the French possessions in Hispaniola, about a third of the attacking forces on this occasion being buccaneers. Considerable booty was obtained on the capture of the city, but the freebooters being unable to obtain their portion from the French commander, returned and put the city to ransom. On their return they were chased by a combined English and Dutch squadron, were obliged to disperse, and lost a considerable proportion of their gains.

After the Peace of Ryswick, in 1697, buccaneers became practically extinct, the major part of the adventurers either taking service with their respective governments, returning home, or settling down as planters. The balance, becoming pirates pure and simple, long infested the Gulf of Mexico (the coasts of Virginia, the Carolinas, and the Bahama islands serving them as ports of call), and were not finally put down till early in the 19th century ; the Lafittes of Barataria, near the mouth of the Mississippi, being probably the last in the trade.[1]

It now only remains to chronicle the events in the South Sea subsequent to the capture of Panama by Morgan. For several years after his retreat no fresh attempts were made to carry the war in that direction until early in 1680, when a party of 330, under Coxon, Sawkins, Sharp, and others, landed in Darien, and under the guidance of Indians marched to the town of Santa Maria, and thence proceeded in canoes upon the river of the same name to the sea. With two small captured vessels and the canoes, they engaged and took a small Spanish squadron, three of which they fitted out and with them blockaded Panama. Disputes however arising, Coxon, with seventy of the men and most of the Indians, returned across the isthmus, while the remainder pursued their voyage to the south. On the death of Captain Sawkins, killed soon afterwards in a skirmish, further disputes arose, another party broke off and returned to the Gulf, leaving Sharp in command, with about 140 men. They took a few prizes, put one or two small towns to ransom, and on Christmas Day, 1680, anchored at Juan Fernandez to refit. In February they attacked Arica, but were repulsed with loss. On their arrival at the isle of La Plata differences again arose, and forty-four more (among whom were William Dampier and Lionel Wafer) quitted the ship and returned north. The ship sailed to the Gulf of Nicoya,

---

[1] Teach (or Blackbeard), England, Low, Roberts, Kidd and Avery were the principal pirate heroes of the 18th century. Their depredations were on a very large scale, and extended from the Atlantic coast of America and the Gulf of Mexico to the west coast of Africa, Madagascar, and the Indian Ocean.

then back to La Plata, during which interval some valuable prizes were made,[1] and finally round Cape Horn to Antigua, where the crew dispersed. Sharp and others on reaching England were, at the instance of the Spanish ambassador, tried for piracy, but acquitted on the ground that the Spanish ships captured by them had fired first, and that therefore the pirates had acted in self-defence.

In August, 1683, the ship *Revenge*, of eighteen guns and seventy men, among whom were Dampier, Wafer, Cook, Davis, and several other noted buccaneers, sailed from the Chesapeake. Near Sierra Leone they took a Danish ship of thirty-six guns, into which they shifted their crew, christening her the *Bachelor's Delight*, and reached in March, 1684, Juan Fernandez, accompanied by another English privateer, the *Nicholas*, Captain Swan, that fell in with them shortly before their arrival. Having taken a few prizes the ships proceeded in company to the Galapagos and then to the Gulf of Nicoya, where Captain Cook died and Davis was elected in his place. After cruising for some time together with moderate success the two vessels separated, the *Nicholas* proceeding to England, by way of the East Indies, while the *Bachelor's Delight* sailed to the island of La Plata, where she encountered the *Cygnet*, Captain Swan, a vessel which (fitted out in London as a trader) had come round Cape Horn and thence up the coast to the Gulf of Nicoya, where she had filled up her crew by a number of buccaneers, who had crossed the isthmus to that point. The two crews at once agreed to keep company, and accordingly sailed to Payta, Guayaquil[2] and Panama, taking several prizes during

[1] One of these prizes, the *San Rosario*, contained no less than 700 pigs or large ingots of silver, which were taken to be tin, and (with one exception only) thrown overboard by the ignorant sailors.

[2] Several hundred negroes were taken in vessels at Guayaquil, the greater part of which were set at liberty, against the advice of Dampier, who wished them to be employed in working the gold mines at Darien for the benefit of the adventurers.

the voyage. After blockading the latter town for some weeks, they were reinforced by Captains Grogniet and L'Escayer, with 200 French and 80 English freebooters from the isthmus, then by Townley, with 180 English from the same quarter, and again by 260 Frenchmen more, which raised their total strength to 960 men, distributed in ten vessels of various sizes, but (with the exception of the *Bachelor's Delight* and the *Cygnet*) carrying no cannon, Davis being elected Admiral. On the 28th May, 1685, the Spanish Treasure Fleet from Lima, numbering six heavily armed vessels, six smaller ones, and two fire ships, hove in sight ; but having received information that the buccaneers' fleet was cruising in the neighbourhood, they had found an opportunity of landing the greater part of the specie and other valuables with which they were laden. A distant cannonade took place between the two fleets, but the buccaneers were daunted by the heavy armament of the Spaniards, who, on their side, were too prudent to provoke an action by which they had nothing to gain. The former then withdrew to the Island of Quibo, where they found another body of pirates. Disputes soon arising between English and French, the former, under Davis, went north and plundered Leon and Rio Lexa, in Nicaragua. Here a fresh split took place, Swan and Townley going in search of the French, while Davis went to the Galapagos, and then cruised along the coast of Peru till the end of 1686, taking several vessels and sacking two or three small towns with profitable results. Some of his men, who desired to secure their plunder, now returned to the West Indies *viâ* Cape Horn, while the remainder who still adhered to Davis remained on the coast till April, 1687, when they encountered first a Spanish frigate, which they drove ashore and burnt, and shortly afterwards a squadron of very superior force, from which they successfully escaped after a running fight which lasted for seven days. In May they once more fell in with Townley and the French buccaneers, and with their re-united forces succeeded in capturing Guayaquil. This was practically the last exploit of Davis and his companions in the South Sea, for after a short visit to the Galapagos to refit they followed Knight round the Horn to the West Indies, where they arrived in the spring of 1688.

It may be interesting here to note that Lionel Wafer, from whose journal an account of this voyage is derived, accompanied Davis in the capacity of surgeon; also that Dampier in Swan's vessel, the *Cygnet*, occupied the post of pilot or quartermaster, a post analogous to that of navigating lieutenant or staff-commander in a man-of-war of the present day, and Ringrose, the author of the last part of this history, that of supercargo and pilot on the same vessel.

On leaving Rio Lexa the *Cygnet*, with two tenders and 340 men, cruised along the coast of Mexico and Central America for some time, her crew landing and skirmishing at intervals with the inhabitants, but they were not fortunate enough to meet the galleon from Manila, the capture of which had been their principal reason for visiting the coast. This disappointment resulted in the usual quarrel, and Townley accordingly went south to join Grogniet. Swan remained on the coast a short time, but more than sixty of his men being cut off [1] on shore by the Spaniards, the most severe defeat in the South Seas ever experienced by the buccaneers, he thought it better to retire, and the *Cygnet* therefore proceeded to Mindanao, in the Philippines, where a mutiny took place which caused Swan and thirty-six others to be left behind, the rest, among whom was Dampier, pursuing their voyage and visiting Celebes, Timor, and New Holland, or Northern Australia. Dampier and some others left her at the Nicobar Islands, and somehow managed to reach England. The *Cygnet* meanwhile just succeeded in reaching Madagascar but in

[1] Among the slain on this occasion was Basil Ringrose, above mentioned.

so crazy a condition that she sank at her anchors immediately after her arrival. Some of the crew settled or took service with the petty chiefs, the remainder returning home as opportunity offered.[1]

Grogniet and the 340 French who had parted company with Davis at Quibo in July, 1685, plundered several towns, and then unfortunately revisited Quibo, where they were discovered by a Spanish squadron in January, 1686, which burnt their vessel while the crew were on shore. They were, however, rescued from their difficulties by Townley, in whose company they went northward to Nicaragua, and sacked Granada. In May, Grogniet and half the French took the opportunity to recross the isthmus. The other adventurers, however, came back to Panama, disembarked, and took the neighbouring town of Lavelia, at which place the valuable cargo of the Lima fleet had been landed the previous year to avoid capture by the buccaneer fleet under Davis. With almost incredible carelessness the viceroy, and the merchants to whom this immense mass of treasure had been consigned, had taken no trouble to remove it to a place of safety, and it consequently fell an easy prey to Townley and his companions, who however lost several of their number in conveying it to the ships. In August they were attacked by three Spanish men-of-war, but were able to give a very good account of them by capturing two and burning the third. They lost, however, the gallant Townley, who died of his wounds a short time afterwards.

In January, Grogniet appeared, and the united forces once more plundered Guayaquil, but their leader was so severely wounded that he died soon after the assault.

In May, Davis rejoined them and remained until his retreat from the South Sea, whereupon, under the command of Le Picard, they set sail for New Spain and landed at Amapalla Bay. Here they destroyed

[1] See note, p. xxxiv.

their ships and marched across to New Segovia, which they took. This was their last exploit. We only know that they finally reached Cape Gracias a Dios, on the Gulf of Mexico, about February, 1688, and that the last buccaneers of the South Sea gradually dispersed and were heard of no more.

The first three parts of this volume, written in Dutch by John Esquemeling, and originally published in Amsterdam in 1678, under the title of *De Americæneche Zee Roovers*, became at once very popular, and were quickly translated into the principal European languages. The translators, however, allowed themselves considerable latitude in incorporating into their respective versions considerable additional matter, chiefly to bring into prominence the special merits of their compatriots, *e.g.*, the French version embodying many exploits of the French filibusters not referred to by the Dutch author, while the English edition makes Morgan the principal hero of the story. Esquemeling's book gives a very reliable account of the principal exploits of the buccaneers down to their final disappearance, with the notable exception of their adventures in the South Sea, of which he makes no mention. This defect is, however, amply supplied by the journal of Mr. Basil Ringrose, published in London, which is now extremely scarce and difficult to meet with. Ringrose in the capacity of pilot personally took part in Sharp's voyage and was killed in a plundering raid; his account is extremely curious and accurate. He also added several sketches and outlines of the principal points and islands along the coast, which have been faithfully reproduced. Captains Sharp and Cowley, a buccaneer well known in his time, also published their journals, but they add but little to what has already been narrated by Ringrose, Dampier, or Wafer.

THE TRANSLATOR TO THE READER.

THE present volume, both for its curiosity and ingenuity, I dare recommend to the perusal of our English nation, whose glorious actions it contains. What relates to the curiosity hereof, this piece, both of Natural and Human History, was no sooner published in the Dutch original than it was snatched up for the most curious libraries of Holland; it was translated into Spanish (two impressions thereof being sent into Spain in one year); it was taken notice of by the learned Academy of Paris; and finally recommended as worthy our esteem by the ingenious author of the Weekly Memorials for the Ingenious, printed here at London about two years ago. Neither all this undeservedly, seeing it enlarges our acquaintance of Natural History, so much prized and enquired for by the learned of this present age, with several observations not easily to be found in other accounts already received from America: and besides, it informs us (with huge novelty) of as great and bold attempts in point of military conduct and valour as ever were performed by mankind; without excepting here either Alexander the Great or Julius Cæsar or the rest of the Nine Worthies of Fame. Of all which actions, as we cannot but confess ourselves to have been ignorant hitherto (the very name of Buccaneers *being as yet known but to few of the ingenious, as their lives, laws and conversation are in a manner unto none), so can they not choose but be admired, out of this ingenious Author, by whosoever is curious to learn the various revolutions of human affairs. But, more especially by our English Nation, as unto whom these things more narrowly appertain. We having here more than half the Book filled with the unparalleled if not inimitable adventures and heroic exploits of our own countrymen and relations, whose undaunted and exemplary courage, when called upon by our King and Country, we ought to emulate.*

From whence it has proceeded that nothing of this kind was ever as yet published in England, I cannot easily determine; except, as some will say, from some secret ragion di Stato. *Let the reason be as it will, this is certain, so much the more we are obliged to this present Author, who, though a stranger to our nation, yet with that candour and fidelity has recorded our actions, as to render the metal of our true English valour to be the more believed and feared abroad, than if these things had been divulged by ourselves at home. From hence peradventure will other nations learn, that the English people are of their genius more inclinable to act than to write; seeing as well they as we have lived unacquainted with these actions of our nation, until such time as a foreign Author to our country came to tell them.*

Besides the merit of this piece for its curiosity, another point of no less esteem is the truth and sincerity wherewith everything seems to be penned. No greater ornament or dignity can be added to History, either human or natural, than truth. All other embellishments, if this be failing, are of little or no esteem; if this be delivered, are either needless or superfluous. What concerns this requisite in our Author, his lines everywhere declare the faithfulness and sincerity of his mind. He writes not by hearsay, but was an eye-witness, as he somewhere tells you, to all and every one of the bold and hazardous attempts which he relates. And these he delivers with such candour of style, such ingenuity of mind, such plainness of words, such conciseness of periods, so much divested of rhetorical hyperboles or the least flourishes of eloquence, so hugely void of passion or national reflections, that he strongly persuades all along to the credit of what he says ; yea, raises the mind of the Reader to believe these things far greater than what he has said; and having read him, leaves only this scruple or concern behind, that you can read him no longer. In a word, such are his deserts that some persons peradventure would not stickle to compare him to the Father of Historians, Philip de Comines : at least, thus much may be said, with all truth imaginable, that he resembles that great Author in many of his excellent qualities.

I know some persons have objected to the greatness of these prodigious Adventures, intimating that the resistance our Buccaneers found in America was everywhere but small. For the Spaniards, say they, in the West Indies, are become of late years nothing less, but rather much more, degenerate than in Europe, the continual peace they have enjoyed in those parts, the defect of military discipline, and European soldiers for their commanders, much contributing hereunto. But more especially and above all other reasons the very luxury of the soil and riches, the extreme heat of those countries and influence of the stars being such as totally incline their bodies to an infinite effeminacy and cowardice of mind.

Unto these reasons I shall only answer in brief, This history will convince them to be manifestly false. For as to the continual peace here alleged, we know that no peace could ever be established beyond the Line, *since the first possession of the West Indies by the Spaniards till the burning of Panama. At that time, or few months before, Sir William Godolphin by his prudent negociation in quality of Ambassador for our most Gracious Monarch concluded at Madrid a peace to be observed even beyond the Line and through the whole extent of the Spanish Dominions in the West Indies. This transaction gave the Spaniards new causes of complaints against our proceedings, that no sooner a peace had been established for those parts of America, but our Forces had taken and burnt both Chagre, St. Catharine, and Panama. But our Reply was convincing, That whereas eight or ten months had been allowed by Articles for the publishing of the said Peace through all the Dominions of both Monarchies in America, those hostilities had been committed, not only without orders from his Majesty of England but also within the space of the said eight or ten months of time. Until that time the Spanish inhabitants of America being, as it were, in a perpetual war with Europe, certain it is, that no Coasts nor Kingdoms in the World have been more frequently infested nor alarmed with the invasions of several nations than theirs. Thus from the very beginning of their conquests in America, both English, French, Dutch, Portuguese, Swedes, Danes, Courlanders and all other Nations that navigate the Ocean, have frequented the West Indies, and filled them with their robberies and assaults. From these occasions have they been in continual watch and ward, and kept their Militia in constant exercise, as also their Garrisons pretty well provided and paid; as fearing every sail they discovered at sea to be Pirates of one nation or another. But much more especially, since that Curaçoa, Tortuga and Jamaica have been inhabited by English, French and Dutch, and bred up that race of huntsmen, than which no other ever was more desperate nor more mortal enemies to the Spaniards, called Buccaneers. Now shall we say that these People, through too long continuation of peace, have utterly abolished the exercises of war, having been all along incessantly vexed with the tumults and alarms thereof?*

In like manner is it false to accuse their defect of military discipline for want of European Commanders. For who knows not that all places, both military and civil, through those vast Dominions of the West Indies are provided out of Spain? And those of the Militia most commonly given to expert Commanders trained up from their infancy in the Wars of Europe, either in Africa,

Milan, Sicily, Naples or Flanders, fighting against either English, French, Dutch, Portuguese or Moors? Yea, their very garrisons, if you search them in those parts, will peradventure be found to be stocked, three parts to four with soldiers both born and bred in the Kingdom of Spain.

From these considerations it may be inferred what little difference ought to be allowed betwixt the Spanish soldiers, inhabitants of the West Indies, and those of Europe. And how little the soil or climate has influenced or caused their courage to degenerate towards cowardice or baseness of mind. As if the very same arguments, deduced from the nature of that climate, did not equally militate against the valour of our famous Buccaneers, and represent this to be of as degenerate metal as theirs!

But nothing can be more clearly evinced than is the valour of the American Spaniards, either soldiers or officers, by the sequel of this history. What men ever fought more desperately than the garrison of Chagre? Their number being 314, and of all these only thirty remaining; of which number scarce ten were unwounded, and among them not one officer found alive? Were not 600 killed upon the spot at Panama, 500 at Gibraltar, almost as many more at Puerto del Principe, all dying with their arms in their hands and facing bravely the Enemy for the defence of their Country and private concerns? Did not those of the town of San Pedro both fortify themselves, lay several ambuscades, and lastly sell their lives as dear as ever any European soldier could do, L'Ollonais being forced to gain step by step his advance unto the town with huge loss both of blood and men? Many other instances might be produced out of this compendious volume of the generous resistance the Spaniards made in several places, though Fortune favoured not their arms.

Next, as to the personal valour of many of their Commanders, what man ever behaved himself more briskly than the Governor of Gibraltar; than the. Governor of Puerto del Principe, both dying for the defence of their towns; than Don Alonso del Campo, and others? Or what examples can easily parallel the desperate courage of the Governor of Chagre, who, though the palisades were fired, the terrepleins were sunk into the ditch, the breaches were entered, the houses all burnt about him, the whole castle taken, his men all killed, yet would not admit of any quarter, but chose rather to die under his arms, being shot into the brain, than surrender himself as a prisoner unto the Buccaneers? What lion ever fought to the last gasp more obstinately than the Governor of Porto Bello, who seeing the town entered by surprisal in the night, one chief castle blown up into the air, all the other forts and castles taken, his own assaulted several ways, both religious men and women placed at the front of the enemy to fix the ladders against the walls, yet spared not to kill as many of the said religious persons as he could; and at last, the walls being scaled, the castle entered and taken, all his own men overcome by fire and sword, who had cast down their arms and begged mercy from the enemy, yet would admit of none for his own life? Yea, with his own hands killed several of his soldiers, to force them to stand to their arms though all were lost. Yea, though his own wife and daughter begged of him upon their knees that he would save his life by craving quarter, though the enemy desired of him the same thing, yet would hearken to no cries nor persuasions, but they were forced to kill him, combating with his arms in his hands, being not otherwise able to take him prisoner as they were desirous to do. Shall these men be said to be influenced with cowardice, who thus acted to the very last scene of their own tragedies? Or shall we rather say, that they wanted not courage, but fortune? It being certainly true that he who is killed in a battle may be equally courageous with him that kills. And that whosoever derogates from the valour of the Spaniards in the West Indies diminishes in like manner the courage of the Buccaneers, his own countrymen, who have seemed to act beyond mortal men in America.

Now, to say something concerning John Esquemeling, the first author of this history. I take him to be a Dutchman, or at least born in Flanders, notwithstanding that the Spanish translation represents him to be native of the Kingdom of France ; his printing this history originally in Dutch, which doubtless must be his native tongue, who otherwise was but an illiterate man, together with the very sound of his name, convincing me thereunto. True it is, he set sail from France and was some years at Tortuga, but neither of these two arguments, drawn from the history, are prevalent. For were he a Frenchman born, how came he to learn the Dutch language so perfectly as to prefer it to his own—especially that not being spoken at Tortuga nor Jamaica, where he resided all the while ?

I hope I have made this English translation something more plain and correct than the Spanish. Some few notorious faults either of the printer or of the interpreter I am sure I have redressed. But the Spanish translator complaining much of the intricacy of style in the original (as flowing from a person who, as hath been said, was no scholar) as he was pardonable, being in great haste, for not rendering his own version so distinct and elaborate as he could desire ; so must I be excused from the one, that is to say, elegance, if I have cautiously declined the other, I mean confusion.

THE BUCCANEERS OF AMERICA.

PART I.

CHAPTER I.

The Author sets forth towards the Western Islands, in the Service of the West India Company of France. They meet with an English frigate, and arrive at the Island of Tortuga.

WE set sail from Havre de Grace, in France, in a ship called *St. John*, the second day of May, in the year 1666. Our vessel was equipped with eight and twenty guns, twenty mariners, and two hundred and twenty passengers, including in this number those whom the Company sent as free passengers, as being in their service. Soon after we came to an anchor under the Cape of Barfleur, there to join seven other ships of the same West India Company, which were to come from Dieppe under the convoy of a man-of-war, mounted with seven and thirty guns and two hundred and fifty men. Of these ships two were bound for Senegal, five for the Caribbee Islands, and ours for the Island of Tortuga. In the same place there gathered unto us about twenty sail of other ships that were bound for Newfoundland, with some Dutch vessels that were going for Nantes, Rochelle, and St. Martins; so that in all we made a fleet of thirty sail. Here we prepared to fight, putting ourselves into a convenient posture of defence, as having notice that four English frigates, of threescore guns each, lay in wait

for us about the Isle of Ornay.   Our Admiral, the
Chevalier Sourdis, having distributed what orders he
thought convenient, we set sail from thence with a favourable gale of wind.   Presently after, some mists arising,
these totally impeded the English frigates from discovering our fleet at sea.   We steered our course as near as
we could under the coast of France, for fear of the enemy.
As we sailed along, we met a vessel of Ostend, who
complained to our Admiral that a French privateer had
robbed him that very morning.   This complaint being
heard, we endeavoured to pursue the said pirate ; but our
labour was in vain, as not being able to overtake him.

Our fleet, as we went along, caused no small fears and
alarms to the inhabitants of the coasts of France, these
judging us to be English, and that we sought some convenient place for landing.   To allay their frights, we used
to hang out our colours ; but, notwithstanding, they would
not trust us.   After this we came to an anchor in the
Bay of Conquet, in Brittany, near the Isle of Ushant,
there to take in water.   Having stored ourselves with
fresh provisions at this place, we prosecuted our voyage,
designing to pass by the Ras of Fonteneau and not
expose ourselves to the Sorlingues, fearing the English
vessels that were cruising thereabouts to meet us.   This
river Ras is of a current very strong and rapid, which,
rolling over many rocks, disgorges itself into the sea on
the coast of France, in the latitude of eight and forty
degrees and ten minutes.   For which reason this passage
is very dangerous, all the rocks as yet being not thoroughly known.

Here I shall not omit to mention the ceremony which
at this passage, and some other places, is used by the
mariners, and by them called Baptism, although it may
seem either little to our purpose or of no use.   The
Master's Mate clothed himself with a ridiculous sort of
garment that reached to his feet, and on his head he put
a suitable cap, which was made very burlesque.   In his

right hand he placed a naked wooden sword, and in his
left a pot full of ink. His face was horribly blacked with
soot, and his neck adorned with a collar of many little
pieces of wood. Being thus apparelled, he commanded
to be called before him every one of them who never
had passed that dangerous place before. And then causing them to kneel down in his presence, he made the sign
of the Cross upon their foreheads with ink, and gave each
one a stroke on the shoulders with his wooden sword
Meanwhile the standers-by cast a bucket of water upon
every man's head ; and this was the conclusion of the
ceremony. But, that being ended, every one of the
baptized is obliged to give a bottle of brandy for his
offering, placing it near the main-mast, and without
speaking a word ; even those who have no such liquor
being not excused from this performance. In case the
vessel never passed that way before, the Captain is
obliged to distribute some wine among the mariners and
other people in the ship. But as for other gifts which
the newly baptized frequently offer, they are divided
among the old seamen, and of them they make a banquet
among themselves.

The Hollanders likewise baptize such as never passed
that way before. And not only at the passage above-
mentioned, but also at the rocks called Berlingues, near
the coast of Portugal, in the latitude of thirty-nine degrees and forty minutes, being a passage very dangerous,
especially by night, when through the obscurity thereof
the rocks are not distinguishable. But their manner of
baptizing is quite distinct from that which we have described above as performed by the French. He, therefore,
that is to be baptized is fastened, and hoisted up three
times at the main-yard's end, as if he were a criminal.
If he be hoisted the fourth time, in the name of the Prince
of Orange or of the Captain of the vessel, his honour is
more than ordinary. Thus they are dipped, every one,
several times into the main ocean. But he that is the

first dipped has the honour of being saluted with a gun. Such as are not willing to fall are bound to pay twelve pence for their ransom ; if he be an officer in the ship, two shillings ; and if a passenger, according to his pleasure.   In case the ship never passed that way before, the Captain is bound to give a small runlet of wine, which, if he does not perform, the mariners may cut off the stem of the vessel. All the profit which accrues by this ceremony is kept by the Master's Mate, who after reaching their port usually lays it out in wine, which is drunk amongst the ancient seamen.   Some say this ceremony was instituted by the Emperor Charles the Fifth ; howsoever, it is not found amongst his Laws.   But here I leave these customs of the sea, and shall return to our voyage.

Having passed the river Ras, we met with very good weather until we came to Cape Finisterre.   Here a huge tempest of wind surprised us, and separated our ship from the rest that were in our company.   This storm continued for the space of eight days, in which time it would move compassion to see how miserably the passengers were tumbled to and fro on all sides of the ship ; insomuch as the mariners in the performance of their duty were compelled to tread upon them everywhere.   This uncouthsome weather being spent, we had again the use of very favourable gales until we came to the Tropic of Cancer.   This Tropic is nothing but an imaginary circle which astrologers have invented in the heavens, and serves as a period to the progress of the sun towards the North Pole.   It is placed in the latitude of three and twenty degrees and thirty minutes, under the line.   Here we were baptized the second time, after the same manner as before.   The French always perform this ceremony at this Tropic, as also under the Tropic of Capricorn, towards the South.   In this part of the world we had very favourable weather, at which we were infinitely gladdened by reason of our great necessity of water. For at this time that element was already so scarce with us that we were stinted to two half-pints per man every day.

Being about the latitude of Barbados, we met an English frigate, or privateer, who first began to give us chase; but finding himself not to exceed us in strength, presently steered away from us. This flight gave us occasion to pursue the said frigate, as we did, shooting at him several guns of eight pound carriage. But at length he escaped, and we returned to our course. Not long after, we came within sight of the Isle of Martinique. Our endeavours were bent towards the coast of the Isle of St. Peter. But these were frustrated by reason of a storm, which took us hereabouts. Hence we resolved to steer to the Island of Guadaloupe. Yet neither this island could we reach by reason of the said storm, and thus we directed our course to the Isle of Tortuga, which was the very same land to which we were bound. We passed along the coast of the Isle of Porto Rico, which is extremely delicious and agreeable to the view, as being adorned with beautiful trees and woods, even to the tops of the mountains. After this, we discovered the Island Hispaniola (of which I shall give a description in this book), and we coasted about it until we came to the Isle of Tortuga, our desired port. Here we anchored the seventh day of July in the same year, not having lost one man in the whole voyage. We unladed the goods that belonged to the Company of the West Indies, and soon after the ship was sent to Cul de Sac with some passengers.

CHAPTER II.

Description of the Island of Tortuga : of the fruits and plants there growing: how the French settled there, at two several times, and cast out the Spaniards, first masters thereof. The Author of this book was twice sold in the said Island.

THE Island of Tortuga is situated on the North side of the famous and great island called Hispaniola, near the Continent thereof and in the latitude of twenty degrees and thirty minutes. Its exact extent is threescore leagues about. The Spaniards, who gave name to this island, called it so from the shape of the land, which in some manner resembles a great sea tortoise, called by them *tortuga de mar*. The country is very mountainous and full of rocks, yet notwithstanding hugely thick of lofty trees that cease not to grow upon the hardest of those rocks without partaking of a softer soil. Hence it comes that their roots, for the greatest part, are seen all over entangled among the rocks, not unlike the branching of ivy against our walls. That part of this island which stretches towards the North is totally uninhabited. The reason is, first, because it has proved to be very incommodious and unhealthy, and, secondly, for the ruggedness of the coast, that gives no access to the shore, unless among rocks almost inaccessible. For this cause it is populated only on the Southern part, which has only one port that may be esteemed indifferently good. Yet this harbour has two several entries, or channels, which afford passage to ships of seventy guns, the port itself being without danger and capable of receiving a great number of vessels. That part which is inhabited is divided into four other parts, of which the first is called the Low-land, or Low-country. This is the chief of them all, because it contains the aforesaid port. The town is called Cayona, and here live the chief and richest planters of the island. The second part is called the Middle Plantation. Its territory, or soil, is hitherto almost new, as being only known to be good for the culture of tobacco. The third is named Ringot. These places are situated towards the Western part of the island. The fourth, and last, is called The Mountain, in which place were made the first plantations that were cultivated upon this island.

As to the wood that grows on the island, we have already said that the trees are exceedingly tall and pleasing to the sight ; whence no man will doubt but they may be applied to several uses with great benefit. Such is the Yellow Saunder, which tree by the inhabitants of this country is called *Bois de Chandelle*, or in English Candlewood, because it burns like a candle, and serves them with light while they use their fishery in the night. Here also grows *Lignum Sanctum*, by others called *Guaiacum*, the virtues of which are very well known. The trees likewise that afford *Gummi Elemi* grow here in great abundance, and in like manner *Radix Chinæ*, or China Root ; yet this is not so good as that which comes from other parts of the Western world. It is very white and soft, and serves for pleasant food to the wild boars when they can find nothing else. This island also is not deficient in Aloes, nor an infinite number of other medicinal herbs, which may please the curiosity of such as are given to their contemplation. Moreover for the building of ships, or any other sort of architecture, here are found, in this spot of Neptune, several sorts of timber very convenient. The fruits, likewise, which here abundantly grow, are nothing inferior, as to their quantity or quality, to what the adjacent islands produce. I shall name only some of the most ordinary and common. Such are magniot,[1] potatoes, Acajou apples, yannas,[2] bacones, paquayes, carosoles, mamayns,[3] ananas and diverse other sorts, which, not to be tedious, I omit to specify. Here grow likewise in huge number those trees called Palmetto, whence is drawn a certain juice which serves the inhabitants instead of wine, and whose leaves cover their houses instead of tiles.

In this island abounds also, with daily increase, the Wild Boar. The Governor has prohibited the hunting of them with dogs, fearing lest, the island being but small, the whole race of those animals in short time should be destroyed. The reason why he thought convenient to preserve those wild beasts was that in case of any invasion of an external enemy the inhabitants might sustain themselves with their food, especially if they were constrained to retire to the woods and mountains. By this means he judged they were enabled to maintain any sudden assault or long persecution. Yet this sort of game is almost impeded by itself, by reason of the many rocks and precipices, which for the greatest part are covered with little shrubs, very green and thick, whence the huntsmen have ofttimes precipitated themselves, and left us the sad experience and grief of many memorable disasters.

At a certain time of the year huge flocks of Wild Pigeons resort to this Island of Tortuga, at which season the inhabitants feed on them very plentifully, having more than they can consume, and leaving totally to their repose all other sorts of fowl, both wild and tame, to the intent that in absence of the pigeons these may supply their place. But as nothing in the universe, though never so pleasant, can be found but what has

[1] Probably the mango. There is, however, a local term, "manihot," applied to cassava.
[2] Probably the yam.
[3] The mammee apple.

something of bitterness joined to it, the very symbol of this truth we see in the aforesaid pigeons. For these, the season being past wherein God has appointed them to afford delicious food to those people, can scarcely be touched with the tongue, they become so extremely lean and bitter even to admiration. The reason of this bitterness is attributed to a certain seed which they eat about that time, as bitter as gall. About the sea shores great multitudes of Crabs [1] are everywhere found, belonging both to the land and sea, and both sorts very big. These are good to feed servants and slaves, who find them very pleasing to the palate, yet withal very hurtful to the sight. Besides which symptom, being eaten too often, they also cause great giddiness in the head, with much weakness of the brain, insomuch that very frequently they are deprived of sight for the space of one quarter of an hour.

The French, having in 1625 established themselves in the Isle of St. Christopher, planted there a sort of trees, of which at present there possibly may be greater quantities. With the timber of those trees they made Longboats and Hoys, which they sent thence westward, well manned and victualled, to discover other islands. These, setting sail from St. Christopher, came within sight of the Island of Hispaniola, where at length they arrived with abundance of joy. Having landed, they marched into the country, where they found huge quantities of cattle, such as cows, bulls, horses and wild boars. But finding no great profit in those animals unless they could enclose them, and knowing likewise the island to be pretty well peopled by the Spaniards, they thought it convenient to enterprize upon and seize the Island of Tortuga. This they performed without any difficulty there being upon the island no more than ten or twelve

---

[1] Land-crabs are abundant in the West Indies. The violet land-crab (*Gecarcinus ruricola*), living in communities, burrowing and travelling great distances, is the principal variety—it is a great delicacy.

Spaniards to guard it. These few men let the French
come in peaceably and possess the island for the space
of six months, without any trouble. In the meanwhile
they passed and repassed with their canoes to Hispaniola,
whence they transported many people, and at last began
to plant the whole Isle of Tortuga. The few Spaniards
remaining there, perceiving the French to increase their
number daily, began at last to repine at their prosperity
and grudge them the possession they had freely given.
Hence they gave notice to others of their own nation,
their neighbours, who sent several great boats, well armed
and manned, to dispossess the French of that island. This
expedition succeeded according to their desires. For the
new possessors, seeing the great number of Spaniards that
came against them, fled with all they had to the woods ;
and hence by night they wafted over with canoes to the
Isle of Hispaniola. This they more easily performed
having no women or children with them, nor any great
substance to carry away. Here they also retired into the
woods, both to seek themselves food, and thence with
secrecy to give intelligence to others of their own faction ;
judging for certain that within a little while they should
be in a capacity to hinder the Spaniards from fortifying
in Tortuga.

Meanwhile the Spaniards of the greater island ceased
not to seek after their new guests, the French, with intent to root them out of the woods, if possible, or cause
them to perish with hunger. But this their design soon
failed, having found that the French were masters both
of good guns, powder and bullets. Here, therefore,
the fugitives waited for a certain opportunity, wherein
they knew the Spaniards were to come from Tortuga,
with arms and great number of men, to join with those
of the greater Island for their destruction. When this
occasion proffered, they, in the meanwhile deserting the
woods where they were, returned to Tortuga, and dis
possessed the small number of Spaniards that remained

at home. Having so done, they fortified themselves as best they could, thereby to prevent the return of the Spaniards, in case they should attempt it. Moreover, they sent immediately to the Governor of St. Christopher, in 1630, craving his aid and relief, and demanding of him to send them a Governor, the better to be united among themselves and strengthened on all occasions. The Governor of St. Christopher received their petition with expressions of much satisfaction, and without any delay sent to them Monsieur le Passeur in quality of a Governor, together with a ship full of men and all other things necessary both for their establishment and defence. No sooner had they received this recruit than the Governor commanded a fortress to be built upon the top of a high rock, whence he could hinder the access of any ships or other vessels that should design to enter the port. To this fort no other access could be had than by almost climbing through a very narrow passage, that was capable only of receiving two persons at once, and those not without difficulty. In the middle of this rock was a great cavity, which now serves for a storehouse ; and, besides, here was great convenience for raising a battery. The fort being finished, the Governor commanded two guns to be mounted, which could not be performed without huge toil and labour, as also a house to be built in the fort ; and, afterwards, the narrow way that led to the said fort to be broken and demolished, leaving no other ascent thereto than by a ladder. Within the fort a plentiful fountain of fresh water gushes out, which perpetually runs with a pure and crystalline stream sufficient to refresh a garrison of a thousand men. Being possessed of these conveniences, and the security these things might promise, the French began to people the island, and each of them to seek his living, some by the exercise of hunting, others by planting tobacco, and others by cruising and robbing upon the coasts of the Spanish Islands—which trade is continued by them to this day.

The Spaniards, notwithstanding, could not behold but with jealous eyes the daily increase of the French in Tortuga, fearing lest in time they might by them be dispossessed also of Hispaniola. Thus taking an opportunity, when many of the French were abroad at sea, and others employed in hunting, with eight hundred men in several canoes, they landed again in Tortuga, almost without being perceived by the French. But finding that the Governor had cut down many trees, for the better discovery of an enemy in case of any assault, also that nothing of consequence could be done without great guns, they consulted about the fittest place for raising a battery. This place was soon concluded to be the top of a mountain which was in sight, seeing that thence alone they could level their guns at the fort, which now lay open to them, since the cutting down of the trees by the new possessors. Hence they resolved to open a way for carriage of some pieces of ordnance to the top. This mountain is somewhat high, and the upper part plain, whence the whole island may be viewed. The sides thereof are very rugged by reason of a huge number of inaccessible rocks surrounding it everywhere ; so that the ascent was very difficult, and would always have been the same, had not the Spaniards undergone the immense labour and toil of making the way aforementioned, as I shall now relate.

The Spaniards had in their company many slaves, and Indians, labouring men, whom they call *Matates*, or, in English, half-yellow men. To these they gave orders to dig a way through the rocks with iron tools. This they performed with the greatest speed imaginable. And through this way, by the help of many ropes and pulleys, they at last made shift to get up two sole cannon pieces, wherewith they made a battery, and intended next day to batter the fort. Meanwhile the French were not ignorant of these designs, but rather prepared themselves for a defence (while the Spaniards were busied about the

battery), sending notice everywhere to their companions
requiring their help. Thus the hunters of the island all
joined together, and with them all the pirates who were
not already too far from home. These landed by night
at Tortuga, lest they should be seen by the Spaniards.
And under the same obscurity of the night, they all
together by a back way climbed up the mountain where
the Spaniards were posted ; which they more easily could
perform as being acquainted with those rocks. They
came thither at the very instant that the Spaniards, who
were above, were preparing to shoot at the fort, not
knowing in the least of their coming. Here they set
upon them, at their backs, with such fury as forced the
greatest part to precipitate themselves from the top to the
bottom, and dash their bodies in pieces. Few or none
escaped this attack, for if any remained alive they were
all put to the sword, without giving quarter to the
meanest. Some Spaniards still kept the bottom of the
mountain, but hearing the shrieks and cries of them
that were killed, and believing some tragical revolution
to be above, fled immediately towards the sea, despair-
ing, through this accident, to ever regain the Isle of
Tortuga.

The Governors of this island always behaved themselves as proprietors and absolute lords thereof until the
year 1664 ; at which time the West India Company of
France took possession of it, and sent thither for their
Governor, Monsieur Ogeron. These planted the colony
for themselves, by the means of their factors and servants,
thinking to drive some considerable trade thence with the
Spaniards, even as the Hollanders do from Curaçoa.
But this design did not answer their expectation. For
with other nations they could drive no trade, by reason
they could not establish any secure commerce from the
beginning with their own. Forasmuch as at the first
institution of this Company in France, they made an
agreement with the pirates, hunters and planters, first

possessors of Tortuga, that these should buy all their
necessaries from the said Company, taking them upon
trust. And although this agreement was put in execution, yet the factors of the Company soon after found that
they could not recover either monies or returns from
those people. Insomuch as they were constrained to
bring some armed men into the island, in behalf of the
Company, to get in some of their payments. But neither
this endeavour nor any other could prevail towards
settling a secure trade with those of the island. And
hereupon the Company recalled their factors, giving
them orders to sell all that was their own in the said
plantation, both the servants belonging to the Company
(which were sold, some for twenty, others for thirty,
pieces of eight), as also all other merchandizes and properties which they had there. With this resolution all
their designs fell to the ground.

In this occasion I was also sold, as being a servant
under the said Company, in whose service I came out of
France. But my fortune was very bad, for I fell into the
hands of the most cruel tyrant and perfidious man that
ever was born of woman, who was then Governor, or
rather Lieutenant General, of that island. This man
treated me with all the hard usages imaginable, even with
that of hunger, with which I thought I should have
perished inevitably. Withal he was willing to let me buy
my freedom and liberty, but not under the rate of three
hundred pieces of eight, I not being master of one, at
that time, in the whole world. At last through the
manifold miseries I endured, as also affliction of mind, I
was thrown into a dangerous fit of sickness. This misfortune, being added to the rest of my calamities, was the
cause of my happiness. For my wicked master, seeing
my condition, began to fear lest he should lose his monies
with my life. Hereupon he sold me the second time to
a surgeon for the price of seventy pieces of eight. Being
in the hands of this second master, I began soon after to

recover my health through the good usage I received
from him, as being much more humane and civil than
that of my first patron. He gave me both clothes and
very good food, and after I had served him but one year
he offered me my liberty, with only this condition, that I
should pay him one hundred pieces of eight when I was
in a capacity of wealth to do so. Which kind proposal of
his I could not choose but accept with infinite joy and
gratitude of mind.

Being now at liberty, though like unto Adam when he
was first created by the hands of his Maker—that is,
naked and destitute of all human necessaries, nor knowing
how to get my living—I determined to enter into the
wicked order of the Pirates, or Robbers at Sea. Into
this Society I was received with common consent both of
the superior and vulgar sort, and among them I continued
until the year 1672. Having assisted them in all their
designs and attempts, and served them in many notable
exploits, of which hereafter I shall give the reader a true
account, I returned to my own native country. But before I begin to relate the things above-mentioned, I shall
say something, for the satisfaction of such as are curious,
of the Island Hispaniola, which lies towards the Western
parts of America, as also give my reader a brief description thereof, according to my slender ability and experience.

CHAPTER III.

Description of the great and famous Island of Hispaniola.

THE very large and rich island called Hispaniola is situate in the latitude of seventeen degrees and a half. The greatest part thereof extends, from East to West, twenty degrees Southern latitude. The circumference is three hundred leagues, the length one hundred and twenty, its breadth almost fifty, being more or less broad or narrow at certain places. I shall not need here to insert how this island was at first discovered, it being known to the world that it was performed by the means of Christopher Columbus, in the year 1492, being sent for this purpose by Ferdinand, the Catholic, then King of Spain. From which time, to this present, the Spaniards have been continually possessors thereof. There are on this island many very good

and strong cities, towns and hamlets; it also abounds
in a great number of pleasant and delicious country-
houses and plantations; all which are owing to the care
and industry of the Spaniards, its inhabitants.

The chief city and metropolis of this island is called
San Domingo, being dedicated to St. Dominic, from
whom it derives this name. It is situated towards the
South, in a place which affords a most excellent prospect,
the country round about being embellished with innumerable rich plantations, also verdant meadows and
fruitful gardens—all which produce plenty and variety of
excellent and pleasant fruits, according to the nature of
those countries. The Governor of the island makes his
residence in this city, which is, as it were, the storehouse
of all the other cities, towns and villages, which hence
export and provide themselves with all necessaries whatsoever for human life. And yet has it this particularity,
above many other cities in other places, that it entertains
no external commerce with any other nation than its own,
the Spaniards. The greatest part of the inhabitants are
rich and substantial merchants, or such as are shop-
keepers and sell by retail.

Another city of this island is named Santiago, or,
in English, St. James, as being consecrated to the
Apostle of that name. This is an open place, without
either walls or castle, situate in the latitude of nineteen
degrees South. The greatest part of the inhabitants
are hunters and planters, the adjacent territory and
soil being very proper for the said exercises of its
constitution. The city is surrounded with large and
delicious fields, as much pleasing to the view as those
of San Domingo; and these abound with all sorts of
beasts, both wild and tame, whence are taken a huge
number of skins and hides, that afford to the owners
a very considerable traffic.

Towards the Southern parts of this island is seen
another city called Nuestra Señora del Alta Gracia.

The territory hereof produces great quantities of cacao, which occasions the inhabitants to make great store of the richest sort of chocolate. Here grows also much ginger and tobacco ; and much tallow is prepared of the beasts which hereabouts are hunted.

The inhabitants of this beautiful island of Hispaniola often go and come in their canoes to the Isle of Savona, not far distant thence, where is their chief fishery, especially of tortoises. Hither those fish constantly resort in huge multitudes at certain seasons of the year, there to lay their eggs, burying them in the sands of the shore. Thus by the heat of the sun, which in those parts is very ardent, they are hatched, and continue the propagation of their species. This island of Savona has little or nothing that is worthy consideration or may merit any particular description, as being so extremely barren, by reason of its sandy soil. True it is, that here grows some small quantity of *lignum sanctum* or *guaiacum.*

Westwards of the city of San Domingo is also situated another great village, called by the name of El Pueblo del Aso, or the Town of Aso. The inhabitants of this town drive a great commerce and traffic with those of another village, which is placed in the very middle of the island, and is called San Juan de Goave, or St. John of Goave. This place is environed with a magnificent prospect of gardens, woods and meadows. Its territory extends above twenty leagues in length, and grazes a huge number of wild bulls and cows. In this village scarce dwell any others than hunters and butchers, who flay the beasts that are killed. These are for the most part a mongrel sort of people of several bloods [1] ; some of which are born of white Euro-

---

[1] The offspring of a negro and Indian, or a person with three-fourths of black blood, is denominated a zambo or sambo; a mixture of half white and half black is strictly the mulatto ; three parts white to one part black forms the quadroon; one-eighth part of black blood marks the mustee or octoroon ; after the octoroon the mixed race are usually considered to be " white-washed," and rank as white. In the British

pean people and negroes, and these are called *Mulattos.*
Others are born of Indians and white people, and such
are termed *Mestizos.* But others are begotten of negroes
and Indians, and these also have their peculiar name,
being called *Alcatraces.* Besides which sorts of people,
there are several other species and races, both here and
in other places of the West Indies, of whom this account
may be given, that the Spaniards love better the negro
women, in those Western parts, or the tawny Indian
females, than their own white European race, whereas
peradventure the negroes and Indians have greater
inclinations to the white women, or those that come near
them, the tawny, than their own. From the said village
are exported yearly vast quantities of tallow and hides,
they exercising no other traffic nor toil. For as to the
lands in this place, they are not cultivated, by reason of
the excessive dryness of the soil. These are the chiefest
places that the Spaniards possess in this island, from the
Cape of Lobos towards St. John de Goave, to the Cape
of Samana, near the sea, on the North side, and from the
Eastern part, towards the sea, called Punta d'Espada.
All the rest of the island is possessed by the French, who
are also planters and hunters.

This island has very good ports for ships, from the
Cape of Lobos to the Cape of Tiburon, which lies on the
Western side thereof. In this space of land there are
no less than four ports, which exceed in goodness,
largeness and security even the very best of England.
Besides these, from the Cape of Tiburon to the Cape of
Donna Maria, there are two very excellent ports, and
from this Cape to the Cape of St. Nicholas there are no
less than twelve others. Every one of these ports has
also the confluence of two or three good rivers, in which

West Indies very few of the negroes are of pure black blood, owing to
the number of convicts and political prisoners who were sent to the
plantations during the earlier settlements of the islands. In Montserrat
(known as little Ireland), which was largely colonized by Irish prisoners,
the negroes universally bear Irish surnames, and retain the Irish accent.

are found several sorts of fish, very pleasing to the palate, and also in great plenty. The country hereabouts is sufficiently watered with large and profound rivers and brooks, so that this part of the land may easily be cultivated without any great fear of droughts, it being certain that better streams are not to be found in any part of the world. The sea coasts and shores are also very pleasant, to which the tortoises resort in huge numbers, there to lay their eggs.

This island was formerly very well peopled on the North side with many towns and villages; but these, being ruined by the Hollanders, were at last for the greatest part deserted by the Spaniards.

CHAPTER IV.

Of the Fruits, Trees and Animals that are found at Hispaniola.

THE spacious fields of this island commonly extend themselves to the length of five or six leagues, the beauty whereof is so pleasing to the eye that, together with the great variety of their natural productions, they infinitely applaud and captivate the senses of the contemplator. For here at once they not only, with diversity of objects, recreate the sight, but, with many of the same, also please the smell, and, with most, contribute abundancy of delights to the taste. With sundry diversities also they flatter and excite the appetite ; but more especially with the multitude of oranges and lemons, here growing both sweet and sour, and those that participate of both tastes, and are only pleasantly tart. Besides which here abundantly grow several other sorts of the same fruit, such as are called citrons, toronjas and limes, in English not improperly called crab-lemons. True it is that, as to the lemons, they do not exceed here the bigness of a hen's egg ; which smallness distinguishes them from those of Spain most frequently used in these our Northern countries. The date-trees, which here are seen to cover the whole extent of very spacious plains, are exceedingly tall in their proportion, which notwithstanding does not offend but rather delight the view. Their height is observed to be from 150 to 200 feet, being wholly destitute of branches to the very tops. Here it is there grows a certain pleasant white substance not unlike that of white cabbage, whence the branches and leaves sprout, and in which also the seed or dates are contained.

Every month one of those branches falls to the ground, and at the same time another sprouts out. But the seed ripens only once in the year. The dates are food extremely coveted by the hedgehogs. The white substance growing at the top of the tree is used by the Spaniards after the same manner for common sustenance as cabbage in Europe, they cutting it into slices, and boiling it in their *ollas*, or stews, with all sorts of meat. The leaves of this sort of date-tree are seven or eight foot in length and three or four in breadth, being very fit to cover houses with. For they defend from rain equally with the best tiles, though never so rudely huddled together. They make use of them also to wrap up smoked flesh with, and to make a certain sort of buckets wherewith to carry water, though no longer durable than the space of six, seven, or eight days. The cabbages of these trees, for so we may call them, are of a greenish colour on the outside, though inwardly very white, whence may be separated a sort of rind, which is very like parchment, being fit to write upon, as we do upon paper. The bodies of these trees are of an huge bulk or thickness, which two men can hardly compass with their arms. And yet they cannot properly be termed woody, but only three or four inches deep in thickness, all the rest of the internal part being very soft, insomuch that, paring off those three or four inches of woody substance, the remaining part of the body may be sliced like new cheese. They wound them three or four foot above the root, and, making an incision or broach in the body, thence gently distils a sort of liquor, which in short time by fermentation becomes as strong as the richest wine, and which easily inebriates if not used with moderation. The French call this sort of palm-trees *Frank-palms*, and they only grow, both here and elsewhere, in saltish grounds.

Besides these palm-trees of which we have made mention, there are also in Hispaniola four other species of palms, which are distinguished by the names of Latanier, Palma Espinosa or Prickle-palm, Palma à Chapelet or Rosary-palm, Palma Vinosa or Wine-palm. The Latanier-palm is not so tall as the Wine-palm, although it has almost the same shape, only that the leaves are very like the fans our women use. They grow mostly in gravelly and sandy ground, their circumference being of seven foot more or less. The body has many prickles or thorns of the length of half a foot, very sharp and pungent. It produces its seed after the same manner as that above-mentioned, which likewise serves for food to the wild beasts.

Another sort of these palm-trees is called Prickle-palm, as we said before, by reason it is infinitely full of prickles, from the root to the very leaves thereof, much more than the precedent. With these prickles some of the barbarous Indians torment their prisoners of war, whom they take in battle. They tie them to a tree, and then taking these thorns, they put them into little pellets of cotton, which they dip in oil, and thus stick them in the sides of the miserable prisoners, as thick as the bristles of a hedgehog ; which of necessity cause an incredible torment to the patient. Afterwards they set them on fire, and if the tormented prisoner sings in the midst of his torments and flames, he is esteemed as a valiant and courageous soldier, who neither fears his enemies nor their torments. But if on the contrary he cries out, they esteem him but as a poltroon or coward, and unworthy of any memory. This custom was told me by an Indian, who said he had used his enemies thus oftentimes. The like cruelties to these, many Christians have seen while they lived among those barbarians. But returning to the Prickle-palm, I shall only tell you that this palm-tree is in this only different from the Latanier, that the leaves are like those of the Frank-palm. Its seed is like that of the other palm-trees, only much bigger and rounder, almost as a farthing, and inwardly

full of little kernels, which are as pleasing to the taste as
our walnuts in Europe. This tree grows for the most
part in the marshes and low grounds of the sea coast.

The Wine-palm is so called from the abundance of wine
which is gathered from it. This palm grows in high and
rocky mountains, not exceeding in tallness the height of
forty or fifty foot, but yet of an extraordinary shape or
form. For from the root to the half of its proportion, it
is only three or four inches thick. But upwards, something above the two-thirds of its height, it is as big and
as thick as an ordinary bucket or milk-pail. Within, it is
full of a certain matter, very like the tender stalk of a
white cabbage, which is very juicy of a liquor that is
much pleasing to the palate. This liquor after fermentation and settling of the grounds reduces itself into a very
good and clear wine, which is purchased with no great
industry. For having wounded the tree with an ordinary
hatchet, they make a square incision or orifice in it,
through which they bruise the said matter until it be
capable of being squeezed out, or expressed with the
hands, they needing no other instrument than this.
With the leaves they make certain vessels, not only to
settle and purify the afore-mentioned liquor, but also to
drink in. It bears its fruit like other palms, but of a
very small shape, being not unlike cherries. The taste
hereof is very good, but of dangerous consequence to the
throat, where it causes huge and extreme pains, that produce malignant quinsies in them that eat it.

The Palma à Chapelet, or Rosary-palm, was thus called
both by the French and Spaniards, because its seed is
very fit to make rosaries or beads to say prayers upon,
the beads being small, hard and capable of being easily
bored for that use. This fourth species grows on the tops
of the highest mountains, and is of an excessive tallness,
but withal very straight, and adorned with very few leaves.

Here grows also in this island a certain sort of Apricot
trees, whose fruit equals in bigness that of our ordinary

melons. The colour is like ashes, and the taste the very same as that of our apricots in Europe, the inward stones of this fruit being of the bigness of a hen's egg. On these the wild boars feed very deliciously, and fatten even to admiration.

The trees called caremites are very like our pear-trees, whose fruits resemble much our Damascene plums or pruants of Europe, being of a very pleasant and agreeable taste and almost as sweet as milk. This fruit is black on the inside, and the kernels thereof, sometimes only two in number, sometimes three, others five, of the bigness of a lupin. This plum affords no less pleasant food to the wild boars than the apricots above-mentioned, only that it is not so commonly to be found upon the island, nor in such quantity as those are.

The Genipa-trees are seen everywhere all over this island, being very like our cherry-trees, although its branches are more dilated. The fruit hereof is of an ash colour, of the bigness of two fists, which interiorly is full of many prickles or points that are involved under a thin membrane or skin, the which, if not taken away at the time of eating, causes great obstructions and gripings of the belly. Before this fruit grows ripe, if pressed, it affords a juice as black as ink, being fit to write with upon paper. But the letters disappear within the space of nine days, the paper remaining as white as if it never had been written upon. The wood of this tree is very strong, solid and hard, good to build ships with, seeing it is observed to last many years in the water without putrefaction.

Besides these, divers other sorts of trees are natives of this delicious island, that produce very excellent and pleasant fruits. Of these I shall omit to name several, knowing there are entire volumes of learned authors that have both described and searched them with greater attention and curiosity than my own. Notwithstanding, I shall continue to make mention of some few more in particular. Such are the Cedars, which trees this part of the world produces in prodigious quantity. The French nation calls them *Acajou;* and they find them very useful for the building of ships and canoes.[1] These canoes are like little wherry-boats, being made of one tree only, excavated, and fitted for the sea. They are withal so swift as for that very property they may be called "Neptune's post-horses." The Indians make these canoes without the use of any iron instruments, by only burning the trees at the bottom near the root, and afterwards governing the fire with such industry that nothing is burnt more than what they would have. Some of them have hatchets, made of flint, wherewith they scrape or pare off whatsoever was burnt too far. And thus, by the sole instrument of fire, they know how to give them that shape which renders them capable of navigating threescore or fourscore leagues with ordinary security.

As to medicinal productions, here is to be found the tree that affords the *gum elemi*, used in our apothecaries' shops. Likewise *guaiacum*, or *lignum sanctum*, *lignum aloes*, or aloe-wood, *cassia lignea*, China-roots, with several others. The tree called *mapou*, besides that it is medicinal, is also used for making of canoes, as being very thick; yet is it much inferior to the *acajou* or cedar, as being somewhat spongy, whereby it sucks in much water, rendering it dangerous in navigation. The tree called *acoma* has its wood very hard and heavy, of the colour of palm. These qualities render it very fit to make oars for the sugar mills. Here are also in great quantities *brasilete*, or brazil-wood, and that which the Spaniards call *mançanilla*.

Brazil-wood is now very well known in the provinces of Holland and the Low Countries. By another name it is called by the Spaniards *Lenna de Peje palo.* It

---

[1] The French term "Acajou" seems to be applied by the buccaneers to cedar wood; it is now, however, almost entirely confined to mahogany.

serves only, or chiefly, for dyeing, and what belongs to that trade. It grows abundantly along the sea coasts of this island, especially in two places called Jacmel and Jaquina. These are two commodious ports or bays, capable of receiving ships of the greatest bulk.

The tree called *mançanilla*, or dwarf-apple-tree,[1] grows near the sea shore, being naturally so low that its branches, though never so short, always touch the water. It bears a fruit something like our sweet-scented apples, which notwithstanding is of a very venomous quality. For these apples being eaten by any person, he instantly changes colour, and such a huge thirst seizes him as all the water of the Thames cannot extinguish, he dying raving mad within a little while after. But what is more, the fish that eat, as it often happens, of this fruit are also poisonous. This tree affords also a liquor, both thick and white, like the fig-tree, which, if touched by the hand, raises blisters upon the skin, and these are so red in colour as if it had been deeply scalded with hot water. One day being hugely tormented with mosquitos or gnats, and as yet unacquainted with the nature of this tree, I cut a branch thereof, to serve me instead of a fan, but all my face swelled the next day and filled with blisters, as if it were burnt to such a degree that I was blind for three days.

Ycao is the name of another sort of tree, so called by the Spaniards, which grows by the sides of rivers. This bears a certain fruit, not unlike our bullace or damson plums. And this food is extremely coveted by the wild boar, when at its perfect maturity, with which they fatten as much as our hogs with the sweetest acorns of Spain. These trees love sandy ground, yet are so low that, their branches being very large, they take up a great circumference, almost couched upon the ground. The trees named Abelcoses bear fruit of like colour with

---

[1] The well-known manchineel, erroneously supposed to be the upas-tree, which latter owes its reputation to a Malay legend.

the Ycaos above-mentioned, but of the bigness of melons, the seeds or kernels being as big as eggs. The substance of this fruit is yellow, and of a pleasant taste, which the poorest among the French eat instead of bread, the wild boar not caring at all for this fruit. These trees grow very tall and thick, being somewhat like our largest sort of pear-trees.

As to the insects which this island produces, I shall only take notice of three sorts of flies, which excessively torment all human bodies, but more especially such as never before, or but a little while, were acquainted with these countries. The first sort of these flies are as big as our common horse-flies in Europe. And these, darting themselves upon men's bodies, there stick and suck their blood till they can no longer fly. Their importunity obliges to make almost continual use of branches of trees wherewith to fan them away. The Spaniards in those parts call them mosquitos or gnats, but the French give them the name of *maranguines*. The second sort of these insects is no bigger than a grain of sand. These make no buzzing noise, as the preceding species does, for which reason it is less avoidable, as being able also through its smallness to penetrate the finest linen or cloth. The hunters are forced to anoint their faces with hogs'-grease, thereby to defend themselves from the stings of these little animals. By night, in their huts or cottages, they constantly for the same purpose burn the leaves of tobacco, without which smoke they were not able to rest. True it is that in the daytime they are not very troublesome, if any wind be stirring; for this, though never so little, causes them to dissipate. The gnats of the third species exceed not the bigness of a grain of mustard.[1] Their colour is red. These sting not at all, but bite so sharply upon the flesh as to create little ulcers therein. Whence it often

---

[1] This is the Bête rouge, one of the greatest plagues of the West Indies.

comes that the face swells and is rendered hideous to the view, through this inconvenience. These are chiefly troublesome by day, even from the beginning of the morning until sun-setting, after which time they take their rest, and permit human bodies to do the same. The Spaniards gave these insects the name of *rojados*, and the French that of *calarodes*.

The insects which the Spaniards call *cochinillas* and the English glow-worms are also to be found in these parts. These are very like such as we have in Europe, unless that they are somewhat bigger and longer than ours. They have two little specks on their heads, which by night give so much light that three or four of those animals, being together upon a tree, it is not discernible at a distance from a bright shining fire. I had on a certain time at once three of these cochinillas in my cottage, which there continued until past midnight, shining so brightly that without any other light I could easily read in any book, although of never so small a print. I attempted to bring some of these insects into Europe, when I came from those parts, but as soon as they came into a colder climate they died by the way. They lost also their shining on the change of air, even before their death. This shining is so great, according to what I have related, that the Spaniards with great reason may well call them from their luminous quality *moscas de fuego*, that is to say fire-flies.

There be also in Hispaniola an excessive number of *grillones* or crickets. These are of an extraordinary magnitude, if compared to ours, and so full of noise that they are ready to burst themselves with singing, if any person comes near them. Here is no lesser number of reptiles, such as serpents and others, but by a particular providence of the Creator these have no poison. Neither do they any other harm than to what fowl they can catch, but more especially to pullets, pigeons and others of this kind. Ofttimes these serpents or snakes are useful in houses to cleanse them of rats and mice. For with great cunning they counterfeit their shrieks, and hereby both deceive and catch them at their pleasure. Having taken them, they in no wise eat the guts of these vermin, but only suck their blood at first. Afterwards throwing away the guts, they swallow almost entire the rest of the body, which, as it should seem, they readily digest into soft excrements, of which they discharge their bellies. Another sort of reptiles belonging to this island is called by the name of *caçadores de moscas*, or fly-catchers. This name was given to this reptile by the Spaniards, by reason they never could experience it lived upon any other food than flies. Hence it cannot be said this creature causes any harm to the inhabitants, but rather benefit, seeing it consumes by its continual exercise of hunting the vexatious and troublesome flies.

Land-tortoises here are also in great quantities. They mostly breed in mud, and fields that are overflown with water. The inhabitants eat them, and testify they are very good food. But a sort of spider which is here found is very hideous. These are as big as an ordinary egg, and their feet as long as those of the biggest sea-crabs. Withal, they are very hairy, and have four black teeth, like those of a rabbit, both in bigness and shape. Notwithstanding, their bites are not venomous, although they can bite very sharply, and do use it very commonly. They breed for the most part in the roofs of houses. This island also is not free from the insect called in Latin *millepes*, and in Greek *scolopendria*, or " Many-feet " : neither is it void of scorpions. Yet, by the providence of nature, neither the one nor the other bears the least suspicion of poison. For although they cease not to bite, yet their wounds require not the application of any medicament for their cure. And although their bites cause some inflammation and swelling at the beginning, however these symptoms disappear of their own accord.

Thus in the whole circumference of Hispaniola, no animal is found that produces the least harm with its venom.

After the insects above-mentioned, I shall not omit to say something of that terrible beast called cayman. This is a certain species of crocodile, wherewith this island very plentifully abounds. Among these caymans some are found to be of a corpulency very horrible to the sight. Certain it is, that such have been seen as had no less than threescore and ten foot in length, and twelve in breadth. Yet more marvellous than their bulk is their cunning and subtlety wherewith they purchase their food. Being hungry, they place themselves near the sides of rivers, more especially at the fords, where cattle come to drink or wade over. Here they lie without any motion, nor stirring any part of their body, resembling an old tree fallen into the river, only floating upon the waters, whither these will carry them. Yet they recede not far from the bank-sides, but continually lurk in the same place, waiting till some wild boar or salvage cow comes to drink or refresh themselves at that place. At which point of time, with huge activity, they assault them, and seizing on them with no less fierceness, they drag the prey into the water and there stifle it. But what is more worthy admiration is, that three or four days before the caymans go upon this design, they eat nothing at all. But, diving into the river, they swallow one or two hundred-weight of stones, such as they can find. With these they render themselves more heavy than before, and make addition to their natural strength (which in this animal is very great), thereby to render their assault the more terrible and secure. The prey being thus stifled, they suffer it to lie four or five days under water untouched. For they could not eat the least bit thereof, unless half rotten. But when it is arrived at such a degree of putrefaction as is most pleasing to their palate, they devour it with great appetite and voracity. If they can lay hold on any hides of beasts, such as the inhabitants ofttimes place in the fields for drying in the sun, they drag them into the water. Here they leave them for some days, well loaden with stones, till the hair falls off. Then they eat them with no less appetite than they would the animals themselves, could they catch them. I have seen myself, many times, like things to these I have related. But besides my own experience, many writers of natural things have made entire treatises of these animals, describing not only their shape, magnitude and other qualities, but also their voracity and brutish inclinations ; which, as I have told you, are very strange. A certain person of good reputation and credit told me that one day he was by the river-side, washing his *baraca*, or tent, wherein he used to lie in the fields. As soon as he began his work, a cayman fastened upon the tent, and with incredible fury dragged it under water. The man, desirous to see if he could save his tent, pulled on the contrary side with all his strength, having in his mouth a butcher's knife (wherewith as it happened he was scraping the canvas) to defend himself in case of urgent necessity. The cayman, being angry at this opposition, vaulted upon his body, out of the river, and drew him with great celerity into the water, endeavouring with the weight of his bulk to stifle him under the banks. Thus finding himself in the greatest extremity, almost crushed to death by that huge and formidable animal, with his knife he gave the cayman several wounds in the belly, wherewith he suddenly expired. Being thus delivered from the hands of imminent fate, he drew the cayman out of the water, and with the same knife opened the body, to satisfy his curiosity. In his stomach he found nearly one hundred-weight of stones, each of them being almost of the bigness of his fist.

The caymans are ordinarily busied in hunting and catching of flies, which they eagerly devour. The occasion is, because close to their skin they have certain little scales, which smell with a sweet scent, something like musk. This aromatic odour is coveted by the flies, and here they come to repose themselves and sting. Thus they both persecute each other continually, with an incredible hatred and antipathy. Their manner of procreating and hatching their young ones is as follows. They approach the sandy banks of some river that lies exposed to the rays of the south sun. Among these sands they lay their eggs, which afterwards they cover with their feet; and here they find them hatched, and with young generation, by the heat only of the sun. These, as soon as they are out of the shell, by natural instinct run to the water. Many times those eggs are destroyed by birds that find them out, as they scrape among the sands. Hereupon the females of the caymans, at such times as they fear the coming of any flocks of birds, ofttimes by night swallow their eggs, and keep them in their stomach till the danger is over. And, from time to time, they bury them again in the sand, as I have told you, bringing them forth again out of their belly till the season is come of being excluded the shell. At this time, if the mother be near at hand, they run to her and play with her as little whelps would do with their dams, sporting themselves according to their own custom. In this sort of sport they will oftentimes run in and out of their mother's belly, even as rabbits into their holes. This I have seen them do many times, as I have spied them at play with their dam over the water upon the contrary banks of some river. At which time I have often disturbed their sport by throwing a stone that way, causing them on a sudden to creep into the mother's bowels, for fear of some imminent danger. The manner of procreating of those animals is always the same as I have related, and at the same time of the year, for they neither meddle nor make with one another but in the month of May. They give them in this country the name of crocodiles, though in other places of the West Indies they go under the name of caymans.

CHAPTER V.

Of all sorts of quadruped Animals and Birds that are found in this Island. As also a relation of the French Buccaneers.

BESIDES the fruits which this island produces, whose plenty, as is held for certain, surpasses all the islands of America, it abounds also very plentifully in all sorts of quadruped animals, such as horses, bulls, cows, wild boars, and others very useful to human kind, not only for common sustenance of life, but also for cultivating the ground and the management of a sufficient commerce.

In this island therefore are still remaining a huge number of wild dogs. These destroy yearly multitudes of all sorts of cattle. For no sooner has a cow brought forth her calf, or a mare foaled, than these wild mastiffs come to devour the young breed, if they find not some resistance from keepers and other domestic dogs. They run up and down the woods and fields commonly in whole troops of fifty, threescore or more, together, being withal so fierce that they ofttimes will assault an entire herd of wild boars, not ceasing to persecute them till they have at last overcome and torn in pieces two or three. One day a French buccaneer caused me to see a strange action of this kind. Being in the fields hunting together, we heard a great noise of dogs, which had surrounded a wild boar. Having tame dogs with us, we left them to the custody of our servants, desirous to see the sport, if possible. Hence my companion and I, each of us, climbed up into several trees, both for security and prospect. The wild boar was all alone, and standing against a tree ; with his tusks he endeavoured to defend himself

from a great number of dogs that had enclosed him, having with his teeth killed and wounded several of them.
This bloody fight continued about an hour, the wild boar
meanwhile attempting many times to escape. At last,
being upon the flight, one of those dogs leaped on his
back, and the rest of the dogs, perceiving the courage of
their companion, fastened likewise upon the boar, and
presently after killed him. This being done, all of them,
the first only excepted, laid themselves down upon the
ground about the prey, and there peaceably continued
till he, the first and most courageous of the troop, had
eaten as much as he could devour. When this dog had
ended his repast and left the dead beast, all the rest fell
in to take their share, till nothing was left that they could
devour. What ought we to infer from this notable action,
performed by the brutish sense of wild animals ? Only
this, that even beasts themselves are not destitute of
knowledge, and that they give us documents how to
honour such as have well deserved, seeing these, being
irrational animals as they were, did reverence and respect
him that exposed his life to the greatest danger, in
vanquishing courageously the common enemy.

The Governor of Tortuga, Monsieur Ogeron, understanding that the wild dogs killed too many of the wild
boars, and that the hunters of that island had much-a-do
to find any, fearing lest that common sustenance of the
isle should fail, caused a great quantity of poison to be
brought from France, therewith to destroy the wild
mastiffs. This was performed in the year 1668, by commanding certain horses to be killed and envenomed, and
laid open in the woods and fields, at certain places where
mostly wild dogs used to resort. This being continued
for the space of six months, there were killed an incredible
number in the said time. And yet all this industry was
not sufficient to exterminate and destroy the race ; yea,
scarce to make any diminution thereof, their number
appearing to be almost as entire as before. These wild

dogs are easily rendered tame among people, even as
tame as the ordinary dogs we breed in houses. Moreover, the hunters of those parts, whensoever they find a
wild bitch with young whelps, commonly take away the
puppies, and bring them to their houses, where they find
them, being grown up, to hunt much better than other
dogs.

But here the curious reader may peradventure enquire
whence or by what accident came so many wild dogs into
those islands ? The occasion was that the Spaniards,
having possessed themselves of these isles, found them
much peopled with Indians. These were a barbarous
sort of people, totally given to sensuality and a brutish
custom of life, hating all manner of labour, and only in-
clined to run from place to place, killing and making war
against their neighbours, not out of any ambition to reign,
but only because they agreed not with themselves in
some common terms of language. Hence perceiving
the dominion of the Spaniards laid a great restriction
upon their lazy and brutish customs, they conceived an
incredible odium against them, such as never was to be
reconciled. But more especially, because they saw them
take possession of their kingdoms and dominions. Hereupon they made against them all the resistance they were
capable of, opposing everywhere their designs to the
utmost of their power, until the Spaniards, finding themselves to be cruelly hated by those Indians, and nowhere secure from their treacheries, resolved to extirpate
and ruin them every one ; especially seeing they could
neither tame them by the civilities of their customs, nor
conquer them with the sword. But the Indians, it being
their ancient custom to make their woods their chiefest
places of defence, at present made these their refuge
whenever they fled from the Spaniards that pursued them.
Hereupon those first conquerors of the New World made
use of dogs to range and search the intricatest thickets
of woods and forests for those their implacable and un-

conquerable enemies. By this means they forced them to leave their ancient refuge and submit to the sword, seeing no milder usage would serve turn. Hereupon they killed some of them, and, quartering their bodies, placed them in the highways, to the intent that others might take warning from such a punishment, not to incur the like danger. But this severity proved to be of ill consequence. For, instead of frighting them and reducing their minds to a civil society, they conceived such horror of the Spaniards and their proceedings, that they resolved to detest and fly their sight for ever. And hence the greatest part died in caves and subterraneous places of the woods and mountains ; in which places I myself have seen many times great numbers of human bones. The Spaniards afterwards, finding no more Indians to appear about the woods, endeavoured to rid themselves of the great number of dogs they had in their houses, whence these animals, finding no masters to keep them, betook themselves to the woods and fields, there to hunt for food to preserve their lives. Thus by degrees they became unacquainted with the houses of their ancient masters and at last grew wild. This is the truest account I can give of the multitudes of wild dogs which are seen to this day in these parts.

But besides the wild mastiffs above-mentioned, here are also huge numbers of wild horses to be seen everywhere. These run up and down in whole herds or flocks all over the Island of Hispaniola. They are but low of stature, short-bodied, with great heads, long necks, and big or thick legs. In a word, they have nothing that is handsome in all their shape. They are seen to run up and down commonly in troops of two or three hundred together, one of them going always before, to lead the multitude. When they meet any person that travels through the woods or fields, they stand still, suffering him to approach till he can almost touch them, and then, suddenly starting, they betake themselves to flight, running away disorderly, as fast as they are able. The hunters catch them with industry, only for the benefit of their skins, although sometimes they preserve their flesh likewise, which they harden with smoke, using it for provisions when they go to sea.

Here would be also wild bulls and cows, in greater number than at present, if by continuation of hunting their race were not much diminished. Yet considerable profit is made even to this day by such as make it their business to kill them. The wild bulls are of a vast corpulency, or bigness of body ; and yet they do no hurt to any person if they be not exasperated, but left to their own repose. The hides which are taken from them are from eleven to thirteen foot long.

The diversity of birds inhabiting the air of this island is so great that I should be troublesome, as well to the reader as myself, if I should attempt to muster up their species. Hence, leaving aside the prolix catalogue of their multitude, I shall content myself only to mention some few of the chiefest. Here is a certain species of pullets in the woods, which the Spaniards call by the name of *pintadas*, which the inhabitants find without any distinction to be as good as those which are bred in houses. It is already known to everybody that the parrots which we have in Europe are transported to us from these parts of the world. Whence may be inferred that, seeing such a number of these talkative birds are preserved among us, notwithstanding the diversity of climates, much greater multitudes are to be found where the air and temperament is natural to them. The parrots make their nests in holes of palmetto-trees, which holes are before made to their hand by other birds. The reason is, forasmuch as they are not capable of excavating any wood, though never so soft, as having their own bills too crooked and blunt. Hence provident nature has supplied them with the labour and industry of another sort of small birds called *carpinteros*, or carpenters.

These are no bigger than sparrows, yet notwithstanding of such hard and piercing bills, that no iron instrument can be made more apt to excavate any tree, though never so solid and hard. In the holes therefore fabricated beforehand by these birds, the parrots get possession, and build their nests, as has been said.

Pigeons of all sorts are also here abundantly provided to the inhabitants by Him that created in the beginning and provided all things. For eating of them, those of this island observe the same seasons as we said before, speaking of the Isle of Tortuga. Betwixt the pigeons of both islands little or no difference is observable, only that these of Hispaniola are something fatter and bigger than those. Another sort of small birds here are called *cabreros*, or goat-keepers. These are very like others called *heronsetas*, and chiefly feed upon crabs of the sea. In these birds are found seven distinct bladders of gall, and hence their flesh is as bitter to the taste as aloes. Crows or ravens, more troublesome to the inhabitants than useful, here make a hideous noise through the whole circumference of the island. Their ordinary food is the flesh of wild dogs, or the carcases of those beasts the buccaneers kill and throw away. These clamorous birds no sooner hear the report of a fowling-piece or musket than they gather from all sides into whole flocks, and fill the air and woods with their unpleasant notes. They are in nothing different from those we see in Europe.

It is now high time to speak of the French nation, who inhabit a great part of this island. We have told, at the beginning of this book, after what manner they came at first into these parts. At present, therefore, we shall only describe their manner of living, customs and ordinary employments. The different callings or professions they follow are generally but three : either to hunt, or plant, or else to rove on the sea in quality of pirates. It is a general and solemn custom amongst them all to seek out for a comrade or companion, whom we may call partner, in their fortunes, with whom they join the whole stock of what they possess, towards a mutual and reciprocal gain. This is done also by articles drawn and signed on both sides, according to what has been agreed between them. Some of these constitute their surviving companion absolute heir to what is left by the death of the first of the two. Others, if they be married, leave their estates to their wives and children; others to other relations. This being done, every one applies himself to his calling, which is always one of the three aforementioned.

The hunters are again sub-divided into two several sorts. For some of these are only given to hunt wild bulls and cows; others hunt only wild boars. The first of these two sorts of hunters are called buccaneers. These not long ago were about the number of six hundred upon this island; but at present there are not reckoned to be above three hundred, more or less. The cause has been the great decrease of wild cattle through the dominions of the French in Hispaniola, which has appeared to be so notable that, far from getting any considerable gain, they at present are but poor in this exercise. When the buccaneers go into the woods to hunt for wild bulls and cows, they commonly remain there the space of a whole twelvemonth or two years, without returning home. After the hunt is over and the spoil divided among them, they commonly sail to the Isle of Tortuga, there to provide themselves with guns, powder, bullets and small shot, with all other necessaries against another going out or hunting. The rest of their gains they spend with great liberality, giving themselves freely to all manner of vices and debauchery, among which the first is that of drunkenness, which they exercise for the most part with brandy. This they drink as liberally as the Spaniards do clear fountain water. Sometimes they buy together a pipe of wine; this they stave at the one end, and never cease drinking till they have made an end of it. Thus they celebrate the festivals of Bacchus so long as they have any money left. For all the tavern-keepers wait for the coming of these lewd buccaneers, even after the same manner that they do at Amsterdam for the arrival of the East India fleet at the Texel. The said buccaneers are hugely cruel and tyrannical towards their servants ; insomuch that commonly these had rather be galley slaves in the Straits, or saw brazil-wood in the rasp-houses of Holland, than serve such barbarous masters.

The second sort of hunters hunt nothing else but wild boars. The flesh of these they salt, and, being thus preserved from corruption, they sell it to the planters. These hunters have also the same vicious customs of life, and are as much addicted to all manner of debauchery as the former. But their manner of hunting is quite different from what is practised in Europe. For these buccaneers have certain places, designed for hunting, where they live for the space of three or four months, and sometimes, though not often, a whole year. Such places are called *Deza Boulan ;* and in these, with only the company of five or six friends, who go along with them, they continue all the time above-mentioned, in mutual friendship. The first buccaneers we spoke of many times make an agreement with certain planters to furnish them with meat all the whole year at a certain price. The payment hereof is often made with two or three hundred-weight of tobacco, in the leaf. But the planters commonly into the bargain furnish them likewise with a servant, whom they send to help. To the servant they afford a sufficient quantity of all necessaries for that purpose, especially of powder, bullets and small shot, to hunt with.

The planters began to cultivate and plant the Isle of Tortuga in the year 1598. The first plantation was of tobacco, which grew to admiration, being likewise of very good quality. Notwithstanding, by reason of the small

circumference of the island, they were then able to plant
but little ; especially there being many pieces of land in
that isle that were not fit to produce tobacco. They
attempted likewise to make sugar, but by reason of the
great expenses necessary to defray the charges, they
could not bring it to any effect. So that the greatest part
of the inhabitants, as we said before, betook themselves
to the exercise of hunting, and the remaining part to that
of piracy. At last the hunters, finding themselves scarce
able to subsist by their first profession, began likewise to
seek out lands that might be rendered fit for culture ; and
in these they also planted tobacco. The first land that
they chose for this purpose was Cul de Sac, whose territory extends towards the Southern part of the island.
This piece of ground they divided into several quarters,
which were called the Great Amea, Niep, Rochelois, the
Little Grave, the Great Grave, and the Augame. Here,
by little and little, they increased so much, that at present
there are above two thousand planters in those fields.
At the beginning they endured very much hardship,
seeing that while they were busied about their husbandry,
they could not go out of the island to seek provisions.
This hardship was also increased by the necessity of
grubbing, cutting down, burning and digging, whereby to
extirpate the innumerable roots of shrubs and trees. For
when the French possessed themselves of that island, it
was wholly overgrown with woods extremely thick, these
being only inhabited by an extraordinary number of wild
boars. The method they took to clear the ground was
to divide themselves into small companies of two or three
persons together, and these companies to separate far
enough from each other, provided with a few hatchets
and some quantity of coarse provision. With these things
they used to go into the woods, and there to build huts
for their habitation, of only a few rafters and boughs of
trees. Their first endeavour was to root up the shrubs
and little trees ; afterwards to cut down the great ones.

These they gathered into heaps, with their branches, and then set them on fire, excepting the roots, which, last of all, they were constrained to grub and dig up after the best manner they could. The first seed they committed to the ground was beans. These in those countries both ripen and dry away in the space of six weeks.

The second fruit, necessary to human life, which here they tried, was potatoes. These do not come to perfection in less time than four or five months. On these they most commonly make their breakfasts every morning. They dress them no otherwise than by boiling them in a kettle with fair water. Afterwards they cover them with a cloth for the space of half an hour, by which manner of dressing they become as soft as boiled chestnuts. Of the said potatoes also they make a drink called Maiz. They cut them into small slices, and cover them with hot water. When they are well imbibed with water, they press them through a coarse cloth, and the liquor that comes out, although somewhat thick, they keep in vessels made for that purpose. Here, after settling two or three days, it begins to work; and, having thrown off its lees, is fit for drink. They use it with great delight, and although the taste is somewhat sour, yet it is very pleasant, substantial and wholesome. The industry of this composition is owing to the Indians, as well as of many others, which the ingenuity of those barbarians caused them to invent both for the preservation and the pleasure of their own life.

The third fruit the newly cultivated land afforded was Mandioca, which the Indians by another name call Cassava. This is a certain root which they plant, but comes not to perfection till after eight or nine months, sometimes a whole year. Being thoroughly ripe, it may be left in the ground the space of eleven or twelve months, without the least suspicion of corruption. But this time being past, the said roots must be converted to use some way or another, otherwise they conceive a total putrefaction. Of these roots of Cassava, in those countries, is made a sort of granulous flour or meal, extremely dry and white, which supplies the want of common bread made of wheat, whereof the fields are altogether barren in that island. For this purpose they have in their houses certain graters made either of copper or tin, wherewith they grate the afore-mentioned roots, just as they do Mirick in Holland. By the by, let me tell you, Mirick is a certain root of a very biting taste, not unlike to strong mustard, wherewith they usually make sauces for some sorts of fish. When they have grated as much Cassava root as will serve turn, they put the gratings into bags or sacks, made of coarse linen, and press out all the moisture, until they remain very dry. Afterwards they pass the gratings through a sieve, leaving them, after sifting, very like sawdust. The meal being thus prepared, they lay it upon planches of iron, which are made very hot, upon which it is converted into a sort of cakes, very thin. These cakes are afterwards placed in the sun, upon the tops of houses, where they are thoroughly and perfectly dried. And lest they should lose any part of their meal, what did not pass the sieve is made up into rolls, five or six inches thick. These are placed one upon another, and left in this posture until they begin to corrupt. Of this corrupted matter they make a liquor, by them called Veycou, which they find very excellent, and certainly is not inferior to our English beer.

Bananas are likewise another sort of fruit, of which is made another excellent liquor, which, both in strength and pleasantness of taste, may be compared with the best wines of Spain. But this liquor of Bananas, as it easily causes drunkenness in such as use it immoderately, so it likewise very frequently inflames the throat, and produces dangerous diseases in that part. Guines agudos is also another fruit whereof they make drink. But this sort of liquor is not so strong as the preceding. Howbeit, both the one and the other are frequently mingled with water, thereby to quench thirst.

After they had cultivated these plantations, and filled them with all sorts of roots and fruits necessary for human life, they began to plant tobacco, for trading. The manner of planting this frequent commodity is as follows. They make certain beds of earth in the field, no larger than twelve foot square. These beds they cover very well with palmetto leaves, to the intent that the rays of the sun may not touch the earth wherein tobacco is sowed. They water them, likewise, when it does not rain, as we do our gardens in Europe. When it is grown about the bigness of young lettuce, they transplant it into straight lines which they make in other spacious fields, setting every plant at the distance of three foot from each other. They observe, likewise, the fittest seasons of the year for these things, which are commonly from January until the end of March, these being the months wherein most rains fall in those countries. Tobacco ought to be weeded very carefully, seeing that the least root of any other herb, coming near it, is sufficient to hinder its growth. When it is grown to the height of one foot and a half or thereabouts, they cut off the tops, thereby to hinder the stalks and leaves from shooting too high upwards, to the intent that the whole plant may receive greater strength from the earth, which affords it all its vigour and taste. While it ripens and comes to full perfection, they prepare in their houses certain apartments of fifty or threescore foot in length, and thirty or forty in breadth. These they fill with branches of trees and rafters, and upon them lay the green tobacco to dry. When it is thoroughly dried, they strip off the leaf from the stalks, and cause it to be rolled up by certain people who are employed in this work and no other. To these they afford for their labour the tenth part of what they make up into rolls. This property is peculiar to tobacco, which therefore I shall not omit, that if, while it is yet in the ground, the leaf be pulled off from

the stalk, it sprouts again, no less than four times in one
year.   Here I should be glad to give an account also of
the manner of making sugar, indigo, and gimbes [1]; but
seeing these things are not planted in those parts whereof we now speak, I have thought fit to pass them over in
silence.

The French planters of the Isle of Hispaniola have
always to this present time been subject to the Governors of Tortuga.   Yet this obedience has not been rendered without much reluctance and grudging on their
side.   In the year 1664 the West India Company of
France laid the foundations of a colony in Tortuga, under
which colony the planters of Hispaniola were compre-
hended and named, as subjects thereto.   This decree
disgusted the said planters very much, they taking it very
ill to be reputed subjects to a private Company of men
who had no authority to make them so ; especially being
in a country which did not belong to the dominions of
the King of France.   Hereupon they resolved to work
no longer for the said Company.   And this resolution of
theirs was sufficient to compel the Company to a total
dissolution of the Colony.   But at last the Governor of
Tortuga, who was pretty well stocked with planters, conceiving he could more easily force them than the West
India Company, found an invention whereby to draw
them to his obedience.   He promised them he would put
off their several sorts of merchandise, and cause such
returns to be made, in lieu of their goods from France,
as they should best like.   Withal, he dealt with the merchants under hand, that all ships whatsoever should come
consigned to him, and no persons should entertain any
correspondence with those planters of Hispaniola ; thinking thereby to avoid many inconveniences, and compel
them through necessity and want of all things to obey.
By this means he not only obtained the obedience he
designed from those people, but also that some merchants

[1] Probably gambier.

who had promised to deal with them and visit them now and then, no longer did it.

Notwithstanding what has been said, in the year 1669 two ships from Holland happened to arrive at the Isle of Hispaniola with all sorts of merchandise necessary in those parts. With these ships presently the planters aforesaid resolved to deal, and with the Dutch nation for the future, thinking hereby to withdraw their obedience from the Governor of Tortuga, and, by frustrating his designs, revenge themselves of what they had endured under his government. Not long after the arrival of the Hollanders, the Governor of Tortuga came to visit the plantation of Hispaniola, in a vessel very well armed. But the planters not only forbade him to come ashore, but with their guns also forced him to weigh anchor, and retire faster than he came. Thus the Hollanders began to trade with these people for all manner of things. But such relations and friends as the Governor had in Hispaniola used all the endeavours they were capable of to impede the commerce. This being understood by the planters, they sent them word that *in case they laid not aside their artifices, for the hindrance of the commerce which was begun with the Hollanders, they should every one assuredly be torn in pieces.* Moreover, to oblige farther the Hollanders and contemn the Governor and his party, they gave greater ladings to the two ships than they could desire, with many gifts and presents to the officers and mariners, whereby they sent them very well contented to their own country. The Hollanders came again very punctually, according to their promise, and found the planters under a greater indignation than before against the Governor; either because of the great satisfaction they had already conceived of this commerce with the Dutch, or that by their means they hoped to subsist by themselves without any further dependence upon the French nation. However, it was suddenly after, they set up another resolution something more

strange than the preceding. The tenour hereof was, that
they would go to the Island of Tortuga, and cut the
Governor in pieces. Hereupon they gathered together
as many canoes as they could, and set sail from Hispaniola, with design not only to kill the Governor, but
also to possess themselves of the whole island. This
they thought they could more easily perform, by reason
of all necessary assistance which they believed would at
any time be sent them from Holland. By which means
they were already determined in their minds to erect
themselves into a new Commonwealth, independent of
the Crown of France. But no sooner had they begun
this great revolution of their little State, when they
received news of a war declared between the two nations
in Europe. This wrought such a consternation in their
minds as caused them to give over that enterprize, and
retire without attempting anything.

In the meanwhile the Governor of Tortuga sent into
France for aid towards his own security, and the reduc-
tion of those people to their former obedience. This
was granted him, and two men-of-war were sent to
Tortuga, with orders to be at his commands. Having
received such a considerable support, he sent them very
well equipped to the Isle of Hispaniola. Being arrived
at the place, they landed part of their forces, with a
design to force the people to the obedience of those
whom they much hated in their hearts. But the
planters, seeing the arrival of those two frigates, and not
being ignorant of their design, fled into the woods, abandoning their houses and many of their goods, which they
left behind. These were immediately rifled and burnt
by the French without any compassion, not sparing the
least cottage they found. Afterwards the Governor began to relent in his anger, and let them know by some
messengers that *in case they would return to his obedience,
he would give ear to some accommodation between them.*
Hereupon the planters, finding themselves destitute of all

human relief and that they could expect no help from any side, surrendered to the Governor upon Articles, which were made and signed on both sides. But these were not too strictly observed, for he commanded two of the chief among them to be hanged. The residue were pardoned, and, moreover, he gave them free leave *to trade with any nation whatsoever they found most fit for their purpose.* With the grant of this liberty they began to recultivate their plantations, which gave them a huge quantity of very good tobacco ; they selling yearly to the sum of twenty or thirty thousand rolls.

In this country the planters have but very few slaves, for want of which they themselves, and some servants they have, are constrained to do all the drudgery. These servants commonly oblige and bind themselves to their masters for the space of three years. But their masters, forsaking all conscience and justice, oftentimes traffic with their bodies, as with horses at a fair ; selling them to other masters, just as they sell negroes brought from the coast of Guinea. Yea, to advance this trade, some persons there are who go purposely into France (the same happens in England and other countries), and travelling through the cities, towns and villages, endeavour to pick up young men or boys, whom they transport, by making them great promises. These, being once allured and conveyed into the islands I speak of, they force to work like horses, the toil they impose upon them being much harder than what they usually enjoin on the negroes, their slaves. For these they endeavour in some manner to preserve, as being their perpetual bond-men ; but as for their white servants, they care not whether they live or die, seeing that they are to continue no longer than three years in their service. These miserable kidnapped people are frequently subject to a certain disease, which in those parts is called coma, being a total privation of all their senses. And this distemper is judged to proceed from their hard usage, together with the change from their native climate into that which is directly opposite. Oftentimes it happens that, among these transported people, such are found as are persons of good quality and tender education. And these, being of a softer constitution, are more suddenly surprised with the disease above-mentioned and with several others belonging to those countries, than those who have harder bodies and have been brought up to all manner of fatigue. Besides the hard usage they endure in their diet, apparel and repose, many times they beat them so cruelly that some of them fall down dead under the hands of their cruel masters. This I have often seen with my own eyes, not without great grief and regret. Of many instances of this nature I shall only give you the following history, as being somewhat remarkable in its circumstances.

It happened that a certain planter of those countries exercised such cruelty towards one of his servants as caused him to run away. Having absconded for some days in the woods from the fury of his tyrannical master, at last he was taken, and brought back to the dominion of this wicked Pharaoh. No sooner had he got him into his hands than he commanded him to be tied to a tree. Here he gave him so many lashes upon his naked back as made his body run an entire stream of gore blood, embruing therewith the ground about the tree. Afterwards, to make the smart of his wounds the greater, he anointed them with juice of lemon mingled with salt and pepper, being ground small together. In this miserable posture he left him tied to the tree for the space of four and twenty hours. These being past, he commenced his punishment again, lashing him as before, with so much cruelty that the miserable wretch, under this torture, gave up the ghost, with these dying words in his mouth : *I beseech the Almighty God, Creator of heaven and earth, that he permit the wicked Spirit to make thee feel as many torments, before thy death, as*

thou hast caused me to feel before mine. A strange thing
and worthy all astonishment and admiration! Scarce
three or four days were past after this horrible fact, when
the Almighty Judge, who had heard the clamours of that
tormented wretch, gave permission to the Author of
Wickedness suddenly to possess the body of that barbarous and inhuman *Amirricide*, who tormented him to
death. Insomuch that those tyrannical hands, wherewith he had punished to death his innocent servant, were
the tormentors of his own body. For with them, after a
miserable manner, he beat himself and lacerated his own
flesh, till he lost the very shape of man which nature had
given him ; not ceasing to howl and cry, without any
rest either by day or night. Thus he continued to do
until he died, in that condition of raving madness wherein he surrendered his ghost to the same Spirit of Darkness who had tormented his body. Many other examples
of this kind I could rehearse, but these, not belonging to
our present discourse, I shall therefore omit.

The planters that inhabit the Caribbee Islands are
rather worse and more cruel to their servants than the
preceding. In the Isle of Saint Christopher dwells one,
whose name is Bettesa, very well known among the
Dutch merchants, who has killed above a hundred of his
servants with blows and stripes. The English do the
same with their servants. And the mildest cruelty they
exercise towards them is that, when they have served six
years of their time (the years they are bound for among
the English being seven complete), they use them with
such cruel hardship as forces them to beg of their masters
to sell them to others, although it be to begin another
servitude of seven years, or at least three or four. I
have known many who after this manner served fifteen
and twenty years before they could obtain their freedom.
Another thing very rigorous among that nation is a law
in those islands, whereby if any man owes to another
above five and twenty shillings, English money, in case

he cannot pay, he is liable to be sold for the space of six or eight months. I shall not trouble the patience of my reader any longer with relations of this kind, as belonging to another subject, different from what I have proposed to myself in this history. Whereupon I shall take my beginning hence to describe the famous actions and exploits of the greatest Pirates of my time, during my residence in those parts. These I shall endeavour to relate without the least note of passion or partiality ; yea, with that candour which is peculiar both to my mind and style : withal assuring my reader I shall give him no stories taken from others upon trust or hearsay, but only those enterprizes to which I was myself an eye-witness.

CHAPTER VI.

Of the Origin of the most famous Pirates of the coasts of America.
A notable exploit of Pierre le Grand.

I HAVE told you in the preceding chapters of this book,
after what manner I was compelled to adventure my life
among the Pirates of America—to which sort of men I
think myself obliged to give this name, for no other
reason than that they are not maintained or upheld in
their actions by any Sovereign Prince. For this is certain, that the Kings of Spain have upon several occasions
sent, by their Ambassadors, to the Kings of France and
England, *complaining of the molestations and troubles
those Pirates often caused upon the coasts of America,
even in the calm of peace.* To whose Ambassadors it has
always been answered : *That such men did not commit
those acts of hostility and piracy as subjects of their
Majesties ; and therefore his Catholic Majesty might proceed against them according as he should find fit.* The
King of France, besides what has been said, added to
this answer : *That he had no fortress nor castle upon the
Isle of Hispaniola, neither did he receive one farthing of
tribute thence.* Moreover, the King of England adjoined:
*That he had never given any patents or commissions to
those of Jamaica, for committing any hostility against the
subjects of his Catholic Majesty.* Neither did he only
give this bare answer, but also, out of his Royal desire to
pleasure the Court of Spain, recalled the Governor of
Jamaica, placing another in his room. All this was not
sufficient to prevent the Pirates of those parts from acting
what mischief they could to the contrary. But before I

commence the relation of their bold and insolent actions, I shall say something of their origin and most common exercises, as also of the chief among them, and their manner of arming before they go out to sea.

The first Pirate that was known upon the Island of Tortuga was named Pierre le Grand, or Peter the Great. He was born at the town of Dieppe, in Normandy. The action which rendered him famous was his taking of the Vice-Admiral of the Spanish flota, near the Cape of Tiburon, upon the Western side of the Island of Hispaniola. This bold exploit he performed alone with only one boat, wherein he had eight and twenty persons, no more, to help him. What gave occasion to this enterprize was that until that time the Spaniards had passed and repassed with all security, and without finding the least opposition, through the Bahama Channel. So that Pierre le Grand set out to sea by the Caicos, where he took this great ship with almost all facility imaginable. The Spaniards they found aboard were all set on shore, and the vessel presently sent into France. The manner how this undaunted spirit attempted and took such an huge ship, I shall give you out of the Journal of a true and faithful author, in the same words as I read. *The Boat*, he says, *wherein Pierre le Grand was with his companions, had now been at sea a long time, without finding anything, according to his intent of piracy, suitable to make a prey. And now their provisions beginning to fail, they could keep themselves no longer upon the ocean, or they must of necessity starve. Being almost reduced to despair, they espied a great ship belonging to the Spanish flota, which had separated from the rest. This bulky vessel they resolved to set upon and take, or die in the attempt. Hereupon they made sail towards her, with design to view her strength. And although they judged the vessel to be far above their forces, yet the covetousness of such a prey, and the extremity of fortune they were reduced to, made them adventure on such an enterprize. Being now come so near that they could not escape without danger of being all killed, the Pirates jointly made an oath to their captain, Pierre le Grand, to behave themselves courageously in this attempt, without the least fear or fainting. True it is, that these rovers had conceived an opinion that they should find the ship unprovided to fight, and that through this occasion they should master her by degrees. It was in the dusk of the evening, or soon after, when this great action was performed. But before it was begun, they gave orders to the surgeon of the boat to bore a hole in the sides thereof, to the intent that, their own vessel sinking under them, they might be compelled to attack more vigorously, and endeavour more hastily to run aboard the great ship. This was performed accordingly; and without any other arms than a pistol in one of their hands and a sword in the other, they immediately climbed up the sides of the ship, and ran altogether into the great cabin, where they found the Captain, with several of his companions, playing at cards. Here they set a pistol to his breast, commanding him to deliver up the ship to their obedience. The Spaniards seeing the Pirates aboard their ship, without scarce having seen them at sea, cried out, "* Jesus bless us! Are these devils, or what are they?" *In the meanwhile some of them took possession of the gun-room, and seized the arms and military affairs they found there, killing as many of the ship as made any opposition. By which means the Spaniards presently were compelled to surrender. That very day the Captain of the ship had been told by some of the Seamen that the boat, which was in view cruizing, was a boat of Pirates. To whom the Captain, slighting their advice, made answer:* "What then? Must I be afraid of such a pitiful thing as that is? No, nor though she were a ship as big and as strong as mine is." *As soon as Pierre le Grand had taken this magnificent prize, he detained in his service as many of the common seamen as he had need of, and the rest he set on shore. This being done, he immediately set sail for France, carrying with him all the riches he found in that huge vessel: here he continued without ever returning to the parts of America.*

The planters and hunters of the Isle of Tortuga had no sooner understood this happy event, and the rich prize those Pirates had obtained, than they resolved to follow their example. Hereupon many of them left their ordinary exercises and common employments, and used what means they could to get either boats or small vessels, wherein to exercise piracy. But not being able either to purchase or build them at Tortuga, at last they resolved to set forth in their canoes and seek them elsewhere. With these, therefore, they cruized at first upon Cape d'Alvarez, whereabouts the Spaniards used much to trade from one city to another in small boats. In these they carry hides, tobacco and other commodities to the port of Havana, which is the metropolis of that island, and to which the Spaniards from Europe frequently resort.

Hereabouts it was that those Pirates at the beginning took a great number of boats, laden with the aforesaid commodities. These boats they used to carry to the Isle of Tortuga, and there sell the whole purchase to the ships that waited in the port for their return, or accidentally happened to be there. With the gain of these prizes they provided themselves with necessaries, wherewithal to undertake other voyages. Some of these voyages were made towards the coast of Campeche, and others towards that of New Spain; in both which places the Spaniards at that time frequently exercised much commerce and trade. Upon those coasts they commonly found a great number of trading vessels and many times ships of great burden. Two of the biggest of these vessels, and two great ships which the Spaniards had laden with plate in the port of Campeche to go to Caracas, they took in less than a month's time, by cruizing to and fro. Being arrived at Tortuga with these prizes, and the whole people of the island admiring their progresses, especially that within the space of two years the riches of the country were much increased, the number also of Pirates augmented so fast, that from these beginnings, within a little space of time, there were to be numbered in that small island and port above twenty ships of this sort of people. Hereupon the Spaniards, not able to bear their robberies any longer, were constrained to put forth to sea two great men-of-war, both for the defence of their own coasts, and to cruize upon the enemies.

CHAPTER VII.

After what manner the Pirates arm their vessels, and how they regulate their voyages.

BEFORE the Pirates go out to sea, they give notice to every one that goes upon the voyage, of the day on which they ought precisely to embark, intimating also to them their obligation of bringing each man in particular so many pounds of powder and bullets as they think necessary for that expedition. Being all come on board, they join together in council, concerning what place they ought first to go to wherein to get provisions—especially of flesh, seeing they scarce eat anything else. And of this the most common sort among them is pork. The next food is tortoises, which they are accustomed to salt a little. Sometimes they resolve to rob such or such hog-yards, wherein the Spaniards often have a thousand heads of swine together. They come to these places in the dark of the night, and having beset the keeper's lodge, they force him to rise, and give them as many heads as they desire, threatening withal to kill him in case he disobeys their commands or makes any noise. Yea, these menaces are oftentimes put in execution, without giving any quarter to the miserable swine-keepers, or any other person that endeavours to hinder their robberies.

Having got provisions of flesh sufficient for their voyage, they return to their ship. Here their allowance, twice a day to every one, is as much as he can eat, without either weight or measure. Neither does the steward of the vessel give any greater proportion of flesh, or anything else to the captain than to the meanest mariner.

The ship being well victualled, they call another council, to deliberate towards what place they shall go, to seek their desperate fortunes. In this council, likewise, they agree upon certain Articles, which are put in writing, by way of bond or obligation, which every one is bound to observe, and all of them, or the chief, set their hands to it. Herein they specify, and set down very distinctly, what sums of money each particular person ought to have for that voyage, the fund of all the payments being the common stock of what is gotten by the whole expedition; for otherwise it is the same law, among these people, as with other Pirates, *No prey, no pay.* In the first place, therefore, they mention how much the Captain ought to have for his ship. Next the salary of the carpenter, or shipwright, who careened, mended and rigged the vessel. This commonly amounts to one hundred or an hundred and fifty pieces of eight,[1] being, according to the agreement, more or less. Afterwards for provisions and victualling they draw out of the same common stock about two hundred pieces of eight. Also a competent salary for the surgeon and his chest of medicaments, which usually is rated at two hundred or two hundred and fifty pieces of eight. Lastly they stipulate in writing what recompense or reward each one ought to have, that is either wounded or maimed in his body, suffering the loss of any limb, by that voyage. Thus they order for the loss of a right arm six hundred pieces of eight, or six slaves; for the loss of a left arm five hundred pieces of eight, or five slaves; for a right leg five hundred pieces of eight, or five slaves; for the left leg four hundred pieces of eight, or four slaves; for an eye one hundred pieces of eight, or one slave; for a finger of the hand the same reward as for the eye. All which sums of money, as I have said before, are taken out of the capital sum or common stock of what is got by their piracy. For a very exact and equal

---

[1] A piece of eight is equivalent to about five shillings.

dividend is made of the remainder among them all.
Yet herein they have also regard to qualities and places.
Thus the Captain, or chief Commander, is allotted five
or six portions to what the ordinary seamen have; the
Master's Mate only two; and other Officers proportionate
to their employment. After whom they draw equal parts
from the highest even to the lowest mariner, the boys
not being omitted. For even these draw half a share, by
reason that, when they happen to take a better vessel
than their own, it is the duty of the boys to set fire to
the ship or boat wherein they are, and then retire to the
prize which they have taken.

They observe among themselves very good orders.
For in the prizes they take, it is severely prohibited to
every one to usurp anything in particular to themselves.
Hence all they take is equally divided, according to what
has been said before. Yea, they make a solemn oath to
each other not to abscond, or conceal the least thing
they find amongst the prey. If afterwards any one is
found unfaithful, who has contravened the said oath,
immediately he is separated and turned out of the society.
Among themselves they are very civil and charitable to
each other. Insomuch that if any wants what another
has, with great liberality they give it one to another.
As soon as these Pirates have taken any prize of ship or
boat, the first thing they endeavour is to set on shore the
prisoners, detaining only some few for their own help
and service, to whom also they give their liberty after
the space of two or three years. They put in very frequently for refreshment at one island or another; but
more especially into those which lie on the Southern side
of the Isle of Cuba. Here they careen their vessels, and
in the meanwhile some of them go to hunt, others to
cruize upon the seas in canoes, seeking their fortune.
Many times they take the poor fishermen of tortoises,
and, carrying them to their habitations, they make them
work so long as the Pirates are pleased.

In the several parts of America are found four distinct species of tortoises. The first hereof are so great that every one reaches the weight of two or three thousand pounds. The scales of the species are so soft that they may easily be cut with a knife. Yet these tortoises are not good to be eaten. The second species is of an indifferent bigness, and are green in colour. The scales of these are harder than the first, and this sort is of a very pleasant taste. The third is very little different in size and bigness from the second, unless that it has the head something bigger. This third species is called by the French *cavana*, and is not good for food. The fourth is named *caret*, being very like the tortoises we have in Europe. This sort keeps most commonly among the rocks, whence they crawl out to seek their food, which is for the greatest part nothing but apples of the sea. These other species above-mentioned feed upon grass, which grows in the water upon the banks of sand. These banks or shelves, for their pleasant green, resemble the delightful meadows of the United Provinces. Their eggs are almost like those of the crocodile, but without any shell, being only covered with a thin membrane or film. They are found in such prodigious quantities along the sandy shores of those countries, that, were they not frequently destroyed by birds, the sea would infinitely abound with tortoises.

These creatures have certain customary places whither they repair every year to lay their eggs. The chief of these places are the three islands called Caymanes, situated in the latitude of twenty degrees and fifteen minutes North, being at the distance of five and forty leagues from the Isle of Cuba, on the Northern side thereof.

It is a thing much deserving consideration how the tortoises can find out these islands. For the greatest part of them come from the Gulf of Honduras, distant thence the whole space of one hundred and fifty leagues. Certain it is, that many times the ships, having lost their

latitude through the darkness of the weather, have steered
their course only by the noise of the tortoises swimming
that way, and have arrived at those isles. When their
season of hatching is past, they retire towards the Island
of Cuba, where are many good places that afford them
food. But while they are at the Islands of Caymanes,
they eat very little or nothing. When they have been
about the space of one month in the seas of Cuba, and
are grown fat, the Spaniards go out to fish for them,
they being then to be taken in such abundance that they
provide with them sufficiently their cities, towns and
villages. Their manner of taking them is by making
with a great nail a certain kind of dart. This they fix
at the end of a long stick or pole, with which they wound
the tortoises, as with a dagger, whensoever they appear
above water to breathe fresh air.

The inhabitants of New Spain and Campeche lade
their principal sorts of merchandises in ships of great
bulk ; and with these they exercise their commerce to
and fro. The vessels from Campeche in winter time
set out towards Caracas, Trinity Isles and Margarita.
For in summer the winds are contrary, though very
favourable to return to Campeche, as they are accustomed
to do at the beginning of that season. The Pirates are
not ignorant of these times, being very dextrous in
searching out all places and circumstances most suitable
to their designs. Hence in the places and seasons afore-
mentioned, they cruize upon the said ships for some
while. But in case they can perform nothing, and that
fortune does not favour them with some prize or other,
after holding a council thereupon, they commonly enterprize things very desperate. Of these their resolutions
I shall give you one instance very remarkable. One
certain Pirate, whose name was Pierre Francois, or Peter
Francis, happened to be a long time at sea with his boat
and six and twenty persons, waiting for the ships that
were to return from Maracaibo towards Campeche. Not

being able to find anything, nor get any prey, at last he resolved to direct his course to Rancherias, which is near the river called De la Plata, in the latitude of twelve degrees and a half North.   In this place lies a rich bank of pearl, to the fishery whereof they yearly send from Cartagena a fleet of a dozen vessels, with a man-of-war for their defence.   Every vessel has at least a couple of negroes in it, who are very dextrous in diving, even to the depth of six fathoms within the sea, whereabouts they find good store of pearls.   Upon this fleet of vessels, though small, called the Pearl Fleet, Pierre François resolved to adventure, rather than go home with empty hands.   They rode at anchor, at that time, at the mouth of the river De la Hacha, the man-of-war being scarce half a league distant from the small ships, and the wind very calm.   Having espied them in this posture, he presently pulled down his sails and rowed along the coast, dissembling to be a Spanish vessel that came from Maracaibo, and only passed that way.   But no sooner was he come to the Pearl Bank, than suddenly he assaulted the Vice-Admiral of the said fleet, mounted with eight guns and threescore men well armed, commanding them to surrender.   But the Spaniards, running to their arms, did what they could to defend themselves, fighting for some while; till at last they were constrained to submit to the Pirate.   Being thus possessed of the Vice-Admiral, he resolved next to adventure with some other stratagem upon the man-of-war, thinking thereby to get strength sufficient to master the rest of the fleet.   With this intent he presently sank his own boat in the river, and, putting forth the Spanish colours, weighed anchor, with a little wind, which then began to stir, having with promises and menaces compelled most of the Spaniards to assist him in his design. But no sooner did the man-of-war perceive one of his fleet to set sail than he did so too, fearing lest the mariners should have any design to run away with the

vessel and riches they had on board. This caused the
Pirates immediately to give over that dangerous enterprize, thinking themselves unable to encounter force to
force with the said man-of-war that now came against
them. Hereupon they attempted to get out of the
river and gain the open seas with the riches they had
taken, by making as much sail as possibly the vessel
would bear. This being perceived by the man-of-war,
he presently gave them chase. But the Pirates, having
laid on too much sail, and a gust of wind suddenly arising,
had their main-mast blown down by the board, which
disabled them from prosecuting their escape.

This unhappy event much encouraged those that were
in the man-of-war, they advancing and gaining upon the
Pirates every moment ; by which means at last they were
overtaken. But these notwithstanding, finding themselves still with two and twenty persons sound, the rest
being either killed or wounded, resolved to defend themselves so long as it were possible. This they performed
very courageously for some while, until being thereunto
forced by the man-of-war, they were compelled to surrender. Yet this was not done without Articles, which
the Spaniards were glad to allow them, as follows : That
they should not use them as slaves, forcing them to carry
or bring stones, or employing them in other labours, for
three or four years, as they commonly employ their
negroes. But that they should set them on shore, upon
free land, without doing them any harm in their bodies.
Upon these Articles they delivered themselves, with all
that they had taken, which was worth only in pearls to
the value of above one hundred thousand pieces of eight,
besides the vessel, provisions, goods and other things.
All which, being put together, would have made to this
Pirate one of the greatest prizes he could desire ; which
he would certainly have obtained, had it not been for the
loss of his main-mast, as was said before.

Another bold attempt, not unlike that which I have

BARTOLOMEW PORTUGUES.

related, nor less remarkable, I shall also give you at present. A certain Pirate, born in Portugal, and from the name of his country called Bartholomew Portugues, was cruizing in his boat from Jamaica (wherein he had only thirty men and four small guns) upon the Cape de Corrientes, in the Island of Cuba. In this place he met with a great ship, that came from Maracaibo and Cartegena, bound for the Havana, well provided with twenty great guns and threescore and ten men, between passengers and mariners. This ship he presently assaulted, but found as strongly defended by them that were on board. The Pirate escaped the first encounter, resolving to attack her more vigorously than before, seeing he had sustained no great damage hitherto. This resolution he boldly performed, renewing his assaults so often that after a long and dangerous fight he became master of the great vessel. The Portuguese lost only ten men and had four wounded, so that he had still remaining twenty fighting men, whereas the Spaniards had double that number. Having possessed themselves of such a ship, and the wind being contrary to return to Jamaica, they resolved to steer their course towards the Cape of Saint Antony (which lies on the Western side of the Isle of Cuba), there to repair themselves and take in fresh water, of which they had great necessity at that time.

Being now very near the cape above-mentioned, they unexpectedly met with three great ships that were coming from New Spain and bound for the Havana. By these, as not being able to escape, they were easily retaken, both ship and Pirates. Thus they were all made prisoners, through the sudden change of fortune, and found themselves poor, oppressed, and stripped of all the riches they had pillaged so little before. The cargo of this ship consisted of one hundred and twenty thousand weight of cacao-nuts, the chief ingredient of that rich liquor called chocolate, and threescore and ten thousand pieces

of eight.   Two days after this misfortune, there happened
to arise a huge and dangerous tempest, which largely
separated the ships from one another.   The great vessel
wherein the Pirates were, arrived at Campeche, where
many considerable merchants came to salute and welcome
the Captain thereof.   These presently knew the Portuguese Pirate, as being him who had committed innumerable excessive insolences upon those coasts, not only
infinite murders and robberies, but also lamentable
incendiums (*i.e.*, fires), which the people of Campeche
still preserved very fresh in their memory.

Hereupon, the next day after their arrival, the magistrates of the city sent several of their officers to demand
and take into custody the criminal prisoners from on
board the ship, with intent to punish them according to
their deserts.   Yet fearing lest the Captain of those
Pirates should escape out of their hands on shore (as he
had formerly done, being once their prisoner in the city
before), they judged it more convenient to leave him
safely guarded on board the ship for the present.   In
the meanwhile they caused a gibbet to be erected, whereupon to hang him the very next day, without any other
form of process than to lead him from the ship to the
place of punishment.   The rumour of this future tragedy
was presently brought to Bartholomew Portugues' ears,
whereby he sought all the means he could to escape that
night.   With this design he took two earthen jars,
wherein the Spaniards usually carry wine from Spain
to the West Indies, and stopped them very well, intending to use them for swimming, as those who are unskilful
in that art do calabashes, a sort of pumpkins, in Spain,
and in other places empty bladders.   Having made this
necessary preparation, he waited for the night, when all
should be asleep, even the sentry that guarded him.
But seeing he could not escape his vigilancy, he secretly
secured a knife, and with the same gave him such a
mortal stab as suddenly deprived him of life and the

possibility of making any noise. At that instant he committed himself to sea, with those two earthen jars beforementioned, and by their help and support, though never having learned to swim, he reached the shore. Being arrived upon land, without any delay he took refuge in the woods, where he hid himself for three days, without daring to appear nor eating any other food than wild herbs.

Those of the city failed not the next day to make a diligent search for him in the woods, where they concluded him to be. This strict enquiry Portugues had the convenience to espy from the hollow of a tree, wherein he lay absconded. Hence perceiving them to return without finding what they sought for, he adventured to sally forth towards the coasts called Del Golfo Triste, forty leagues distant from the city of Campeche. Hither he arrived within a fortnight after his escape from the ship. In which space of time, as also afterwards, he endured extreme hunger, thirst, and fears of falling again into the hands of the Spaniards. For during all this journey he had no other provision with him than a small calabash, with a little water ; neither did he eat anything else than a few shell-fish, which he found among the rocks near the sea-shore. Besides that, he was compelled to pass some rivers, not knowing well to swim. Being in this distress, he found an old board, which the waves had thrown upon the shore, wherein stuck a few great nails. These he took, and with no small labour whetted against a stone, until he had made them capable of cutting like knives, though very imperfectly. With these, and no better instruments, he cut down some branches of trees, which with twigs and osiers he joined together, and made as well as he could a boat, or rather a raft, wherewith he rafted over the rivers. Thus he arrived finally at the Cape of Golfo Triste, as was said before, where he happened to find a certain vessel of Pirates, who were great comrades of his own, and were lately come from Jamaica.

To these Pirates he instantly related all his adversities and misfortunes, and withal demanded of them that they would fit him with a boat and twenty men.   With which company alone he promised to return to Campeche and assault the ship that was in the river, which he had been taken by and escaped from fourteen days before.   They readily granted his request, and equipped him a boat with the said number of men.   With this small company he set forth towards the execution of his design, which he bravely performed eight days after he separated from his comrades at the Cape of Golfo Triste.   For being arrived at the river of Campeche, with undaunted courage and without any rumour of noise he assaulted the ship before-mentioned.   Those that were on board were persuaded this was a boat from land, that came to bring contraband goods ; and hereupon were not in any posture of defence. Thus the Pirates, laying hold on this occasion, assaulted them without any fear of ill success, and in short space of time compelled the Spaniards to surrender.

Being now masters of the ship, they immediately weighed anchor and set sail, determining to fly from the port, lest they should be pursued by other vessels. This they did with extremity of joy, seeing themselves possessors of such a brave ship.   Especially Portugues, their captain, who now by a second turn of Fortune's wheel was become rich and powerful again, who had been so lately in that same vessel a poor miserable prisoner and condemned to the gallows.   With this great booty he designed in his mind greater things ; which he might well hope to obtain, seeing he had found in the vessel great quantity of rich merchandise still remaining on board, although the plate had been transported into the city.   Thus he continued his voyage towards Jamaica for some days.   But coming near the Isle of Pinos, on the South side of the Island of Cuba, Fortune suddenly turned her back upon him once more, never to show him her countenance again.   For a horrible storm arising at

ROCK. BRASILIANO

sea occasioned the ship to split against the rocks or banks called Jardines. Insomuch that the vessel was totally lost, and Portugues, with his companions, escaped in a canoe. After this manner he arrived at Jamaica, where he remained no long time, being only there till he could prepare himself to seek his fortune anew, which from that time proved always adverse to him.

Nothing less rare and admirable than the preceding are the actions of another Pirate, who at present lives at Jamaica, and who has on sundry occasions enterprized and achieved things very strange. The place of his birth was the city of Groningen, in the United Provinces; but his own proper name is not known : the Pirates, his companions, having only given him that of Roche Brasiliano by reason of his long residence in the country of Brazil, whence he was forced to flee, when the Portuguese retook those countries from the West India Company of Amsterdam, several nations then inhabiting at Brazil (as English, French, Dutch and others) being constrained to seek new fortunes.

This fellow at that conjuncture of time retired to Jamaica, where being at a stand how to get a livelihood, he entered the Society of Pirates. Under these he served in quality of a private mariner for some while, in which degree he behaved himself so well that he was both beloved and respected by all, as one that deserved to be their Commander for the future. One day certain mariners happened to engage in a dissension with their Captain ; the effect whereof was that they left the boat. Brasiliano followed the rest, and by these was chosen for their conductor and leader, who also fitted him out a boat or small vessel, wherein he received the title of Captain.

Few days were past from his being chosen Captain, when he took a great ship that was coming from New Spain, on board of which he found great quantity of plate, and both one and the other he carried to Jamaica.

This action gave him renown, and caused him to be both esteemed and feared, every one apprehending him much abroad. Howbeit, in his domestic and private affairs he had no good behaviour nor government over himself; for in these he would oftentimes shew himself either brutish or foolish. Many times being in drink, he would run up and down the streets, beating or wounding whom he met, no person daring to oppose him or make any resistance.

To the Spaniards he always showed himself very barbarous and cruel, only out of an inveterate hatred he had against that nation. Of these he commanded several to be roasted alive upon wooden spits, for no other crime than that they would not shew him the places or hogyards, where he might steal swine. After many of these cruelties, it happened as he was cruizing upon the coasts of Campeche, that a dismal tempest suddenly surprised him. This proved to be so violent that at last his ship was wrecked upon the coasts, the mariners only escaping with their muskets and some few bullets and powder, which were the only things they could save of all that was in the vessel. The place where the ship was lost was precisely between Campeche and the Golfo Triste. Here they got on shore in a canoe, and marching along the coast with all the speed they could, they directed their course towards Golfo Triste, as being a place where the Pirates commonly used to repair and refresh themselves. Being upon this journey and all very hungry and thirsty, as is usual in desert places, they were pursued by some Spaniards, being a whole troop of a hundred horsemen. Brasiliano no sooner perceived this imminent danger than he animated his companions, telling them : " *We had better, fellow soldiers, choose to die under our arms fighting, as becomes men of courage, than surrender to the Spaniards, who, in case they overcome us, will take away our lives with cruel torments.*" The Pirates were no more than thirty in number, who, notwithstanding, seeing their brave Commander oppose himself with courage to the enemy, resolved to do the like. Hereupon they faced the troop of Spaniards, and discharged their muskets against them with such dexterity, that they killed one horseman with almost every shot. The fight continued for the space of an hour, till at last the Spaniards were put to flight by the Pirates. They stripped the dead, and took from them what they thought most convenient for their use. But such as were not already dead, they helped to quit the miseries of life with the ends of their muskets.

Having vanquished the enemy, they all mounted on several horses they found in the field, and continued the journey aforementioned, Brasiliano having lost but two of his companions in this bloody fight, and had two others wounded. As they prosecuted their way, before they came to the port, they espied a boat from Campeche, well manned, that rode at anchor, protecting a small number of canoes that were lading wood. Hereupon they sent a detachment of six of their men to watch them; and these the next morning possessed themselves of the canoes. Having given notice to their companions, they went all on board, and with no great difficulty took also the boat, or little man-of-war, their convoy. Thus having rendered themselves masters of the whole fleet, they wanted only provisions, which they found but very small aboard those vessels. But this defect was supplied by the horses, which they instantly killed and salted with salt which by good fortune the wood-cutters had brought with them. Upon which victuals they made shift to keep themselves, until such time as they could procure better.

These very same Pirates, I mean Brasiliano and his companions, took also another ship that was going from New Spain to Maracaibo, laden with divers sorts of merchandise, and a very considerable number of pieces of eight, which were designed to buy cacao-nuts for their lading home. All these prizes they carried into Jamaica, where they safely arrived, and, according to their custom, wasted in a few days in taverns all they had gained, by giving themselves to all manner of debauchery. Such of these Pirates are found who will spend two or three thousand pieces of eight in one night, not leaving themselves peradventure a good shirt to wear on their backs in the morning. My own master would buy, on like occasions, a whole pipe of wine, and, placing it in the street, would force every one that passed by to drink with him; threatening also to pistol them, in case they would not do it. At other times he would do the same with barrels of ale or beer. And, very often, with both his hands, he would throw these liquors about the streets, and wet the clothes of such as walked by, without regarding whether he spoiled their apparel or not, were they men or women.

Among themselves, and to each other, these Pirates are extremely liberal and free. If any one of them has lost all his goods, which often happens in their manner of life, they freely give him, and make him partaker of what they have. In taverns and ale-houses they always have great credit; but in such houses at Jamaica they ought not to run very deep in debt, seeing the inhabitants of that island easily sell one another for debt. Thus it happened to my patron, or master, to be sold for a debt of a tavern, wherein he had spent the greatest part of his money. This man had, within the space of three months before, three thousand pieces of eight in ready cash, all which he wasted in that short space of time, and became as poor as I have told you.

But now to return to our discourse, I must let my reader know that Brasiliano, after having spent all that he had robbed, was constrained to go to sea again, to seek his fortune once more. Thus he set forth towards the coast of Campeche, his common place of rendezvous. Fifteen days after his arrival there, he put himself into a canoe, with intent to espy the port of that city, and see if he could rob any Spanish vessel. But his fortune was so bad, that both he and all his men were taken prisoners, and carried into the presence of the Governor. This man immediately cast them into a dungeon, with full intention to hang them every person. And doubtless he had performed his intent, were it not for a stratagem that Brasiliano used, which proved sufficient to save their lives. He wrote therefore a letter to the Governor, making him believe it came from other Pirates that were abroad at sea, and withal telling him : *He should have a care how he used those persons he had in his custody. For in case he caused them any harm, they did swear unto him they would never give quarter to any person of the Spanish nation that should fall into their hands.*

Because these Pirates had been many times at Campeche, and in many other towns and villages of the West Indies belonging to the Spanish dominions, the Governor began to fear what mischief they might cause by means of their companions abroad, in case he should punish them. Hereupon he released them out of prison, exacting only an oath of them beforehand, that they would leave their exercise of piracy for ever. And withal he sent them as common mariners, or passengers in the galleons to Spain. They got in this voyage altogether five hundred pieces of eight, whereby they tarried not long there after their arrival. But providing themselves with some few necessaries, they all returned to Jamaica within a little while. Whence they set forth again to sea, committing greater robberies and cruelties than ever they had done before ; but more especially abusing the poor Spaniards that happened to fall into their hands, with all sorts of cruelty imaginable.

The Spaniards perceiving they could gain nothing upon this sort of people, nor diminish their number, which rather increased daily, resolved to diminish the number of their ships wherein they exercised trading to and fro. But neither was this resolution of any effect, or did them any good service. For the Pirates, finding not so many ships at sea as before, began to gather into greater companies, and land upon the Spanish dominions, ruining whole cities, towns and villages ; and withal pillaging, burning and carrying away as much as they could find possible.

The first Pirate who gave a beginning to these invasions by land, was named Lewis Scot, who sacked and pillaged the city of Campeche. He almost ruined the town, robbing and destroying all he could ; and, after he had put it to the ransom of an excessive sum of money, he left it. After Scot came another named Mansvelt, who enterprized to set footing in Granada, and penetrate with his piracies even to the South Sea. Both which things he effected, till at last, for want of provision, he was constrained to go back. He assaulted the Isle of Saint Catharine, which was the first land he took, and upon it some few prisoners. These showed him the way towards Cartagena, which is a principal city situate in the kingdom of New Granada. But the bold attempts and actions of John Davis, born at Jamaica, ought not to be forgotten in this history, as being some of the most remarkable thereof, especially his rare prudence and valour, wherewith he behaved himself in the aforementioned kingdom of Granada. This Pirate having cruized a long time in the Gulf of Pocatauro upon the ships that were expected from Cartagena bound for Nicaragua, and not being able to meet any of the said ships, resolved at last to land in Nicaragua, leaving his ship concealed about the coast.

This design he presently put in execution. For taking fourscore men, out of fourscore and ten which he had in all (the rest being left to keep the ship), he divided them equally into three canoes. His intent was to rob the churches, and rifle the houses of the chief citizens of the aforesaid town of Nicaragua. Thus, in the obscurity of the night, they mounted the river which leads to that city, rowing with oars in their canoes. By day they concealed themselves and boats under the branches of trees that were upon the banks. These grow very thick and intricate along the sides of the rivers in those countries, as also along the sea-coast. Under which, likewise, those who remained behind absconded from their vessel, lest they should be seen either by fishermen or Indians. After this manner they arrived at the city the third night, where the sentry, who kept the post of the river, thought them to be fishermen that had been fishing in the lake. And as the greatest part of the Pirates are skilful in the Spanish tongue, so he never doubted thereof as soon as he heard them speak. They had in their company an Indian, who had run away from his master because he would make him a slave after having served him a long time. This Indian went first on shore, and, rushing at the sentry, he instantly killed him. Being animated with this success, they entered into the city, and went directly to three or four houses of the chief citizens, where they knocked with dissimulation. These believing them to be friends opened the doors, and the Pirates suddenly possessing themselves of the houses, robbed all the money and plate they could find. Neither did they spare the churches and most sacred things, all which were pillaged and profaned without any respect or veneration.

In the meanwhile great cries and lamentation were heard about the town, of some who had escaped their hands ; by which means the whole city was brought into an uproar and alarm. Hence the whole number of citizens rallied together, intending to put themselves in defence. This being perceived by the Pirates, they instantly put themselves to flight, carrying with them all that they had robbed, and likewise some prisoners. These they led away, to the intent that, if any of them should happen to be taken by the Spaniards, they might make use of them for ransom. Thus they got to their ship, and with all speed imaginable put out to sea, forcing the prisoners, before they would let them go, to procure them as much flesh as they thought necessary for their voyage to Jamaica. But no sooner had they weighed anchor, than they saw on shore a troop of about five hundred Spaniards, all being very well armed, at the sea-side. Against these they let fly several guns, where-with they forced them to quit the sands and retire to-wards home, with no small regret to see those Pirates carry away so much plate of their churches and houses, though distant at least forty leagues from the sea.

These Pirates robbed on this occasion above four thousand pieces of eight in ready money, besides great quantities of plate uncoined and many jewels. All which was computed to be worth the sum of fifty thousand pieces of eight, or more. With this great booty they arrived at Jamaica, soon after the exploit. But as this sort of people are never masters of their money but a very little while, so were they soon constrained to seek more, by the same means they had used before. This adventure caused Captain John Davis, presently after his return, to be chosen Admiral of seven or eight boats of Pirates ; he being now esteemed by common consent an able conductor for such enterprizes as these were. He began the exercise of this new command by directing his fleet towards the coasts of the North of Cuba, there to wait for the fleet which was to pass from New Spain. But, not being able to find anything by this design, they determined to go towards the coasts of Florida. Being arrived there, they landed part of their men, and sacked a small city, named Saint Augustine of Florida, the castle of which place had a garrison of two hundred men, which, notwithstanding, could not prevent the pillage of the city, they effecting it without receiving the least damage from either soldiers or townsmen.

Hitherto we have spoken in the first part of this book

of the constitution of the Islands of Hispaniola and Tortuga, their peculiarities and inhabitants, as also of the fruits to be found in those countries. In the second part of this work we shall bend our discourse to describe the actions of two of the most famous Pirates, who committed many horrible crimes and inhuman cruelties against the Spanish nation.

The End of the First Part.

FRANCIS LOLONOIS.

PART II.

CHAPTER I.

Origin of Francis L'Ollonais, and beginning of his robberies.

FRANCIS L'OLLONAIS was a native of that territory in France which is called Les Sables d'Ollone, or the Sands of Ollone. In his youth he was transported to the Caribbee Islands, in quality of a servant or slave, according to the custom of France and other countries ; of which we have already spoken in the first part of this book. Being out of his time, when he had obtained his freedom, he came to the Isle of Hispaniola. Here he placed himself for some while among the hunters, before he began his robberies against the Spaniards ; whereof I shall make mention at present, until his unfortunate death.

At first he made two or three voyages in quality of a common mariner, wherein he behaved himself so courageously as to deserve the favour and esteem of the Governor of Tortuga, who was then Monsieur de la Place. Insomuch that this gentleman gave him a ship, and made him captain thereof, to the intent he might seek his fortune. This Dame shewed herself very favourable to him at the beginning, for in a short while he pillaged great riches. But, withal, his cruelties against the Spaniards were such that the very fame of them made him known through the whole Indies. For which reason the Spaniards, in his time, whensoever they

were attacked by sea, would choose rather to die or sink
fighting than surrender, knowing they should have no
mercy nor quarter at his hands.   But as Fortune is seldom constant, so after some time she turned her back
upon him.   The beginning of whose disasters was, that in
a huge storm he lost his ship upon the coasts of Campeche.   The men were all saved ; but coming upon dry
land, the Spaniards pursued them, and killed the greatest
part of them, wounding also L'Ollonais, their captain.
Not knowing how to escape, he thought to save his life
by a stratagem.   Hereupon he took several handfuls of
sand and mingled them with the blood of his own
wounds, with which he besmeared his face and other
parts of his body.   Then hiding himself dextrously
among the dead, he continued there till the Spaniards
had quitted the field.

After they were gone, he retired into the woods, and
bound up his wounds as well as he could.   These being
by the help of Nature pretty well healed, he took his
way to the city of Campeche, having perfectly disguised
himself in Spanish habit.   Here he spoke with certain
slaves, to whom he promised their liberty, in case they
would obey him and trust in his conduct.   They accepted
his promises, and stealing one night a canoe from one of
their masters, they went to sea with the Pirate.   The
Spaniards in the meanwhile had made prisoner several
of his companions, whom they kept in close dungeons in
the city, while L'Ollonais went about the town and saw all
that passed.   These were often asked by the Spaniards,
" *What is become of your Captain ?* " to whom they
constantly answered, " *He is dead.*"   With which news
the Spaniards were hugely gladdened, and made great
demonstrations of joy, kindling bonfires, and, like those
that knew nothing to the contrary, giving thanks to God
Almighty for their deliverance from such a cruel Pirate.
L'Ollonais, having seen these joys for his death, made
haste to escape with the slaves above-mentioned, and

came safe to Tortuga, the common place of refuge of all
sorts of wickedness, and the seminary, as it were, of all
manner of Pirates and thieves. Though now his fortune
was but low, yet he failed not of means to get another
ship, which with craft and subtlety he obtained, and in it
one and twenty persons. Being well provided with arms
and other necessaries, he set forth towards the Isle of
Cuba, on the South side whereof lies a small village,
which is called De los Cayos. The inhabitants of this
town drive a great trade in tobacco, sugar and hides;
and all in boats, as not being able to make use of ships
by reason of the little depth of that sea.

L'Ollonais was greatly persuaded he should get here
some considerable prey; but by the good fortune of some
fishermen who saw him, and the mercy of the Almighty,
they escaped his tyrannical hands. For the inhabitants
of the town of Cayos dispatched immediately a messenger
overland to Havana, complaining to the Governor that
L'Ollonais was come to destroy them, with two canoes.
The Governor could very hardly be persuaded of the
truth of this story, seeing he had received letters from
Campeche that he was dead. Notwithstanding, at the
importunity of the petitioners he sent a ship to their
relief, with ten guns and fourscore and ten persons, well
armed; giving them withal this express command: *They
should not return unto his presence without having totally
destroyed those Pirates.* To this effect he gave them
also a negro, who might serve them for a hangman; his
orders being that *They should immediately hang every one
of the said Pirates, excepting L'Ollonais their Captain,
whom they should bring alive to Havana.* This ship
arrived at Cayos; of whose coming the Pirates were
advertised beforehand; and, instead of flying, went to
seek the said vessel in the river Estera, where she rode at
anchor. The Pirates apprehended some fishermen, and
forced them, by night, to shew the entry of the port,
hoping soon to obtain a greater vessel than their two

canoes, and thereby to mend their fortune.   They arrived,
after two o'clock in the morning, very near the ship.
And the watch on board the ship asking them : *Whence
they came, and if they had seen any Pirates abroad*, they
caused one of the prisoners to answer : *They had seen no
Pirates, nor anything else.*   Which answer brought them
into persuasion that they were fled away, having heard
of their coming.

But they experienced very soon the contrary; for
about break of day the Pirates began to assault the vessel
on both sides with their two canoes.   This attack they
performed with such vigour that, although the Spaniards
behaved themselves as they ought and made as good
defence as they could, shooting against them likewise
some great guns, yet they were forced to surrender, after
being beaten by the Pirates, with swords in hand, down
under the hatches.   Hence L'Ollonais commanded them
to be brought up one by one, and in this order caused their
heads to be struck off.   Among the rest came up the
negro, designed to be the Pirates' executioner by the
Governor of Havana.   This fellow implored mercy at
his hands very dolefully, desiring not to be killed, and
telling L'Ollonais he was constituted hangman of that ship ;
and that, in case he would spare him, he would tell him
faithfully all that he should desire to know.   L'Ollonais
made him confess as many things as he thought fit to
ask him ; and, having done, commanded him to be
murdered with the rest.   Thus he cruelly and barbarously put them all to death, reserving of the whole number only one alive, whom he sent back to the Governor
of Havana, with this message given him in writing :
*I shall never henceforward give quarter to any Spaniard
whatsoever ; and I have great hopes I shall execute on your
own person the very same punishment I have done upon
them you sent against me.   Thus I have retaliated the
kindness you designed to me and my companions.*   The
Governor was much troubled to understand these sad

and withal insolent news ; which occasioned him to swear, in the presence of many, he would never grant quarter to any Pirate that should fall into his hands. But the citizens of Havana desired him not to persist in the execution of that rash and rigorous oath, *seeing the Pirates would certainly take occasion thence to do the same ; and they had an hundred times more opportunity of revenge than he : that, being necessitated to get their livelihood by fishery, they should hereafter always be in danger of losing their lives.* By these reasons he was persuaded to bridle his anger, and remit the severity of his oath aforementioned.

Now L'Ollonais had got himself a good ship, but withal very few provisions and people in it. Hereupon, to secure both the one and the other, he resolved to use his customary means of cruizing from one port to another. This he did for some while, till at last not being able to procure anything, he determined to go to the port of Maracaibo. Here he took by surprize a ship that was laden with plate and other merchandize, being outward bound to buy cacao-nuts. With these prizes he returned to Tortuga, where he was received with no small joy by the inhabitants, they congratulating his happy success and their own private interest. He continued not long there, but pitched upon new designs of equipping a whole fleet, sufficient to transport five hundred men, with all other necessaries. With these preparations he resolved to go to the Spanish dominions, and pillage both cities, towns and villages, and finally take Maracaibo itself. For this purpose, he knew the Island of Tortuga would afford him many resolute and courageous men, very fit for such enterprizes. Besides that, he had in his service several prisoners, who were exactly acquainted with the ways and places he designed upon.

CHAPTER II.

L'Ollonais equips a fleet to land upon the Spanish islands of America, with intent to rob, sack and burn whatever he met.

OF this his design L'Ollonais gave notice to all the Pirates who at that conjuncture of time were either at home or abroad. By which means he got together in a little while above four hundred men. Besides which, there was at that present in the Isle of Tortuga another Pirate, whose name was Michael de Basco. This man by his piracy had got riches sufficient to live at ease, and go no more abroad to sea ; having withal the office of Major of the Island. Yet seeing the great preparations that L'Ollonais made for this expedition, he entered into a straight league of friendship with him, and proffered him that, in case he would make him his chief captain by land (seeing he knew the country very well and all its avenues), he would take part in his fortunes, and go along with him. They both agreed upon articles, with great joy of L'Ollonais, as knowing that Basco had performed great actions in Europe, and had gained the repute of a good soldier. He gave him therefore the command he desired, and the conduct of all his people by land. Thus they all embarked in eight vessels, that of L'Ollonais being the greatest, as having ten guns of various carriage.

All things being in readiness, and the whole company on board, they set sail together about the end of April, having a considerable number of men for those parts, that is in all six hundred and threescore persons. They directed their course towards that part which is

called Bayala, situated on the North side of the Island of
Hispaniola. Here they also took into their company a
certain number of French hunters, who voluntarily offered
themselves to go along with them. And here likewise
they provided themselves with victuals and other necessaries for that voyage.

Hence they set sail again the last day of July, and
steered directly towards the Eastern Cape of the Isle,
called Punta d' Espada. Hereabouts they suddenly
espied a ship that was coming from Porto Rico, and
bound for New Spain, being laden with cacao-nuts.
L'Ollonais, the Admiral, presently commanded the rest of
the fleet they should wait for him near the Isle of Savona,
situate on the Eastern side of Cape Punta d' Espada,
forasmuch as he alone intended to go and take the said
vessel. The Spaniards, although they had been in sight
now fully two hours, and knew them to be Pirates, yet
they would not flee, but rather prepared to fight ; as
being well armed, and provided of all things necessary
thereto. Thus the combat began between L'Ollonais and
the Spanish vessel, which lasted three hours ; and these
being past, they surrendered to him. This ship was
mounted with sixteen guns, and had fifty fighting men
on board. They found in her *one hundred and twenty
thousand weight of cacao, forty thousand pieces of eight,
and the value of ten thousand more in jewels.* L'Ollonais
sent the vessel presently to Tortuga to be unladed, with
orders to return with the said ship as soon as possible to
the Isle of Savona, where he would wait for their coming.
In the meanwhile the rest of the fleet, being arrived at the
said Island of Savona, met with another Spanish vessel
that was coming from Comana with military provisions to
the Isle of Hispaniola ; and also with money to pay the
garrisons of the said island. This vessel also they took
without any resistance, although mounted with eight
guns. Here were found seven thousand weight of powder, great number of muskets and other things of this

kind, together with twelve thousand pieces of eight in ready money.

These forementioned events gave good encouragement to the Pirates, as judging them very good beginnings to the business they had in hand, especially finding their fleet pretty well recruited within a little while. For the first ship that was taken being arrived at Tortuga, the Governor ordered to be instantly unladen, and soon after sent her back with fresh provisions and other necessaries to L'Ollonais. This ship he chose for his own, and gave that which he commanded to his comrade Antony du Puis. Thus having received new recruits of men, in lieu of them he had lost in taking the prizes above-mentioned and by sickness, he found himself in a good condition to prosecute his voyage. All being well animated and full of courage, they set sail for Maracaibo, which port is situated in the province of New Venezuela, in the latitude of twelve degrees and some minutes North. This island is in length twenty leagues, and twelve in breadth. To this port also belong the Islands of Onega and Monges. The East side thereof is called Cape St. Roman, and the Western side Cape of Caquibacoa. The gulf is called by some the Gulf of Venezuela ; but the Pirates usually call it the Bay of Maracaibo.

At the beginning of this gulf are two islands, which extend for the greatest part from East to West. That which lies towards the East is called Isla de las Vigilias, or the Watch Isle, because in the middle thereof is to be seen a high hill, upon which stands a house wherein dwells perpetually a watchman. The other is called Isla de las Palomas, or the Isle of Pigeons. Between these two islands runs a little sea, or rather a lake, of fresh water, being threescore leagues in length and thirty in breadth ; which disgorges into the ocean, and dilates itself about the two islands afore-mentioned. Between them is found the best passage for ships, the channel of this passage being no broader than the flight of a great gun of eight pound carriage, more or less. Upon the Isle of Pigeons stands a castle, to impede the entry of any vessels; all such as come in being necessitated to approach very near the castle, by reason of two banks of sand that lie on the other side, with only fourteen foot water. Many other banks of sand are also found in this lake, as that which is called El Tablazo, or The Great Table, which is no deeper than ten foot; but this lies forty leagues within the lake. Others there are that are no more than six, seven or eight foot in depth. All of them are very dangerous, especially to such mariners as are little acquainted with this lake. On the West side hereof is situated the city of Maracaibo, being very pleasant to the view, by reason its houses are built along the shore, having delicate prospects everywhere round about. The city may possibly contain three or four thousand persons, the slaves being included in this number; all which make a town of reasonable bigness. Among these are judged to be eight hundred persons, more or less, able to bear arms, all of them Spaniards. Here are also one Parish Church, of very good fabric and well adorned, four monasteries and one hospital. The city is governed by a Deputy-Governor, who is substituted here by the Governor of Caracas, as being his dependency. The commerce or trading here exercised consists for the greatest part in hides and tobacco. The inhabitants possess great numbers of cattle, and many plantations, which extend for the space of thirty leagues within the country; especially on that side that looks towards the great and populous town of Gibraltar. At which place are gathered huge quantities of cacao-nuts, and all other sorts of garden fruits; which greatly serve for the regalement and sustenance of the inhabitants of Maracaibo, whose territories are much drier than those of Gibraltar. To this place those of Maracaibo send great quantities of flesh; they making returns in oranges, lemons, and several other fruits. For the inhabitants of Gibraltar have great scarcity of provisions of flesh, their fields being not capable of feeding cows or sheep.

Before the city of Maracaibo lies a very spacious and secure port, wherein may be built all sort of vessels ; as having great convenience of timber, which may be transported thither at very little charge. Near the town lies also a small island called Borrica, which serves them to feed great numbers of goats, of which cattle the inhabitants of Maracaibo make greater use of their skins than their flesh or milk ; they making no great account of these two, unless while they are as yet but tender and young kids. In the fields about the town are fed some numbers of sheep, but of a very small size. In some of the islands that belong to the lake, and in other places hereabouts, inhabit many savage Indians, whom the Spaniards call Bravos, or Wild. These Indians could never agree as yet, nor be reduced to any accord with the Spaniards, by reason of their brutish and untamable nature. They dwell for the most part towards the Western side of the lake, in little huts that are built upon trees which grow in the water, the cause hereof being only to exempt themselves as much as possible from the innumerable quantity of mosquitos or gnats which infest those parts, and by which they are tormented night and day. Towards the East side of the said lake are also to be seen whole towns of fishermen, who likewise are constrained to live in huts, built upon trees, like the former. Another reason of thus dwelling is the frequent inundations of waters : for after great rains, the land is often overflowed for the space of two or three leagues, there being no less than five and twenty great rivers that feed this lake. The town of Gibraltar is also frequently drowned by these inundations, insomuch that the inhabitants are constrained to leave their houses and retire to their plantations.

Gibraltar is situated at the side of the lake, forty

leagues or thereabouts within it, and receives its necessary provisions of flesh, as has been said, from Maracaibo.
The town is inhabited by fifteen hundred persons, more
or less, whereof four hundred may be capable of bearing
arms. The greatest part of the inhabitants keep open
shops, wherein they exercise one mechanic trade or other.
All the adjacent fields about this town are cultivated with
numerous plantations of sugar and cacao, in which are
many tall and beautiful trees, of whose timber houses
may be built, and also ships. Among these trees are
found great store of handsome and proportionable cedars,
being seven or eight foot in circumference, which serve
there very commonly to build boats and ships. These
they build after such manner as to bear only one great
sail ; and such vessels are called Piraguas. The whole
country round about is sufficiently furnished with rivers
and brooks, which are very useful to the inhabitants in
time of droughts, they opening in that occasion many
little channels, through which they lead the rivulets to
water their fields and plantations. They plant in like
manner great quantity of tobacco, which is much
esteemed in Europe ; and for its goodness, is called
there Tabaco de Sacerdotes, or Priest's Tobacco. They
enjoy nigh twenty leagues of jurisdiction, which is
bounded and defended by very high mountains that are
perpetually covered with snow. On the other side of
these mountains is situated a great city called Merida, to
which the town of Gibraltar is subject. All sort of merchandize is carried from this town to the aforesaid city,
upon mules ; and that but at one season of the year, by
reason of the excessive cold endured in those high mountains. Upon the said mules great returns are made in
flour of meal, which comes from towards Peru by the
way of Estaffe.

Thus far I thought it convenient to make a short
description of the aforesaid lake of Maracaibo, and its
situation ; to the intent my reader might the better be

enabled to comprehend what I shall say concerning what was acted by the Pirates in this place, the history whereof I shall presently begin.

As soon as L'Ollonais arrived at the Gulf of Venezuela, he cast anchor with his whole fleet, out of sight of the watch-tower of the Island of Vigilias, or Watch-Isle. The next day, very early, he set sail hence, with all his ships, for the lake of Maracaibo ; where being arrived, they cast anchor the second time. Soon after, they landed all their men, with design to attack in the first place the castle or fortress that commanded the bar, and is there-fore called De la Barra. This fort consists only of several great baskets of earth, placed upon a rising ground, upon which are planted sixteen great guns, with several other heaps of earth round about, for covering the men within. The Pirates having landed at the distance of a league from this fort, began to advance by degrees towards it. But the Governor thereof, having espied their landing, had placed an ambuscade of some of his men, with design to cut them off behind, while he meant to attack them in the front. This ambuscade was found out by the Pirates ; and, hereupon getting before, they assaulted and defeated it so entirely that not one man could retreat to the castle. This obstacle being removed, L'Ollonais with all his com-panions advanced in great haste towards the fort. And after a fight of almost three hours, wherein they behaved themselves with desperate courage, such as this sort of people are used to show, they became masters thereof, having made use of no other arms than their swords and pistols. And while they were fighting, those who were routed in the ambuscade, not being able to get into the castle, retired towards the city of Maracaibo in great confusion and disorder, crying : *The Pirates will presently be here with two thousand men and more.* This city having formerly been taken by such kind of people as these were, and sacked even to the

remotest corners thereof, preserved still in its memory a
fresh *Idea* of that misery. Hereupon, as soon as they
heard this dismal news, they endeavoured to escape as
fast as they could towards Gibraltar in their boats and
canoes, carrying with them all the goods and money they
could. Being come to Gibraltar, they dispersed the
rumour that the fortress was taken, and that nothing had
been saved, nor any persons able to escape the fury of
the Pirates.

The castle being taken by the Pirates, as was said
before, they presently made sign to the ships of the
victory they had obtained ; to the end they should come
farther in, without apprehension of any danger. The
rest of that day was spent in ruining and demolishing
the said castle. They nailed the guns, and burnt as
much as they could not carry away ; burying also the
dead, and sending on board the fleet such as were
wounded. The next day very early in the morning
they weighed anchor, and directed their course all together towards the city of Maracaibo, distant only six
leagues more or less from the fort. But the wind being
very scarce, that day they could advance but little, as
being forced to expect the flowing of the tide. The
next morning they came within sight of the town, and
began to make preparations for landing under the pro-
tection of their own guns; being persuaded the Spaniards
might have laid an ambuscade among the trees and
woods. Thus they put their men into canoes, which for
that purpose they brought with them, and landed where
they thought most convenient, shooting in the meanwhile
very furiously with their great guns. Of the people that
were in the canoes, half only went on shore, the other
half remained on board the said canoes. They fired
with their guns from the ships as fast as was possible
towards the woody part of the shore ; but could see, and
were answered by, nobody. Thus they marched in good
order into the town, whose inhabitants, as I told you

before, were all retired into the woods, and towards Gibraltar, with their wives, children and families. Their houses they left well provided with all sort of victuals, such as flour, bread, pork, brandy, wines and good store of poultry. With these things the Pirates fell to ban- queting and making good cheer ; for in four weeks before they had had no opportunity of filling their stomachs with such plenty.

They instantly possessed themselves of the best houses in the town, and placed sentries everywhere they thought convenient. The great church served them for their main *corps du garde.* The next day they sent a body of one hundred and sixty men to find out some of the in- habitants of the town, whom they understood were hidden in the woods not far thence. These returned that very night, bringing with them twenty thousand pieces of eight, several mules laden with household goods and merchandize, and twenty prisoners, between men, women and children. Some of these prisoners were put to the rack, only to make them confess where they had hidden the rest of their goods ; but they could extort very little from them. L'Ollonais, who never used to make any great account of murdering, though in cold blood, ten or twelve Spaniards, drew his cutlass and hacked one to pieces in the presence of all the rest, saying : *If you do not confess and declare where you have hidden the rest of your goods, I will do the like to all your companions.* At last, amongst these horrible cruelties and inhuman threats, one was found who promised to conduct him and show the place where the rest of the Spaniards were hidden. But those that were fled, having intelligence that one had discovered their lurking holes to the Pirates, changed place, and buried all the remnant of their riches under ground ; insomuch that the Pirates could not find them out, unless some other person of their own party should reveal them. Besides that the Spaniards, flying from one place to another every day and often changing woods, were jealous even of each other; insomuch as the father scarce presumed to trust his own son.

Finally, after that the Pirates had been fifteen days in Maracaibo, they resolved to go towards Gibraltar. But the inhabitants of this place, having received intelligence thereof beforehand, as also that they intended afterwards to go to Merida, gave notice of this design to the Governor thereof, who was a valiant soldier and had served his king in Flanders in many military offices. His answer was: *He would have them take no care ; for he hoped in a little while to exterminate the said Pirates.* Whereupon he transferred himself immediately to Gibraltar, with four hundred men well armed, ordering at the same time the inhabitants of the said town to put themselves in arms ; so that in all he made a body of eight hundred fighting men. With the same speed he commanded a battery to be raised towards the sea, whereon he mounted twenty guns, covering them all with great baskets of earth. Another battery likewise he placed in another place, mounted with eight guns. After this was done, he barricaded a highway or narrow passage into the town, through which the Pirates of necessity ought to pass ; opening at the same time another, through much dirt and mud, in the wood, which was totally unknown to the Pirates.

The Pirates, not knowing anything of these preparations, having embarked all their prisoners and what they had robbed, took their way towards Gibraltar. Being come within sight of the place, they perceived the Royal standard hanging forth, and that those of the town had a mind to fight and defend their houses. L'Ollonais, seeing this resolution, called a council of war, to deliberate what he ought to do in such case ; propounding withal to his officers and mariners, that the difficulty of such an enterprize was very great, seeing the Spaniards had had so much time to put themselves in a posture of defence, and had got a good body of men together, with many martial provisions. *But notwithstanding*, said he, *have a good courage. We must either defend ourselves like good soldiers, or lose our lives with all the riches we have got. Do as I shall do, who am your Captain. At other times we have fought with fewer men than we have in our company at present, and yet we have overcome greater numbers than there possibly can be in this town. The more they are, the more glory we shall attribute unto our fortune, and the greater riches we shall increase unto it.* The Pirates were under this suspicion, that all those riches which the inhabitants of Maracaibo had absconded, were transported to Gibraltar, or at least the greatest part thereof. After this speech they all promised to follow him and obey very exactly his commands. To whom L'Ollonais made answer : *'Tis well; but know ye withal that the first man who shall show any fear, or the least apprehension thereof, I will pistol him with my own hands.*

With this resolution they cast anchor near the shore, at the distance of one quarter of a league from the town. The next day, before sunrise, they were all landed, being to the number of three hundred and fourscore men, well provided, and armed every one with a cutlass and one or two pistols ; and withal sufficient powder and bullet for thirty charges. Here, upon the shore, they all shook hands with one another in testimony of good courage, and began their march, L'Ollonais speaking these words to them : *Come, my brothers, follow me, and have a good courage.* They followed their way with a guide they had provided. But he, believing he led them well, brought them to the way which the Governor had obstructed with barricades. Through this not being able to pass, they went to the other, which was newly made in the wood among the mire, to which the Spaniards could shoot at pleasure. Notwithstanding, the Pirates being full of courage, cut down multitude of branches

of trees, and threw them in the dirt upon the way, to the
end they might not stick so fast in it. In the meanwhile,
those of Gibraltar fired at them with their great guns so
furiously that they could scarce hear or see one another
through the noise and smoke. Being now past the
wood, they came upon firm ground, where they met with
a battery of six guns, which immediately the Spaniards
discharged against them, all being loaded with small bullets and pieces of iron. After this, the Spaniards sallying
forth set upon them with such fury, as caused the Pirates
to give way and retire ; very few of them daring to
advance towards the fort. They continued still firing
against the Pirates, of whom they had already killed and
wounded many. This made them go back to seek
some other way through the middle of the wood ; but
the Spaniards having cut down many trees to hinder the
passage, they could find none, and thus were forced to
return to that they had left. Here the Spaniards continued to fire as before ; neither would they sally out of
their batteries to attack the Pirates any more. Hereby
L'Ollonais and his companions, not being able to grimp
up the baskets of earth, were compelled to make use of
an old stratagem ; wherewith at last they deceived and
overcame the Spaniards.

L'Ollonais retired suddenly with all his men, making
show as if he fled. Hereupon the Spaniards, crying out,
They flee, they flee ; let us follow them, sallied forth with
great disorder, to pursue the fugitive Pirates. After
they had drawn them some distance from their batteries,
which was their only design, they turned upon them unexpectedly with swords in hand, and killed above two
hundred men. And thus fighting their way through
those who remained alive, they possessed themselves of
the batteries. The Spaniards that remained abroad gave
themselves up for lost, and consequently took their flight
to the woods. The other part that was in the battery of
eight guns surrendered themselves upon conditions of

obtaining quarter for their lives.   The Pirates, being now
become masters of the whole town, pulled down the
Spanish colours, and set up their own, taking prisoners
at the same time as many as they could find.   These
they carried to the great church, whither also they transferred many great guns, wherewith they raised a battery
to defend themselves, fearing lest the Spaniards that
were fled should rally more of their own party and come
upon them again.   But the next day, after they were all
fortified, all their fears disappeared.   They gathered all
the dead, with intent to allow them burial, finding the
number of above five hundred Spaniards killed, besides
those that were wounded within the town and those that
died of their wounds in the woods, where they sought
for refuge.   Besides which, the Pirates had in their
custody above one hundred and fifty prisoners, and nigh
five hundred slaves, many women and children.

Of their own companions the Pirates found only forty
dead, and almost as many more wounded.   Whereof the
greatest part died afterwards, through the constitution of
the air, which brought fevers and other accidents upon
them.   They put all the Spaniards that were slain into
two great boats, and carrying them one quarter of a
league within the sea, they sank the boats.   These things
being done, they gathered all the plate, household stuff
and merchandize they could rob or thought convenient
to carry away.   But the Spaniards who had anything as
yet left to them, hid it very carefully.   Soon after, the
Pirates, as if they were unsatisfied with the great riches
they had got, began to seek for more goods and merchandize, not sparing those who lived in the fields, such
as hunters and planters.   They had scarce been eighteen
days upon the place, when the greatest part of the
prisoners they had taken died of hunger.   For in the
town very few provisions, especially of flesh, were to be
found.   Howbeit, they had some quantity of flour of
meal, although perhaps something less than what was

sufficient. But this the Pirates had taken into their
custody to make bread for themselves. As to the swine,
cows, sheep and poultry that were found upon the place,
they took them likewise for their own sustenance, without allowing any share thereof to the poor prisoners.
For these they only provided some small quantity of
mules' and asses' flesh, which they killed for that purpose.
And such as could not eat of that loathsome provision
were constrained to die of hunger, as many did, their
stomachs not being accustomed to such unusual sustenance. Only some women were found, who were allowed
better cheer by the Pirates, because they served them
in their sensual delights, to which those robbers are
hugely given. Among those women, some had been
forced, others were volunteers; though almost all had
rather taken up that vice through poverty and hunger,
more than any other cause. Of the prisoners many also
died under the torments they sustained, to make them
confess where they had hidden their money or jewels.
And of these, some because they had none nor knew of
any, and others for denying what they knew, endured
such horrible deaths.

Finally, after having been in possession of the town
four entire weeks, they sent four of the prisoners, remaining alive, to the Spaniards that were fled into the
woods, demanding of them a ransom for not burning the
town. The sum hereof they constituted *ten thousand
pieces of eight*, which, unless it were sent to them, they
threatened to fire and reduce into ashes the whole village.
For bringing in of this money they allowed them only
the space of two days. These being past, and the
Spaniards not having been able to gather so punctually
such a sum, the Pirates began to set fire to many places
of the town. Thus the inhabitants, perceiving the
Pirates to be in earnest, begged of them to help to
extinguish the fire; and withal promised the ransom
should be readily paid. The Pirates condescended to

their petition, helping as much as they could to stop the progress of the fire. Yet, though they used the best endeavours they possibly could, one part of the town was ruined, especially the church belonging to the monastery, which was burnt even to dust. After they had received the sum above-mentioned, they carried on board their ships all the riches they had robbed, together with a great number of slaves which had not as yet paid their ransom. For all the prisoners had sums of money set upon them, and the slaves were also commanded to be redeemed. Hence they returned to Maracaibo, where being arrived they found a general consternation in the whole city. To which they sent three or four prisoners to tell the governor and inhabitants : *They should bring them thirty thousand pieces of eight on board their ships, for a ransom of their houses ; otherwise they should be entirely sacked anew and burnt.*

Among these debates a certain party of Pirates came on shore to rob, and these carried away the images, the pictures and bells of the great church, on board the fleet. The Spaniards, who were sent to demand of those that were fled the sum afore-mentioned, returned with orders to make some agreement with the Pirates. This they performed, and concluded with the Pirates they would give for their ransom and liberty the sum of twenty thousand pieces of eight and five hundred cows. The condition hereof being that they should commit no farther acts of hostility against any person, but should depart thence presently after payment of the money and cattle. The one and the other being delivered, they set sail with the whole fleet, causing great joy to the inhabitants of Maracaibo to see themselves quit of this sort of people. Notwithstanding, three days after they resumed their fears and admiration, seeing the Pirates to appear again and re-enter the port they had left with all their ships. But these apprehensions soon vanished, by only hearing the errand of one of the Pirates, who came on shore to tell them from L'Ollonais : *They should send him a skilful Pilot to conduct one of his greatest ships over the dangerous bank that lies at the entry of the lake.* Which petition, or rather command, was instantly granted.

The Pirates had now been full two months in those towns, wherein they committed those cruel and insolent actions we have told you of. Departing therefore thence, they took their course towards the island Hispaniola, and arrived thither in eight days, casting anchor in a port called Isla de la Vaca, or Cow Island. This isle is inhabited by French buccaneers, who most commonly sell the flesh they hunt to Pirates and others who now and then put in there with intent of victualling or trading with them. Here they unladed the whole cargo of riches they had robbed ; the usual storehouse of the Pirates being commonly under the shelter of the buccaneers. Here also they made a dividend amongst them of all their prizes and gains, according to that order and degree which belonged to every one, as hath been mentioned above. Having cast up the account and made exact calculation of all they had purchased, they found in ready money two hundred and threescore thousand pieces of eight. Whereupon, this being divided, every one received to his share in money, and also in pieces of silk, linen and other commodities, the value of above one hundred pieces of eight. Those who had been wounded in this expedition received their part before all the rest ; I mean, such recompences as I spoke of in the first Book, for the loss of their limbs which many sustained. Afterwards they weighed all the plate that was uncoined, reckoning after the rate of ten pieces of eight for every pound. The jewels were prized with much variety, either at too high or too low rates ; being thus occasioned by their own ignorance. This being done, every one was put to his oath again, that he had not concealed anything nor subtracted from the common stock. Hence they proceeded to the dividend of what shares belonged to such as were dead amongst them, either in battle or otherwise. These shares were given to their friends to be kept entire for them, and to be delivered in due time to their nearest relations, or whomsoever should appear to be their lawful heirs.

The whole dividend being entirely finished, they set sail thence for the Isle of Tortuga. Here they arrived one month after, to the great joy of most that were upon the island. For as to the common Pirates, in three weeks they had scarce any money left them; having spent it all in things of little value, or at play either at cards or dice. Here also arrived, not long before them, two French ships laden with wine and brandy and other things of this kind; whereby these liquors, at the arrival of the Pirates, were sold indifferent cheap. But this lasted not long; for soon after they were enhanced extremely, a gallon of brandy being sold for four pieces of eight. The Governor of the island bought of the Pirates the whole cargo of the ship laden with cacao, giving them for that rich commodity scarce the twentieth part of what it was worth. Thus they made shift to lose and spend the riches they had got in much less time than they were purchased by robbing. The taverns, according to the custom of Pirates, got the greatest part thereof; insomuch that soon after they were constrained to seek more by the same unlawful means they had obtained the preceding.

CHAPTER III.

L'Ollonais makes new preparations to take the city of St. James de Leon ; as also that of Nicaragua, where he miserably perishes.

L'OLLONAIS had got himself very great esteem and repute at Tortuga by this last voyage, by reason he brought them home such considerable profit. And now he needed take no great care how to gather men to serve under his colours, seeing more came in voluntarily to proffer their service to him than he could employ, every one reposing such great confidence in his conduct for seeking their fortunes, that they judged it a matter of the greatest security imaginable to expose themselves in his company to the hugest dangers that might possibly occur. He resolved therefore for a second voyage, to go with his officers and soldiers towards the parts of Nicaragua, and pillage there as many towns as he could meet.

Having published his new preparations, he had all his men together at the time appointed, being about the number of seven hundred, more or less. Of these he put three hundred on board the ship he took at Maracaibo, and the rest in other vessels of lesser burden, which were five more : so that the whole number were in all six ships. The first port they went to was in the Island of Hispaniola, to a place called Bayaha, where they determined to victual the fleet and take in provisions. This being done, they set sail thence, and steered their course to a port called Matamana, lying on the South side of the Isle of Cuba. Their intent was to take here all the canoes they could meet, these coasts

being frequented by an huge number of fishermen of
tortoises, who carry them thence to Havana.   They
took as many of the said canoes, to the great grief of
those miserable people, as they thought necessary for
their designs.   For they had great necessity of these
small bottoms, by reason the port whither they designed
to go was not of depth sufficient to bear ships of any
burden.   Hence they took their course towards the cape
called Gracias à Dios, situate upon the continent in
latitude fifteen degrees North, at the distance of one
hundred leagues from the island De los Pinos.   But
being out at sea they were taken with a sad and
tedious calm, and by the agitation of the waves alone
were thrown into the Gulf of Honduras.   Here they
laboured very much to regain what they had lost, but all
in vain ; both the waters in their course, and the winds,
being contrary to their endeavours.   Besides that the
ship wherein L'Ollonais was embarked could not follow
the rest ; and what was worse, they wanted already provisions.   Hereupon they were forced to put into the
first port or bay they could reach, to revictual their fleet.
Thus they entered with their canoes into a river called
Xagua, inhabited by Indians, whom they totally robbed
and destroyed ; they finding amongst their goods great
quantity of millet, many hogs and hens.   Not contented
with what they had done, they determined to remain
there until the bad weather was over, and to pillage all
the towns and villages lying along the coast of the gulf.
Thus they passed from one place to another, seeking as
yet more provisions, by reason they had not what they
wanted for the accomplishment of their designs.   Having
searched and rifled many villages, where they found no
great matter, they came at last to Puerto Cavallo.   In
this port the Spaniards have two several storehouses,
which serve to keep the merchandizes that are brought
from the inner parts of the country until the arrival of
the ships.   There was in the port at that occasion a

Spanish ship mounted with four and twenty guns and sixteen pateraras or mortar-pieces. This ship was immediately seized by the Pirates ; and then, drawing near the shore, they landed and burnt the two store-houses, with all the rest of the houses belonging to the place. Many inhabitants likewise they took prisoners, and committed upon them the most insolent and in-human cruelties that ever heathens invented, putting them to the cruellest tortures they could imagine or devise. It was the custom of L'Ollonais that, having tormented any persons and they not confessing, he would instantly cut them in pieces with his hanger, and pull out their tongues ; desiring to do the same, if possible, to every Spaniard in the world. Oftentimes it happened that some of these miserable prisoners, being forced thereunto by the rack, would promise to discover the places where the fugitive Spaniards lay hidden ; which being not able afterwards to perform, they were put to more enormous and cruel deaths than they who were dead before.

The prisoners being all dead and annihilated (except-ing only two, whom they reserved to show them what they desired), they marched hence to the town of San Pedro, or St. Peter, distant ten or twelve leagues from Puerto Cavallo, having in their company three hundred men, whom L'Ollonais led, and leaving behind him Moses van Vin for his lieutenant to govern the rest in his absence. Being come three leagues upon their way, they met with a troop of Spaniards, who lay in ambus-cade for their coming. These they set upon with all the courage imaginable, and at last totally defeated, howbeit they behaved themselves very manfully at the beginning of the fight. But not being able to resist the fury of the Pirates, they were forced to give way and save them-selves by flight, leaving many Pirates dead upon the place and wounded, as also some of their own party maimed by the way. These L'Ollonais put to death with-

out mercy, having asked them what questions he thought
fit for his purpose.

There were still remaining some few prisoners who
were not wounded. These were asked by L'Ollonais if
any more Spaniards did lie farther on in ambuscade?
To whom they answered, there were. Then he commanded them to be brought before him, one by one, and
asked if there was no other way to be found to the town
but that? This he did out of a design to excuse, if
possible, those ambuscades. But they all constantly
answered him, they knew none. Having asked them
all, and finding they could show him no other way,
L'Ollonais grew outrageously passionate; insomuch that
he drew his cutlass, and with it cut open the breast of
one of those poor Spaniards, and pulling out his heart
with his sacrilegious hands, began to bite and gnaw it
with his teeth, like a ravenous wolf, saying to the rest:
*I will serve you all alike, if you show me not another
way.*

Hereupon those miserable wretches promised to show
him another way; but withal they told him, it was
extremely difficult and laborious. Thus, to satisfy that
cruel tyrant, they began to lead him and his army. But
finding it not for his purpose, even as they told him, he
was constrained to return to the former way, swearing
with great choler and indignation: *Mort Dieu, les
Espagnols me le payeront* (*By God's death the Spaniards
shall pay me for this*).

The next day he fell into another ambuscade; the
which he assaulted with such horrible fury that in less
than an hour's time he routed the Spaniards, and killed
the greatest part of them. The Spaniards were persuaded that by these ambuscades they should better be
able to destroy the Pirates, assaulting them by degrees;
and for this reason had posted themselves in several
places. At last he met with a third ambuscade, where
was placed a party of Spaniards both stronger and to

The Cruelty of Lolonois

LOLONOIS

greater advantage than the former. Yet, notwithstanding, the Pirates, by throwing with their hands little fireballs in great number, and continuing to do so for some time, forced this party, as well as the preceding, to flee. And this with such great loss of men as that, before they could reach the town, the greatest part of the Spaniards were either killed or wounded. There was but one path which led to the town. This path was very well barricaded with good defences; and the rest of the town round about was planted with certain shrubs or trees named Raqueltes, very full of thorns and these very sharp-pointed. This sort of fortification seemed stronger than the triangles which are used in Europe, when an army is of necessity to pass by the place of an enemy, it being almost impossible for the Pirates to traverse those shrubs. The Spaniards that were posted behind the said defences, seeing the Pirates come, began to shoot at them with their great guns. But these, perceiving them ready to fire, used to stoop down, and when the shot was made, fall upon the defendants with fireballs in hands and naked swords, killing with these weapons many of the town. Yet, notwithstanding, not being able to advance any farther, they were constrained to retire for the first time. Afterwards they returned to the attack again, with fewer men than before; and observing not to shoot till they were very near, they gave the Spaniards a charge so dexterously, that with every shot they killed an enemy.

The attack continuing thus eager on both sides till night, the Spaniards were compelled to hang forth a white flag, in token of truce and that they desired to come to a parley. The only conditions they required for delivering the town were: *That the Pirates should give the inhabitants quarter for two hours.* This short space of time they demanded, with intent to carry away and abscond as much of their goods and riches as they could, as also to flee to some other neighbouring town. Upon the agreement of this article they entered the town, and continued there the two hours above-mentioned, without committing the least act of hostility, or causing any trouble to the inhabitants. But no sooner that time was passed, than L'Ollonais ordered the inhabitants should be followed and robbed of all they had carried away ; and not only goods, but their persons likewise to be made all prisoners. Notwithstanding, the greatest part of their merchandize and goods were in such manner absconded as the Pirates could not find them ; they meeting only a few leathern sacks that were filled with anil or indigo.

Having stayed at this town some few days, and according to their usual customs committed there most horrid insolencies, they at last quitted the place, carrying away with them all that they possibly could, and reducing the town totally into ashes. Being come to the seaside, where they left a party of their own comrades, they found these had busied themselves in cruizing upon the fishermen that lived thereabouts or came that way from the river of Guatemala. In this river also was expected a ship that was to come from Spain. Finally they resolved to go towards the islands that lie on the other side of the gulf, there to cleanse and careen their vessels. But in the meanwhile they left two canoes before the coast, or rather the mouth of the river of Guatemala, to the intent they should take the ship which, as I said before, was expected from Spain.

But their chief intention of going to those islands was to seek provisions, as knowing the tortoises of those places are very excellent and pleasant food. As soon as they arrived there, they divided into troops, each party choosing a fit post for that fishery. Every one of them undertook to knit a net with the rinds of certain trees, called in those parts Macoa. Of these rinds they make also ropes and cables for the service of ships : insomuch that no vessel can be in need of such things whensoever they can but find the said trees. There are also in those parts many places where they find pitch,[1] which is gathered thereabouts in great abundance. The quantity hereof is so great that, running down the sea-coasts, being melted by the heat of the sun, it congeals in the water into great heaps, and represents the shape of small islands. This pitch is not like that we have in the countries of Europe, but is hugely like, both in colour and shape, that froth of the sea which is called by the naturalists bitumen. But in my judgment this matter is nothing else but wax, which stormy weather has cast into the sea, being part of that huge quantity which in the neighbouring terri- tories is made by the bees. Thus from places far distant from the sea it is also brought to the sea-coast by the winds and rolling waves of great rivers ; being likewise mingled with sand, and having the smell of black amber, such as is sent us from the Orient. In those parts are found great quantities of the said bees, who make their honey in trees ; whence it happens that the honey-combs being fixed to the bodies of the trees, when tempests arise they are torn away, and by the fury of the winds carried into the sea, as has been said before. Some naturalists are willing to say that between the honey and the wax is made a separation by means of the salt water, whence proceeds also the good amber. This opinion is rendered the more probable because the said amber being found and tasted, it affords the like taste as wax does.

But now, returning to my discourse, I shall let you know that the Pirates made in those islands all the haste to equip their vessels they could possibly, by reason they had news the Spanish ship which they expected was come. They spent some time in cruizing upon the coasts of Yucatan, whereabouts inhabit many Indians, who seek for the amber above-mentioned in those seas.

---

[1] One of the largest pitch or asphalt lakes is to be seen in the British island of Trinidad, a very good description of which is to be found in C. Kingsley's "At Last." Similar deposits on a small scale are not uncommon in the West Indian Islands, which are mostly of volcanic origin.

But seeing we are come to this place, I shall here, by the by, make some short remarks on the manner of living of these Indians, and the divine worship which they practise.

The Indians of the coasts of Yucatan have now been above one hundred years under the dominion of the Spaniards. To this nation they performed all manner of service ; for, whensoever any of them had need of a slave or servant, they sent to seek one of these Indians to serve them as long as they pleased. By the Spaniards they were initiated at first in the principles of Christian faith and religion. Being thus made a part of Christianity, they used to send them every Sunday and holiday through the whole year a priest to perform divine service among them. Afterwards, for what reasons are not known, but certainly through evil temptations of the Father of Idolatry, the Devil, they suddenly cast off Christian religion again, and abandoned the true divine worship, beating withal and abusing the priest was sent them. This provoked the Spaniards to punish them according to their deserts, which they did by casting many of the chief of these Indians into prison. Every one of those barbarians had, and has still, a god to himself, whom he serves and worships. It is a thing that deserves all admiration, to consider how they use in this particular a child that is newly born into the world. As soon as this is issued from the womb of the mother, they carry it to the temple. Here they make a circle or hole, which they fill with ashes, without mingling anything else with them. Upon this heap of ashes they place the child naked, leaving it there a whole night alone, not without great danger ; nobody daring to come near it. In the meanwhile the temple is open on all sides, to the intent all sorts of beasts may freely come in and out. The next day the father and relations of the infant return thither, to see if the track or step of any animal appears to be printed in the ashes. Not finding any, they leave the child there until some beast hath approached the infant, and left behind him the mark of his feet. To this animal, whatsoever it be, they consecrate the creature newly born, as unto its god ; which he is bound to worship and serve all his life, esteeming the said beast as his patron and protector in all cases of danger or necessity. They offer to their gods sacrifices of fire, wherein they burn a certain gum called by them copal, whose smoke affords a very delicious smell. When the infant is grown up, the parents thereof tell him and show him whom he ought to worship, serve and honour as his own proper god. This being known, he goes to the temple, where he makes offerings to the said beast. Afterwards, if in the course of his life any one has injured him, or any evil happens to him, he complains thereof to that beast, and sacrifices to it for revenge. Whence many times comes that those who have done the injury of which he complains are found to be bitten, killed, or otherwise hurt by such animals.

After this superstitious and idolatrous manner do live those miserable and ignorant Indians, that inhabit all the islands of the Gulf of Honduras, as also many of them that dwell upon the continent of Yucatan. In the territories of which country are found most excellent ports for the safety of ships, where those Indians most commonly love to build their houses. These people are not very faithful one to another, and likewise use strange ceremonies at their marriages. Whensoever any one pretends to marry a young damsel, he first applies himself to her father or nearest relation. He then examines him very exactly concerning the manner of cultivating their plantations and other things at his pleasure. Having satisfied the questions that were put to him by the father-in-law, he gives the young man a bow and arrow. With these things he repairs to the young maid, and presents her with a garland of green leaves, interweaved with sweet-smelling flowers. This she is obliged

to put upon her head, and lay aside that which she wore
before that time ; it being the custom of the country that
all virgins go perpetually crowned with flowers. This
garland being received and put upon the head, every one
of the relations and friends go to advise with others,
among themselves, whether that marriage will be useful
and of likely happiness, or not. Afterwards the aforesaid
relations and friends meet together at the house of the
damsel's father, and there they drink of a certain liquor
made of maize, or Indian wheat. And here before the
whole company the father gives his daughter in marriage
to the bridegroom. The next day the newly-married
bride comes to her mother, and in her presence pulls off
the garland and tears it in pieces, with great cries and
bitter lamentations, according to the custom of the
country. Many other things I could relate at large of
the manner of living and customs of those Indians ; but
these I shall omit, thereby to follow my discourse.

Our Pirates therefore had many canoes of the Indians
in the Isle of Sambale, five leagues distant from the
coasts of Yucatan. In the aforesaid island is found great
quantity of amber, but more especially when any storm
arises from towards the East, whence the waves bring
many things and very different. Through this sea no
vessels can pass, unless very small, the waters being too
shallow. In the lands that are surrounded by this sea is
found huge quantity of Campeche wood (*i.e.* logwood),
and other things of this kind, that serve for the art of
dyeing, which occasions them to be much esteemed in
Europe, and doubtless would be much more, in case we
had the skill and science of the Indians, who are so
industrious as to make a dye or tincture that never
changes its colour nor fades away.

After that the Pirates had been in that gulf three
entire months, they received advice that the Spanish
ship was come. Hereupon they hastened to the port,
where the ship lay at anchor unlading the merchandize

it brought, with design to assault her as soon as it were possible. But before this attempt they thought it convenient to send away some of their boats from the mouth of the river, to seek for a small vessel which was expected ; having notice that she was very richly laden, the greatest part of the cargo being plate, indigo and cochineal. In the meanwhile the people of the ship that was in the port had notice given that the Pirates designed upon them. Hereupon they prepared all things very well for the defence of the said vessel, which was mounted with forty-two guns, had many arms on board and other necessaries, together with one hundred and thirty fighting men. To L'Ollonais all this seemed but little ; and thus he assaulted her with great courage, his own ship carrying only twenty-two guns, and having no more than a small saëtia, or flyboat, for help. But the Spaniards defended themselves after such manner as they forced the Pirates to retire. Notwithstanding, while the smoke of the powder continued very thick, as amidst a dark fog or mist, they sent four canoes very well manned, and boarded the ship with great agility, whereby they compelled the Spaniards to surrender.

The ship being taken, they found not in her what they thought, as being already almost wholly unladed. All the treasure they here got consisted only in fifty bars of iron, a small parcel of paper, some earthen jars full of wine, and other things of this kind ; all of small importance.

Presently after, L'Ollonais called a council of the whole fleet, wherein he told them he intended to go to Guatemala. Upon this point they divided into several sentiments ; some of them liking the proposal very well, and others disliking it as much—especially a certain party of them, who were but new in those exercises of piracy, and who had imagined at their setting forth from Tortuga that pieces of eight were gathered as easily as pears from a tree. But having found at last most things contrary to

their expectation, they quitted the fleet, and returned
whence they set out. Others, on the contrary, affirmed
they had rather die of hunger, than return home without
a great deal of money.

But the major part of the company, judging the propounded voyage little fit for their purpose, separated from
L'Ollonais and the rest. Among these was ringleader
one Moses Vanclein, who was captain of the ship taken
at Puerto Cavallo. This fellow took his course towards
Tortuga, designing to cruize to and fro in those seas.
With him also joined another comrade of his own, by
name Pierre le Picard, who, seeing the rest to leave
L'Ollonais, thought fit to do the same. These runaways
having thus parted company, steered their course homewards, coasting along the continent, till they came at
last to Costa Rica. Here they landed a strong party of
men near the river of Veraguas, and marched in good
order to the town of the same name. This place they
took and totally pillaged, notwithstanding that the
Spaniards made a strong and warlike resistance. They
brought away some of the inhabitants as prisoners, with
all that they had robbed, which was of no great importance, the reason hereof being the poverty of the place,
which exercises no manner of trade than only working in
the mines, where some of the inhabitants constantly
attend. Yet no other persons seek for the gold than
only slaves. These they compel to dig, whether they
live or die, and wash the earth that is taken out in the
neighbouring rivers ; where oftentimes they find pieces
of gold as big as peas. Finally, the Pirates found in
this robbery no greater value than seven or eight pounds
weight of gold. Hereupon they returned back, giving
over the design they had to go farther on to the town of
Nata, situated upon the coasts of the South sea. Hitherto they designed to march, knowing the inhabitants to
be rich merchants, who had their slaves at work in the
mines of Veraguas. But from this enterprize they were

deterred by the multitude of Spaniards whom they saw gather on all sides to fall upon them ; whereof they had timely advice beforehand.

L'Ollonais, thus abandoned by his companions, remained alone in the Gulf of Honduras, by reason his ship was too great to get out at the time of the reflux of those seas, which the smaller vessels could more easily do. There he sustained great want of all sorts of provisions ; insomuch as they were constrained to go ashore every day, to seek wherewithal to maintain themselves. And not finding anything else, they were forced to kill monkeys and other animals such as they could find, for their sustenance.

At last having found, in the latitude of the Cape of Gracias à Dios, certain little islands called De las Pertas, here, near these isles, his ship fell upon a bank of sand, where it stuck so fast that no art could be found to get her off into deep water again, notwithstanding they unladed all the guns, iron and other weighty things as much as possibly they could : but all they could do was to little or no effect. Hereupon they were necessitated to break the ship in pieces, and with some of the planks and nails build themselves a boat, wherewith to get away from those islands. Thus they began their work ; and while they are employed about it, I shall pass to describe succinctly the isles aforementioned and their inhabitants.

The islands called De las Pertas are inhabited by Indians, who are properly savages, not having at any time known or conversed with any civil people. They are tall in stature and very nimble in running, which they perform almost as fast as horses. At diving also in the sea they are very dexterous and hardy. From the bottom of the sea I saw them take up an anchor that weighed six hundred pound, by tying a cable to it with great dexterity, and pulling it from a rock. They use no other arms than such as are made of wood, without any iron, unless that some instead thereof fix a crocodile

tooth, which serves for a point.   They have neither bows
nor arrows among them, as other Indians have ; but their
common weapon is a sort of lances, that are long a fathom
and a half.   In these islands there are many plantations
surrounded with woods, whence they gather great abundance of fruits.   Such are potatoes, bananas, racoven,
ananas and many others, which the constitution of the
soil affords.   Near these plantations they have no houses
to dwell in, as in other places of the Indies.   Some are
of opinion that these Indians eat human flesh, which seems
to be confirmed by what happened when L'Ollonais was
there.   Two of his companions, the one being a Frenchman and the other a Spaniard, went into the woods,
where having straggled up and down some while, they
met with a troop of Indians that began to pursue them.
They defended themselves as well as they could with
their swords ; but at last were forced to flee.   This the
Frenchman performed with great agility; but the Spaniard,
being not so swift as his companion, was taken by those
barbarians, and heard of no more.   Some days after, they
attempted to go into the woods to see what was become
of their companion.   To this effect twelve Pirates set
forth very well armed, amongst whom was the Frenchman, who conducted them, and shewed them the place
where he left his companion.   Here they found, near the
place, that the Indians had kindled a fire ; and, at a small
distance thence, they found the bones of the said Spaniard
very well roasted.   Hence they inferred that they had
roasted the miserable Spaniard, of whom they found
more, some pieces of flesh ill scraped off from the bones,
and one hand, which had only two fingers remaining.

They marched farther on, seeking for Indians.   Of
these they found a great number together, who endeavoured to escape, seeing the Pirates so strong and well
armed.   But they overtook some of them, and brought
on board their ships five men and four women.   With
these they used all the means they could invent to make

themselves be understood and gain their affections ;
giving them certain small trifles, as knives, beads and
the like things. They gave them also victuals and
drink ; but nothing of either would they taste. It was
also observable that all the while they were prisoners on
board the ships, they spoke not one word to each other
among themselves. Thus the Pirates, seeing these poor
Indians were much afraid of them, presented them again
with some small things, and let them go. When they
departed, they made signs, giving them to understand
they would come again. But they soon forgot their
benefactors, and were never heard nor seen more.
Neither could any notice afterwards be had of these
Indians or any others in the whole island after that time.
Which occasioned the Pirates to suspect that both those
that were taken, and all the rest of the island, did all
swim away by night to some other little neighbouring
islands, especially considering they could never set eyes
on any Indian more ; neither was there ever seen any
boat or other vessel in the whole circumference of the
island.

In the meanwhile the Pirates were very desirous to
see their long-boat finished, which they were building
with the timber of the ship that struck upon the sands.
Yet, considering their work would be but long, they
began to cultivate some pieces of ground. Here they
sowed French beans, which came to maturity in six
weeks' time, and many other fruits. They had good
provision of Spanish wheat, bananas, racoven and other
things. With the wheat they made bread, and baked it
in portable ovens, which they had brought with them to
this effect. Thus they feared not hunger in those desert
places. After this manner they employed themselves
for the space of five or six months. Which time being
passed, and the long-boat finished, they determined to
go to the river of Nicaragua, to see if they could take
some few canoes, and herewith return to the said islands

and fetch away their companions that remained behind, by reason the boat they had built was not capable of transporting so many men together. Hereupon, to avoid any disputes that might arise, they cast lots among themselves, determining thereby who should go, or stay, in the island.

The lot fell only upon one half of the people of the lost vessel ; who embarked upon the long-boat they had built, and also the skiff which they had before ; the other half remaining on shore. L'Ollonais having set sail, arrived in a few days at the mouth of the river of Nicaragua. Here suddenly his ill-fortune assailed him, which of long time had been reserved for him, as a punishment due to the multitude of horrible crimes, which in his licentious and wicked life he had committed. Here he met with both Spaniards and Indians, who jointly together set upon him and his companions, and used them so roughly that the greatest part of the Pirates were killed upon the place. L'Ollonais, with those that remained alive, had much ado to escape on board their boats aforementioned. Yet notwithstanding this great loss of men, he resolved not to return to seek those he had left at the Isle of Pertas, without taking some boats, such as he looked for. To this effect he determined to go farther on to the coasts of Cartagena, with design to seek for canoes. But God Almighty, the time of His Divine justice being now already come, had appointed the Indians of Darien to be the instruments and executioners thereof. The Indians of Darien are esteemed as bravos, or wild savage Indians, by the neighbouring Spaniards, who never could reduce them to civility. Hither L'Ollonais came (being rather brought by his evil conscience that cried for punishment of his crimes), thinking to act in that country his former cruelties. But the Indians within a few days after his arrival took him prisoner and tore him in pieces alive, throwing his body limb by limb into the fire, and his ashes into the air ; to the intent no trace nor memory might remain of such an infamous, inhuman creature. One of his companions gave me an exact account of the aforesaid tragedy; affirming withal that he himself had escaped the same punishment, not without the greatest of difficulties. He believed also that many of his comrades who were taken prisoners in that encounter by the Indians of Darien were after the same manner as their cruel captain torn in pieces and burned alive. Thus ends the history of the life and miserable death of that infernal wretch L'Ollonais, who, full of horrid, execrable and enormous deeds, and also debtor to so much innocent blood, died by cruel and butcherly hands, such as his own were in the course of his life.

Those that remained in the island De las Pertas, waiting for the return of them who got away, only to their great misfortune, hearing no news of their captain nor companions, at last embarked themselves upon the ship of a certain Pirate who happened to pass that way. This fellow was come from Jamaica with intent to land at the Cape of Gracias à Dios, and hence to mount the river with his canoes, and take the city of Cartagena. These two parcels of Pirates being now joined together were infinitely gladdened at the presence and society of one another. Those because they found themselves delivered from their miseries, poverty and necessities, wherein now they had lived the space of ten entire months—these, because they were now considerably strengthened, whereby to effect with greater satisfaction their intended designs. Hereupon, as soon as they were arrived at the aforesaid Cape of Gracias à Dios, they all put themselves into canoes, and with these vessels mounted the river, being in number five hundred men; leaving only five or six persons in every ship to keep them. They took no provisions with them, as being persuaded they should find everywhere sufficient. But these their own hopes were found totally vain,

as not being grounded in God Almighty. For He
ordained it so that the Indians having perceived
their coming, were all fled before them, not leaving in
their houses nor plantations, which for the most part
border upon the sides of rivers, anything of necessary
provisions or victuals. Hereby, in few days after they
had quitted their ships, they were reduced to such necessity and hunger as nothing could be more extreme.
Notwithstanding, the hopes they had conceived of
making their fortunes very soon animated them for the
present, being contented in this affliction with a few
green herbs, such as they could gather as they went upon
the banks of the river.

Yet all this courage and vigour of mind could not last
above a fortnight. After which, their hearts, as well as
their bodies, began to fail for hunger ; insomuch as they
found themselves constrained to quit the river and betake
themselves to the woods, seeking out some small villages
where they might find relief for their necessity. But all
was in vain : for, having ranged up and down the woods
for some days without finding the least comfort to their
hungry desires, they were forced to return again to the
river. Where being come, they thought it convenient to
descend to the sea-coasts where they had left their ships,
not being able to find in the present enterprize what they
sought for. In this laborious journey they were reduced
to such extremity that many of them devoured their own
shoes, the sheaths of their swords, knives and other
things of this kind, being almost ravenous, and fully
desirous to meet some Indians, intending to sacrifice
them unto their teeth. At last they arrived at the coast
of the sea, where they found some comfort and relief to
their former miseries, and also means to seek more. Yet
notwithstanding, the greatest part of them perished
through faintness and other diseases contracted by
hunger ; which occasioned also the remaining part to
disperse. Till at last by degrees many or most of them

fell into the same pit that L'Ollonais did. Of him, and of his companions I have hitherto given my reader a compendious narrative ; which now I shall continue with the actions and exploits of Captain Henry Morgan, who may not undeservedly be called the second L'Ollonais, as not being unlike or inferior to him either in achievements against the Spaniards or in robberies of many innocent people.

CHAPTER IV.

Of the Origin and Descent of Captain Henry Morgan—his Exploits and a continuation of the most remarkable actions of his life.

CAPTAIN HENRY MORGAN was born in the Kingdom of England, and there in the principality of Wales. His father was a rich yeoman, or farmer, and of good quality in that country, even as most who bear that name in Wales are known to be. Morgan, being as yet young, had no inclinations to follow the calling of his father; and therefore left his country, and came towards the sea-coasts to seek some other employ more suitable to his humour, that aspired to something else. There he found entertainment in a certain port where several ships lay at anchor, that were bound for the Isle of Barbados. With these ships he resolved to go in the service of one, who, according to what is commonly practised in those parts by the English and other nations, sold him as soon as he came on shore. He served his time at Barbados, and when he had obtained his liberty, thence transferred himself to the Island of Jamaica, there to seek new fortunes. Here he found two vessels of Pirates that were ready to go to sea. Being destitute of employ, he put himself into one of these ships, with intent to follow the exercises of that sort of people. He learned in a little while their manner of living; and so exactly, that having performed three or four voyages with some profit and good success, he agreed with some of his comrades, who had gotten by the same voyages a small parcel of money, to join stocks and buy a ship. The vessel being bought,

they unanimously chose him to be the captain and commander thereof.

With this ship, soon after, he set forth from Jamaica
to cruize upon the coasts of Campeche ; in which voyage
he had the fortune to take several ships, with which
he returned triumphant to the same island. Here he
found at the same time an old Pirate, named Mansvelt
(of whom we have already made mention in the first
part of this book), who was then busied in equipping
a considerable fleet of ships with design to land upon
the Continent, and pillage whatever came in his way.
Mansvelt, seeing Captain Morgan return with so many
prizes, judged him, from his actions, to be of undaunted
courage ; and hereupon was moved to choose him for
his Vice-Admiral in that expedition. Thus having fitted
out fifteen ships, between great and small, they set sail
from Jamaica with five hundred men, both Walloons and
French. With this fleet they arrived not long after at
the Isle of St. Catharine, situated near the Continent of
Costa Rica, in the latitude of twelve degrees and a
half North, and distant thirty-five leagues from the
river of Chagre, between North and South. Here they
made their first descent, landing most of their men presently after.

Being now come to try their arms and fortune, they
in a short while forced the garrison that kept the island
to surrender and deliver into their hands all the forts and
castles belonging thereunto. All these they instantly
demolished, reserving only one, wherein they placed one
hundred men of their own party, and all the slaves they
had taken from the Spaniards. With the rest of their
men they marched to another small island near that of
St. Catharine, and adjoining so near to it, that with a
bridge they could get over. In few days they made a
bridge, and passed thither, conveying also over it all the
pieces of ordnance which they had taken upon the great
island. Having ruined and destroyed, with sword and

fire, both the islands, leaving what orders were necessary at the castle above-mentioned, they put forth to sea again with the Spaniards they had taken prisoners. Yet these they set on shore, not long after, upon the firm land, near a place called Porto Bello. After this they began to cruize upon the coasts of Costa Rica, till finally they came to the river of Colla, designing to rob and pillage all the towns they could find in those parts, and afterwards to pass to the village of Nata, to do the same.

The President or Governor of Panama, having had advice of the arrival of these Pirates and the hostilities they committed everywhere, thought it his duty to set forth to their encounter with a body of men. His coming caused the Pirates to retire suddenly with all speed and care, especially seeing the whole country alarmed at their arrival, and that their designs were known and consequently could be of no great effect at that present. Hereupon they returned to the Isle of St. Catharine, to visit the hundred men they had left in garrison there. The Governor of these men was a certain Frenchman named Le Sieur Simon, who behaved himself very well in that charge, while. Mansvelt was absent. Insomuch that he had put the great island in a very good posture of defence; and the little one he had caused to be cultivated with many fertile plantations, which were sufficient to revictual the whole fleet with provisions and fruits, not only for present refreshment, but also in case of a new voyage. Mansvelt's inclinations were very much bent to keep these two islands in perpetual possession, as being very commodious, and profitably situated for the use of the Pirates, chiefly because they were so near the Spanish dominions, and easily to be defended against them; as I shall represent in the third part of this history more at large, in a copper plate, delineated for this purpose.

Hereupon Mansvelt determined to return to Jamaica, with design to send some recruit to the Isle of St.

Catharine, that in case of any invasion of the Spaniards, the Pirates might be provided for a defence. As soon as he arrived, he propounded his mind and intentions to the Governor of that island ; but he liked not the propositions of Mansvelt, fearing lest by granting such things he should displease his Master, the King of England, besides, that giving him the men he desired, and other necessaries for that purpose, he must of necessity diminish and weaken the forces of that island whereof he was Governor. Mansvelt seeing the unwillingness of the Governor of Jamaica, and that of his own accord he could not compass what he desired, with the same intent and designs went to the Isle of Tortuga. But there, before he could accomplish his desires, or put in execution what was intended, death suddenly surprised him, and put a period to his wicked life ; all things hereby remaining in suspense, until the occasion which I shall hereafter relate.

Le Sieur Simon, who remained at the Isle of St. Catharine in quality of Governor thereof, receiving no news from Mansvelt, his Admiral, was greatly impatient, and desirous to know what might be the cause thereof. In the meanwhile Don John Perez de Guzman, being newly come to the government of Costa Rica, thought it no ways convenient for the interest of the King of Spain that that island should remain in the hands of the Pirates. And hereupon he equipped a considerable fleet, which he sent to the said island to retake it. But before he came to use any great violence, he wrote a letter to Le Sieur Simon, wherein he gave him to understand, if he would surrender the island to his Catholic Majesty, he should be very well rewarded ; but in case of refusal, severely punished when he had forced him to do it. Le Sieur Simon, seeing no appearance or probability of being able to defend it alone, nor any emolument that by so doing could accrue either to him or his people, after some small resistance delivered up

the island into the hands of its true lord and master,
under the same articles they had obtained it from the
Spaniards.   Few days after the surrender of the island,
there arrived from Jamaica an English ship which the
Governor of the said island had sent underhand, wherein
was a good supply of people, both men and women.   The
Spaniards from the castle having espied this ship, put
forth the English colours, and persuaded Le Sieur Simon
to go on board, and conduct the said ship into a port
they assigned him.   This he performed immediately with
dissimulation, whereby they were all made prisoners.   A
certain Spanish engineer has published, before me, an
exact account and relation of the retaking of the Isle of
St. Catharine by the Spaniards ; which printed paper
being fallen into my hands, I have thought it fit to be
inserted here.

*A true Relation and particular Account of the Victory
obtained by the Arms of his Catholic Majesty against
the English Pirates, by the direction and valour of
Don John Perez de Guzman, Knight of the Order
of St. James, Governor and Captain-General of
Terra Firma and the Province of Veraguas.*

THE Kingdom of Terra Firma, which of itself is sufficiently strong to repulse and extirpate great fleets, but
more especially the Pirates of Jamaica, had several ways
notice, under several hands, imparted to the Governor
thereof, that fourteen English vessels did cruize upon the
coasts belonging to his Catholic Majesty.   The 14th day
of July, 1665, news came to Panama, that the English
Pirates of the said fleet were arrived at Puerto de Naos,
and had forced the Spanish garrison of the Isle of
St. Catharine, whose Governor was Don Estevan del
Campo ; and that they had possessed themselves of the
said island, taking prisoners the inhabitants, and destroying all that ever they met.   Moreover, about the same

time Don John Perez de Guzman received particular information of these robberies from the relation of some Spaniards who escaped out of the island (and whom he ordered to be conveyed to Porto Bello), who more distinctly told him, that the aforementioned Pirates came into the island the 2nd day of May, by night, without being perceived by anybody ; and that the next day, after some disputes by arms, they had taken the fortresses and made prisoners all the inhabitants and soldiers, not one excepted, unless those that by good fortune had escaped their hands. This being heard by Don John, he called a council of war, wherein he declared the great progress the said Pirates had made in the dominions of his Catholic Majesty. Here likewise he propounded : *That it was absolutely necessary to send some forces to the Isle of St. Catharine, sufficient to retake it from the Pirates ; the honour and interest of his Majesty of Spain being very narrowly concerned herein. Otherwise the Pirates by such conquests might easily in course of time possess themselves of all the countries thereabouts.* To these reasons some were found who made answer : *That the Pirates, as not being able to subsist in the said island, would of necessity consume and waste themselves, and be forced to quit it, without any necessity of retaking it. That consequently it was not worth the while to engage in so many expenses and troubles as might be foreseen this would cost.* Notwithstanding these reasons to the contrary, Don John, as one who was an expert and valiant soldier, gave order that a quantity of provisions should be conveyed to Porto Bello, for the use and service of the militia. And neither to be idle nor negligent in his master's affairs, he transported himself thither, with no small danger to his life. Here he arrived the 7th day of July, with most things necessary to the expedition in hand ; where he found in the port a good ship, called *St. Vincent*, that belonged to the Company of the Negroes. This ship being of itself a strong vessel and well mounted with guns, he manned and victualled very well and sent to the Isle of St. Catharine, constituting Captain Joseph Sanchez Ximenez, mayor of the city of Porto Bello, commander thereof. The people he carried with him were two hundred threescore and ten soldiers, and thirty-seven prisoners of the same island, besides four-and-thirty Spaniards belonging to the garrison of Porto Bello, nine-and-twenty mulattos of Panama, twelve Indians very dexterous at shooting with bows and arrows, seven expert and able gunners, two lieutenants, two pilots, one surgeon, and one religious man of the Order of St. Francis for their chaplain.

Don John soon after gave his orders to every one of the officers, instructing them how they ought to behave themselves, telling them withal that the Governor of Cartagena would assist and supply them with more men, boats, and all things else they should find necessary for that enterprize ; to which effect he had already written to the said Governor. On the 24th day of the said month Don John commanded the ship to weigh anchor, and sail out of the port. Then seeing a fair wind to blow, he called before him all the people designed for that expedition, and made them a speech, encouraging them to fight against the enemies of their country and religion, but more especially against those inhuman Pirates who had heretofore committed so many horrid and cruel actions against the subjects of his Catholic Majesty. Withal, promising to every one of them most liberal rewards : but especially to such as should behave themselves as they ought in the service of their king and country. Thus Don John bid them farewell ; and immediately the ship weighed anchor, and set sail under a favourable gale of wind. The 22nd of the said month they arrived at Cartagena, and presented a letter to the Governor of the said city from the noble and valiant Don John ; who received it, with testimonies of great affection to the person of Don John and his Majesty's service. And seeing their resolute courage to be conformable to his desires and expectation, he promised them his assistance, which should be with one frigate, one galleon, one boat, and one hundred and twenty-six men, the one half out of his own garrison, and the other half mulattos. Thus all of them being well provided with necessaries, they set forth from the port of Cartagena, the 2nd day of August ; and the 10th of the said month they arrived within sight of the Isle of St. Catharine, towards the Western point thereof. And although the wind was contrary, yet they reached the port, and came to an anchor within it ; having lost one of their boats, by foul weather, at the rock called Quita Signos.

The Pirates, seeing our ships come to an anchor, gave them presently three guns with bullets ; the which were soon answered in the same coin. Hereupon the Mayor Joseph Sanchez Ximenez sent on shore to the Pirates one of his officers, to require them in the name of the Catholic King, his Master, to surrender the island, seeing they had taken it in the midst of peace between the two crowns of Spain and England ; and that in case they would be obstinate, he would certainly put them all to the sword. The Pirates made answer, That island had once before belonged to the Government and dominions of the King of England ; and that, instead of surrendering it, they preferred to lose their lives.

On Friday, the 13th of the said month, three negroes, from the enemy, came swimming aboard our Admiral. These brought intelligence, that all the Pirates that were upon the island were only threescore and twelve in number ; and that they were under a great consternation, seeing such considerable forces come against them. With this intelligence the Spaniards resolved to land, and advance towards the fortresses, the which ceased not to fire as many great guns against them as they possibly could ; which were corresponded in the same manner on our side till dark night. On Sunday, the 15th of the said month, which was the day of the Assumption of Our Lady, the weather being very calm and clear, the Spaniards began to advance thus. The ship named *St. Vincent*, which rode Admiral, discharged two whole broadsides upon the battery called the Conception. The ship called *St. Peter*, that was Vice-Admiral, discharged likewise her guns against the other battery named St. James. In the meanwhile our people were landed in small boats, directing their course towards the point of the battery last mentioned, and thence they marched towards the gate called Cortadura. The lieutenant Frances de Cazeres, being desirous to view the strength of the enemy, with only fifteen men, was compelled to retreat in all haste, by reason of the great guns which played so furiously upon the place where he stood, they shooting not only pieces of iron and small bullets, but also the organs of the church, discharging in every shot three-score pipes at a time.

Notwithstanding this heat of the enemy, Captain Don Joseph Ramirez de Leyva, with threescore men, made a strong attack, wherein they fought on both sides very desperately, till at last he overcame and forced the Pirates to surrender the fort he had taken in hand.

On the other side, Captain John Galeno, with four-score and ten men, passed over the hills, to advance that way towards the castle of St. Teresa. In the meanwhile the Mayor Don Joseph Sanchez Ximenez, as commander-in-chief, with the rest of his men set forth from the battery of St. James, passing the fort with four boats, and landing in despite of the enemy. About this same time Captain John Galeno began to advance with the men he led to the forementioned fortress. So that our men made three attacks upon the enemy, on three several sides, at one and the same time, with great courage and valour. Thus the Pirates, seeing many of their men already killed and that they could in no manner subsist any longer, retreated towards Cortadura, where they surrendered themselves and likewise the whole island into our hands. Our people possessed themselves of all, and set up the Spanish colours, as soon as they had rendered thanks to God Almighty for the victory obtained on such a signalized day. The number of dead were six men of the enemy's, with many wounded, and three-score and ten prisoners. On our side was found only one man killed, and four wounded.

There was found upon the island eight hundred pound of powder, two hundred and fifty pound of small bullets, with many other military provisions. Among the prisoners were taken also two Spaniards, who had borne arms under the English against his Catholic Majesty. These were commanded to be shot to death the next day by order of the Mayor. The 10th day of September arrived at the isle an English vessel, which being seen at a great distance by the Mayor, he gave order to Le Sieur Simon, who was a Frenchman, to go and visit the said ship, and tell them that were on board the island belonged still to the English. He performed the commands, and found in the said ship only fourteen men, one woman and her daughter; who were all instantly made prisoners.

The English Pirates were all transported to Porto Bello; excepting only three, who by order of the Governor were carried to Panama, there to work in the castle of St. Jerome. This fortification is an excellent piece of workmanship, and very strong; being raised in the middle of the port, of quadrangular form, and of very hard stone. Its elevation or height is eighty-eight geometrical feet, the walls being fourteen and the curtains seventy-five feet diameter. It was built at the expense of several private persons, the Governor of the city furnishing the greatest part of the money; so that it did not cost his Majesty any sum at all.

CHAPTER V.

Some account of the Island of Cuba. Capt. Morgan attempts to preserve the Isle of St. Catharine as a refuge and nest to Pirates ; but fails of his designs. He arrives at and takes the village of El Puerto del Principe.

CAPTAIN MORGAN, seeing his predecessor and Admiral Mansvelt was dead, endeavoured as much as he could, and used all the means that were possible, to preserve and keep in perpetual possession the Isle of St. Catharine, seated near that of Cuba. His principal intent was to consecrate it as a refuge and sanctuary to the Pirates of those parts, putting it in a sufficient condition of being a convenient receptacle or storehouse of their preys and robberies. To this effect he left no stone unmoved whereby to compass his designs, writing for the same purpose to several merchants that lived in Virginia and New England, and persuading them to send him provisions and other necessary things towards the putting the said island in such a posture of defence as it might neither fear any external dangers nor be moved at any suspicions of invasion from any side that might attempt to disquiet it. At last all his thoughts and cares proved ineffectual by the Spaniards retaking the said island. Yet, notwithstanding, Captain Morgan retained his ancient courage, which instantly put him upon new designs. Thus he equipped at first a ship, with intention to gather an entire fleet, both as great and as strong as he could compass. By degrees he put the whole matter in execution, and gave order to every member of his fleet, they should meet at a certain port of Cuba. Here he determined to call a council and deliberate concerning what were best to be done, and what place first they should fall upon. Leaving these new preparations in this condition, I shall here give my reader some small account of the aforementioned Isle of Cuba, in whose ports this expedition was hatched, seeing I omitted to do it in its proper place.

The Island of Cuba lies from East to West, in the latitude and situation of twenty to three and twenty degrees North, being in length one hundred and fifty German leagues and about forty in breadth. Its fertility is equal to that of the Island of Hispaniola. Besides which, it affords many things proper for trading and commerce, such as are hides of several beasts, particularly those that in Europe are called Hides of Havana. On all sides it is surrounded with a great number of small islands, which go altogether under the name of Cayos. Of these little islands the Pirates make great use, as of their own proper ports of refuge. Here most commonly they make their meetings and hold their councils, how to assault more easily the Spaniards. It is thoroughly irrigated on all sides with the streams of plentiful and pleasant rivers, whose entries form both secure and spacious ports, besides many other harbours for ships, which along the calm shores and coasts adorn many parts of this rich and beautiful island ; all which contribute very much to its happiness, by facilitating the exercise of trade, whereunto they invite both natives and aliens. The chief of these ports are Santiago, Bayame, Santa Maria, Espiritu Santo, Trinidad, Xagoa, Cabo de Corrientes and others, all which are seated on the south side of the island. On the northern side hereof are found the following : La Havana, Puerto Mariano, Santa Cruz, Mata Ricos and Barracoa.

This island has two principal cities, by which the whole country is governed, and to which all the towns and villages thereof give obedience. The first of these

is named Santiago, or St. James, being seated on the
south side, and having under its jurisdiction one half of the
island.   The chief magistrates hereof are a Bishop and a
Governor, who command over the villages and towns
belonging to the half above-mentioned.   The chief of
these are, on the southern side Espiritu Santo, Puerto
del Principe and Bayame ; on the north side it has
Barracoa and the town called De los Cayos.   The
greatest part of the commerce driven at the aforementioned city of Santiago comes from the Canary Islands,
whither they transport great quantity of tobacco, sugar,
and hides : which sorts of merchandize are drawn to the
head city from the subordinate towns and villages.   In
former times the city of Santiago was miserably sacked
by the Pirates of Jamaica and Tortuga, notwithstanding
that it is defended by a considerable castle.

The city and port De la Havana lies between the
north and west side of the island.   This is one of the
most renowned and strongest places of all the West
Indies.   Its jurisdiction extends over the other half of
the island, the chief places under it being Santa Cruz
on the northern side and La Trinidad on the south.
Hence is transported huge quantity of tobacco, which is
sent in great plenty to New Spain and Costa Rica, even
as far as the South Sea ; besides many ships laden with
this commodity that are consigned to Spain and other
parts of Europe, not only in the leaf but also in rolls.
This city is defended by three castles, very great and
strong ; two of which lie towards the port, and the other
is seated upon a hill that commands the town.   'Tis
esteemed to contain ten thousand families, more or less ;
among which number of people the merchants of this
place trade in New Spain, Campeche, Honduras and
Florida.   All the ships that come from the parts afore-
mentioned, as also from Caracas, Cartagena and Costa
Rica, are necessitated to take their provisions in at
Havana, wherewith to make their voyage for Spain ;

this being the necessary and straight course they ought to steer for the South of Europe and other parts. The plate-fleet of Spain, which the Spaniards call Flôta, being homeward bound, touches here yearly, to take in the rest of their full cargo, as hides, tobacco and Campeche-wood.

Captain Morgan had been no longer than two months in the above-mentioned ports of the South of Cuba, when he had got together a fleet of twelve sail, between ships and great boats ; wherein he had seven hundred fighting men, part of which were English and part French. They called a council, and some were of opinion 'twere convenient to assault the city of Havana, under the obscurity of the night. Which enterprize, they said, might easily be performed, especially if they could but take a few of the ecclesiastics, and make them prisoners. Yea, that the city might be sacked, before the castles could put themselves in a posture of defence. Others propounded, according to their several opinions, other attempts. Notwithstanding, the former proposal was rejected, because many of the Pirates had been prisoners at other times in the said city ; and these affirmed nothing of consequence could be done, unless with fifteen hundred men. Moreover, that with all this number of people they ought first to go to the island De los Pinos, and land them in small boats about Matamano, fourteen leagues distant from the aforesaid city, whereby to accomplish by these means and order their designs.

Finally, they saw no possibility of gathering so great a fleet ; and hereupon, with that they had, they concluded to attempt some other place. Among the rest was found, at last, one who propounded they should go and assault the town of El Puerto del Principe. This proposition he endeavoured to persuade, by saying he knew that place very well, and that, being at a distance from the sea, it never was sacked by any Pirates ; whereby the inhabitants were rich, as exercising their trade for ready money with those of Havana, who kept here an established commerce which consisted chiefly in hides. This proposal was presently admitted by Captain Morgan and the chief of his companions. And hereupon they gave order to every captain to weigh anchor and set sail, steering their course towards that coast that lies nearest to El Puerto del Principe. Hereabouts is to be seen a bay, named by the Spaniards El Puerto de Santa Maria. Being arrived at this bay, a certain Spaniard, who was prisoner on board the fleet, swam ashore by night, and came to the town of Puerto del Principe, giving account to the inhabitants of the design the Pirates had against them. This he affirmed to have overheard in their discourse, while they thought he did not understand the English tongue. The Spaniards, as soon as they received this fortunate advice, began instantly to hide their riches, and carry away what movables they could. The Governor also immediately raised all the people of the town, both freemen and slaves ; and with part of them took a post by which of necessity the Pirates were to pass. He commanded likewise many trees to be cut down and laid amidst the ways to hinder their passage. In like manner he placed several ambuscades, which were strengthened with some pieces of cannon, to play upon them on their march. He gathered in all about eight hundred men, of which he distributed several into the aforementioned ambuscades, and with the rest he begirt the town, displaying them upon the plain of a spacious field, whence they could see the coming of the Pirates at length.

Captain Morgan, with his men, being now upon the march, found the avenues and passages to the town impenetrable. Hereupon they took their way through the wood, traversing it with great difficulty, whereby they escaped divers ambuscades. Thus at last they came into the plain aforementioned, which, from its

figure, is called by the Spaniards, La Savana, or the
Sheet. The Governor, seeing them come, made a detachment of a troop of horse, which he sent to charge
them in the front, thinking to disperse them, and, by
putting them to flight, pursue them with his main body.
But this design succeeded not as it was intended. For
the Pirates marched in very good rank and file, at the
sound of their drums and with flying colours. When
they came near the horse, they drew into the form of
a semicircle, and thus advanced towards the Spaniards,
who charged them like valiant and courageous soldiers
for some while. But seeing that the Pirates were very
dextrous at their arms, and their Governor, with many
of their companions, killed, they began to retreat towards
the wood. Here they designed to save themselves with
more advantage ; but, before they could reach it, the
greatest part of them were unfortunately killed by the
hands of the Pirates. Thus they left the victory to
these new-come enemies, who had no considerable loss
of men in this battle, and but very few wounded, howbeit the skirmish continued for the space of four hours.
They entered the town, though not without great resistance of such as were within ; who defended themselves as
long as was possible, thinking by their defence to hinder
the pillage. Hereupon many, seeing the enemy within
the town, shut themselves up in their own houses, and
thence made several shot against the Pirates, who, perceiving the mischief of this disadvantage, presently
began to threaten them, saying : *If you surrender not
voluntarily, you shall soon see the town in a flame, and
your wives and children torn in pieces before your faces.*
With these menaces the Spaniards submitted entirely to
the discretion of the Pirates, believing they could not
continue there long, and would soon be forced to dis-
lodge.

As soon as the Pirates had possessed themselves of
the town, they enclosed all the Spaniards, both men,

women, children and slaves, in several churches; and gathered all the goods they could find by way of pillage. Afterwards they searched the whole country round about the town, bringing in day by day many goods and prisoners, with much provision. With this they fell to banqueting among themselves and making great cheer after their customary way, without remembering the poor prisoners, whom they permitted to starve in the churches. In the meanwhile they ceased not to torment them daily after an inhuman manner, thereby to make them confess where they had hid their goods, moneys and other things, though little or nothing was left them. To this effect they punished also the women and little children, giving them nothing to eat; whereby the greatest part perished.

When they could find no more to rob, and that provisions began to grow scarce, they thought it convenient to depart and seek new fortunes in other places. Hence they intimated to the prisoners: *They should find moneys to ransom themselves, else they should be all transported to Jamaica. Which being done, if they did not pay a second ransom for the town, they would turn every house into ashes.* The Spaniards, hearing these severe menaces, nominated among themselves four fellow-prisoners to go and seek for the above-mentioned contributions. But the Pirates, to the intent they should return speedily with the ransoms prescribed, tormented several in their presence, before they departed, with all rigour imaginable. After few days, the Spaniards returned from the fatigue of their unreasonable commissions, telling Captain Morgan: *We have run up and down, and searched all the neighbouring woods and places we most suspected, and yet have not been able to find any of our own party, nor consequently any fruit of our embassy. But if you are pleased to have a little longer patience with us, we shall certainly cause all that you demand to be paid within the space of fifteen days.* Captain Morgan was contented, as it should seem, to grant them this petition. But, not long after, there came into the town seven or eight Pirates, who had been ranging in the woods and fields, and got thereabouts some considerable booty. These brought among other prisoners a certain negro, whom they had taken with letters about him. Captain Morgan having perused them, found they were from the Governor of Santiago, being written to some of the prisoners ; wherein he told them : *They should not make too much haste to pay any ransom for their town or persons, or any other pretext. But, on the contrary, they should put off the Pirates as well as they could with excuses and delays ; expecting to be relieved by him within a short while, when he would certainly come to their aid.* This intelligence being heard by Captain Morgan, he immediately gave orders that all they had robbed should be carried on board the ships. And, withal, he intimated to the Spaniards that the very next day they should pay their ransoms, forasmuch as he would not wait one moment longer, but reduce the whole town to ashes in case they failed to perform the sum he demanded.

With this intimation Captain Morgan made no mention to the Spaniards of the letters he had intercepted. Whereupon they made him answer, that it was totally impossible for them to give such a sum of money in so short a space of time ; seeing their fellow-townsmen were not to be found in all the country thereabouts. Captain Morgan knew full well their intentions, and, withal, thought it not convenient to remain there any longer time. Hence he demanded of them only five hundred oxen or cows, together with sufficient salt wherewith to salt them. Hereunto he added only this condition, that they should carry them on board his ships, which they promised to do. Thus he departed with all his men, taking with him only six of the principal prisoners, as pledges of what he intended. The next day the Spaniards brought the cattle and salt to the ships, and required the prisoners. But Captain Morgan refused to deliver them till such time as they had helped his men to kill and salt the beeves. This was likewise performed in great haste, he not caring to stay there any longer, lest he should be surprised by the forces that were gathering against him. Having received all on board his vessels, he set at liberty the prisoners he had kept as hostages of his demands. While these things were in agitation, there happened to arise some dissensions between the English and the French. The occasion of their discord was as follows : A certain Frenchman being employed in killing and salting one of the beeves, an English Pirate came to him and took away the marrow-bones he had taken out of the ox; which sort of meat these people esteem very much. Hereupon they challenged one another. Being come to the place of duel, the Englishman drew his sword treacherously against the Frenchman, wounding him in the back, before he had put himself into a just posture of defence ; whereby he suddenly fell dead upon the place. The other Frenchmen, desirous to revenge this base action, made an insurrection against the English. But Captain Morgan soon extinguished this flame, by commanding the criminal to be bound in chains, and thus carried to Jamaica ; promising to them all he would see justice done upon him. For although it was permitted him to challenge his adversary, yet it was not lawful to kill him treacherously, as he did.

As soon as all things were in readiness, and on board the ships, and likewise the prisoners set at liberty, they sailed thence, directing their course to a certain island, where Captain Morgan intended to make a dividend of what they had pillaged in that voyage. Being arrived at the place assigned, they found near the value of fifty thousand pieces of eight, both in money and goods. The sum being known, it caused a general resentment and grief, to see such a small booty; which was not sufficient to pay their debts at Jamaica. Hereupon Captain Morgan propounded to them, they should think upon some other enterprize and pillage before they returned home. But the Frenchmen not being able to agree with the English, separated from their company, leaving Captain Morgan alone with those of his own nation; notwithstanding all the persuasions he used to induce them to continue in his company. Thus they parted with all external signs of friendship; Captain Morgan reiterating his promises to them that he would see justice done upon the criminal. This he performed : for being arrived at Jamaica, he caused him to be hanged; which was all the satisfaction the French Pirates could expect.

CHAPTER VI.

Captain Morgan resolves to attack and plunder the city of Porto Bello. To this effect he equips a fleet, and, with little expense and small forces, takes the said place.

SOME nations may think that the French having deserted Captain Morgan, the English alone could not have sufficient courage to attempt such great actions as before. But Captain Morgan, who always communicated vigour with his words, infused such spirits into his men as were able to put every one of them instantly upon new designs; they being all persuaded by his reasons, that the sole execution of his orders would be a certain means of obtaining great riches. ꞌ This persuasion had such influence upon their minds, that with inimitable courage they all resolved to follow him. The same likewise did a certain Pirate of Campeche, who in this occasion joined with Captain Morgan, to seek new fortunes under his conduct, and greater advantages than he had found before. Thus Captain Morgan in a few days gathered a fleet of nine sail, between ships and great boats, wherein he had four hundred and threescore military men.

After that all things were in a good posture of readiness, they put forth to sea, Captain Morgan imparting the design he had in his mind to nobody for that present. He only told them on several occasions, that he held as indubitable he should make a good fortune by that voyage, if strange occurrences altered not the course of his designs. They directed their course towards the continent, where they arrived in few days upon the coast of Costa Rica, with all their fleet entire. No sooner had they discovered land than Captain Morgan declared his intentions to the Captains, and presently after to all the rest of the company. He told them he intended in that expedition to plunder Porto Bello, and that he would perform it by night, being resolved to put the whole city to the sack, not the least corner escaping his diligence. Moreover, to encourage them, he added : This enterprize could not fail to succeed well, seeing he had kept it secret in his mind without revealing it to anybody ; whereby they could not have notice of his coming. To this proposition some made answer : They had not a sufficient number of men wherewith to assault so strong and great a city. But Captain Morgan replied : *If our number is small, our hearts are great. And the fewer persons we are, the more union and better shares we shall have in the spoil.* Hereupon, being stimulated with the ambition of those vast riches they promised themselves from their good success, they unanimously concluded to venture upon that design. But, now, to the intent my reader may better comprehend the incomparable boldness of this exploit, it may be necessary to say something beforehand of the city of Porto Bello.

The city which bears this name in America is seated in the Province of Costa Rica, under the latitude of ten degrees North, at the distance of fourteen leagues from the Gulf of Darien, and eight westwards from the port called Nombre de Dios. It is judged to be the strongest place that the King of Spain possesses in all the West Indies, excepting two, that is to say Havana and Cartagena. Here are two castles, almost inexpugnable, that defend the city, being situated at the entry of the port ; so that no ship or boat can pass without permission. The garrison consists of three hundred soldiers, and the town constantly inhabited by four hundred families, more or less. The merchants dwell not here, but only reside for awhile, when the galleons come

or go from Spain ; by reason of the unhealthiness of the
air, occasioned by certain vapours that exhale from the
mountains. Notwithstanding, their chief warehouses are
at Porto Bello, howbeit their habitations be all the year
long at Panama, whence they bring the plate upon mules
at such times as the fair begins, and when the ships,
belonging to the Company of Negroes, arrive here to sell
slaves.

Captain Morgan, who knew very well all the avenues
of this city, as also all the neighbouring coasts, arrived
in the dusk of the evening at the place called Puerto de
Naos, distant ten leagues towards the west of Porto
Bello. Being come to this place, they mounted the river
in their ships, as far as another harbour called Puerto
Pontin ; where they came to an anchor. Here they put
themselves immediately into boats and canoes, leaving
in the ships only a few men to keep them and conduct
them the next day to the port. About midnight they
came to a certain place called Estera longa Lemos, where
they all went on shore, and marched by land to the first
posts of the city. They had in their company a certain
Englishman, who had been formerly a prisoner in those
parts, and who now served them for a guide. To him,
and three or four more, they gave commission to take
the sentry, if possible, or kill him upon the place. But
they laid hands on him and apprehended him with such
cunning, that he had no time to give warning with his
musket, or make any other noise. Thus they brought
him, with his hands bound, to Captain Morgan, who
asked him : *How things went in the city, and what forces
they had* : with many other circumstances, which he was
desirous to know. After every question, they made him
a thousand menaces to kill him, in case he declared not
the truth. Thus they began to advance towards the
city, carrying always the said sentry bound before them.
Having marched about one quarter of a league, they
came to the castle that is near the city, which presently

they closely surrounded, so that no person could get either in or out of the said fortress.

Being thus posted under the walls of the castle, Captain Morgan commanded the sentry whom they had taken prisoner, to speak to those that were within, charging them to surrender, and deliver themselves up to his discretion ; otherwise they should be all cut to pieces, without giving quarter to any one. But they would hearken to none of these threats, beginning instantly to fire ; which gave notice to the city, and this was suddenly alarmed. Yet, notwithstanding, although the Governor and soldiers of the said castle made as great resistance as could be performed, they were constrained to surrender to the Pirates. These no sooner had taken the castle, than they resolved to be as good as their words, in putting the Spaniards to the sword, thereby to strike a terror into the rest of the city. Hereupon, having shut up all the soldiers and officers as prisoners into one room, they instantly set fire to the powder (whereof they found great quantity), and blew up the whole castle into the air, with all the Spaniards that were within. This being done, they pursued the course of their victory, falling upon the city, which as yet was not in order to receive them. Many of the inhabitants cast their precious jewels and moneys into wells and cisterns or hid them in other places underground, to excuse, as much as were possible, their being totally robbed. One party of the Pirates being assigned to this purpose, ran immediately to the cloisters, and took as many religious men and women as they could find. The Governor of the city not being able to rally the citizens, through the huge confusion of the town, retired to one of the castles remaining, and thence began to fire incessantly at the Pirates. But these were not in the least negligent either to assault him or defend themselves with all the courage imaginable. Thus it was observable that, amidst the horror of the assault, they made very few shot in

vain. For aiming with great dexterity at the mouths of
the guns, the Spaniards were certain to lose one or two
men every time they charged each gun anew.

The assault of this castle where the Governor was continued very furious on both sides, from break of day until
noon. Yea, about this time of the day the case was very
dubious which party should conquer or be conquered. At
last the Pirates, perceiving they had lost many men and
as yet advanced but little towards the gaining either this
or the other castles remaining, thought to make use of
fireballs, which they threw with their hands, designing,
if possible, to burn the doors of the castle. But going
about to put this into execution, the Spaniards, from the
wall let fall great quantities of stones and earthen pots
full of powder and other combustible matter, which forced
them to desist from that attempt. Captain Morgan seeing this generous defence made by the Spaniards, began
to despair of the whole success of the enterprize. Hereupon many faint and calm meditations came into his
mind ; neither could he determine which way to turn
himself in that straitness of affairs. Being involved in
these thoughts, he was suddenly animated to continue the
assault, by seeing the English colours put forth at one of
the lesser castles, then entered by his men, of whom he
presently after spied a troop that came to meet him, pro-
claiming victory with loud shouts of joy. This instantly
put him upon new resolutions of making new efforts to
take the rest of the castles that stood out against him ;
especially seeing the chief citizens were fled to them, and
had conveyed thither great part of their riches, with all
the plate belonging to the churches, and other things
dedicated to divine service.

To this effect, therefore, he ordered ten or twelve
ladders to be made, in all possible haste, so broad that
three or four men at once might ascend by them. These
being finished, he commanded all the religious men and
women whom he had taken prisoners to fix them against

the walls of the castle. Thus much he had beforehand threatened the Governor to perform, in case he delivered not the castle. But his answer was : *He would never surrender himself alive.* Captain Morgan was much persuaded that the Governor would not employ his utmost forces, seeing religious women and ecclesiastical persons, exposed in the front of the soldiers to the greatest dangers. Thus the ladders, as I have said, were put into the hands of religious persons of both sexes ; and these were forced, at the head of the companies, to raise and apply them to the walls. But Captain Morgan was fully deceived in his judgment of this design. For the Governor, who acted like a brave and courageous soldier, refused not, in performance of his duty, to use his utmost endeavours to destroy whoever came near the walls. The religious men and women ceased not to cry to him and beg of him by all the Saints of Heaven he would deliver the castle, and hereby spare both his and their own lives. But nothing could prevail with the obstinacy and fierceness that had possessed the Governor's mind. Thus many of the religious men and nuns were killed before they could fix the ladders. Which at last being done, though with great loss of the said religious people, the Pirates mounted them in great numbers, and with no less valour ; having fireballs in their hands, and earthen pots full of powder. All which things, being now at the top of the walls, they kindled and cast in among the Spaniards.

This effort of the Pirates was very great: insomuch as the Spaniards could no longer resist nor defend the castle, which was now entered. Hereupon they all threw down their arms, and craved quarter for their lives. Only the Governor of the city would admit or crave no mercy ; but rather killed many of the Pirates with his own hands, and not a few of his own soldiers, because they did not stand to their arms. And although the Pirates asked him if he would have quarter, yet he constantly answered :

By no means : I had rather die as a valiant soldier than be hanged as a coward. They endeavoured, as much as they could, to take him prisoner. But he defended himself so obstinately that they were forced to kill him ; notwithstanding all the cries and tears of his own wife and daughter, who begged of him upon their knees he would demand quarter and save his life. When the Pirates had possessed themselves of the castle, which was about night, they enclosed therein all the prisoners they had taken, placing the women and men by themselves, with some guards upon them. All the wounded were put into a certain apartment by itself, to the intent their own complaints might be the cure of their own diseases ; for no other was afforded them.

This being done, they fell to eating and drinking after their usual manner ; that is to say, committing in both these things all manner of debauchery and excess. After such manner they delivered themselves up to all sort of debauchery, that if there had been found only fifty courageous men, they might easily have retaken the city, and killed all the Pirates. The next day, having plundered all they could find, they began to examine some of the prisoners (who had been persuaded by their companions to say they were the richest of the town), charging them severely to discover where they had hidden their riches and goods. But not being able to extort anything out of them, as they were not the right persons who possessed any wealth, they at last resolved to torture them. This they performed with such cruelty that many of them died upon the rack, or presently after. Soon after, the President of Panama had news brought him of the pillage and ruin of Porto Bello. This intelligence caused him to employ all his care and industry to raise forces, with design to pursue and cast out the Pirates thence. But these cared little for what extraordinary means the President used, as having their ships near at hand, and being determined to set fire to the city, and retreat. They had now been at Porto Bello fifteen days, in which space of time they had lost many of their men, both by unhealthiness of the country and the extravagant debaucheries they had committed.

Hereupon they prepared for a departure, carrying on board their ships all the pillage they had got. But, before all, they provided the fleet with sufficient victuals for the voyage. While these things were getting ready, Captain Morgan sent an injunction to the prisoners, that they should pay him a ransom for the city, or else he would by fire consume it to ashes, and blow up all the castles into the air. Withal, he commanded them to send speedily two persons to seek and procure the sum he demanded, which amounted to one hundred thousand pieces of eight. To this effect, two men were sent to the President of Panama, who gave him an account of all these tragedies. The President having now a body of men in a readiness, set forth immediately towards Porto Bello, to encounter the Pirates before their retreat. But these people, hearing of his coming, instead of flying away, went out to meet him at a narrow passage through which of necessity he ought to pass. Here they placed an hundred men very well armed ; who, at the first encounter, put to flight a good party of those of Panama. This accident obliged the President to retire for that time, as not being yet in a posture of strength to proceed any farther. Presently after this encounter, he sent a message to Captain Morgan, to tell him : *That in case he departed not suddenly with all his forces from Porto Bello, he ought to expect no quarter for himself nor his companions, when he should take them, as he hoped soon to do.* Captain Morgan, who feared not his threats, knowing he had a secure retreat in his ships which were near at hand, made him answer : *He would not deliver the castles, before he had received the contribution-money he had demanded. Which in case it were not paid down, he would certainly burn the whole city, and then leave it ; demolishing beforehand the castles, and killing the prisoners.*

The Governor of Panama perceived by this answer that no means would serve to mollify the hearts of the Pirates, nor reduce them to reason. Hereupon he determined to leave them ; as also those of the city, whom he came to relieve, involved in the difficulties of making the best agreement they could with their enemies. Thus, in few days more, the miserable citizens gathered the contribution wherein they were fined, and brought the entire sum of one hundred thousand pieces of eight to the Pirates, for a ransom of the cruel captivity they were fallen into. But the President of Panama, by these transactions, was brought into an extreme admiration, considering that four hundred men had been able to take such a great city, with so many strong castles : especially seeing they had no pieces of cannon, nor other great guns, wherewith to raise batteries against them. And what was more, knowing that the citizens of Porto Bello had always great repute of being good soldiers themselves, and who had never wanted courage in their own defence. This astonishment was so great, that it occasioned him, for to be satisfied herein, to send a messenger to Captain Morgan, desiring him to send him some small pattern of those arms wherewith he had taken with such violence so great a city. Captain Morgan received this messenger very kindly, and treated him with great civility. Which being done, he gave him a pistol and a few small bullets of lead, to carry back to the President, his Master, telling him withal : *He desired him to accept that slender pattern of the arms wherewith he had taken Porto Bello, and keep them for a twelvemonth ; after which time he promised to come to Panama and fetch them away.* The Governor of Panama returned the present very soon to Captain Morgan, giving him thanks for the favour of lending him such weapons as he needed not, and withal sent him a ring of gold, with this message : *That he desired him not to give himself the labour of coming to Panama, as he had done to Porto Bello; for he did certify to him, he should not speed so well here as he had done there.*

After these transactions, Captain Morgan (having provided his fleet with all necessaries, and taken with him the best guns of the castles, nailing the rest which he could not carry away) set sail from Porto Bello with all his ships. With these he arrived in few days at the Island of Cuba, where he sought out a place wherein with all quiet and repose he might make the dividend of the spoil they had got. They found in ready money two hundred and fifty thousand pieces of eight, besides all other merchandizes, as cloth linen, silks, and other goods. With this rich booty they sailed again thence to their common place of rendezvous, Jamaica. Being arrived, they passed here some time in all sorts of vices and debauchery, according to their common manner of doing, spending with huge prodigality what others had gained with no small labour and toil.

CHAPTER VII.

*Captain Morgan takes the city of Maracaibo, on the coast of
New Venezuela. Piracies committed in those Seas. Ruin
of three Spanish ships, that were set forth to hinder the robberies of the Pirates.*

Not long after the arrival of the Pirates at Jamaica,
being precisely that short time they needed to lavish
away all the riches above-mentioned, they concluded upon
another enterprize whereby to seek new fortunes. To
this effect Captain Morgan gave orders to all the commanders of his ships to meet together at the island called
De la Vaca, or Cow Isle, seated on the south side of the
Isle of Hispaniola, as has been mentioned above. As
soon as they came to this place, there flocked to them
great numbers of other Pirates, both French and English,
by reason the name of Captain Morgan was now rendered
famous in all the neighbouring countries, for the great
enterprizes he had performed. There was at that present at Jamaica an English ship newly come from New
England, well mounted with thirty-six guns. This vessel
likewise, by order of the Governor of Jamaica, came to
join with Captain Morgan to strengthen his fleet, and
give him greater courage to attempt things of huge consequence. With this supply Captain Morgan judged
himself sufficiently strong, as having a ship of such port,
being the greatest of his fleet, in his company. Notwithstanding, there being in the same place another great
vessel that carried twenty-four iron guns, and twelve of
brass, belonging to the French, Captain Morgan endeavoured as much as he could to join this ship in like

manner to his own. But the French, not daring to repose any trust in the English, of whose actions they were
not a little jealous, denied absolutely to consent to any
such thing.

The French Pirates belonging to this great ship had
accidentally met at sea an English vessel; and being
then under an extreme necessity of victuals, they had
taken some provisions out of the English ship without
paying for them, having peradventure no ready money
on board. Only they had given them bills of exchange,
for Jamaica and Tortuga, to receive money there for
what they had taken. Captain Morgan having notice of
this accident, and perceiving he could not prevail with
the French Captain to follow him in that expedition,
resolved to lay hold on this occasion as a pretext to ruin
the French, and seek his own revenge. Hereupon he
invited, with dissimulation, the French commander and
several of his men to dine with him on board the great
ship that was come from Jamaica, as was said before.
Being come thither, he made them all prisoners, pretending the injury aforementioned done to the English vessel
in taking away some few provisions without pay.

This unjust action of Captain Morgan was soon followed by divine punishment, as we may very rationally
conceive. The manner I shall instantly relate. Captain
Morgan, presently after he had taken the French
prisoners abovesaid, called a council to deliberate what
place they should first pitch upon, in the course of this
new expedition. At this council it was determined to
go to the Isle of Savona, there to wait for the *flota* which
was then expected from Spain, and take any of the
Spanish vessels that might chance to straggle from the
rest. This resolution being taken, they began on board
the great ship to feast one another for joy of their new
voyage and happy council, as they hoped it would prove.
In testimony hereof, they drank many healths, and discharged many guns, as the common sign of mirth among

seamen used to be. Most of the men being drunk, by
what accident is not known the ship suddenly was blown
up into the air, with three hundred and fifty Englishmen,
besides the French prisoners above-mentioned that were
in the hold. Of all which number, there escaped only
thirty men, who were in the great cabin at some distance
from the main force of the powder. Many more 'tis
thought might have escaped, had they not been so much
overtaken with wine.

The loss of such a great ship brought much consternation and conflict of mind upon the English. They
knew not whom to blame ; but at last the accusation was
laid upon the French prisoners, whom they suspected to
have fired the powder of the ship wherein they were, out
of design to revenge themselves, though with the loss of
their own lives. Hereupon they sought to be revenged
on the French anew, and accumulate new accusations
against the former, whereby to seize the ship and all
that was in it. With this design they forged another
pretext against the said ship, by saying the French
designed to commit piracy upon the English. The
grounds of this accusation were given them by a commission from the Governor of Barracoa, found on board
the French vessel, wherein were these words : *That the
said Governor did permit the French to trade in all
Spanish ports, etc. . . . As also to cruize upon the English
Pirates in what place soever they could find them, because
of the multitude of hostilities which they had committed
against the subjects of his Catholic Majesty, in time of
peace betwixt the two Crowns.* This Commission for
trade was interpreted by the English as an express order
to exercise piracy and war against them, notwithstanding
it was only a bare licence for coming into the Spanish
ports ; the cloak of which permission were those words
inserted : *That they should cruize upon the English.*
And although the French did sufficiently expound the
true sense of the said Commission, yet they could not

clear themselves to Captain Morgan, nor his council. But, in lieu hereof, the ship and men were seized and sent to Jamaica. Here they also endeavoured to obtain justice and the restitution of their ship, by all the means possible. But all was in vain : for instead of justice, they were long time detained in prison, and threatened with hanging.

Eight days after the loss of the said ship, Captain Morgan commanded the bodies of the miserable wretches who were blown up to be searched for, as they floated upon the waters of the sea. This he did, not out of any design of affording them Christian burial, but only to obtain the spoil of their clothes and other attire. And if any had golden rings on their fingers, these were cut off for purchase, leaving them in that condition exposed to the voracity of the monsters of the sea. At last they set sail for the Isle of Savona, being the place of their assignation. They were in all fifteen vessels, Captain Morgan commanding the biggest, which carried only fourteen small guns. The number of men belonging to this fleet were nine hundred and threescore. In few days after, they arrived at the Cape called Cabo de Lobos, on the south side of the Isle of Hispaniola, between Cape Tiburon and Cape Punta d' Espada. Hence they could not pass, by reason of contrary winds that continued the space of three weeks, notwithstanding all the endeavours Captain Morgan used to get forth, leaving no means unattempted thereunto. At the end of this time they doubled the cape, and presently after spied an English vessel at a distance. Having spoken with her, they found she came from England, and bought of her, for ready money, some provisions they stood in need of.

Captain Morgan proceeded in the course of his voyage, till he came to the port of Ocoa. Here he landed some of his men, sending them into the woods to seek water and what provisions they could find, the better to spare such as he had already on board his fleet. They killed many beasts, and among other animals some horses. But the Spaniards, being not well satisfied at their hunting, attempted to lay a stratagem for the Pirates. To this purpose they ordered three or four hundred men to come from the city of San Domingo, not far distant from this port, and desired them to hunt in all the parts thereabouts adjoining the sea, to the intent that if any Pirates should return, they might find no subsistence. Within a few days the same Pirates returned, with design to hunt. But finding nothing to kill, a party of them, being about fifty in number, straggled farther on into the woods. The Spaniards, who watched all their motions, gathered a great herd of cows, and set two or three men to keep them. The Pirates having spied this herd, killed a sufficient number thereof ; and although the Spaniards could see them at a distance, yet they would not hinder their work for the present. But as soon as they attempted to carry them away, they set upon them with all fury imaginable, crying : *Mata, mata !* that is, *Kill, kill.* Thus the Pirates were soon compelled to quit the prey, and retreat towards their ships as well as they could. This they performed, notwithstanding, in good order, retiring from time to time by degrees ; and when they had any good opportunity, discharging full volleys of shot upon the Spaniards. By this means the Pirates killed many of the enemies, though with some loss on their own side.

The rest of the Spaniards, seeing what damage they had sustained, endeavoured to save themselves by flight, and carry off the dead bodies and wounded of their companions. The Pirates perceiving them to flee, could not content themselves with what hurt they had already done, but pursued them speedily into the woods, and killed the greatest part of those that were remaining. The next day Captain Morgan, being extremely offended at what had passed, went himself with two hundred men

The Towne of Puerto del Principe taken & sackt

into the woods, to seek for the rest of the Spaniards. But finding nobody there, he revenged his wrath upon the houses of the poor and miserable rustics that inhabit scatteringly those fields and woods ; of which he burnt a great number. With this he returned to his ships, something more satisfied in his mind, for having done some considerable damage to the enemy ; which was always his most ardent desire.

The huge impatience wherewith Captain Morgan had waited now this long while for some of the ships, which were not yet arrived, made him resolve to set sail without them, and steer his course for the Isle of Savona, the place he had always designed. Being arrived there, and not finding any of his ships yet come, he was more impatient and concerned than before, fearing their loss, or that he must proceed without them. Notwithstanding, he waited for their arrival some few days longer. In the meanwhile, having no great plenty of provisions, he sent a crew of one hundred and fifty men to the Isle of Hispaniola, to pillage some towns that were near the city of San Domingo. But the Spaniards, having had intelligence of their coming, were now so vigilant and in such good posture of defence, that the Pirates thought it not convenient to assault them, choosing rather to return empty-handed to Captain Morgan's presence than to perish in that desperate enterprize.

At last Captain Morgan, seeing the other ships did not come, made a review of his people, and found only five hundred men, more or less. The ships that were wanting were seven, he having only eight in his company, of which the greatest part were very small. Thus having hitherto resolved to cruize upon the coasts of Caracas, and plunder all the towns and villages he could meet, finding himself at present with such small forces, he changed his resolution, by the advice of a French Captain that belonged to his fleet. This Frenchman had served L'Ollonais in like enterprizes, and was at the taking of Maracaibo ; whereby he knew all the entries, passages, forces and means how to put in execution the same again in the company of Captain Morgan, to whom, having made a full relation of all, he concluded to sack it again the second time, as being himself persuaded, with all his men, of the facility the Frenchman propounded. Hereupon they weighed anchor, and steered their course towards Curaçoa. Being come within sight of that island, they landed at another, which is near it, and is called Ruba, seated about twelve leagues from Curaçoa, towards the west. This island is defended but by a slender garrison, and is inhabited by Indians, who are subject to the Crown of Spain, and speak Spanish, by reason of the Roman Catholic religion, which is here cultivated by some few priests that are sent from time to time from the neighbouring continent.

The inhabitants of this isle exercise a certain commerce or trade with the Pirates that go and come this way. These buy of the islanders sheep, lambs and kids, which they exchange unto them for linen, thread and other things of this kind. The country is very dry and barren, the whole substance thereof consisting in those three things above-mentioned, and in a small quantity of wheat, which is of no bad quality. This isle produces a great number of venomous insects, as vipers, spiders and others. These last are so pernicious here, that if any man is bitten by them, he dies mad. And the manner of recovering such persons, is to tie them very fast both hands and feet, and in this condition to leave them for the space of four and twenty hours without eating or drinking the least thing imaginable. Captain Morgan, as was said, having cast anchor before this island, bought of the inhabitants many sheep, lambs and also wood, which he needed for all his fleet. Having been there two days he set sail again, in the time of the night, to the intent they might not see what course he steered.

The next day they arrived at the sea of Maracaibo, having always great care of not being seen from Vigilias, for which reason they anchored out of the sight of the watch-tower. Night being come, they set sail again towards the land, and the next morning by break of day found themselves directly over against the bar of the lake above-mentioned. The Spaniards had built another fort since the action of L'Ollonais, whence they did now fire continually against the Pirates, while they were putting their men into boats to land. The dispute continued very hot on both sides, being managed with huge courage and valour from morning till dark night. This being come, Captain Morgan, in the obscurity thereof, drew nigh the fort; which having examined, he found nobody in it, the Spaniards having deserted it not long before. They left behind them a match kindled near a train of powder, wherewith they designed to blow up the Pirates and the whole fortress, as soon as they were in it. This design had taken effect, had the Pirates failed to discover it the space of one quarter of an hour. But Captain Morgan prevented the mischief by snatching away the match with all speed, whereby he saved both his own and his companions' lives. They found here great quantity of powder, whereof he provided his fleet; and afterwards demolished part of the walls, nailing sixteen pieces of ordnance, which carried from twelve to four and twenty pound of bullet. Here they found also great number of muskets and other military provisions.

The next day they commanded the ships to enter the bar ; among which, they divided the powder, muskets and other things they found in the fort, These things being done, they embarked again, to continue their course towards Maracaibo. But the waters were very low, whereby they could not pass a certain bank that lies at the entry of the lake. Hereupon they were compelled to put themselves into canoes and small boats with which they arrived the next day before Maracaibo, having no other defence than some small pieces which they could carry in the said boats.   Being landed, they ran immediately to the fort called De la Barra, which they found in like manner as the preceding, without any person in it: for all were fled before them into the woods, leaving also the town without any people, except a few miserable poor folk who had nothing to lose.

As soon as they had entered the town the Pirates searched every corner thereof, to see if they could find any people that were hidden who might offend them unawares.   Not finding anybody, every party, according as they came out of their several ships, chose what houses they pleased to themselves, the best they could find.   The church was deputed for the common *corps de garde*, where they lived after their military manner, committing many insolent actions.   The next day after their arrival, they sent a troop of one hundred men to seek for the inhabitants and their goods.   These returned the next day following, bringing with them to the number of thirty persons, between men, women and children, and fifty mules laden with several good merchandize. All these miserable prisoners were put to the rack, to make them confess where the rest of the inhabitants were and their goods.   Amongst other tortures then used, one was to stretch their limbs with cords, and at the same time beat them with sticks and other instruments.   Others had burning matches placed betwixt their fingers, which were thus burnt alive.   Others had slender cords or matches twisted about their heads, till their eyes burst out of the skull.   Thus all sort of inhuman cruelties were executed upon those innocent people.   Those who would not confess, or who had nothing to declare, died under the hands of those tyrannical men.   These tortures and racks continued for the space of three whole weeks ; in which time they ceased not to send out, daily, parties of men to seek for more people

to torment and rob ; they never returning home without
booty and new riches.

Captain Morgan, having now got by degrees into his
hands about one hundred of the chief families, with all
their goods, at last resolved to go to Gibraltar, even as
L'Ollonais had done before. With this design he equipped
his fleet, providing it very sufficiently with all necessary
things. He put likewise on board all the prisoners ;
and, thus weighing anchor, set sail for the said place,
with resolution to hazard the battle. They had sent
before them some prisoners to Gibraltar, to denounce to
the inhabitants they should surrender : otherwise Captain
Morgan would certainly put them all to the sword, without giving quarter to any person he should find alive.
Not long after, he arrived with his fleet before Gibraltar,
whose inhabitants received him with continual shooting
of great cannon-bullets. But the Pirates, instead of
fainting hereat, ceased not to encourage one another,
saying : *We must make one meal upon bitter things, before we come to taste the sweetness of the sugar this place
affords.*

The next day, very early in the morning, they landed
all their men. And being guided by the Frenchman
above-mentioned, they marched towards the town, not by
the common way but crossing through the woods ; which
way the Spaniards scarce thought they would have come.
For, at the beginning of their march, they made appearance
as if they intended to come the next and open way that
led to the town, hereby the better to deceive the Spaniards. But these remembering as yet full well what hostilities L'Ollonais had committed upon them but two years
before, thought it not safe to expect the second brunt,
and hereupon were all fled out of the town as fast
as they could, carrying with them all their goods and
riches, as also all the powder, and having nailed all the
great guns : insomuch as the Pirates found not one person
in the whole city, excepting only one poor and innocent

man who was born a fool. This man they asked whither
the inhabitants were fled, and where they had absconded
their goods. To all which questions and the like he
constantly made answer: *I know nothing, I know nothing.*
But they presently put him to the rack, and tortured
him with cords; which torments forced him to cry out:
*Do not torture me any more, but come with me and I will
show you my goods and my riches.* They were persuaded,
as it should seem, he was some rich person who had
disguised himself under those clothes so poor as also that
innocent tongue. Hereupon they went along with him;
and he conducted them to a poor and miserable cottage,
wherein he had a few earthen dishes, and other things of
little or no value; and amongst these, three pieces of
eight, which he had concealed with some other trumpery
underground. After this, they asked him his name; and
he readily made answer: *My name is Don Sebastian
Sanchez, and I am brother to the Governor of Maracaibo.*
This foolish answer, it must be conceived, these men,
though never so inhuman, took for a certain truth. For
no sooner had they heard it, but they put him again upon
the rack, lifting him up on high with cords, and tying huge
weights to his feet and neck; besides which cruel and
stretching torment, they burnt him alive, applying palm-
leaves burning to his face, under which miseries he died
in half-an-hour. After his death they cut the cords
wherewith they had stretched him, and dragged him
forth into the adjoining woods, where they left him without burial.

The same day they sent out a party of Pirates to seek
for the inhabitants, upon whom they might employ their
inhuman cruelties. These brought back with them an
honest peasant with two daughters of his, whom they had
taken prisoners, and whom they intended to torture as
they used to do with others, in case they showed not the
places where the inhabitants had absconded themselves.
The peasant knew some of the said places, and hereupon

seeing himself threatened with the rack, went with the
Pirates to show them. But the Spaniards perceiving
their enemies to range everywhere up and down the
woods, were already fled thence much farther off into
the thickest parts of the said woods, where they built
themselves huts, to preserve from the violence of the
weather those few goods they had carried with them.
The Pirates judged themselves to be deceived by the
said peasant; and hereupon, to revenge their wrath upon him, notwithstanding all the excuses he could make,
and his humble supplications for his life, they hanged
him upon a tree.

After this, they divided into several parties, and went
to search the plantations. For they knew the Spaniards
that were absconded could not live upon what they found
in the woods, without coming now and then to seek provisions at their own country houses. Here they found a
certain slave, to whom they promised mountains of gold,
and that they would give him his liberty by transporting
him to Jamaica, in case he would show them the places
where the inhabitants of Gibraltar lay hidden. This
fellow conducted them to a party of Spaniards, whom they
instantly made all prisoners, commanding the said slave
to kill some of them before the eyes of the rest; to the
intent that by this perpetrated crime he might never
be able to leave their wicked company. The negro,
according to their orders, committed many murders and
insolent actions upon the Spaniards, and followed the
unfortunate traces of the Pirates, who after the space
of eight days, returned to Gibraltar with many prisoners
and some mules laden with riches. They examined
every prisoner by himself (who were in all about two
hundred and fifty persons) where they had absconded the
rest of their goods, and if they knew of their fellow-
townsmen. Such as would not confess were tormented
after a most cruel and inhuman manner. Among the
rest, there happened to be a certain Portuguese, who by

the information of a negro was reported, though falsely, to be very rich. This man was commanded to produce his riches. But his answer was, he had no more than one hundred pieces of eight in the whole world, and that these had been stolen from him two days before, by a servant of his. Which words, although he sealed with many oaths and protestations, yet they would not believe him. But dragging him to the rack, without any regard to his age, as being threescore years old, they stretched him with cords, breaking both his arms behind his shoulders.

This cruelty went not alone. For he not being able or willing to make any other declaration than the abovesaid, they put him to another sort of torment that was worse and more barbarous than the preceding. They tied him with small cords by his two thumbs and greattoes to four stakes that were fixed in the ground at a convenient distance, the whole weight of his body being pendent in the air upon those cords. Then they thrashed upon the cords with great sticks and all their strength, so that the body of this miserable man was ready to perish at every stroke, under the severity of those horrible pains. Not satisfied as yet with this cruel torture, they took a stone which weighed above two hundred pound, and laid it on his belly, as if they intended to press him to death. At which time they also kindled palm-leaves, and applied the flame to the face of this unfortunate Portuguese, burning with them the whole skin, beard and hair. At last these cruel tyrants, seeing that neither with these tortures nor others they could get anything out of him, they untied the cords, and carried him, being almost half dead, to the church, where was their *corps du garde*. Here they tied him anew to one of the pillars thereof, leaving him in that condition, without giving him either to eat or drink, except very sparingly, and so little as would scarce sustain life, for some days. Four or five being past, he desired that one of the prisoners might have the liberty to come to him, by whose means he promised he would endeavour to raise some money to satisfy their demands. The prisoner whom he required was brought to him; and he ordered him to promise the Pirates five hundred pieces of eight for his ransom. But they were both deaf and obstinate at such a small sum, and, instead of accepting it, did beat him cruelly with cudgels, saying unto him: *Old fellow, instead of five hundred you must say five hundred thousand pieces of eight; otherwise you shall here end your life.* Finally, after a thousand protestations that he was but a miserable man, and kept a poor tavern for his living, he agreed with them for the sum of one thousand pieces of eight. These he raised in few days, and having paid them to the Pirates, got his liberty; although so horribly maimed in his body, that 'tis scarce to be believed he could survive many weeks after.

Several other tortures besides these were exercised upon others, which this Portuguese endured not. If with this they were minded to show themselves merciful to those wretches, thus lacerated in the most tender parts of their bodies, their mercy was to run them through and through with their swords; and by this means rid them soon of their pains and life. Otherwise, if this were not done, they used to lie four or five days under the agonies of death, before dying. Others were crucified by these tyrants, and with kindled matches were burnt between the joints of their fingers and toes. Others had their feet put into the fire, and thus were left to be roasted alive. At last, having used both these and other cruelties with the white men, they began to practice the same over again with the negroes, their slaves; who were treated with no less inhumanity than their masters.

Among these slaves was found one who promised Captain Morgan to conduct him to a certain river belonging to the lake, where he should find a ship and four boats richly laden with goods that belonged to the inhabi-

tants of Maracaibo. The same slave discovered likewise
the place where the Governor of Gibraltar lay hidden, together with the greatest part of the women of the town.
But all this he revealed, through great menaces wherewith they threatened to hang him, in case he told not
what he knew.   Captain Morgan sent away presently
two hundred men in two *saëties*, or great boats, towards
the river above-mentioned, to seek for what the slave had
discovered.   But he himself, with two hundred and fifty
more, undertook to go and take the Governor.   This
gentleman was retired to a small island seated in the
middle of the river, where he had built a little fort, after
the best manner he could, for his defence.   But hearing
that Captain Morgan came in person with great forces
to seek him, he retired farther off to the top of a mountain not much distant from that place ; unto which
there was no ascent, but by a very narrow passage.
Yea, this was so straight, that whosoever did pretend to
gain the ascent, must of necessity cause his men to pass
one by one.   Captain Morgan spent two days before he
could arrive at the little island above-mentioned.   Thence
he designed to proceed to the mountain where the
Governor was posted, had he not been told of the im-
possibility he should find in the ascent, not only of the
narrowness of the path that led to the top, but also because the Governor was very well provided with all sorts
of ammunition above.   Besides that, there was fallen a
huge rain, whereby all the baggage belonging to the
Pirates, and their powder, was wet.   By this rain also
they had lost many of their men at the passage over a
river that was overflown.   Here perished likewise some
women and children, and many mules laden with plate
and other goods ; all which they had taken in the fields
from the fugitive inhabitants.   So that all things were in
a very bad condition with Captain Morgan, and the
bodies of his men as much harassed, as ought to be inferred from this relation.   Whereby, if the Spaniards in

that juncture of time had had but a troop of fifty men well armed with pikes or spears, they might have entirely destroyed the Pirates, without any possible resistance on their sides. But the fears which the Spaniards had conceived from the beginning were so great, that only hearing the leaves on the trees to stir, they often fancied them to be Pirates. Finally, Captain Morgan and his people, having upon this march sometimes waded up to their middles in water for the space of half or whole miles together, they at last escaped for the greatest part. But of the woman and children they brought home prisoners, the major part died.

Thus twelve days after they set forth to seek the Governor, they returned to Gibraltar with a great number of prisoners. Two days after arrived also the two *saëties* that went to the river, bringing with them four boats and some prisoners. But as to the greatest part of the merchandize that were in the said boats, they found them not, the Spaniards having unladed and secured them, as having intelligence beforehand of the coming of the Pirates. Whereupon they designed also, when the merchandize were all taken out, to burn the boats. Yet the Spaniards made not so much haste as was requisite to unlade the said vessels, but that they left both in the ship and boats great parcels of goods, which, they being fled from thence, the Pirates seized, and brought thereof a considerable booty to Gibraltar. Thus, after they had been in possession of the place five entire weeks, and committed there infinite number of murders, robberies, and suchlike insolences, they concluded upon their departure. But before this could be performed, for the last proof of their tyranny, they gave orders to some prisoners to go forth into the woods and fields, and collect a ransom for the town ; otherwise they would certainly burn every house down to the ground. Those poor afflicted men went forth as they were sent. And after they had searched every corner of the adjoining fields and

woods, they returned to Captain Morgan, telling him they
had scarce been able to find anybody.   But that to such
as they had found, they had proposed his demands ; to
which had they made answer that the Governor had
prohibited them to give any ransom for not burning the
town.   But notwithstanding any prohibition to the contrary, they beseeched him to have a little patience, and
among themselves they would collect to the sum of
five thousand pieces of eight.   And for the rest, they
would give him some of their own townsmen as hostages,
whom he might carry with him to Maracaibo, till such
time as he had received full satisfaction.

Captain Morgan having now been long time absent
from Maracaibo, and knowing the Spaniards had had
sufficient time wherein to fortify themselves, and hinder
his departure out of the lake, granted them their proposition above-mentioned ; and, withal, made as much haste
as he could to set things in order for his departure.   He
gave liberty to all the prisoners, having beforehand put
them every one to the ransom ; yet he detained all the
slaves with him.   They delivered to him four persons
that were agreed upon for hostages of what sums of
money more he was to receive from them ; and they
desired to have the slave of whom we made mention
above, intending to punish him according to his deserts.
But Captain Morgan would not deliver him, being persuaded they would burn him alive.   At last they weighed
anchor, and set sail with all the haste they could, directing
their course towards Maracaibo.   Here they arrived in
four days, and found all things in the same posture they
had left them when they departed.   Yet here they received news, from the information of a poor distressed
old man, who was sick and whom alone they found in
the town, that three Spanish men-of-war were arrived at
the entry of the lake, and there waited for the return
of the Pirates out of those parts.   Moreover, that the
castle at the entry thereof was again put into a good pos-

ture of defence, being well provided with great guns and
men and all sorts of ammunition.

This relation of the old man could not choose but
cause some disturbance in the mind of Captain Morgan,
who now was careful how to get away through those narrow passages of the entry of the lake. Hereupon he sent
one of his boats, the swiftest he had, to view the entry,
and see if things were as they had been related. The
next day the boat came back, confirming what was said,
and assuring they had viewed the ships so near that they
had been in great danger of the shot they had made at
them. Hereunto they added that the biggest ship was
mounted with forty guns, the second with thirty, and the
smallest with four and twenty. These forces were much
beyond those of Captain Morgan ; and hence they caused
a general consternation in all the Pirates, whose biggest
vessel had not above fourteen small guns. Every one
judged Captain Morgan to despond in his mind and be
destitute of all manner of hopes, considering the difficulty
either of passing safely with his little fleet amidst those
great ships and the fort, or that he must perish. How
to escape any other way by sea or by land, they saw no
opportunity nor convenience. Only they could have
wished that those three ships had rather come over the
lake to seek them at Maracaibo, than to remain at the
mouth of the strait where they were. For at that
passage they must of necessity fear the ruin of their fleet,
which consisted only for the greatest part of boats.

Hereupon, being necessitated to act as well as he could,
Captain Morgan resumed new courage, and resolved to
show himself as yet undaunted with these terrors. To
this intent he boldly sent a Spaniard to the Admiral of
those three ships, demanding of him a considerable
tribute or ransom for not putting the city of Maracaibo
to the flame. This man (who doubtless was received by
the Spaniards with great admiration of the confidence
and boldness of those Pirates) returned two days after,

bringing to Captain Morgan a letter from the said
Admiral, whose contents were as follows.

Letter of Don Alonso del Campo y Espinosa, Admiral of the Spanish Fleet, unto Captain Morgan,
commander of the pirates.

*HAVING understood by all our friends and neighbours the
unexpected news, that you have dared to attempt and commit hostilities in the countries, cities, towns and villages
belonging to the dominions of his Catholic Majesty,
my Sovereign Lord and Master; I let you understand
by these lines, that I am come to this place, according
to my obligation, nigh unto that castle which you took
out of the hands of a parcel of cowards; where I have put
things into a very good posture of defence, and mounted
again the artillery which you had nailed and dismounted.
My intent is to dispute with you your passage out of the
lake, and follow and pursue you everywhere, to the end
you may see the performance of my duty. Notwithstanding, if you be contented to surrender with humility all that
you have taken, together with the slaves and all other
prisoners, I will let you freely pass, without trouble or
molestation; upon condition that you retire home presently
to your own country. But in case that you make any
resistance or opposition unto these things that I proffer unto
you, I do assure you I will command boats to come from
Caracas, wherein I will put my troops, and coming to
Maracaibo, will cause you utterly to perish, by putting
you every man to the sword. This is my last and absolute
resolution. Be prudent, therefore, and do not abuse my
bounty with ingratitude. I have with me very good soldiers,
who desire nothing more ardently than to revenge on you
and your people all the cruelties and base infamous actions
you have committed upon the Spanish nation in America.
Dated on board the Royal Ship named the* Magdalen, *lying*

at anchor at the entry of the Lake of Maracaibo, this 24th day of April, 1669.

Don Alonso del Campo y Espinosa.

As soon as Captain Morgan had received this letter, he called all his men together in the market-place of Maracaibo ; and, after reading the contents thereof, both in French and English, he asked their advice and resolutions upon the whole matter, and whether they had rather surrender all they had purchased, to obtain their liberty, than fight for it ?

They answered all unanimously : They had rather fight, and spill the very last drop of blood they had in their veins, than surrender so easily the booty they had got with so much danger of their lives. Among the rest, one was found who said to Captain Morgan : *Take you care for the rest, and I will undertake to destroy the biggest of those ships with only twelve men. The manner shall be, by making a brulot, or fire-ship, of that vessel we took in the river of Gibraltar. Which, to the intent she may not be known for a fire-ship, we will fill her decks with logs of wood, standing with hats and Montera-caps, to deceive their fight with the representation of men. The same we will do at the port-holes that serve for the guns, which shall be filled with counterfeit cannon. At the stern we will hang out the English colours, and persuade the enemy she is one of our best men-of-war that goes to fight them.* This proposition, being heard by the *Junta* (*i.e.*, council), was admitted and approved of by every one ; howbeit their fears were not quite dispersed.

For notwithstanding what had been concluded there, they endeavoured the next day to see if they could come to an accommodation with Don Alonso. To this effect Captain Morgan sent him two persons, with these following propositions. First : *That he would quit Maracaibo, without doing any damage to the town, nor exacting any ransom for the firing thereof.* Secondly : *That he would*

*set at liberty one half of the slaves, and likewise all other
prisoners, without ransom.* Thirdly : *That he would
send home freely the four chief inhabitants of Gibraltar,
which he had in his custody as hostages for the contributions those people had promised to pay.* These propositions from the Pirates, being understood by Don Alonso,
were instantly rejected every one, as being dishonourable
for him to grant. Neither would he hear any word more
of any other accommodation ; but sent back this message :
*That in case they surrendered not themselves voluntarily
into his hands within the space of two days, under the
conditions which he had offered them by his letter, he
would immediately come and force them to do it.*

No sooner had Captain Morgan received this message
from Don Alonso, than he put all things in order to fight,
resolving to get out of the lake by main force, and without surrendering anything. In the first place, he commanded all the slaves and prisoners to be tied and
guarded very well. After this, they gathered all the
pitch, tar and brimstone they could find in the whole
town, therewith to prepare the fire-ship above-mentioned.
Likewise they made several inventions of powder and
brimstone, with great quantities of palm-leaves, very well
anointed with tar. They covered very well their counterfeit cannon, laying under every piece thereof many
pounds of powder. Besides which, they cut down many
outworks belonging to the ship, to the end the powder
might exert its strength the better. Thus they broke
open also new port-holes ; where, instead of guns they
placed little drums, of which the negroes make use.
Finally, the decks were handsomely beset with many
pieces of wood dressed up in the shape of men with hats,
or monteras, and likewise armed with swords, muskets
and bandoliers.

The brulot or fire-ship, being thus fitted to their
purpose, they prepared themselves to go to the entry of
the port. All the prisoners were put into one great boat,

and in another of the biggest they placed all the women,
plate, jewels and other rich things which they had.   Into
others they put all the bales of goods and merchandize,
and other things of greatest bulk.   Each of these boats
had twelve men on board, very well armed.   The brulot
had orders to go before the rest of the vessels, and presently to fall foul with the great ship.   All things being
in readiness, Captain Morgan exacted an oath of all his
comrades, whereby they protested to defend themselves
against the Spaniards, even to the last drop of blood,
without demanding quarter at any rate : promising them
withal, that whosoever thus behaved himself should be
very well rewarded.

With this disposition of mind and courageous resolution,
they set sail to seek the Spaniards, on the 30th day of
April, 1669.   They found the Spanish fleet riding at
anchor in the middle of the entry of the lake.   Captain
Morgan, it being now late and almost dark, commanded
all his vessels to come to an anchor ; with design to
fight thence even all night, if they should provoke him
thereunto.   He gave orders that a careful and vigilant
watch should be kept on board every vessel till the morning, they being almost within shot, as well as within fight,
of the enemy.   The dawning of the day being come,
they weighed anchors, and set sail again, steering their
course directly towards the Spaniards; who observing
them to move, did instantly the same.   The fire-ship,
sailing before the rest, fell presently upon the great ship,
and grappled to her sides in a short while.   Which by
the Spaniards being perceived to be a fire-ship, they attempted to escape the danger by putting her off ; but in
vain, and too late.   For the flame suddenly seized her
timber and tackling, and in a short space consumed all
the stern, the forepart sinking into the sea, whereby she
perished.   The second Spanish ship, perceiving the
Admiral to burn, not by accident but by industry of the
enemy, escaped towards the castle, where the Spaniards

themselves caused her to sink; choosing this way of losing their ship, rather than to fall into the hands of those Pirates, which they held for inevitable. The third, as having no opportunity nor time to escape, was taken by the Pirates. The seamen that sank the second ship near the castle, perceiving the Pirates to come towards them to take what remains they could find of their ship-wreck (for some part of the bulk was extant above water), set fire in like manner to this vessel, to the end the Pirates might enjoy nothing of that spoil. The first ship being set on fire, some of the persons that were in her swam towards the shore. These the Pirates would have taken up in their boats; but they would neither ask nor admit of any quarter, choosing rather to lose their lives than receive them from the hands of their persecutors, for such reasons as I shall relate hereafter.

The Pirates were extremely gladdened at this signal victory, obtained in so short a time and with so great inequality of forces; whereby they conceived greater pride in their minds than they had before. Hereupon they all presently ran ashore, intending to take the castle. This they found very well provided both with men, great cannon and ammunition; they having no other arms than muskets and a few fire-balls in their hands. Their own artillery they thought incapable, for its smallness, of making any considerable breach in the walls. Thus they spent the rest of that day, firing at the garrison with their muskets till the dusk of the evening, at which time they attempted to advance nearer to the walls, with intent to throw in the fire balls. But the Spaniards, resolving to sell their lives as dear as they could, continued firing so furiously at them, that they thought it not convenient to approach any nearer nor persist any longer in that dispute. Thus having experienced the obstinacy of the enemy, and seeing thirty of their own men already dead, and as many more wounded, they retired to their ships.

The Spaniards believing the Pirates would return the next day to renew the attack, as also make use of their own cannon against the castle, laboured very hard all night to put all things in order for their coming. But more particularly they employed themselves that night in digging down and making plain some little hills and eminent places, whence possibly the castle might be offended.

But Captain Morgan intended not to come ashore again, busying himself the next day in taking prisoners some of the men who still swam alive upon the waters, and hoping to get part of the riches that were lost in the two ships that perished. Among the rest, he took a certain pilot, who was a stranger and who belonged to the lesser ship of the two, with whom he held much discourse, enquiring of him several things. Such questions were : What number of people those three ships had had in them ? Whether they expected any more ships to come ? From what port they set forth the last time, when they came to seek them out ? His answer to all these questions was as follows, which he delivered in the Spanish tongue : *Noble sir, be pleased to pardon and spare me, that no evil be done to me, as being a stranger to this nation I have served, and I shall sincerely inform you of all that passed till our arrival at this lake. We were sent by orders from the Supreme Council of State in Spain, being six men-of-war well-equipped into these seas, with instructions to cruize upon the English pirates, and root them out from these parts by destroying as many of them as we could. These orders were given, by reason of the news brought to the Court of Spain of the loss and ruin of Porto Bello, and other places. Of all which damages and hostilities committed here by the English very dismal lamentations have oftentimes penetrated the ears both of the Catholic King and Council, to whom belongs the care and preservation of this New World. And although the Spanish Court has many times by their Ambassadors sent complaints hereof to the King of England, yet it has been the constant answer of his Majesty of Great Britain, That he never gave any Letters-patent nor Commissions for the acting any hostility whatsoever against the subjects of the King of Spain.   Hereupon the Catholic King, being resolved to avenge his subjects and punish these proceedings, commanded six men-of-war to be equipped, which he sent into these parts under the command of Don Augustin de Bustos, who was constituted Admiral of the said fleet. He commanded the biggest ship thereof, named* Nuestra Señora de la Soledad, *mounted with eight and forty great guns and eight small ones.   The Vice-Admiral was Don Alonso del Campo y Espinosa, who commanded the second ship, called* La Concepcion, *which carried forty-four great guns and eight small ones.   Besides which vessels, there were also four more; whereof the first was named the* Magdalen, *and was mounted with thirty-six great guns and twelve small ones, having on board two hundred and fifty men.   The second was called* St. Lewis, *with twenty-six great guns, twelve small ones and two hundred men. The third was called* La Marquesa, *which carried sixteen great guns, eight small ones and one hundred and fifty men.   The fourth and last,* Nuestra Señora del Carmen, *with eighteen great guns, eight small ones and likewise two hundred and fifty men.*

We were now arrived at Cartagena, when the two greatest ships received orders to return into Spain, as being judged too big for cruizing upon these coasts.   With the four ships remaining, Don Alonso del Campo y Espinosa departed thence towards Campeche, to seek out the English. We arrived at the port of the said city, where being surprised by a huge storm that blew from the north, we lost one of our four ships; being that which I named in the last place among the rest.   Hence we set sail for the Isle of Hispaniola; in sight of which we came within few days, and directed our course to the port of San Domingo.   Here we received intelligence there had passed that way a fleet

*from Jamaica, and that some men thereof having landed at
a place called Alta Gracia, the inhabitants had taken one
of them prisoner, who confessed their whole design was to
go and pillage the city of Caracas. With these news Don
Alonso instantly weighed anchor, and set sail thence, crossing over to the continent, till we came in sight of Caracas.
Here we found not the English; but happened to meet
with a boat which certified us they were in the Lake of
Maracaibo, and that the fleet consisted of seven small ships
and one boat.*

*Upon this intelligence we arrived here; and coming nigh
unto the entry of the lake, we shot off a gun to demand a
pilot from the shore. Those on land perceiving that we
were Spaniards, came willingly to us with a pilot, and
told us that the English had taken the city of Maracaibo,
and that they were at present at the pillage of Gibraltar.
Don Alonso, having understood this news, made a handsome speech to all his soldiers and mariners, encouraging
them to perform their duty, and withal promising to
divide among them all they should take from the English.
After this, he gave order that the guns which we had taken
out of the ship that was lost should be put into the castle,
and there mounted for its defence, with two pieces more
out of his own ship, of eighteen pounds port each. The
pilots conducted us into the port, and Don Alonso commanded the people that were on shore to come to his presence, to whom he gave orders to repossess the castle, and
re-inforce it with one hundred men more than it had before its being taken by the English. Not long after, we
received news that you were returned from Gibraltar to
Maracaibo; to which place Don Alonso wrote you a Letter,
giving you account of his arrival and design, and withal
exhorting you to restore all that you had taken. This you
refused to do; whereupon he renewed his promises and
intentions to his soldiers and seamen. And having given
a very good supper to all his people, he persuaded them
neither to take nor give any quarter to the English that*

*should fall into their hands. This was the occasion of
so many being drowned, who dared not to crave any
quarter for their lives, as knowing their own intentions
of giving none. Two days before you came against us, a
certain negro came on board Don Alonso's ship, telling
him: Sir, be pleased to have great care of yourself; for
the English have prepared a fire-ship with design to burn
your fleet. But Don Alonso would not believe this intelligence, his answer being: How can that be ? Have
they, peradventure, wit enough to build a fire-ship ? or
what instruments have they to do it withal ?*

The pilot above-mentioned having related so distinctly
all the aforesaid things to Captain Morgan, was very well
used by him, and, after some kind proffers made to
him, remained in his service. He discovered moreover
to Captain Morgan, that in the ship which was sunk,
there was a great quantity of plate, even to the value of
forty thousand pieces of eight. And that this was certainly the occasion they had oftentimes seen the Spaniards
in boats about the said ship. Hereupon Captain Morgan ordered that one of his ships should remain there
to watch all occasions of getting out of the said vessel
what plate they could. In the meanwhile he himself,
with all his fleet, returned to Maracaibo, where he refitted the great ship he had taken of the three afore-mentioned. And now being well accommodated, he chose it
for himself, giving his own bottom to one of his captains.

After this he sent again a messenger to the Admiral,
who was escaped on shore and got into the castle, demanding of him a tribute or ransom of fire for the town
of Maracaibo ; which being denied, he threatened he
would entirely consume and destroy it. The Spaniards,
considering how unfortunate they had been all along
with those Pirates, and not knowing after what manner
to get rid of them, concluded among themselves to pay
the said ransom, although Don Alonso would not consent

Hereupon they sent to Captain Morgan to ask what sum he demanded. He answered them he would have thirty thousand pieces of eight, and five hundred beeves, to the intent his fleet might be well victualled with flesh. This ransom being paid, he promised in such case he would give no farther trouble to the prisoners, nor cause any ruin or damage to the town. Finally, they agreed with him upon the sum of twenty thousand pieces of eight, besides the five hundred beeves. The cattle the Spaniards brought in the next day, together with one part of the money. And while the pirates were busied in salting the flesh, they returned with the rest of the whole sum of twenty thousand pieces of eight, for which they had agreed.

But Captain Morgan would not deliver for that present the prisoners, as he had promised to do, by reason he feared the shot of the artillery of the castle at his going forth of the lake. Hereupon he told them he intended not to deliver them till such time as he was out of that danger, hoping by this means to obtain a free passage. Thus he set sail with all his fleet in quest of that ship which he had left behind, to seek for the plate of the vessel that was burnt. He found her upon the place, with the sum of fifteen thousand pieces of eight, which they had secured out of the wreck, besides many other pieces of plate, as hilts of swords and other things of this kind; also great quantity of pieces of eight that were melted and run together by the force of the fire of the said ship.

Captain Morgan scarce thought himself secure, neither could he contrive how to evade the damages the said castle might cause to his fleet. Hereupon he told the prisoners it was necessary they should agree with the Governor to open the passage with security for his fleet; to which point, if he should not consent, he would certainly hang them all up in his ships. After this warning the prisoners met together to confer upon the persons

they should depute to the said Governor Don Alonso ;
and they assigned some few among them for that embassy.   These went to him, beseeching and supplicating
the Admiral he would have compassion and pity on those
afflicted prisoners who were as yet, together with their
wives and children, in the hands of Captain Morgan ;
and that to this effect he would be pleased to give his
word to let the whole fleet of Pirates freely pass, without
any molestation, forasmuch as this would be the only
remedy of saving both the lives of them that came with
this petition, as also of those who remained behind in
captivity ; all being equally menaced with the sword and
gallows, in case he granted not this humble request.
But Don Alonso gave them for answer a sharp repre-
hension of their cowardice, telling them : *If you had been
as loyal to your King in hindering the entry of these
Pirates as I shall do their going out, you had never caused
these troubles, neither to yourselves, nor to our whole
nation ; which have suffered so much through your pusill-
animity.   In a word, I shall never grant your request ;
but shall endeavour to maintain that respect which is due
to my King, according to my duty.*

Thus the Spaniards returned to their fellow-prisoners
with much consternation of mind, and no hopes of obtaining their request ; telling Captain Morgan what answer
they had received.   His reply was : *If Don Alonso
will not let me pass, I will find means how to do it without
him.*   Hereupon he began presently to make a dividend
of all the booty they had taken in that voyage, fearing lest
he might not have an opportunity of doing it in another
place, if any tempest should arise and separate the ships,
as also being jealous that any of the commanders might
run away with the best part of the spoil which then lay
much more in one vessel than another.   Thus they all
brought in, according to their laws, and declared what
they had ; having beforehand made an oath not to conceal the least thing from the public.   The   accounts

being cast up, they found to the value of two hundred and fifty thousand pieces of eight in money and jewels, besides the huge quantity of merchandize and slaves : all which booty was divided into every ship or boat, according to its share.

The dividend being made, the question still remained on foot, how they should pass the castle and get out of the Lake. To this effect they made use of a stratagem, of no ill invention, which was as follows. On the day that preceeded the night wherein they determined to get forth, they embarked many of their men in canoes, and rowed towards the shore, as if they designed to land them. Here they concealed themselves under the branches of trees that hung over the coast for a while till they had laid themselves down along in the boats. Then the canoes returned to the ships, with the appearance only of two or three men rowing them back, all the rest being concealed at the bottom of the canoes. Thus much only could be perceived from the castle ; and this action of false-landing of men, for so we may call it, was repeated that day several times. Hereby the Spaniards were brought into persuasion the Pirates intended to force the castle by scaling it, as soon as night should come. This fear caused them to place most of their great guns on that side which looks towards the land, together with the main force of their arms, leaving the contrary side belonging to the sea almost destitute of strength and defence.

Night being come, they weighed anchor, and by the light of the moon, without setting sail, committed themselves to the ebbing tide, which gently brought them down the river, till they were nigh the castle. Being now almost over against it, they spread their sails with all the haste they could possibly make. The Spaniards, perceiving them to escape, transported with all speed their guns from the other side of the castle, and began to fire very furiously at the Pirates. But these having a favourable wind were almost past the danger before those of the castle could put things into convenient order of offence. So that the Pirates lost not many of their men, nor received any considerable damage in their ships. Being now out of the reach of the guns, Captain Morgan sent a canoe to the castle with some of the prisoners ; and the Governor thereof gave them a boat that every one might return to his own home. Notwithstanding, he detained the hostages he had from Gibraltar, by reason those of that town were not as yet come to pay the rest of the ransom for not firing the place. Just as he departed Captain Morgan ordered seven great guns with bullets to be fired against the castle, as it were to take his leave of them. But they answered not so much as with a musket-shot.

The next day after their departure, they were surprised with a great tempest, which forced them to cast anchor in the depth of five or six fathom water. But the storm increased so much that they were compelled to weigh again and put out to sea, where they were in great danger of being lost. For if on either side they should have been cast on shore, either to fall into the hands of the Spaniards, or of the Indians, they would certainly have obtained no mercy. At last the tempest being spent, the wind ceased ; which caused much content and joy in the whole fleet.

While Captain Morgan made his fortune by pillaging the towns above-mentioned, the rest of his companions, who separated from his fleet at the Cape de Lobos to take the ship of which was spoken before, endured much misery, and were very unfortunate in all their attempts. For being arrived at the Isle of Savona, they did not find Captain Morgan there, nor any one of their companions. Neither had they the good fortune to find a letter which Captain Morgan at his departure left behind him in a certain place, where in all probability they would meet with it. Thus, not knowing what course to steer, they at last concluded to pillage some town or other, whereby to seek their fortune. They were in all four hundred men, more or less, who were divided into four ships and one boat. Being ready to set forth they constituted an Admiral among themselves, by whom they might be directed in the whole affair. To this effect they chose a certain person who had behaved himself very courageously at the taking of Porto Bello, and whose name was Captain Hansel. This commander resolved to attempt the taking of the town of Comana, seated upon the continent of Caracas, nearly threescore leagues from the west side of the Isle of Trinidad. Being arrived there, they landed their men, and killed some few Indians that were near the coast. But approaching the town, the Spaniards, having in their company many Indians, disputed them the entry so briskly, that with great loss and in great confusion they were forced to retire towards their ships. At last they arrived at Jamaica, where the rest of their companions who came with Captain Morgan, ceased not to mock and jeer them for their ill success at Comana, often telling them : *Let us see what money you brought from Comana, and if it be as good silver as that which we bring from Maracaibo.*

The End of the Second Part.

PART III.

CHAPTER I.

*Captain Morgan goes to the Isle of Hispaniola to equip a new fleet,
with intent to pillage again upon the coasts of the West
Indies.*

CAPTAIN MORGAN perceived now that fortune favoured
his arms, by giving good success to all his enterprizes,
which occasioned him, as it is usual in human affairs, to
aspire to greater things, trusting she would always be
constant to him. Such was the burning of Panama;
wherein fortune failed not to assist him, in like manner as
she had done before, crowning the event of his actions
with victory, howbeit she had led him thereto through
thousands of difficulties. The history hereof I shall
now begin to relate, as being so very remarkable in
all its circumstances that peradventure nothing more
deserving memory may occur to be read by future ages.

Not long after Captain Morgan arrived at Jamaica,
he found many of his chief officers and soldiers reduced
to their former state of indigence through their im-
moderate vices and debauchery. Hence they ceased not
to importune him for new invasions and exploits, thereby
to get something to expend anew in wine, as they
had already wasted what was secured so little before.
Captain Morgan being willing to follow fortune while
she called him, hereupon stopped the mouths of many
of the inhabitants of Jamaica, who were creditors to

his men for large sums of money, with the hopes and promises he gave them, of greater achievements than ever, by a new expedition he was going about. This being done, he needed not give himself much trouble to levy men for this or any other enterprize, his name being now so famous through all those islands, that that alone would readily bring him in more men than he could well employ. He undertook therefore to equip a new fleet of ships; for which purpose he assigned the south side of the Isle of Tortuga, as a place of rendezvous. With this resolution, he wrote divers letters to all the ancient and expert Pirates there inhabiting, as also to the Governor of the said isle, and to the planters and hunters of Hispaniola, giving them to understand his intentions, and desiring their appearance at the said place, in case they intended to go with him. All these people had no sooner understood his designs than they flocked to the place assigned in huge numbers, with ships, canoes and boats, being desirous to obey his commands. Many, who had not the convenience of coming to him by sea, traversed the woods of Hispaniola, and with no small difficulties arrived there by land. Thus all were present at the place assigned, and in readiness, against the 24th day of October, 1670.

Captain Morgan was not wanting to be there according to his punctual custom, who came in his ship to the same side of the island, to a port called by the French Port Couillon, over against the island De la Vaca, this being a place which he had assigned to others. Having now gathered the greatest part of his fleet, he called a council, to deliberate about the means of finding provisions sufficient for so many people. Here they concluded to send four ships and one boat, manned with four hundred men, over to the continent, to the intent they should rifle some country towns and villages, and in these get all the corn or maize they could gather. They set sail for the continent, towards the river De la Hacha, with design to assault a small village, called La Rancheria, where is usually to be found the greatest quantity of maize of all those parts thereabouts. In the meanwhile Captain Morgan sent another party of his men to hunt in the woods, who killed there a huge number of beasts, and salted them. The rest of his companions remained in the ships, to clean, fit and rig them out to sea, so that at the return of those who were sent abroad, all things might be in readiness to weigh anchor, and follow the course of their designs.

CHAPTER II.

What happened in the river De la Hacha.

THE four ships abovementioned, after they had set sail from Hispaniola, steered their course till they came within sight of the river De la Hacha, where they were suddenly overtaken with a tedious calm.   Being thus within sight of land becalmed for some days, the Spaniards inhabiting along the coast, who had perceived them to be enemies, had sufficient time to prepare themselves for the assault, at least to hide the best part of their goods, to the end that, without any care of preserving them, they might be in readiness to retire, when they found themselves unable to resist the force of the Pirates, by whose frequent attempts upon those coasts they had already learnt what they had to do in such cases.   There was in the river at that present a good ship, which was come from Cartagena to lade maize, and was now when the Pirates came almost ready to depart.   The men belonging to this ship endeavoured to escape, but not being able to do it, both they and the vessel fell into their hands.   This was a fit booty for their mind, as being good part of what they came to seek for with so much care and toil.   The next morning about break of day they came with their ships towards the shore, and landed their men, although the Spaniards made huge resistance from a battery which they had raised on that side, where of necessity they had to land : but notwithstanding what defence they could make, they were forced to retire towards a village, to which the Pirates followed them. Here the Spaniards, rallying again, fell upon them with great fury, and maintained a strong combat, which lasted till night was come ; but then, perceiving they had lost great number of men, which was no smaller on the Pirates' side, they retired to places more occult in the woods.

The next day when the Pirates saw they were all fled, and the town left totally empty of people, they pursued them as far as they could possibly. In this pursuit they overtook a party of Spaniards, whom they made all prisoners and exercised the most cruel torments, to discover where they had hidden their goods : some were found who by the force of intolerable tortures confessed ; but others who would not do the same were used more barbarously than the former. Thus, in the space of fifteen days that they remained there, they took many prisoners, much plate and moveable goods, with all other things they could rob, with which booty they resolved to return to Hispaniola. Yet not contented with what they had already got, they dispatched some prisoners into the woods to seek for the rest of the inhabitants, and to demand of them a ransom for not burning the town. To this they answered, they had no money nor plate, but in case they would be satisfied with a certain quantity of maize, they would give as much as they could afford. The Pirates accepted this proffer, as being more useful to them at that occasion than ready money, and agreed they should pay four thousand hanegs, or bushels, of maize. These were brought in three days after, the Spaniards being desirous to rid themselves as soon as possible of that inhuman sort of people. Having laded them on board their ships, together with all the rest of their booty, they returned to the Island of Hispaniola, to give account to their leader Captain Morgan of all they had performed.

They had now been absent five entire weeks, about the commission aforementioned, which long delay occasioned Captain Morgan almost to despair of their return, fearing lest they were fallen into the hands of the Spaniards, especially considering that the place whereto they went could easily be relieved from Cartagena and Santa Maria, if the inhabitants were at all careful to alarm the country : on the other side he feared lest they should have made some great fortune in that voyage, and with it escaped to some other place. But at last seeing his ships return, and in greater number than they had departed, he resumed new courage, this sight causing both in him and his companions infinite joy. This was much increased when, being arrived, they found them full laden with maize, whereof they stood in great need for the maintenance of so many people, by whose help they expected great matters through the conduct of their commander.

After Captain Morgan had divided the said maize, as also the flesh which the hunters brought in, among all the ships, according to the number of men that were in every vessel, he concluded upon the departure, having viewed beforehand every ship, and observed their being well equipped and clean. Thus he set sail, and directed his course towards Cape Tiburon, where he determined to take his measures and resolution, of what enterprize he should take in hand. No sooner were they arrived there than they met with some other ships that came newly to join them from Jamaica. So that now the whole fleet consisted of thirty-seven ships, wherein were two thousand fighting men, besides mariners and boys ; the Admiral hereof was mounted with twenty-two great guns, and six small ones, of brass ; the rest carried some twenty, some sixteen, some eighteen, and the smallest vessel at least four, besides which they had great quantity of ammunition and fire-balls, with other inventions of powder.

Captain Morgan finding himself with such a great number of ships, divided the whole fleet into two squadrons, constituting a Vice-Admiral, and other officers and commanders of the second squadron, distinct from the former. To every one of these he gave letters patent, or commissions, to act all manner of hostility against the Spanish nation, and take of them what ships they could, either abroad at sea or in the harbours, in like manner as if they were open and declared enemies (as he termed it) of the King of England, his pretended master. This being done, he called all his captains and other officers together, and caused them to sign some articles of common agreement between them, and in the name of all. Herein it was stipulated that he should have the hundredth part of all that was gotten to himself alone : That every captain should draw the shares of eight men, for the expenses of his ship, besides his own : That the surgeon, besides his ordinary pay, should have two hundred pieces of eight, for his chest of medicaments : And every carpenter, above his common salary, should draw one hundred pieces of eight. As to recompences and rewards, they were regulated in this voyage much higher than was expressed in the first part of this book. Thus, for the loss of both legs, they assigned one thousand five hundred pieces of eight or fifteen slaves, the choice being left to the election of the party ; for the loss of both hands, one thousand eight hundred pieces of eight or eighteen slaves ; for one leg, whether the right or the left, six hundred pieces of eight or six slaves ; for a hand, as much as for a leg ; and for the loss of an eye, one hundred pieces of eight or one slave. Lastly, unto him that in any battle should signalize himself, either by entering the first any castle, or taking down the Spanish colours and setting up the English, they constituted fifty pieces of eight for a reward. In the head of these articles it was stipulated that all these extraordinary salaries, recompences and rewards should be paid out of the first spoil or purchase they should take, according as every one should then occur to be either rewarded or paid.

This contract being signed, Captain Morgan commanded his Vice-admirals and Captains to put all things in order, every one in his ship, to go and attempt one of three places, either Cartagena, Panama or Vera Cruz ; but the lot fell upon Panama as being believed to be the richest of all three : notwithstanding this city being situated at such distance from the Northern sea, as they knew not well the avenues and entries necessary to approach it, they judged it necessary to go beforehand to the isle of St. Catharine, there to find and provide themselves with some persons who might serve them for guides in this enterprize ; for in the garrison of that island are commonly employed many banditti and outlaws belonging to Panama and the neighbouring places, who are very expert in the knowledge of all that country. But before they proceeded any farther, they caused an act to be published through the whole fleet, containing that in case they met with any Spanish vessel, the first captain who with his men should enter and take the said ship, should have for his reward the tenth part of whatsoever should be found within her.

CHAPTER III.

Captain Morgan leaves the Island of Hispaniola, and goes to that of St. Catharine, which he takes.

CAPTAIN MORGAN and his companions weighed anchor from the Cape of Tiburon, the 16th day of December in the year 1670. Four days after they arrived within sight of the Isle of St. Catharine, which was now in possession of the Spaniards again, as was said in the Second Part of this history, and to which they commonly banish all the malefactors of the Spanish dominions in the West Indies. In this island are found huge quantities of pigeons at certain seasons of the year; it is watered continually by four rivulets or brooks, whereof two are always dry in the summer season. Here is no manner of trade nor commerce exercised by the inhabitants, neither do they give themselves the trouble to plant more fruits than what are necessary for the sustentation of human life; howbeit the country would be sufficient to make very good plantations of tobacco, which might render considerable profit, were it cultivated for that use.

As soon as Captain Morgan came near the island with his fleet, he sent before one of his best sailing vessels to view the entry of the river and see if any other ships were there who might hinder him from landing; as also fearing lest they should give intelligence of his arrival to the inhabitants of the island, and they by this means prevent his designs.

The next day before sunrise, all the fleet came to anchor near the island, in a certain bay called Aguada

Grande : upon this bay the Spaniards had lately built a battery, mounted with four pieces of cannon. Captain Morgan landed with a thousand men, more or less, and disposed them into squadrons, beginning his march through the woods, although they had no other guides than some few of his own men who had been there before when Mansvelt took and ransacked the island. The same day they came to a certain place where the Governor at other times kept his ordinary residence : here they found a battery called *The Platform*, but nobody in it, the Spaniards having retired to the lesser island, which, as was said before, is so near the great one that a short bridge only may conjoin them.

This lesser island aforesaid was so well fortified with forts and batteries round it as might seem impregnable. Hereupon, as soon as the Spaniards perceived the pirates to approach, they began to fire upon them so furiously that they could advance nothing that day, but were contented to retreat a little, and take up their rest upon the grass in the open fields, which afforded no strange beds to these people, as being sufficiently used to such kind of repose : what most afflicted them was hunger, having not eaten the least thing that whole day. About midnight it began to rain so hard that those miserable people had much ado to resist so much hardship, the greatest part of them having no other clothes than a pair of seaman's trousers or breeches, and a shirt, without either shoes or stockings. Thus finding themselves in great extremity, they began to pull down a few thatched houses to make fires withal : in a word, they were in such condition that one hundred men, indifferently well armed, might easily that night have torn them all in pieces. The next morning about break of day the rain ceased, at which time they began to dry their arms, which were entirely wet, and proceed on their march. But not long after, the rain commenced anew, rather harder than before, as if the skies were melted into waters, which caused them to cease from advancing towards the forts, whence the Spaniards continually fired at the Pirates, seeing them to approach.

The Pirates were now reduced to great affliction and danger of their lives through the hardness of the weather, their own nakedness, and the great hunger they sustained. For a small relief hereof, they happened to find in the fields an old horse, which was both lean and full of scabs and blotches, with galled back and sides. This horrid animal they instantly killed and flayed, and divided into small pieces among themselves as far as it would reach, for many could not obtain one morsel, which they roasted and devoured without either salt or bread, more like ravenous wolves than men. The rain as yet ceased not to fall, and Captain Morgan perceived their minds to relent, hearing many of them say they would return on board the ships. Amongst these fatigues both of mind and body, he thought it convenient to use some sudden and almost unexpected remedy : to this effect he commanded a canoe to be rigged in all haste, and the colours of truce to be hanged out of it. This canoe he sent to the Spanish governor of the island with this message : *That if within a few hours he delivered not himself and all his men into his hands, he did by that messenger swear to him, and all those that were in his company, he would most certainly put them all to the sword, without granting quarter to any.*

After noon the canoe returned with this answer : *That the Governor desired two hours' time to deliberate with his officers in a full council about that affair ; which being past, he would give his positive answer to the message.* The time now being elapsed, the said Governor sent two canoes with white colours, and two persons, to treat with Captain Morgan ; but before they landed, they demanded of the Pirates two persons as hostages of their security. These were readily granted by Captain Morgan, who delivered to them two of his captains, for a mutual pledge

of the security required.   With this the Spaniards propounded to Captain Morgan, that their Governor in a
full assembly had resolved to deliver up the island,
not being provided with sufficient forces to defend it
against such an armada or fleet.   But withal he desired
that Captain Morgan would be pleased to use a certain
stratagem of war, for the better saving of his own credit,
and the reputation of his officers both abroad and at
home, which should be as follows : That Captain Morgan would come with his troops by night, near the bridge
that joined the lesser island to the great one, and there
attack the fort of St. Jerome : that at the same time all
the ships of his fleet would draw near the castle of Santa
Teresa, and attack it by sea, landing in the meanwhile
some more troops, near the battery called St. Matthew :
that these troops which were newly landed should by
this means intercept the Governor by the way, as he endeavoured to pass to St. Jerome's fort, and then take
him prisoner, using the formality, as if they forced him
to deliver the said castle ; and that he would lead the
English into it, under the fraud of being his own troops ;
that on one side and the other there should be continual
firing at one another, but without bullets, or at least into
the air, so that no side might receive any harm by this
device ; that thus having obtained two such considerable forts, the chief of the isle, he needed not take care
for the rest, which of necessity must fall by course into
his hands.

These propositions, every one, were granted by
Captain Morgan, upon condition they should see them
faithfully observed, for otherwise they should be used
with all rigour imaginable : this they promised to do, and
hereupon took their leaves, and returned to give account
of their negotiation to the Governor.   Presently after
Captain Morgan commanded the whole fleet to enter the
port, and his men to be in readiness to assault that
night the castle of St. Jerome.   Thus the false alarm or

battle began, with incessant firing of great guns from both the castles against the ships, but without bullets, as was said before. Then the Pirates landed, and assaulted by night the lesser island, which they took, as also possession of both the fortresses, forcing all the Spaniards, in appearance, to fly to the church. Before this assault, Captain Morgan had sent word to the Governor he should keep all his men together in a body, otherwise if the Pirates met any straggling Spaniards in the streets, they should certainly shoot them.

The island being taken by this unusual stratagem, and all things put in due order, the Pirates began to make a new war against the poultry, cattle and all sort of victuals they could find. This was their whole employ for some days, scarce thinking of anything else than to kill those animals, roast and eat, and make good cheer, as much as they could possibly attain unto. If wood was wanting, they presently fell upon the houses, and, pulling them down, made fires with the timber, as had been done before in the field. The next day they numbered all the prisoners they had taken upon the whole island, which were found to be in all four hundred and fifty persons, between men, women and children, viz., one hundred and ninety soldiers, belonging to the garrison; forty inhabitants, who were married; forty-three children; thirty-four slaves, belonging to the King, with eight children; eight banditti; thirty-nine negroes, belonging to private persons, with twenty-seven female blacks and thirty-four children. The Pirates disarmed all the Spaniards, and sent them out immediately to the plantations, to seek for provisions, leaving the women in the church, there to exercise their devotions.

Soon after they took a review of the whole island, and all the fortresses belonging thereunto, which they found to be nine in all, as follows: the fort of St. Jerome, nearest to the bridge, had eight great guns, of 12, 6 and 8 pound carriage, together with six pipes of muskets,

every pipe containing ten muskets. Here they found
still sixty muskets, with sufficient quantity of powder and
all other sorts of ammunition. The second fortress,
called St. Matthew, had three guns, of 8 pound carriage
each. The third and chief among all the rest, named
Santa Teresa, had twenty great guns, of 18, 12, 8 and 6
pound carriage, with ten pipes of muskets, like those
we said before, and ninety muskets remaining, besides
all other warlike ammunition. This castle was built with
stone and mortar, with very thick walls on all sides, and
a large ditch round about it of twenty foot depth, which
although it was dry was very hard to get over. Here
was no entry but through one door, which corresponded
to the middle of the castle. Within it was a mount or
hill, almost inaccessible, with four pieces of cannon at
the top, whence they could shoot directly into the port.
On the sea side this castle was impregnable, by reason of
the rocks which surrounded it and the sea beating furiously upon them. In like manner, on the side of the
land, it was so commodiously seated on a mountain that
there was no access to it, but by a path of three or four
foot broad. The fourth fortress was named St. Augustine, having three guns, of 8 and 6 pound carriage. The
fifth, named La Plattaforma de la Concepcion, had only
two guns, of eight pound carriage. The sixth, by
name San Salvador, had likewise no more than two
guns. The seventh, being called Plattaforma de los
Artilleros, had also two guns. The eighth, called Santa
Cruz, had three guns. The ninth, which was called St.
Joseph's Fort, had six guns, of 12 and 8 pound carriage,
besides two pipes of muskets and sufficient ammunition.

In the store-house were found above thirty thousand
pounds of powder, with all other sorts of ammunition,
which were transported by the Pirates on board the ships.
All the guns were stopped and nailed, and the fortresses
demolished, excepting that of St. Jerome, where the
Pirates kept their guard and residence. Captain Morgan

enquired if any banditti were there from Panama or
Porto Bello; and hereupon three were brought before
him, who pretended to be very expert in all the avenues
of those parts. He asked them if they would be his
guides, and show him the securest ways and passages to
Panama; which, if they performed, he promised them
equal shares in all they should pillage and rob in that
expedition, and that afterwards he would set them at
liberty, by transporting them to Jamaica. These propositions pleased the banditti very well, and they readily
accepted his proffers, promising to serve him very faithfully in all he should desire; especially one of these
three, who was the greatest rogue, thief and assassin
among them, and who had deserved for his crimes rather
to be broken alive upon the wheel than punished with
serving in a garrison. This wicked fellow had a great
ascendancy over the other two banditti, and could domi-
neer and command over them as he pleased, they not
daring to refuse obedience to his orders.

Hereupon Captain Morgan commanded four ships and
one boat to be equipped and provided with all things
necessary, to go and take the castle of Chagre, seated
upon the river of that name. Neither would he go himself with his whole fleet, fearing lest the Spaniards should
be jealous of his farther designs upon Panama. In these
vessels he caused to embark four hundred men, who
went to put in execution the orders of their chief commander Captain Morgan, while he himself remained behind in the Island of St. Catharine, with the rest of the
fleet, expecting to hear the success of their arms.

CHAPTER IV.

Captain Morgan takes the castle of Chagre, with four hundred men sent for this purpose from the Isle of St. Catharine.

CAPTAIN MORGAN sending these four ships and a boat to the river of Chagre, chose for Vice-Admiral thereof a certain person named Captain Brodely. This man had been a long time in those quarters, and committed many robberies upon the Spaniards when Mansvelt took the Isle of St. Catharine, as was related in the Second Part of this history. He, being therefore well acquainted with those coasts, was thought a fit person for this exploit, his actions likewise having rendered him famous among the Pirates, and their enemies the Spaniards. Captain Brodely being chosen chief commander of these forces, in three days after he departed from the presence of Captain Morgan arrived within sight of the said castle of Chagre, which by the Spaniards is called St. Lawrence. This castle is built upon a high mountain, at the entry of the river, and surrounded on all sides with strong palisades or wooden walls, being very well terre-pleined, and filled with earth, which renders them as secure as the best walls made of stone or brick. The top of this mountain is in a manner divided into two parts, between which lies a ditch, of the depth of thirty foot. The castle itself has but one entry, and that by a drawbridge which passes over the ditch aforementioned. On the land side it has four bastions, that of the sea containing only two more. That part thereof which looks towards the South is totally inaccessible and impossible to be climbed, through the infinite asperity of the mountain.

The North side is surrounded by the river, which hereabouts runs very broad. At the foot of the said castle,
or rather mountain, is seated a strong fort, with eight
great guns, which commands and impedes the entry of
the river. Not much lower are to be seen two other
batteries, whereof each hath six pieces of cannon, to defend likewise the mouth of the said river. At one side
of the castle are built two great store-houses, in which
are deposited all sorts of warlike ammunition and merchandize, which are brought thither from the inner parts
of the country. Near these houses is a high pair of
stairs, hewed out of the rock, which serves to mount to
the top of the castle. On the West side of the said
fortress lies a small port, which is not above seven or
eight fathom deep, being very fit for small vessels and of
very good anchorage. Besides this, there lies before the
castle, at the entry of the river, a great rock, scarce to be
perceived above water, unless at low tide.

No sooner had the Spaniards perceived the Pirates to
come than they began to fire incessantly at them with
the biggest of their guns. They came to an anchor in a
small port, at the distance of a league more or less from
the castle. The next morning very early they went on
shore, and marched through the woods, to attack the
castle on that side. This march continued until two
o'clock in the afternoon, before they could reach the
castle, by reason of the difficulties of the way, and its
mire and dirt. And although their guides served them
exactly, notwithstanding they came so near the castle at
first that they lost many of their men with the shot from
the guns, they being in an open place where nothing
could cover nor defend them. This much perplexed the
Pirates in their minds, they not knowing what to do, nor
what course to take, for on that side of necessity they
must make the assault, and being uncovered from head
to foot, they could not advance one step without great
danger. Besides that, the castle, both for its situation

and strength, caused them much to fear the success of that enterprize. But to give it over they dared not, lest they should be reproached and scorned by their companions.

At last, after many doubts and disputes among themselves, they resolved to hazard the assault and their lives after a most desperate manner. Thus they advanced towards the castle, with their swords in one hand and fire-balls in the other. The Spaniards defended themselves very briskly, ceasing not to fire at them with their great guns and muskets continually, crying withal : *Come on, ye English dogs, enemies to God and our King ; let your other companions that are behind come on too ; ye shall not go to Panama this bout.* After the Pirates had made some trial to climb up the walls, they were forced to retreat, which they accordingly did, resting themselves until night. This being come, they returned to the assault, to try if by the help of their fire-balls they could overcome and pull down the pales before the wall. This they attempted to do, and while they were about it there happened a very remarkable accident, which gave them the opportunity of the victory. One of the Pirates was wounded with an arrow in his back, which pierced his body to the other side. This instantly he pulled out with great valour at the side of his breast ; then taking a little cotton that he had about him, he wound it about the said arrow, and putting it into his musket, he shot it back into the castle. But the cotton being kindled by the powder, occasioned two or three houses that were within the castle, being thatched with palm-leaves, to take fire, which the Spaniards perceived not so soon as was necessary. For this fire meeting with a parcel of powder, blew it up, and thereby caused great ruin, and no less consternation to the Spaniards, who were not able to account for this accident, not having seen the beginning thereof.

Thus the Pirates, perceiving the good effect of the

arrow and the beginning of the misfortune of the Spaniards, were infinitely gladdened thereat. And while they were busied in extinguishing the fire, which caused great confusion in the whole castle, having not sufficient water wherewithal to do it, the Pirates made use of this opportunity, setting fire likewise to the palisades. Thus the fire was seen at the same time in several parts about the castle, which gave them huge advantage against the Spaniards. For many breaches were made at once by the fire among the pales, great heaps of earth falling down into the ditch. Upon these the Pirates climbed up, and got over into the castle, notwithstanding that some Spaniards, who were not busied about the fire, cast down upon them many flaming pots, full of combustible matter and odious smells, which occasioned the loss of many of the English.

The Spaniards, notwithstanding the great resistance they made, could not hinder the palisades from being entirely burnt before midnight. Meanwhile the Pirates ceased not to persist in their intention of taking the castle. To which effect, although the fire was great, they would creep upon the ground, as nigh unto it as they could, and shoot amidst the flames, against the Spaniards they could perceive on the other side, and thus cause many to fall dead from the walls. When day was come, they observed all the moveable earth that lay between the pales to be fallen into the ditch in huge quantity. So that now those within the castle did in a manner lie equally exposed to them without, as had been on the contrary before. Whereupon the Pirates continued shooting very furiously against them, and killed great numbers of Spaniards. For the Governor had given them orders not to retire from those posts which corresponded to the heaps of earth fallen into the ditch, and caused the artillery to be transported to the breaches.

Notwithstanding, the fire within the castle still continued, and now the Pirates from abroad used what means they could to hinder its progress, by shooting incessantly against it. One party of the Pirates was employed only to this purpose, and another commanded to watch all the motions of the Spaniards, and take all opportunities against them. About noon the English happened to gain a breach, which the Governor himself defended with twenty-five soldiers. Here was performed a very courageous and warlike resistance by the Spaniards, both with muskets, pikes, stones and swords. Yet notwithstanding, through all these arms the Pirates forced and fought their way, till at last they gained the castle. The Spaniards who remained alive cast themselves down from the castle into the sea, choosing rather to die precipitated by their own selves (few or none surviving the fall) than ask any quarter for their lives. The Governor himself retreated to the *corps du garde*, before which were placed two pieces of cannon. Here he intended still to defend himself, neither would he demand any quarter. But at last he was killed with a musket shot, which pierced his skull into the brain.

The Governor being dead, and the *corps du garde* surrendered, they found still remaining in it alive to the number of thirty men, whereof scarce ten were not wounded. These informed the Pirates that eight or nine of their soldiers had deserted their colours, and were gone to Panama to carry news of their arrival and invasion. These thirty men alone were remaining of three hundred and fourteen, wherewith the castle was garrisoned, among which number not one officer was found alive. These were all made prisoners, and compelled to tell whatsoever they knew of their designs and enterprizes. Among other things they declared that the Governor of Panama had notice sent him three weeks ago from Cartagena, how that the English were equipping a fleet at Hispaniola, with design to come and take the said city of Panama. Moreover, that this their intention had been known by a person, who was run away from the Pirates, at the river De la Hacha, where they provided their fleet with corn. That, upon this news, the said Governor had sent one hundred and sixty four men to strengthen the garrison of that castle, together with much provision and warlike ammunition ; the ordinary garrison whereof did only consist of one hundred and fifty men. So that in all they made the number aforementioned of three hundred and fourteen men, being all very well armed. Besides this they had declared that the Governor of Panama had placed several ambuscades all along the river of Chagre ; and that he waited for their coming, in the open fields of Panama, with three thousand six hundred men.

The taking of this castle of Chagre cost the Pirates excessively dear, in comparison to the small numbers they used to lose at other times and places. Yea, their toil and labour here far exceeded what they sustained at the conquest of the Isle of St. Catharine and its adjacent. For coming to number their men, they found they had lost above one hundred, besides those that were wounded, whose number exceeded seventy. They commanded the Spaniards that were prisoners to cast all the dead bodies of their own men down from the top of the mountain to the seaside, and afterwards to bury them. Such as were wounded were carried to the church belonging to the castle, of which they made a hospital, and where also they shut up the women.

Captain Morgan remained not long time behind at the Isle of St. Catharine, after taking the castle of Chagre ; of which he had notice presently sent him. Yet notwithstanding, before he departed thence, he caused to be embarked all the provisions that could be found, together with great quantities of maize or Indian wheat, and cassava, whereof in like manner is made bread in those parts. He commanded likewise great store of provisions should be transported to the garrison of the aforesaid castle of Chagre, from what parts soever they could be got. At a certain place of the island they cast into the sea all the guns belonging thereto, with a design to return and leave that island well garrisoned, for the perpetual possession of Pirates. Notwithstanding he ordered all the houses and forts to be set on fire, excepting only the castle of St. Teresa, which he judged to be the strongest and securest wherein to fortify himself at his return from Panama. He carried with him all the prisoners of the island, and thus set sail for the river of Chagre, where he arrived in the space of eight days. Here the joy of the whole fleet was so great, when they spied the English colours upon the castle that they minded not their way into the river, which occasioned them to lose four of their ships at the entry thereof, that wherein Captain Morgan went being one of the four. Yet their fortune was so good as to be able to save all the men and goods that were in the said vessels. Yea, the ships likewise had been preserved, if a strong northerly wind had not risen on that occasion, which cast the ships upon the rock abovementioned, that lies at the entry of the said river.

Captain Morgan was brought into the castle with great acclamations of triumph and joy of all the Pirates, both of those who were within, and also them that were but newly come. Having understood the whole transactions of the conquest, he commanded all the prisoners to begin to work, and repair what was necessary. Especially in setting up new palisades, or pales, round about the forts depending on the castle. There were still in the river some Spanish vessels, called by them *chatten*, which serve for the transportation of merchandize up and down the said river, as also for going to Porto Bello and Nicaragua. These are commonly mounted with two great guns of iron and four other small ones of brass. All these vessels they seized on, together with four little ships they found there, and all the canoes, In the castle they left a garrison of five hundred men, and in the ships within the river one hundred and fifty more. These things being done, Captain Morgan departed to-wards Panama, at the head of one thousand two hundred men. He carried very small provisions with him, being in good hopes he should provide himself sufficiently among the Spaniards, whom he knew to lie in ambuscade at several places by the way.

CHAPTER V.

Captain Morgan departs from the Castle of Chagre, at the head of one thousand two hundred men, with design to take the city of Panama.

CAPTAIN MORGAN set forth from the castle of Chagre, towards Panama, the 18th day of August[1] in the year 1670. He had under his conduct one thousand two hundred men, five boats with artillery and thirty-two canoes, all which were filled with the said people. Thus he steered his course up the river towards Panama. That day they sailed only six leagues, and came to a place called De los Bracos. Here a party of his men went on shore, only to sleep some few hours and stretch their limbs, they being almost crippled with lying too much crowded in the boats. After they had rested a while, they went abroad, to see if any victuals could be found in the neighbouring plantations. But they could find none, the Spaniards being fled and carrying with them all the provisions they had. This day, being the first of their journey, there was amongst them such scarcity of victuals that the greatest part were forced to pass with only a pipe of tobacco, without any other refreshment.

The next day, very early in the morning, they continued their journey, and came about evening to a place called Cruz de Juan Gallego. Here they were compelled to leave their boats and canoes, by reason the river was

---

[1] " August " is probably intended for " January," for we note (p. 3 of 3rd part) that the assembly at Tortuga was on the 24th of October, 1670, that (p. 11) they sailed from Teburon on 16th December, 1670, and that (p. 70) they left Panama on the 24th February, 1671.

very dry for want of rain, and the many obstacles of trees that were fallen into it.

The guides told them that about two leagues farther on the country would be very good to continue the journey by land. Hereupon they left some companies, being in all one hundred and sixty men, on board the boats to defend them, with intent they might serve for a place of refuge, in case of necessity.

The next morning, being the third day of their journey, they all went ashore, excepting those above mentioned who were to keep the boats. To these Captain Morgan gave very strict orders, under great penalties, that no man, upon any pretext whatsoever, should dare to leave the boats and go ashore. This he did, fearing lest they should be surprised and cut off by an ambuscade of Spaniards, that might chance to lie thereabouts in the neighbouring woods, which appeared so thick as to seem almost impenetrable. Having this morning begun their march they found the ways so dirty and irksome, that Captain Morgan thought it more convenient to transport some of the men in canoes (though it could not be done without great labour) to a place farther up the river, called Cedro Bueno. Thus they re-embarked, and the canoes returned for the rest that were left behind. So that about night they found themselves altogether at the said place. The Pirates were extremely desirous to meet any Spaniards, or Indians, hoping to fill their bellies with what provisions they should take from them. For now they were reduced almost to the very extremity of hunger.

On the fourth day, the greatest part of the Pirates marched by land, being led by one of the guides. The rest went by water, farther up with the canoes, being conducted by another guide, who always went before them with two of the said canoes, to discover on both sides the river the ambuscades of the Spaniards. These had also spies, who were very dextrous, and could at any

time give notice of all accidents or of the arrival of the
Pirates, six hours at least before they came to any place.
This day about noon they found themselves near a post,
called Torna Cavallos.   Here the guide of the canoes
began to cry aloud he perceived an ambuscade.   His
voice caused infinite joy to all the Pirates, as persuading
themselves they should find some provisions wherewith
to satiate their hunger, which was very great.   Being
come to the place, they found nobody in it, the Spaniards
who were there not long before being every one fled, and
leaving nothing behind unless it were a small number of
leather bags, all empty, and a few crumbs of bread
scattered upon the ground where they had eaten.   Being
angry at this misfortune, they pulled down a few little
huts which the Spaniards had made, and afterwards fell
to eating the leathern bags, as being desirous to afford
something to the ferment of their stomachs, which now
was grown so sharp that it did gnaw their very bowels,
having nothing else to prey upon.   Thus they made a
huge banquet upon those bags of leather, which doubtless
had been more grateful unto them, if divers quarrels had
not risen concerning who should have the greatest share.
By the circumference of the place, they conjectured five
hundred Spaniards, more or less, had been there.   And
these, finding no victuals, they were now infinitely
desirous to meet, intending to devour some of them
rather than perish.   Whom they would certainly in that
occasion have roasted or boiled, to satisfy their famine,
had they been able to take them.

After they had feasted themselves with those pieces of
leather, they quitted the place, and marched farther on,
till they came about night to another post called Torna
Munni.   Here they found another ambuscade, but as
barren and desert as the former.   They searched the
neighbouring woods, but could not find the least thing to
eat.   The Spaniards having been so provident as not to
leave behind them anywhere the least crumb of sus-

tenance, whereby the Pirates were now brought to the extremity aforementioned. Here again he was happy, that had reserved since noon any small piece of leather whereof to make his supper, drinking after it a good draught of water for his greatest comfort. Some persons, who never were out of their mothers' kitchens, may ask how these Pirates could eat, swallow and digest those pieces of leather, so hard and dry. To whom I only answer : That could they once experiment what hunger, or rather famine, is, they would certainly find the manner, by their own necessity, as the Pirates did. For these first took the leather, and sliced it in pieces. Then did they beat it between two stones, and rub it, often dipping it in the water of the river, to render it by these means supple and tender. Lastly, they scraped off the hair, and roasted or broiled it upon the fire. And being thus cooked they cut it into small morsels, and eat it, helping it down with frequent gulps of water, which by good fortune they had near at hand.

They continued their march the fifth day, and about noon came to a place called Barbacoa. Here likewise they found traces of another ambuscade, but the place totally as unprovided as the two preceeding were. At a small distance were to be seen several plantations, which they searched very narrowly, but could not find any person, animal or other thing that was capable of relieving their extreme and ravenous hunger. Finally, having ranged up and down and searched a long time, they found a certain grotto which seemed to be but lately hewn out of a rock, in which they found two sacks of meal, wheat and like things, with two great jars of wine, and certain fruits called Platanos. Captain Morgan knowing that some of his men were now, through hunger, reduced almost to the extremity of their lives, and fearing lest the major part should be brought into the same condition, caused all that was found to be distributed amongst them who were in greatest neces-

sity. Having refreshed themselves with these victuals,
they began to march anew with greater courage than
ever. Such as could not well go for weakness were
put into the canoes, and those commanded to land that
were in them before. Thus they prosecuted their
journey till late at night, at which time they came to
a plantation where they took up their rest. But without eating anything at all ; for the Spaniards, as before,
had swept away all manner of provisions, leaving not
behind them the least signs of victuals.

On the sixth day they continued their march, part of
them by land through the woods, and part by water in
the canoes. Howbeit they were constrained to rest
themselves very frequently by the way, both for the
ruggedness thereof and the extreme weakness they were
under. To this they endeavoured to occur, by eating
some leaves of trees and green herbs, or grass, such as
they could pick, for such was the miserable condition
they were in. This day, at noon, they arrived at a
plantation, where they found a barn full of maize. Immediately they beat down the doors, and fell to eating of
it dry, as much as they could devour. Afterwards they
distributed great quantity, giving to every man a good
allowance thereof. Being thus provided, they prosecuted
their journey, which having continued for the space of
an hour or thereabouts, they met with an ambuscade
of Indians. This they no sooner had discovered, but they
threw away their maize, with the sudden hopes they conceived of finding all things in abundance. But after all
this haste, they found themselves much deceived, they
meeting neither Indians, nor victuals, nor anything else
of what they had imagined. They saw notwithstanding
on the other side of the river a troop of a hundred Indians,
more or less, who all escaped away through the agility of
their feet. Some few Pirates there were who leapt into
the river, the sooner to reach the shore to see if they
could take any of the said Indians prisoners. But all

was in vain ; for being much more nimble on their feet than the Pirates, they easily baffled their endeavours. Neither did they only baffle them, but killed also two or three of the Pirates with their arrows, shouting at them at a distance, and crying : *Ha ! perros, á la savana, á la savana. Ha ! ye dogs, go to the plain, go to the plain.*

This day they could advance no farther, by reason they were necessitated to pass the river hereabouts to continue their march on the other side. Hereupon they took up their repose for that night. Howbeit their sleep was not heavy nor profound, for great murmurings were heard that night in the camp, many complaining of Captain Morgan and his conduct in that enterprize, and being desirous to return home. On the contrary, others would rather die there than go back one step from what they had undertaken. But others who had greater courage than any of these two parties did laugh and joke at all their discourses. In the meanwhile they had a guide who much comforted them, saying : *It would not be long before they met with people, from whom they should reap some considerable advantage.*

The seventh day in the morning they all made clean their arms, and every one discharged his pistol or musket, without bullet, to examine the security of their firelocks. This being done, they passed to the other side of the river in the canoes, leaving the post where they had rested the night before, called Santa Cruz. Thus they proceeded on their journey till noon, at which time they arrived at a village called Cruz. Being at a great distance as yet from the place, they perceived much smoke to arise out of the chimneys. The sight hereof afforded them great joy and hopes of finding people in the town, and afterwards what they most desired, which was plenty of good cheer. Thus they went on with as much haste as they could, making several arguments to one another upon those external signs, though all like castles built in the air. *For*, said they, *there is smoke coming out of every house, therefore they are making good fires, to roast and boil what we are to eat.* With other things to this purpose.

At length they arrived there in great haste, all sweating and panting, but found no person in the town, nor anything that was eatable wherewith to refresh themselves, unless it were good fires to warm themselves, which they wanted not. For the Spaniards before their departure, had every one set fire to his own house, excepting only the store-houses and stables belonging to the King.

They had not left behind them any beast whatsoever, either alive or dead. This occasioned much confusion in their minds, they not finding the least thing to lay hold on, unless it were some few cats and dogs, which they immediately killed and devoured with great appetite. At last in the King's stables they found by good fortune fifteen or sixteen jars of Peru wine, and a leather sack full of bread. But no sooner had they began to drink of the said wine when they fell sick, almost every man. This sudden disaster made them think that the wine was poisoned, which caused a new consternation in the whole camp, as judging themselves now to be irrecoverably lost. But the true reason was, their huge want of sustenance in that whole voyage, and the manifold sorts of trash which they had eaten upon that occasion. Their sickness was so great that day as caused them to remain there till the next morning, without being able to prosecute their journey as they used to do, in the afternoon. This village is seated in the latitude of 9 degrees and 2 minutes, North, being distant from the river of Chagre twenty-six Spanish leagues, and eight from Panama. Moreover, this is the last place to which boats or canoes can come; for which reason they built here store-houses, wherein to keep all sorts of merchandize, which hence to and from Panama are transported upon the backs of mules.

Here, therefore, Captain Morgan was constrained to

leave his canoes and land all his men, though never so weak in their bodies. But lest the canoes should be surprized, or take up too many men for their defence, he resolved to send them all back to the place where the boats were, excepting one, which he caused to be hidden, to the intent it might serve to carry intelligence according to the exigence of affairs. Many of the Spaniards and Indians belonging to this village were fled to the plantations thereabouts. Hereupon Captain Morgan gave express orders that none should dare to go out of the village, except in whole companies of a hundred together. The occasion hereof was his fear lest the enemies should take an advantage upon his men, by any sudden assault. Notwithstanding, one party of English soldiers, stickled not to contravene these commands, being tempted with the desire of finding victuals. But these were soon glad to fly into the town again, being assaulted with great fury by some Spaniards and Indians, who snatched up one of the Pirates, and carried him away prisoner. Thus the vigilance and care of Captain Morgan was not sufficient to prevent every accident that might happen.

On the eighth day, in the morning, Captain Morgan sent two hundred men before the body of his army, to discover the way to Panama, and see if they had laid any ambuscades therein. Especially considering that the places by which they were to pass were very fit for that purpose, the paths being so narrow that only ten or twelve persons could march in a file, and oftentimes not so many. Having marched about the space of ten hours, they came to a place called Quebrada Obscura. Here, all on a sudden, three or four thousand arrows were shot at them, without being able to perceive whence they came, or who shot them. The place whence it was presumed they were shot was a high rocky mountain, excavated from one side to the other, wherein was a grotto that went through it, only capable of admitting one horse, or other beast laded. This multitude of arrows caused a huge alarm among the Pirates, especially because they could not discover the place whence they were discharged. At last, seeing no more arrows to appear, they marched a little farther, and entered into a wood. Here they perceived some Indians to fly as fast as they could possible before them, to take the advantage of another post, and thence observe the march of the Pirates. There remained notwithstanding one troop of Indians upon the place, with full design to fight and defend themselves. This combat they performed with huge courage, till such time as their captain fell to the ground wounded, who although he was now in despair of life, yet his valour being greater than his strength, would demand no quarter, but, endeavouring to raise himself, with undaunted mind laid hold of his azagaya, or javelin, and struck at one of the Pirates. But before he could second the blow, he was shot to death with a pistol. This was also the fate of many of his companions, who like good and courageous soldiers lost their lives with their captain, for the defence of their country.

The Pirates endeavoured, as much as was possible, to lay hold on some of the Indians and take them prisoners. But they being infinitely swifter than the Pirates, every one escaped, leaving eight Pirates dead upon the place and ten wounded. Yea, had the Indians been more dextrous in military affairs, they might have defended that passage and not let one sole man to pass. Within a little while after they came to a large campaign field open, and full of variegated meadows. From here they could perceive at a distance before them a parcel of Indians, who stood on the top of a mountain, very near the way by which the Pirates were to pass. They sent a troop of fifty men, the nimblest they could pick out, to see if they could catch any of them, and afterwards force them to declare whereabouts their companions had their mansions. But all their industry was in vain, for they escaped through their nimbleness, and presently afterwards showed themselves in another place, hallooing to the English, and crying : *Á la savana, á la savana cornudos, perros Ingleses;* that is, *To the plain, to the plain, ye cuckolds, ye English dogs !* While these things passed, the ten Pirates that were wounded a little before were dressed and plastered up.

At this place there was a wood, and on each side thereof a mountain. The Indians had possessed themselves of the one, and the Pirates took possession of the other that was opposite to it. Captain Morgan was persuaded that in the wood the Spaniards had placed an ambuscade, as lying so conveniently for that purpose. Hereupon he sent before two hundred men to search it. The Spaniards and Indians perceiving the Pirates to descend the mountains, did so too, as if they designed to attack them. But being got into the wood, out of sight of the Pirates, they disappeared, and were seen no more, leaving the passage open to them.

About night there fell a great rain, which caused the Pirates to march the faster and seek everywhere for houses wherein to preserve their arms from being wet. But the Indians had set fire to every one thereabouts, and transported all their cattle to remote places, to the end that the pirates, finding neither houses nor victuals, might be constrained to return homewards. Notwithstanding, after diligent search, they found a few little huts belonging to shepherds, but in them nothing to eat. These not being capable of holding many men, they placed in them out of every company a small number, who kept the arms of all the rest of the army. Those who remained in the open field endured much hardship that night, the rain not ceasing to fall until the morning.

The next morning, about break of day, being the ninth of this tedious journey, Captain Morgan continued his march while the fresh air of the morning lasted. For the clouds then hanging as yet over their heads were much more favourable to them than the scorching rays of the sun, by reason the way was now more difficult and laborious than all the preceding. After two hours' march, they discovered a troop of about twenty Spaniards, who observed the motions of the Pirates. They endeavoured to catch some of them, but could lay hold on none, they suddenly disappearing, and absconding themselves in caves among the rocks, totally unknown to the Pirates. At last they came to a high mountain, which, when they ascended, they discovered from the top thereof the South Sea. This happy sight, as if it were the end of their labours, caused infinite joy among all the Pirates. Hence they could descry also one ship, and six boats, which were set forth from Panama, and sailed towards the islands of Tovago and Tovagilla. Having descended this mountain, they came to a vale, in which they found great quantity of cattle, whereof they killed good store. Here while some were employed in killing and flaying of cows, horses, bulls and chiefly asses, of which there was greatest number, others busied themselves in kindling of fires and getting wood wherewith to roast them. Thus cutting the flesh of these animals into convenient pieces, or gobbets, they threw them into the fire, and, half carbonadoed or roasted, they devoured them with incredible haste and appetite. For such was their hunger that they more resembled cannibals than Europeans at this banquet, the blood many times running down from their beards to the middle of their bodies.

Having satisfied their hunger with these delicious meats, Captain Morgan ordered them to continue the march. Here again he sent before the main body fifty men, with intent to take some prisoners, if possibly they could. For he seemed now to be much concerned that in nine days time he could not meet one person who might inform him of the condition and forces of the Spaniards. About evening they discovered a troop of two hundred Spaniards, more or less, who hallooed to the Pirates, but these could not understand what they said.

A little while after they came the first time within sight of the highest steeple of Panama. This steeple they no sooner had discovered than they began to show signs of extreme joy, casting up their hats into the air, leaping for mirth, and shouting, even just as if they had already obtained the victory and entire accomplishment of their designs. All their trumpets were sounded and every drum beaten, in token of this universal acclamation and huge alacrity of their minds. Thus they pitched their camp for that night with general content of the whole army, waiting with impatience for the morning, at which time they intended to attack the city. This evening there appeared fifty horse, who came out of the city, hearing the noise of the drums and trumpets of the Pirates, to observe, as it was thought, their motions. They came almost within musket-shot of the army, being preceded by a trumpet that sounded marvellously well. Those on horseback hallooed aloud to the Pirates, and threatened them, saying, *Perros ! nos veremos*, that is, *Ye dogs ! we shall meet ye.* Having made this menace, they returned into the city, excepting only seven or eight horsemen who remained hovering thereabouts, to watch what motions the Pirates made. Immediately after, the city began to fire and ceased not to play with their biggest guns all night long against the camp, but with little or no harm to the Pirates, whom they could not conveniently reach. About this time also the two hundred Spaniards whom the pirates had seen in the afternoon appeared again within sight, making resemblance as if they would block up the passages, to the intent no Pirates might escape the hands of their forces. But the Pirates, who were now in a manner besieged, instead of conceiving any fear of their blockades, as soon as they had placed sentries about their camp, began every one to open their satchels, and without any preparation of napkins or plates, fell to eating very heartily the remaining pieces of bulls and horses flesh which they had re-

served since noon. This being done, they laid themselves down to sleep upon the grass with great repose
and huge satisfaction, expecting only with impatience
the dawning of the next day.

On the tenth day, betimes in the morning, they put all
their men in convenient order, and with drums and trumpets sounding, continued their march directly towards the
city. But one of the guides desired Captain Morgan
not to take the common highway that led thither, fearing
lest they should find in it much resistance and many
ambuscades. He presently took his advice, and chose
another way that went through the wood, although very
irksome and difficult. Thus the Spaniards, perceiving
the Pirates had taken another way, which they scarce
had thought on or believed, were compelled to leave their
stops and batteries, and come out to meet them. The
Governor of Panama put his forces in order, consisting of
two squadrons, four regiments of foot, and a huge number of wild bulls, which were driven by a great number
of Indians, with some negroes and others, to help them.

The Pirates, being now upon their march, came to the
top of a little hill, whence they had a large prospect of
the city and campaign country underneath. Here they
discovered the forces of the people of Panama, extended
in battle array, which, when they perceived to be so
numerous, they were suddenly surprised with great fear,
much doubting the fortune of the day. Yea, few or none
there were but wished themselves at home, or at least
free from the obligation of that engagement, wherein
they perceived their lives must be so narrowly concerned.
Having been some time at a stand, in a wavering condition of mind, they at last reflected upon the straits they
had brought themselves into, and that now they ought of
necessity either to fight resolutely or die, for no quarter
could be expected from an enemy against whom they had
committed so many cruelties on all occasions. Hereupon
they encouraged one another, and resolved either to

conquer, or spend the very last drop of blood in their
bodies. Afterwards they divided themselves into three
battalions, or troops, sending before them one of two
hundred buccaneers, which sort of people are infinitely
dextrous at shooting with guns. Thus the Pirates left
the hill and descended, marching directly towards the
Spaniards, who were posted in a spacious field, waiting
for their coming. As soon as they drew near them, the
Spaniards began to shout, and cry, *Viva el Rey! God
save the King!* and immediately their horse began to
move against the Pirates. But the field being full of
quags and very soft under foot, they could not ply to
and fro and wheel about, as they desired. The two hundred buccaneers who went before, every one putting one
knee to the ground, gave them a full volley of shot,
wherewith the battle was instantly kindled very hot.
The Spaniards defended themselves very courageously,
acting all they could possibly perform, to disorder the
Pirates. Their foot, in like manner, endeavoured to
second the horse, but were constrained by the Pirates to
separate from them. Thus finding themselves frustrated
of their designs, they attempted to drive the bulls against
them at their backs, and by this means put them into
disorder. But the greatest part of that wild cattle ran
away, being frightened with the noise of the battle. And
some few that broke through the English companies
did no other harm than to tear the colours in pieces ;
whereas the buccaneers, shooting them dead, left not
one to trouble them thereabouts.

The battle having now continued for the space of
two hours, at the end thereof the greatest part of the
Spanish horse was ruined and almost all killed. The
rest fled away. Which being perceived by the foot, and
that they could not possibly prevail, they discharged the
shot they had in their muskets, and throwing them on
the ground, betook themselves to flight, every one which
way he could run. The Pirates could not possibly follow

them, as being too much harassed and wearied with the long journey they had lately made. Many of them, not being able to fly whither they desired, hid themselves for that present among the shrubs of the sea-side. But very unfortunately ; for most of them being found out by the Pirates, were instantly killed, without giving quarter to any. Some religious men were brought prisoners before Captain Morgan ; but he being deaf to their cries and lamentations, commanded them all to be immediately pistoled, which was accordingly done. Soon after they brought a captain to his presence, whom he examined very strictly about several things ; particularly, wherein consisted the forces of those of Panama. To which he answered : Their whole strength did consist in four hundred horse, twenty-four companies of foot, each being of one hundred men complete, sixty Indians and some negroes, who were to drive two thousand wild bulls and cause them to run over the English camp, and thus by breaking their files put them into a total disorder and con-fusion. He discovered more, that in the city they had made trenches, and raised batteries in several places, in all which they had placed many guns, and that at the entry of the highway which led to the city they had built a fort, which was mounted with eight great guns of brass, and defended by fifty men.

Captain Morgan, having heard this information, gave orders instantly they should march another way. But before setting forth, he made a review of all his men, whereof he found both killed and wounded a considerable number, and much greater than had been believed. Of the Spaniards were found six hundred dead upon the place, besides the wounded and prisoners. The Pirates were nothing discouraged, seeing their number so much diminished, but rather filled with greater pride than be-fore, perceiving what huge advantage they had obtained against their enemies. Thus having rested themselves some while, they prepared to march courageously towards

the city, plighting their oaths to one another in general
they would fight till never a man was left alive. With
this courage they recommenced their march, either to
conquer or be conquered, carrying with them all the
prisoners.

They found much difficulty in their approach to the
city. For within the town the Spaniards had placed
many great guns, at several quarters thereof, some of
which were charged with small pieces of iron, and others
with musket-bullets. With all these they saluted the
Pirates, at their drawing nigh to the place, and gave them
full and frequent broadsides, firing at them incessantly.
Whence it came to pass that unavoidably they lost, at
every step they advanced, great numbers of men. But
neither these manifest dangers of their lives, nor the
sight of so many of their own as dropped down continually at their sides, could deter them from advancing
farther, and gaining ground every moment upon the
enemy. Thus, although the Spaniards never ceased to
fire and act the best they could for their defence, yet
notwithstanding they were forced to deliver the city
after the space of three hours' combat. And the Pirates,
having now possessed themselves thereof, both killed and
destroyed as many as attempted to make the least opposition against them. The inhabitants had caused the
best of their goods to be transported to more remote and
occult places. Howbeit they found within the city as
yet several warehouses, very well stocked with all sorts
of merchandize, as well silks and cloths as linen, and
other things of considerable value. As soon as the first
fury of their entrance into the city was over, Captain
Morgan assembled all his men at a certain place which
he assigned, and there commanded them under very
great penalties that none of them should dare to drink or
taste any wine. The reason he gave for this injunction
was, because he had received private intelligence that it
had been all poisoned by the Spaniards. Howbeit it was

the opinion of many that he gave these prudent orders
to prevent the debauchery of his people, which he foresaw
would be very great at the beginning, after so much
hunger sustained by the way—fearing withal lest the
Spaniards, seeing them in wine, should rally their forces
and fall upon the city, and use them as inhumanly as
they had used the inhabitants before.

CHAPTER VI.

Captain Morgan sends several canoes and boats to the South Sea. He sets fire to the City of Panama. Robberies and cruelties committed there by the Pirates till their return to the Castle of Chagre.

CAPTAIN MORGAN, as soon as he had placed guards at several quarters where he thought necessary, both within and without the city of Panama, immediately commanded twenty-five men to seize a great boat, which had stuck in the mud of the port for want of water at a low tide, so that she could not put out to sea. The same day, about noon, he caused certain men privately to set fire to several great edifices of the city, nobody knowing whence the fire proceeded nor who were the authors thereof, much less what motives persuaded Captain Morgan thereto, which are as yet unknown to this day. The fire increased so fast that before night the greatest part of the city was in a flame. Captain Morgan endeavoured to make the public believe the Spaniards had been the cause thereof, which suspicions he surmised among his own people, perceiving they reflected upon him for that action. Many of the Spaniards, as also some of the Pirates, used all the means possible either to extinguish the flame, or by blowing up houses with gunpowder, and pulling down others, to stop its progress. But all was in vain; for in less than half an hour it consumed a whole street. All the houses of this city were built with cedar, being of very curious and magnificent structure, and richly adorned within, especially with hangings and paintings, whereof part was already transported out of the Pirates way, and another great part was consumed by the voracity of the fire.

There belonged to this city (which is also the head of a bishopric) eight monasteries, whereof seven were for men and one for women, two stately churches and one hospital. The churches and monasteries were all richly adorned with altar-pieces and paintings, huge quantity of gold and silver, with other precious things ; all which the ecclesiastics had hidden and concealed. Besides which ornaments, here were to be seen two thousand houses of magnificent and prodigious building, being all or the greatest part inhabited by merchants of that country, who are vastly rich. For the rest of the inhabitants of lesser quality and tradesmen, this city contained five thousand houses more. Here were also great number of stables, which served for the horses and mules, that carry all the plate, belonging as well to the King of Spain as to private men, towards the coast of the North Sea. The neighbouring fields belonging to this city are all cultivated with fertile plantations and pleasant gardens, which afford delicious prospects to the inhabitants the whole year long.

The Genoese had in this city of Panama a stately and magnificent house, belonging to their trade and commerce of negroes. This building likewise was commanded by Captain Morgan to be set on fire ; whereby it was burnt to the very ground. Besides which pile of building, there were consumed to the number of two hundred warehouses, and great number of slaves, who had hid themselves therein, together with an infinite multitude of sacks of meal. The fire of all which houses and buildings was seen to continue four weeks after the day it began. The Pirates in the meanwhile, at least the greatest parts of them, camped some time without the city, fearing and expecting that the Spaniards would come and fight them anew. For it was known that they had an incomparable number of men more than the Pirates were. This occasioned them to keep the field, thereby to pre-

serve their forces united, which now were very much
diminished by the losses of the preceding battles ; as also
because they had a great many wounded, all which they
had put into one of the churches which alone remained
standing, the rest being consumed by the fire. Moreover,
beside these decreases of their men, Captain Morgan had
sent a convoy one hundred and fifty men to the Castle
of Chagre, to carry the news of his victory obtained
against Panama.

They saw many times whole troops of Spaniards cruize
to and fro in the campaign fields, which gave them occasion to suspect their rallying anew. Yet they never had
the courage to attempt anything against the Pirates.
In the afternoon of this fatal day Captain Morgan re-
entered again the city with his troops, to the intent that
every one might take up his lodgings, which now they
could hardly find, very few houses having escaped the
desolation of the fire. Soon after they fell to seeking
very carefully among the ruins and ashes for utensils of
plate or gold, which peradventure were not quite wasted
by the flames. And of such things they found no small
number in several places, especially in wells and
cisterns, where the Spaniards had hid them from the
covetous search of the Pirates.

The next day Captain Morgan dispatched away two
troops of Pirates, of one hundred and fifty men each,
being all very stout soldiers and well armed, with orders to seek for the inhabitants of Panama who were
escaped from the hands of their enemies. These men,
having made several excursions up and down the
campaign fields, woods and mountains, adjoining to
Panama, returned after two days' time, bringing with
them above two hundred prisoners, between men,
women and slaves. The same day returned also the
boat above mentioned, which Captain Morgan had
sent into the South Sea, bringing with her three other
boats, which they had taken in a little while. But all

these prizes they could willingly have given, yea, although they had employed greater labour into the bargain, for one certain galleon, which miraculously escaped their industry, being very richly laden with all the King's plate and great quantity of riches of gold, pearl, jewels and other most precious goods, of all the best and richest merchants of Panama. On board of this galleon were also the religious women, belonging to the nunnery of the said city, who had embarked with them all the ornaments of their church, consisting in great quantity of gold, plate and other things of great value.

The strength of this galleon was nothing considerable, as having only seven guns, and ten or twelve muskets for its whole defence, being on the other side very ill provided of victuals and other necessaries, with great want of fresh water, and having no more sails than the uppermost sails of the main mast. This description of the said ship, the Pirates received from certain persons, who had spoken with seven mariners belonging to the galleon, at such time as they came ashore in the cock-boat, to take in fresh water. Hence they concluded for certain they might easily have taken the said vessel, had they given her chase, and pursued her, as they ought to have done, especially considering the said galleon could not long subsist abroad at sea. But they were impeded from following this vastly rich prize, by gluttony and drunkenness, having plentifully debauched themselves with several sorts of rich wines they found there ready to their hands. So that they chose rather to satiate their appetite with the things abovementioned, than to lay hold on the occasion of such a huge advantage, although this only prize would certainly have been of far greater value and consequence to them than all they secured at Panama, and other places thereabouts. The next day, repenting of their negligence, and being totally wearied of the vices and debaucheries aforesaid, they sent forth to sea another boat well armed, to pursue with all speed imaginable the said galleon. But their present care and diligence was in vain, the Spaniards who were on board the said ship having received intelligence of the danger they were in one or two days before, while the Pirates were cruizing so near them, whereupon they fled to places more remote and unknown to their enemies.

Notwithstanding, the Pirates found in the ports of the islands of Tavoga and Tavogilla several boats that were laden with many sorts of very good merchandize : all which they took and brought to Panama ; where, being arrived, they made an exact relation of all that had passed while they were abroad to Captain Morgan. The prisoners confirmed what the Pirates had said, adding thereto, that they undoubtedly knew whereabouts the said galleon might be at that present, but that it was very probable they had been relieved before now from other places. These relations stirred up Captain Morgan anew to send forth all the boats that were in the port of Panama, with design to seek and pursue the said galleon till they could find her. The boats aforesaid, being in all four, set sail from Panama, and having spent eight days in cruizing to and fro, and searching several ports and creeks, they lost all their hopes of finding what they so earnestly sought for. Hereupon they resolved to return to the isles of Tavoga and Tavogilla. Here they found a reasonable good ship, that was newly come from Payta, being laden with cloth, soap, sugar and biscuit, with twenty thousand pieces of eight in ready money. This vessel they instantly seized, not finding the least resistance from any person within her. Near to the said ship was also a boat, whereof in like manner they possessed themselves. Upon the boat they laded great part of the merchandizes they had found in the ship, together with some slaves they had taken in the said islands. With this purchase they returned to Panama, something better satisfied of their voyage, yet withal much discontented they could not meet with the galleon.

The convoy which Captain Morgan had sent to the castle of Chagre returned much about the same time, bringing with them very good news. For while Captain Morgan was upon his journey to Panama, those he had left in the castle of Chagre had sent forth to sea two boats to exercise piracy. These happened to meet with a Spanish ship, which they began to chase within sight of the castle. This being perceived by the Pirates that were in the castle, they put forth Spanish colours, thereby to allure and deceive the ship that fled before the boats. Thus the poor Spaniards, thinking to refuge themselves under the castle and the guns thereof, by flying into the port, were caught in a snare and made prisoners, where they thought to find defence. The cargo which was found on board the said vessel, consisted in victuals and provisions, that were all eatable things. Nothing could be more opportune than this prize for the castle, where they had begun already to experience great scarcity of things of this kind.

This good fortune of the garrison of Chagre gave occasion to Captain Morgan to remain longer time than he had determined at Panama. And hereupon he ordered several new excursions to be made into the whole country round about the city. So that while the Pirates at Panama were employed in these expeditions, those at Chagre were busied in exercising piracy upon the North Sea. Captain Morgan used to send forth daily parties of two hundred men, to make inroads into all the fields and country thereabouts, and when one party came back, another consisting of two hundred more was ready to go forth. By this means they gathered in a short time a huge quantity of riches, and no lesser number of prisoners. These, being brought into the city, were presently put to the most exquisite tortures imaginable, to make them confess both other people's goods and their own. Here it happened, that one poor and miserable wretch was found in the house of a gentleman of great quality, who had put on, amidst that confusion of things, a pair of taffety breeches belonging to his master with a little silver key hanging at the strings thereof. This, being perceived by the Pirates they immediately asked him where was the cabinet of the said key? His answer was: he knew not what was become of it, but only that finding those breeches in his master's house, he had made bold to wear them. Not being able to extort any other confession out of him, they first put him upon the rack, wherewith they inhumanly disjointed his arms. After this, they twisted a cord about his forehead, which they wrung so hard, that his eyes appeared as big as eggs, and were ready to fall out of his skull. But neither with these torments could they obtain any positive answer to their demands. Whereupon they soon after hung him up, giving him infinite blows and stripes, while he was under that intolerable pain and posture of body. Afterwards they cut off his nose and ears, and singed his face with burning straw, till he could speak nor lament his misery no longer. Then losing all hopes of hearing any confession from his mouth, they commanded a negro to run him through with a lance, which put an end to his life and a period to their cruel and inhuman tortures. After this execrable manner did many others of those miserable prisoners finish their days, the common sport and recreation of these Pirates being these and other tragedies not inferior.

They spared, in these their cruelties, no sex nor condition whatsoever. For as to religious persons and priests, they granted them less quarter than to others, unless they could produce a considerable sum of money, capable of being a sufficient ransom. Women themselves were no better used, and Captain Morgan, their leader and commander, gave them no good example in this point. For as soon as any beautiful woman was brought as a prisoner to his presence, he used all the means he could, both of rigour and mildness, to bend her to his pleasure : for a confirmation of which assertion, I shall here give my reader a short history of a lady, whose virtue and constancy ought to be transmitted to posterity, as a memorable example of her sex.

Among the prisoners that were brought by the Pirates from the islands of Tavoga and Tavogilla, there was found a gentlewoman of good quality, as also no less virtue and chastity, who was wife to one of the richest merchants of all those countries. Her years were but few, and her beauty so great as peradventure I may doubt whether in all Europe any could be found to surpass her perfections either of comeliness or honesty. Her husband, at that present, was absent from home, being gone as far as the kingdom of Peru, about great concerns of commerce and trade, wherein his employments did lie. This virtuous lady, likewise, hearing that Pirates were coming to assault the city of Panama, had absented herself thence in the company of other friends and relations, thereby to preserve her life, amidst the dangers which the cruelties and tyrannies of those hard-hearted enemies did seem to menace to every citizen. But no sooner had she appeared in the presence of Captain Morgan than he commanded they should lodge her in a certain apartment by herself, giving her a negress, or black woman, to wait upon her, and that she should be treated with all the respect and regale due to her quality. The poor afflicted lady did beg, with multitude of sobs and tears, she might be suffered to lodge among the other prisoners, her relations, fearing lest that unexpected kindness of the commander might prove to be a design upon her chastity. But Captain Morgan would by no means hearken to her petition, and all he commanded, in answer thereto, was, she should be treated with more particular care than before, and have her victuals carried from his own table.

This lady had formerly heard very strange reports concerning the Pirates, before their arrival at Panama, intimating to her, as if they were not men, but, as they said, heretics, who did neither invoke the Blessed Trinity, nor believe in Jesus Christ. But now she began to have better thoughts of them than ever before, having experienced the manifold civilities of Captain Morgan, especially hearing him many times to swear by the name of God, and of Jesus Christ, in whom, she was persuaded, they did not believe. Neither did she now think them to be so bad, or to have the shapes of beasts, as from the relations of several people she had oftentimes heard. For as to the name of *robbers* or *thieves*, which was commonly given them by others, she wondered not much at it, seeing, as she said, that among all nations of the universe, there were to be found some wicked men, who naturally coveted to possess the goods of others. Conformable to the persuasion of this lady was the opinion of another woman, of weak understanding, at Panama, who used to say, before the Pirates came thither, she desired very much and had a great curiosity to see one of those men called Pirates ; for as much as her husband had often told her, that they were not men, like others, but rather irrational beasts. This silly woman, at last happened to see the first of them, cried out aloud, saying : *Jesus bless me ! these thieves are like us Spaniards.*

This false civility of Captain Morgan, wherewith he used this lady, was soon after changed into barbarous cruelty. For, three or four days being past, he came to see her, and the virtuous lady constantly repulsed him, with all the civility imaginable and many humble and modest expressions of her mind. But Captain Morgan still persisted in his disorderly request, presenting her withal with much pearl, gold and all that he had got that was precious and valuable in that voyage. But the lady being in no manner willing to consent thereto, nor accept his presents, and showing herself in all respects like Susannah for constancy, he presently changed note, and began to speak to her in another tone, threatening her with a thousand cruelties and hard usages at his hands. To all these things she gave this resolute and positive answer, than which no other could be extorted from her : *Sir, my life is in your hands ; but as to my body, in relation to that which you would persuade me to, my soul shall sooner be separated from it, through the violence of your arms, then I shall condescend to your request.* No sooner had Captain Morgan understood this heroic resolution of her mind than he commanded her to be stripped of the best of her apparel, and imprisoned in a darksome and stinking cellar. Here she had allowed her an extremely small quantity of meat and drink, wherewith she had much ado to sustain her life for a few days.

Under this hardship the constant and virtuous lady ceased not to pray daily to God Almighty, for constancy and patience against the cruelties of Captain Morgan. But he being now throughly convinced of her chaste resolutions, as also desirous to conceal the cause of her confinement and hard usage, since many of the Pirates, his companions, did compassionate her condition, laid many false accusations to her charge, giving to understand she held intelligence with the Spaniards, and corresponded with them by letters, abusing thereby his former lenity and kindness. I myself was an eye witness to these things here related, and could never have judged such constancy of mind and virtuous chastity to be found in the world, if my own eyes and ears had not informed me thereof. But of this incomparable lady I shall say something more hereafter in its proper place ; whereupon I shall leave her at present, to continue my history.

Captain Morgan, having now been at Panama the full space of three weeks, commanded all things to be put in order for his departure. To this effect, he gave orders to every company of his men, to seek out for so many beasts of carriage as might suffice to convey the whole spoil of the city to the river where his canoes lay. About this time a great rumour was spread in the city, of a considerable number of Pirates who intended to leave Captain Morgan ; and that, by taking a ship which was in the port, they determined to go and rob upon the South Sea till they had got as much as they thought fit, and then return homewards by the way of the East Indies into Europe. For which purpose, they had already gathered great quantity of provisions, which they had hidden in private places, with sufficient store of powder, bullets and all other sorts of ammunition : likewise some great guns, belonging to the town, muskets and other things, wherewith they designed not only to equip the said vessel but also to fortify themselves and raise batteries in some island or other, which might serve them for a place of refuge.

This design had certainly taken effect as they intended, had not Captain Morgan had timely advice thereof given him by one of their comrades. Hereupon he instantly commanded the mainmast of the said ship should be cut down and burnt, together with all the other boats that were in the port. Hereby the intentions of all or most of his companions were totally frustrated. After this Captain Morgan sent forth many of the Spaniards into the adjoining fields and country, to seek for money wherewith to ransom not only themselves but also all the rest of the prisoners, as likewise the ecclesiastics, both secular and regular. Moreover he commanded all the artillery of the town to be spoiled, that is to say, nailed and stopped up. At the same time he sent out a strong company of men to seek for the Governor of Panama, of whom intelligence was brought that he had laid several ambuscades in the way, by which he ought to pass at his return. But those who were sent upon this design returned soon after, saying they had not found any sign or appearance of any such ambuscades ; for a confirmation whereof, they brought with them some prisoners they had taken, who declared that the said Governor had had an intention of making some opposition by the way, but that the men whom he had designed to effect it were unwilling to undertake any such enterprize; so that for want of means, he could not put his design in execution.

On the 24th of February of the year 1671 Captain Morgan departed from the city of Panama, or rather from the place where the said city of Panama did stand; of the spoils whereof he carried with him one hundred and seventy-five beasts of carriage, laden with silver, gold and other precious things, besides six hundred prisoners, more or less, between men, women, children and slaves. That day they came to a river that passes through a delicious campaign field, at the distance of a league from Panama. Here Captain Morgan put all his forces into good order of martial array, in such manner that the prisoners were in the middle of the camp, surrounded on all sides with Pirates. At which present conjuncture nothing else was to be heard but lamentations, cries, shrieks and doleful sighs, of so many women and children, who were persuaded Captain Morgan designed to transport them all, and carry them into his own country for slaves. Besides that, among all those miserable prisoners, there was extreme hunger and thirst endured at that time; which hardship and misery Captain Morgan designedly caused them to sustain, with intent to excite them more earnestly to seek for money wherewith to ransom themselves, according to the tax he had set upon every one. Many of the women begged of Captain Morgan upon their knees, with infinite sighs and tears, he would permit them to return to Panama, there to live in company of their dear husbands and children, in little huts of straw which they would erect, seeing they had no houses until the rebuilding of the city. But his answer was: he came not thither to hear lamentations and cries, but rather to seek money. Therefore they ought to seek out for that in

the first place, wherever it were to be had, and bring it
to him, otherwise he would assuredly transport them all
to such places whither they cared not to go.

The next day, when the march began, those lamentable cries and shrieks were renewed, in so much as it
would have caused compassion in the hardest heart to
hear them.   But Captain Morgan, a man little given
to mercy, was not moved therewith in the least.   They
marched in the same order as was said before ; one party
of the Pirates preceding in the van, the prisoners in the
middle, and the rest of the Pirates in the rear-guard, by
whom the miserable Spaniards were, at every step,
punched and thrust in their backs and sides, with the
blunt end of their arms, to make them march the faster.
That beautiful and virtuous lady, of whom we made
mention heretofore for her unparalleled constancy and
chastity, was led prisoner by herself, between two Pirates
who guarded her.   Her lamentations now did pierce the
skies, seeing herself carried away into foreign captivity,
often crying to the Pirates, and telling them : *That she
had given order to two religious persons, in whom she had
relied, to go to a certain place, and fetch so much money as
her ransom did amount to.   That they had promised
faithfully to do it, but having obtained the said money,
instead of bringing it to her, they had employed it another
way, to ransom some of their own and particular friends.*
This ill action of theirs was discovered by a slave, who
brought a letter to the said lady.   Her complaints, and
the cause thereof, being brought to the ears of Captain
Morgan, he thought fit to enquire thereinto.   Having
found the thing to be true, especially hearing it confirmed
by the confession of the said religious men, though under
some frivolous excuses, of having diverted the money
but for a day or two, within which time they expected
more sums to repay it, he gave liberty to the said lady,
whom otherwise he designed to transport to Jamaica.
But in the meanwhile he detained the said religious men,

as prisoners in her place, using them according to the deserts of their incompassionate intrigues.

As soon as Captain Morgan arrived, upon his march, at the town called Cruz, situated on the banks of the river Chagre, as was mentioned before, he commanded an order to be published among the prisoners, that within the space of three days every one of them should bring in his ransom, under the penalty aforementioned of being transported to Jamaica. In the meanwhile he gave orders, for so much rice and maize to be collected thereabouts as was necessary for the victualling all his ships. At this place some of the prisoners were ransomed, but many others could not bring in their moneys in so short time. Hereupon he continued his voyage, leaving the village on the 5th day of March next following, and carrying with him all the spoil that ever he could transport. From this village he likewise led away some new prisoners, who were inhabitants of the said place. So that these prisoners were added to those of Panama who had not as yet paid their ransoms, and all transported. But the two religious men, who had diverted the money belonging to the lady, were ransomed three days after their imprisonment, by other persons who had more compassion for their condition than they had showed for hers. About the middle of the way to the castle of Chagre, Captain Morgan commanded them to be placed in due order, according to their custom, and caused every one to be sworn, that they had reserved nor concealed nothing privately to themselves, even not so much as the value of sixpence. This being done, Captain Morgan having had some experience that those lewd fellows would not much stickle to swear falsely in points of interest, he commanded every one to be searched very strictly, both in their clothes and satchels and everywhere it might be presumed they had reserved anything. Yea, to the intent this order might not be ill taken by his companions, he permitted himself to be searched, even to the very soles of his shoes. To this effect, by common consent, there was assigned one out of every company, to be the searchers of all the rest. The French Pirates that went on this expedition with Captain Morgan, were not well satisfied with this new custom of searching. Yet their number being less than that of the English, they were forced to submit to it, as well as the others had done before them. The search being over, they re-embarked in their canoes and boats, which attended them on the river, and arrived at the castle of Chagre on the 9th day of the said month of March. Here they found all things in good order, excepting the wounded men, whom they had left there at the time of their departure. For of these the greatest number were dead, through the wounds they had received.

From Chagre, Captain Morgan sent presently after his arrival, a great boat to Porto Bello, wherein were all the prisoners he had taken at the Isle of St. Catharine, demanding by them a considerable ransom for the castle of Chagre, where he then was, threatening otherwise to ruin and demolish it even to the ground. To this message those of Porto Bello made answer : They would not give one farthing towards the ransom of the said castle, and that the English might do with it as they pleased. This answer being come, the dividend was made of all the spoil they had purchased in that voyage. Thus every company, and every particular person therein included, received their portion of what was got : or rather, what part thereof Captain Morgan was pleased to give them. For so it was, that the rest of his companions, even of his own nation, complained of his proceedings in this particular, and feared not to tell him openly to his face, that he had reserved the best jewels to himself. For they judged it impossible that no greater share should belong to them than two hundred pieces of eight *per capita*, of so many valuable booties and robberies as they had obtained. Which small sum they thought too little reward for so much labour and such huge and manifest dangers as they had so often exposed their lives to. But Captain Morgan was deaf to all these and many other complaints of this kind, having designed in his mind to cheat them of as much as he could.

At last Captain Morgan finding himself obnoxious to many obloquies and detractions among his people, began to fear the consequence thereof, and hereupon thinking it unsafe to remain any longer time at Chagre, he commanded the ordnance of the said castle to be carried on board his ship. Afterwards he caused the greatest part of the walls to be demolished, and the edifices to be burnt, and as many other things spoiled and ruined as could conveniently be done in a short while. These orders being performed, he went secretly on board his own ship, without giving any notice of his departure to his companions, nor calling any council, as he used to do. Thus he set sail, and put out to sea, not bidding anybody adieu, being only followed by three or four vessels of the whole fleet. These were such (as the French Pirates believed) as went shares with Captain Morgan, towards the best and greatest part of the spoil which had been concealed from them in the dividend. The Frenchmen could very willingly have revenged this affront upon Captain Morgan and those that followed him, had they found themselves with sufficient means to encounter him at sea. But they were destitute of most things necessary thereto. Yea, they had much ado to find sufficient victuals and provisions for their voyage to Jamaica, he having left them totally unprovided of all things.

CHAPTER VII.

Of a voyage made by the Author, along the coasts of Costa Rica, at his return towards Jamaica. What happened most remarkable in the said voyage. Some observations made by him at that time.

CAPTAIN MORGAN left us all in such a miserable condition, as might serve for a lively representation of what reward attends wickedness at the latter end of life. Whence we ought to have learned how to regulate and amend our actions for the future. However it was, our affairs being reduced to such a posture, every company that was left behind, whether English or French, were compelled to seek what means they could to help themselves. Thus most of them separated from each other, and several companies took several courses, at their return homewards. As for that party to which I belonged, we steered our voyage along the coast of Costa Rica, where we intended to purchase some provisions, and careen our vessel in some secure place or other. For the boat wherein we were, was now grown so foul as to be rendered totally unfit for sailing. In few days we arrived at a great port, called Boca del Toro, where are always to be found huge quantity of good and eatable tortoises. The circumference hereof is ten leagues, more or less, being surrounded with little islands, under which vessels may ride very secure from the violence of the winds.

The said islands are inhabited by Indians, who never could be subjugated by the Spaniards, and hence they give them the name of *Indios bravos*, or Wild Indians.

They are divided, according to the variety of idioms of their language, into several customs and fashions of people, whence arise perpetual wars against one another. Towards the east side of this port are found some of them, who formerly did much trade with the Pirates, selling to them the flesh of divers animals which they hunt in their countries, as also all sorts of fruits that the land produces. The exchange of which commodities was iron instruments, that the Pirates brought with them, beads and other toys, whereof they made great account for wearing, more than of precious jewels, which they knew not nor esteemed in the least. This commerce afterwards failed, because the Pirates committed many barbarous inhumanities against them, killing many of their men on a certain occasion, and taking away their women. These abuses gave sufficient cause for a perpetual cessation of all friendship and commerce between them and the Pirates.

We went ashore, with design to seek provisions, our necessity being now almost extreme. But our fortune was so bad that we could find nothing else than a few eggs of crocodiles, wherewith we were forced to content ourselves for that present. Hereupon we left those quarters, and steered our course eastwards. Being upon this tack, we met with three boats more of our own companions, who had been left behind by Captain Morgan. These told us they had been able to find no relief for the extreme hunger they sustained ; moreover, that Captain Morgan himself and all his people were already reduced to such misery, that he could afford them no more allowance than once a day, and that very short too.

We therefore hearing from these boats that little or no good was like to be done by sailing farther eastward, changed our course, and steered towards the west. Here we found an excessive quantity of tortoises, more than we needed for the victualling our boats, should we be never so long without any other flesh or fish. Having

provided ourselves with this sort of victuals, the next
thing we wanted was fresh water.   There was enough to
be had in the neighbouring islands, but we scarce dared
to land on them, by reason of the enmity above mentioned between us Pirates and those Indians.   Notwithstanding, necessity having no law, we were forced to do
as we could, rather than as we desired to do.   And
hereupon we resolved to go all of us together to one of
the said islands.   Being landed, one party of our men
went to range in the woods, while another filled the
barrels with water.   Scarce one whole hour was past,
after our people were got ashore, when suddenly the
Indians came upon us, and we heard one of our men cry :
Arm ! Arm ! We presently took up our arms, and
began to fire at them as hot as we could.   This caused
them to advance no farther, and in a short while put
them to flight, sheltering themselves in the woods.   We
pursued them some part of the way, but not far, by
reason we then esteemed rather to get in our water than
any other advantages upon the enemy.   Coming back,
we found two Indians dead upon the shore, whereof
the habiliments of one gave us to understand he was a
person of quality amongst them.   For he had about his
body a girdle, or sash, very richly woven ; and on his
face he wore a beard of massive gold—I mean, a small
planch of gold hung down at his lips by two strings
(which penetrated two little holes, made there on purpose), that covered his beard, or served instead thereof.
His arms were made of sticks of palmetto-trees, being
very curiously wrought, at one end whereof was a kind
of hook, which seemed to be hardened with fire.   We
could willingly have had opportunity to speak with some
of these Indians, to see if we could reconcile their minds
to us, and by this means renew the former trade with them,
and obtain provisions.   But this was a thing impossible,
through the wildness of their persons and savageness of
their minds.   Notwithstanding, this encounter hindered

us not from filling our barrels with water, and carrying them aboard.

The night following we heard from the shore huge cries and shrieks among the Indians. These lamentations caused us to believe, because they were heard so far, they had called in much more people to aid them against us; as also, that they lamented the death of those two men who were killed the day before. These Indians never come upon the waters of the sea, neither have they ever given themselves to build canoes or any other sort of vessels for navigation—not so much as fisher-boats, of which art of fishery they are totally ignorant. At last, having nothing else to hope for in these parts, we resolved to depart thence for Jamaica, whither we designed to go. Being set forth, we met with contrary winds, which caused us to make use of our oars, and row as far as the river of Chagre. When we came near it, we perceived a ship that made towards us, and began to give us chase. Our apprehensions were that it was a ship from Cartagena, which might be sent to rebuild and retake possession of the castle of Chagre, now all the Pirates were departed thence. Hereupon we set all our sail and ran before the wind, to see if we could escape or refuge ourselves in any place. But the vessel, being much swifter and cleaner than ours, easily got the wind of us, and stopped our course. Then approaching near us, we discovered what they were, and knew them to be our former comrades, in the same expedition of Panama, who were but lately set out from Chagre. Their design was to go to Nombre de Dios, and thence to Cartagena, to seek some purchase or other, in or about that frequented port. But the wind at that present being contrary to their intention, they concluded to go in our company towards the same place where we were before, called Boca del Toro.

This accident and encounter retarded our journey, in the space of two days, more than we could regain in a

whole fortnight. This was the occasion that obliged us
to return to our former station, where we remained for a
few days. Thence we directed our course for a place
called Boca del Dragon, there to make provisions of flesh,
especially of a certain animal which the Spaniards call
manati,[1] and the Dutch, *sea-cows*, because the head,
nose and teeth of this beast are very like those of a cow.
They are found commonly in such places, as under the
depth of the waters are very full of grass, on which, it is
thought, they pasture. These animals have no ears, and
only in place of them are to be seen two little holes, scarce
capable of receiving the little finger of a man. Near to
the neck they have two wings, under which are seated
two udders or breasts, much like the breasts of a woman.
The skin is very close and united together, resembling
the skin of a Barbary, or Guinea Dog. This skin upon
the back is of the thickness of two fingers, which, being
dried, is as hard as any whale-bone, and may serve to
make walking-staffs with. The belly is in all things like
that of a cow, as far as the kidneys, or reins. Their
manner of engendering, likewise, is the same with the
usual manner of a land cow, the male of this kind being
in similitude almost one and the same thing with a bull.
Yet, notwithstanding, they conceive and breed but once.
But the space of time that they go with calf, I could not
as yet learn. These fishes have the sense of hearing
extremely acute, in so much that in taking them the
fishermen ought not to make the least noise, nor row,
unless it be very slightly. For this reason they make
use of certain instruments for rowing, which the Indians
call *pagayos*, and the Spaniards name *caneletas*, with
which although they row, yet it is performed without any
noise that can fright the fish. While they are busied in

[1] The name manati was first applied to this animal by the early
Spanish colonists in regard to the hand-like use of its fore limbs; a
good description of it is to be found in Dampier's Letters. It is of the
order Sirenia; there are two varieties—one (M. Latirostris) inhabits the
West Indies and Florida, the other (M. australis) the coast of Brazil.

this fishery, they do not speak to one another, but all is transacted by signs. He that darts them with the javelin, uses it after the same manner as when they kill tortoises. Howbeit, the point of the said javelin is somewhat different, having two hooks at the extremity, and these longer than that of the other fishery. Of these fishes, some are found to be of the length of twenty to twenty-four foot. Their flesh is very good to eat, being very like in colour that of a land cow, but in taste, that of pork. It contains much fat, or grease, which the Pirates melt and keep in earthen pots, to make use thereof instead of oil.

On a certain day, wherein we were not able to do any good at this sort of fishery, some of our men went into the woods to hunt, and others to catch other fish. Soon after we espied a canoe, wherein were two Indians. These no sooner had discovered our vessels than they rowed back with all the speed they could towards the land, being unwilling to trade or have anything to do with us Pirates. We followed them to the shore, but through their natural nimbleness, being much greater than ours, they retired into the woods before we could overtake them. Yea, what was more admirable, they drew on shore, and carried with them their canoe into the wood, as easily as if it were made of straw, although it weighed above two thousand pounds. This we knew by the canoe itself, which we found afterwards, and had much ado to get into the water again, although we were in all eleven persons to pull at it.

We had at that time in our company a certain pilot, who had been divers times in those quarters. This man, seeing this action of the Indians, told us that, some few years before, a squadron of Pirates happened to arrive at that place. Being there, they went in canoes, to catch a certain sort of little birds, which inhabits the sea-coast, under the shade of very beautiful trees, which here are to be seen. While they were busied at that work, certain

Indians who had climbed up into the trees to view their actions, seeing now the canoes underneath, leaped down into the sea, and with huge celerity seized some of the canoes and Pirates that kept them, both which they transported so nimbly into the remotest parts of the woods, that the prisoners could not be relieved by their companions. Hereupon the admiral of the said squadron landed presently after with five hundred men, to seek and rescue the men he had lost. But they saw such an excessive number of Indians flock together to oppose them, as obliged them to retreat with all possible diligence to their ships, concluding among themselves that if such forces as those could not perform anything towards the recovery of their companions, they ought to stay no longer time there. Having heard this history, we came away thence, fearing some mischief might befall us, and bringing with us the canoe aforementioned. In this we found nothing else but a fishing-net, though not very large, and four arrows, made of palm-tree, of the length of seven foot each and of the figure, or shape, as follows.

These arrows, we believed, to be their arms. The canoe we brought away was made of cedar, but very roughly hewn and polished, which caused us to think that those people have no instruments of iron.

We left that place, and arrived in twenty four hours at another called Rio de Zuera, where we found some few houses belonging to the city of Cartagena. These houses are inhabited by Spaniards, whom we resolved to visit, not being able to find any tortoises, nor yet any of their eggs. The inhabitants were all fled from the said houses, having left no victuals, nor provisions behind them, in so much that we were forced to content ourselves with a certain

fruit, which there is called platano. Of these platanos
we filled our boats, and continued our voyage, coasting
along the shore. Our design was to find out some creek
or bay, wherein to careen our vessel, which now was
very leaky on all sides. Yea, in such a dangerous condition, that both night and day we were constrained to
employ several men at the pump, to which purpose we
made use of all our slaves. This voyage lasted a whole
fortnight, all which time we lay under the continual
frights of perishing every moment. At last we arrived
at a certain port, called The Bay of Bleevelt, being so
named from a Pirate who used to resort thither, with the
same design that we did. Here one party of our men
went into the woods to hunt, while another undertook to
refit and careen our vessel.

Our companions who went abroad to hunt found hereabouts porcupines, of a huge and monstrous bigness.
But their chief exercise was killing of monkeys, and
certain birds called by the Spaniards *faisanes*, or pheasants. The toil and labour we had in this employment
of shooting, seemed at least to me, to be sufficiently com-
pensated with the pleasure of killing the said monkeys.
For at these we usually made fifteen to sixteen shots
before we could kill three or four of them, so nimbly
would they escape our hands and aim, even after being
desperately wounded. On the other side, it was delightful to see the female monkeys carry their little ones upon
their backs, even just as negresses do their children.
Likewise, if shooting at a parcel of them, any monkey
happens to be wounded, the rest of the company will
flock about him, and lay their hands upon the wound,
to hinder the blood from issuing forth. Others will
gather moss that grows upon the trees, and thrust it into
the wound, and hereby stop the blood. At other times
they will gather such or such herbs, and, chewing them
in their mouth, apply them after the manner of a poultice,
or cataplasm. All which things did cause in me great

admiration, seeing such strange actions in those irrational creatures, which testified the fidelity and love they had for one another.

On the 9th day after our arrival at that place, our women-slaves being busied in their ordinary employments of washing dishes, sewing, drawing water out of wells, which we had made on the shore, and the like things, we heard great cries of one of them, who said she had seen a troop of Indians appear towards the woods, whereby she began immediately to cry out: *Indians, Indians.* We, hearing this rumour, ran presently to our arms, and their relief. But, coming to the wood, we found no person there, excepting two of our women-slaves killed upon the place, with the shot of arrows. In their bodies we saw so many arrows sticking as might seem they had been fixed there with particular care and leisure ; for otherwise we knew that one of them alone was sufficient to bereave any human body of life. These arrows were all of a rare fashion and shape, their length being eight foot, and their thickness of a man's thumb. At one of the extremities hereof, was to be seen a hook made of wood, and tied to the body of the arrow with a string. At the other end was a certain case, or box, like the case of a pair of tweezers, in which we found certain little pebbles or stones. The colour thereof was red, and very shining, as if they had been locked up some considerable time. All which, we believed, were arms belonging to their captains and leaders.

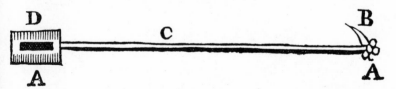

A. *A marcasite, which was tied to the extremity of the arrow.*
B. *A hook, tied to the same extremity.*
C. *The arrow.*
D. *The case, at the other end.*

These arrows were all made without instruments of iron. For whatsoever the Indians make, they harden it first very artificially with fire, and afterwards polish it with flints.

As to the nature of these Indians, they are extremely robust of constitution, strong and nimble at their feet. We sought them carefully up and down the woods, but could not find the least trace of them, neither any of their canoes, nor floats, whereof they make use to go out to fish. Hereupon we retired to our vessels, where, having embarked all our goods, we put off from the shore, fearing lest finding us there they should return in any considerable number, and overpowering our forces tear us all in pieces.

CHAPTER VIII.

The Author departs towards the Cape of Gracias à Dios. Of the
Commerce which here the Pirates exercise with the Indians.
His arrival at the Island De los Pinos ; and finally, his
return to Jamaica.

THE fear we had, more than usual, of those Indians
above mentioned, by reason of the death of our two
women-slaves, of which we told you in the former chapter, occasioned us to depart as fast as we could from that
place. We directed our course thence, towards the Cape
of Gracias à Dios, where we had fixed our last hopes of
finding provisions. For thither do usually resort many
Pirates, who entertain a friendly correspondence and
trade with the Indians of those parts. Being arrived at
the said cape, we hugely rejoiced, and gave thanks to
God Almighty, for having delivered us out of so many
dangers, and brought us to this place of refuge, where we
found people who showed us most cordial friendship, and
provided us with all necessaries whatsoever.

The custom of this island is such that, when any
Pirates arrive there, every one has the liberty to buy for
himself an Indian woman, at the price of a knife, or any
old axe, wood-bill or hatchet. By this contract the
woman is obliged to remain in the custody of the Pirate
all the time he stayeth there. She serves him in the
meanwhile, and brings him victuals of all sorts, that the
country affords. The Pirate moreover has liberty to go
when he pleases, either to hunt, or fish, or about any
other divertisements of his pleasure ; but withal is not to
commit any hostility, or depredation upon the inhabitants,

seeing the Indians bring him in all that he stands in need of, or that he desires.

Through the frequent converse and familiarity these Indians have with the Pirates, they sometimes go to sea with them, and remain among them for whole years, without returning home. Whence it comes that many of them can speak English, and French, and some of the Pirates their Indian language. They are very dextrous at darting with the javelin, whereby they are very useful to the Pirates, towards the victualling their ships, by the fishery of tortoises, and *manitas*, a sort of fish so called by the Spaniards. For one of these Indians is alone sufficient to victual a vessel of an hundred persons. We had among our crew two Pirates who could speak very well the Indian language. By the help of these men, I was so curious as to enquire into their customs, lives and policy, whereof I shall give you here a brief account.

This island contains about thirty leagues in circumference, more or less. It is governed after the form of a little commonwealth, they having no king nor sovereign prince among them. Neither do they entertain any friendship or correspondence with other neighbouring islands, much less with the Spaniards. They are in all but a small nation, whose number does not exceed sixteen or seventeen hundred persons. They have among them some few negroes, who serve them in quality of slaves. These happened to arrive there, swimming, after shipwreck made upon that coast. For being bound for Terra Firma, in a ship that carried them to be sold in those parts, they killed the captain and mariners, with design to return to their country. But through their ignorance in marinery, they stranded their vessel hereabouts. Although, as I said before, they make but a small nation, yet they live divided, as it were, into two several provinces. Of these, the one sort employ themselves in cultivating the ground, and making several plantations. But the others are so lazy that they have not courage to build themselves huts, much less houses, to dwell in. They frequent chiefly the sea-coast, wandering disorderly up and down, without knowing, or caring so much as to cover their bodies from the rains, which are very frequent in those parts, unless it be with a few palm-leaves. These they put upon their heads, and keep their backs always turned to the wind that blows. They use no other clothes than an apron, tied to their middle ; such aprons are made of the rinds of trees, which they strongly beat upon stones till they are softened. Of these same they make use for bed-clothes, to cover themselves when they sleep. Some make to themselves bed-clothes of cotton, but these are but few in number. Their usual arms are nothing but azagayas, or spears, which they make fit for their use with points of iron or teeth of crocodiles.

They know, after some manner, that there is a God, yet they live without any religion or divine worship. Yea, as far as I can learn, they believe not in nor serve the devil, as many other nations of America do both believe, invoke and worship him. Hereby they are not so much tormented by him, as other nations are. Their ordinary food, for the greatest part, consists in several fruits ; such as are called bananas, racoven, ananas, potatos, cassava ; as also crabs, and some few fish of other sorts, which they kill in the sea with darts. As to their drink, they are something expert in making certain pleasant and delicate liquors. The commonest among them is called *achioc*. This is made of a certain seed of palm-tree, which they bruise, and afterwards steep or infuse in hot water, till it be settled at the bottom. This liquor being strained off has a very pleasant taste, and is very nourishing. Many other sorts of liquors they prepare, which I shall omit for brevity. Only I shall say something, in short, of that which is made of *platanos*. These they knead betwixt their hands with hot water, and afterwards put into great calabashes, which they fill up with cold water, and leave in repose for the space of eight days, during which time it ferments as well as the best sort of wine.   This liquor they drink for pleasure, and as a great regale, in so much that when these Indians invite their friends or relations they cannot treat them better than to give them some of this pleasant drink.

They are very unskilful in dressing of victuals ; and hence it is that they very seldom treat one another with banquets.   For this purpose, when they go or send to any house, to invite others, they desire them to come and drink of their liquors.   Before the invited persons come to their house, those that expect them comb their hair very well, and anoint their faces with oil of palm, mingled with a certain black tincture which renders them very hideous.   The women, in like manner, daub their faces with another sort of stuff, which cause them to look as red as crimson.   And such are the greatest civilities they use in their ornaments and attire.   Afterwards, he that invites the other takes his arms, which are three or four *azagayas*, and goes out of his cottage the space of three or four hundred steps, to wait for and receive the persons that are to come to visit him.   As soon as they draw near him, he falls down upon the ground, lying flat on his face, in which posture he remains without any motion, as if he were dead.   Being thus prostrate before them, the invited friends take him up and set him upon his feet, and thus they go altogether to the hut.   Here the persons who are invited use the same ceremony, falling down on the ground, as the inviter did before.   But he lifts them up one by one, and, giving them his hand, conducts them into his cottage, where he causes them to sit.   The women on these occasions perform few or no ceremonies.

Being thus brought into the house, they are presented every one with a calabash full of the liquor abovementioned, made of *platanos*, which is very thick, almost like water-gruel, or children's pap, wherein is contained four quarts, more or less, of the said liquor. These they are to drink off as well as they can, and get down at any rate. The calabashes being emptied into their stomachs, the master of the house, with many ceremonies, goes about the room, and gathers his calabashes. And this drinking hitherto is reckoned but for one welcome, whereas every invitation ought to contain several welcomes. Afterwards, they begin to drink of the clear liquor abovementioned, for which they were called to this treat. Hereunto follow many songs and dances and a thousand caresses to the women that are present.

They do not marry any young maid without the consent of her parents. Hereupon, if any one desires to take a wife, he is first examined by the damsel's father concerning several points relating to good husbandry. These are most commonly : whether he can make *azagayas*, darts for fishing or spin a certain thread which they use about their arrows. Having answered to satisfaction, the examiner calls to his daughter, for a little calabash full of the liquor above mentioned. Of this he drinks first ; then gives the cup to the young man ; and he finally to the bride, who drinks it up ; and with this only ceremony the marriage is made. When any one drinks to the health of another, the second person ought to drink up the liquor which the other person has left in the calabash. But in case of marriage, as was said before, it is consumed alone among those three, the bride obtaining the greatest part to her share.

When the woman lies in, neither she nor her husband observe the time, as is customary among the Caribbees. But as soon as the woman is delivered, she goes instantly to the next river, brook or fountain, and washes the new-born creature, swaddling it up afterwards in certain rollers, or swaddling bands, which there are called *cabalas*. This being done, she goes about her ordinary labour, as before. At their entertainments it is usual, that when the man dies, his wife buries him with all his *azagayas*, aprons and jewels that he used to wear at his ears. Her next obligation is, to come every day to her husband's grave, bringing him meat and drink for a whole year together. Their years they reckon by the moons, allowing fifteen to every year, which make their entire circle, as our twelve months do ours.

Some historians, writing of the Caribbee Islands, affirm that this ceremony of carrying victuals to the dead is generally observed among them. Moreover, that the devil comes to the sepulchres, and carries away all the meat and drink which is placed there. But I myself am not of this opinion, seeing I have oftentimes with my own hands taken away these offerings, and eaten them instead of other victuals. To this I was moved, because I knew that the fruits used on these occasions were the choicest and ripest of all others, as also the liquors of the best sort they made use of for their greatest regale and pleasure. When the widow has thus completed her year, she opens the grave, and takes out all her husband's bones. These she scrapes and washes very well, and afterwards dries against the beams of the sun. When they are sufficiently dried, she ties them all together, and puts them into a *cabala*, being a certain pouch or satchel, and is obliged for another year to carry them upon her back in the daytime, and to sleep upon them in the night, until the year be completely expired. This ceremony being finished, she hangs up the bag and bones against the post of her own door, in case she be mistress of any house. But having no house of her own, she hangs them at the door of her next neighbour, or relation.

The widows cannot marry a second time, according to the laws or customs of this nation, until the space of the two years above mentioned be completed. The men are bound to perform no such ceremonies towards their wives. But if any Pirate marries an Indian Woman, she is bound to do with him, in all things, as if he were an Indian man born. The negroes that are upon this Island, live here in all respects according to the customs of their own country. All these things I have thought fit to take notice of in this place, though briefly, as judging them worthy the curiosity of some judicious and inquisitive persons. Now I shall continue the account of our voyage.

After we had refreshed and provided ourselves, as well as we could, at the island aforesaid, we departed thence, and steered our course towards the island De los Pinos. Here we arrived in fifteen days, and were constrained to refit again our vessel, which now the second time was very leaky and not fit for sailing any farther. Hereupon we divided ourselves, as before, and some went about that work of careening the ship, while others betook themselves to fishing. In this last we were so successful as to take in six or seven hours as much fish as would abundantly suffice to feed a thousand persons. We had in our company some Indians from the cape of Gracias à Dios, who were very dextrous both in hunting and fishing. With the help of these men we killed likewise, in a short while, and salted, a huge number of wild cows, sufficient both to satiate our hungry appetites and to victual our vessel for the sea. These cows were formerly brought into this island by the Spaniards, with design they should here multiply and stock the country with cattle of this kind. We salted, in like manner, a vast number of tortoises, whereof in this island huge quantities are to be found. With these things our former cares and troubles began to dissipate, and our minds to be so far recreated as to forget the miseries we had lately endured. Hereupon, we began to call one another again by the name of brothers, which was customary amongst us but had been disused in our miseries and scarce remembered without regret.

All the time we continued here, we feasted ourselves very plentifully, without the least fear of enemies. For as to the Spaniards that were upon the island, they were here in mutual league and friendship with us. Thus we were only constrained to keep watch and ward every night, for fear of the crocodiles, which are here in great plenty all over the island. For these, when they are hungry, will assault any man whatsoever, and devour him ; as it happened in this conjuncture to one of our companions. This man being gone into the wood, in company with a negro, they fell into a place where a crocodile lay concealed. The furious animal, with incredible agility, assaulted the Pirate, and fastening upon his leg, cast him upon the ground, the negro being fled, who should assist him. Yet he, notwithstanding, being a robust and courageous man, drew forth a knife he had then about him, and with the same, after a dangerous combat, overcame and killed the crocodile. Which having done, he himself, both tired with the battle, and weakened with the loss of blood, that ran from his wounds, lay for dead upon the place, or at least beside his senses. Being found in this posture some while after by the negro, who returned to see what was become of his master, he took him upon his back, and brought him to the sea-side, distant thence the space of a whole league, Here we received him into a canoe, and conveyed him on board our ship.

After this misfortune, none of our men dared be so bold as to enter the woods without good company. Yea, we ourselves, desirous to revenge the disaster of our companion, went in troops the next day to the woods, with design to find out crocodiles to kill. These animals would usually come every night to the sides of our ship, and make resemblance of climbing up into the vessel. One of these, on a certain night, we seized with an iron hook, but he instead of flying to the bottom, began to mount the ladder of the ship, till we killed him with other instruments. Thus, after we had remained there some considerable time, and refitted ourselves with all things necessary, we set sail thence for Jamaica. Here we arrived within few days, after a prosperous voyage, and found Captain Morgan, who was got home before us, but had seen as yet none of his companions whom he left behind, we being the first that arrived there after him.

The said Captain at that present was very busy, endeavouring to persuade and levy people to transport to the isle of St. Catharine, which he designed to fortify and hold as his own, thinking to make it a common refuge to all sorts of Pirates, or at least of his own nation, as was said before. But he was soon hindered in the prosecution of this design, by the arrival of a man-of-war from England. For this vessel brought orders from his Majesty of Great Britain, to recall the Governor of Jamaica from his charge over that island, to the court of England, there to give an account of his proceedings and behaviour in relation to the Pirates whom he had maintained in those parts, to the huge detriment of the subjects of the King of Spain. To this purpose, the said man-of-war brought over also a new Governor of Jamaica, to supply the place of the preceding. This gentleman, being possessed of the government of the island, presently after gave notice to all the ports thereof, by several boats which he sent forth to that intent, of the good and entire correspondence which his master the King of England designed henceforwards to maintain in those Western parts of the world towards his Catholic Majesty and all his subjects and dominions. And that to this effect, for the time to come, he had received from his Sacred Majesty and Privy Council strict and severe orders, not to permit any Pirate whatsoever to set forth from Jamaica, to commit any hostility or depredation upon the Spanish nation, or dominions, or any other people of those neighbouring islands.

No sooner these orders were sufficiently divulged than the Pirates, who as yet were abroad at sea, began to fear them, insomuch that they dared not return home to the said island. Hereupon they kept the seas as long as they could, and continued to act as many hostilities as came in their way. Not long after, the same Pirates took and ransacked a considerable town, seated in the Isle of Cuba, called La Villa de los Cayos, of which we made mention in the description of the said island. Here they committed again all sorts of hostility, and inhuman and barbarous cruelties. But the new Governor of Jamaica behaved himself so constant to his duty, and the orders he had brought from England, that he apprehended several of the chief actors herein, and condemned them to be hanged, which was accordingly done. From this severity many others still remaining abroad took warning, and retired to the isle of Tortuga, lest they should fall into his hands. Here they joined in society with the French Pirates, inhabitants of the said island, in whose company they continue to this day.

CHAPTER IX.

The Relation of the shipwreck, which Monsieur Bertram Ogeron, Governor of the Isle of Tortuga, suffered near the Isles of Guadanillas. How both he and his companions fell into the hands of the Spaniards. By what arts he escaped their hands, and preserved his life. The enterprize which he undertook against Porto Rico, to deliver his people. The unfortunate success of that design.

AFTER the expedition of Panama abovementioned, the inhabitants of the French islands in America, in the year 1673 (while the war was so fierce in Europe between France and Holland) gathered a considerable fleet, to go and possess themselves of the islands belonging to the States-General of the United Provinces in the West Indies. To this effect, their admiral called together and levied all the Pirates and volunteers that would, by any inductions whatsoever, sit down under his colours. With the same design the Governor of Tortuga caused to be built in that island a good strong man-of-war, to which vessel he gave the name of *Ogeron*. This ship he provided very well with all sorts of ammunition, and manned with five hundred buccaneers, all resolute and courageous men, as being the vessel he designed for his own safety. Their first intention was to go and take the Isle of Curaçoa, belonging to the said States of Holland. But this design met with very ill success, by reason of a shipwreck, which impeded the course of their voyage.

Monsieur Ogeron set sail from the port of Tortuga as soon as all things were in readiness, with intent to join the rest of the said fleet and pursue the enterprize aforementioned. Being arrived on the West side of the Island of St. John de Puerto Rico, he was suddenly surprized with a violent storm. This increased to such a degree, that it caused his new frigate to strike against the rocks that neighbour upon the islands, called Guadanillas, where the vessel broke into a thousand pieces. Yet being near the land of Porto Rico, all his men escaped, by saving their lives in boats, which they had at hand.

The next day, all being now got on shore, they were discovered by Spaniards who inhabit the island. These instantly took them to be French Pirates, whose intent was to take the said island anew, as they had done several times before. Hereupon they alarmed the whole country, and, gathering their forces together, marched out to their encounter. But they found them unprovided of all manner of arms, and consequently not able to make any defence, craving for mercy at their hands, and begging quarter for their lives, as the custom is. Yet notwithstanding, the Spaniards, remembering the horrible and cruel actions those Pirates had many times committed against them, would have no compassion on their condition. But answering them *Ha! ye thievish dogs, here's no quarter for you;* they assaulted them with all the fury imaginable, and killed the greatest part of the company. At last perceiving they made no resistance, nor had any arms to defend themselves, they began to relent in their cruelty, and stay their blows, taking prisoners as many as remained alive. Yet still they would not be persuaded but that those unfortunate were come thither with design to take again and ruin the island.

Hereupon they bound them with cords, by two and two or three and three together, and drove them through the woods, into the campaign, or open fields. Being come thus far with them, they asked them : What was become of their captain and leader ? Unto these questions they constantly made answer : he was drowned in the shipwreck at sea ; although they knew full well it was false. For Monsieur Ogeron, being unknown to the Spaniards, behaved himself among them as if he were a fool and had no common use of reason. Notwithstanding, the Spaniards, scarce believing what the prisoners had answered, used all the means they could possibly to find him, but could not compass their desires. For Monsieur Ogeron kept himself very close, to all the features and mimical actions that might become any innocent fool. Upon this account, he was not tied as the rest of his companions, but let loose, to serve the divertisement and laughter of the common soldiers. These now and then would give him scraps of bread and other victuals, whereas the rest of the prisoners had never sufficient wherewith to satisfy their hungry stomachs. For as to the allowance they had from the Spaniards, their enemies, it was scarce enough to preserve them alive.

It happened there was found among the French Pirates a certain surgeon, who had done some remarkable service to the Spaniards. In consideration of these merits, he was unbound, and set at liberty, to go freely up and down, even as Monsieur Ogeron did. To this surgeon Monsieur Ogeron, having a fit opportunity thereto, declared his resolution of hazarding his life, to attempt an escape from the cruelty and hard usage of those enemies. After mature deliberation, they both performed it, by flying to the woods, with design there to make something or other that might be navigable, whereby to transport themselves elsewhere, although to this effect they neither had nor could obtain any other thing in the world that could be serviceable in building of vessels than one hatchet. Thus they joined company, and began their march towards the woods that lay nearest the sea-coast. Having travelled all day long, they came about evening to the sea-side almost unexpectedly. Here they found themselves without anything to eat, nor any secure place wherein to rest their wearied limbs.

At last they perceived nigh the shore a huge quantity of fishes, called by the Spaniards *corlabados*. These frequently approach the sands of the shore, in pursuit of other little fishes that serve them for their food. Of these they took as many as they thought necessary, and, by rubbing two sticks tediously together, they kindled fire, wherewith they made coals to roast them. The next day they began to cut down and prepare timber, wherewith to make a kind of small boat, in which they might pass over to the Isle of Santa Cruz, which belongs to the French.

While they were busied about their work, they discovered, at a great distance, a certain canoe, which steered directly towards the place where they were. This occasioned in their minds some fears lest they should be found, and taken again by the Spaniards; and hereupon they retired into the woods, till such time as they could see thence and distinguish what people were in the canoe. But at last, as their good fortune would have it, they perceived them to be no more than two men, who in their disposition and apparel seemed to be fishermen. Having made this discovery, they concluded unanimously betwixt themselves to hazard their lives, and overcome them, and afterwards seize the canoe. Soon after they perceived one of them, who was a mulatto, to go with several calabashes hanging at his back towards a spring, not far distant from the shore, to take in fresh water. The other, who was a Spaniard, remained behind, waiting for his return. Seeing them divided, they assaulted the mulatto first, and discharging a great blow on his head with the hatchet, they soon bereaved him of life. The Spaniard, hearing the noise, made instantly towards the canoe, thinking to escape. But this he could not perform so soon, without being overtaken by the two, and there massacred by their hands. Having now compassed their design, they went to seek for the corpse of the mulatto, which they carried on board the canoe. Their intent was to convey them into the middle of the sea, and there cast them overboard, to be consumed by the fish, and by this means conceal this fact from being known to the Spaniards, either at a short or long distance of time.

These things being done, they took in presently as much fresh water as they could, and set sail to seek some place of refuge. That day they steered along the coast of Porto Rico, and came to the cape called by the Spaniards Cabo Roxo. Hence they traversed directly to the Isle of Hispaniola, where so many of their own comrades and companions were to be found. Both the currents of the waters and winds were very favourable to this voyage, in so much that in a few days they arrived at a place called Samana, belonging to the said island, where they found a party of their own people.

Monsieur Ogeron, being landed at Samana, gave orders to the surgeon to levy all the people he could possibly in those parts, while he departed to revisit his government of Tortuga. Being arrived at the said port, he used all his endeavours to gather what vessels and men he could to his assistance. So that within a few days he compassed a good number of both, very well equipped and disposed to follow and execute his designs. These were to go to the Island of St. John de Puerto Rico, and deliver his fellow prisoners, whom he had left in the miserable condition as was said before. After having embarked all the people which the surgeon had levied at Samana, he made them a speech, exhorting them to have good courage, and telling them : *You may all expect great spoil and riches from this enterprize, and therefore let all fear and cowardice be set on side. On the contrary, fill your hearts with courage and valour, for thus you will find yourselves soon satisfied, of what, at present, bare hopes do promise.* Every one relied much on these promises of Monsieur Ogeron, and, from his words, conceived no small joy in their minds. Thus they set

sail from Tortuga, steering their course directly for the
coasts of Porto Rico.   Being come within sight of land,
they made use only of their lower sails, to the intent they
might not be discovered at so great a distance by the
Spaniards, till they came somewhat near the place where
they intended to land.

The Spaniards, notwithstanding this caution, had
intelligence beforehand of their coming, and were prepared for a defence, having posted many troops of horse
all along the coast, to watch the descent of the French
Pirates.   Monsieur Ogeron, perceiving their vigilance,
gave order to the vessels to draw near the shore, and
shoot off many great guns, whereby he forced the cavalry
to retire to places more secure within the woods.   Here
lay concealed many companies of foot, who had prostrated
themselves upon the ground.   Meanwhile the Pirates
made their descent at leisure, and began to enter among
the trees, scarce suspecting any harm to be there, where
the horsemen could do no service.   But no sooner were
they fallen into this ambuscade than the Spaniards arose
with great fury, and assaulted the French so courageously
that in a short while they destroyed great part of them.
And thus leaving great numbers of dead on the place, the
rest with difficulty escaped by retreating in all haste to
their ships.

Monsieur Ogeron, although he escaped this danger,
yet could willingly have perished in the fight, rather than
suffer the shame and confusion the unfortunate success
of this enterprize was like to bring upon his reputation,
especially considering that those whom he had attempted
to set at liberty were now cast into greater miseries
through this misfortune.   Hereupon they hastened to set
sail, and go back to Tortuga the same way they came,
with great confusion in their minds, much diminished in
their number, and nothing laden with those spoils, the
hopes whereof had possessed their hearts, and caused
them readily to follow the promises of unfortunate Mon-

sieur Ogeron.   The Spaniards were very vigilant, and kept their posts near the sea-side, till such time as the fleet of Pirates was totally out of sight.   In the meanwhile they made an end of killing such of their enemies as being desperately wounded could not escape by flight. In like manner, they cut off several limbs from the dead bodies, with design to show them to the former prisoners, for whose redemption these others had crossed the seas.

The fleet being departed, the Spaniards kindled bonfires all over the island, and made great demonstrations of joy for the victory they had obtained.   But the French prisoners who were there before had more hardship showed them from that day than ever.   Of their misery and misusage was a good eye witness, Jacob Binkes, Governor at that time in America for the States-General of the United Provinces.   For he happened to arrive in that conjuncture at the Island of Porto Rico, with some men-of-war, to buy provisions and other necessaries for his fleet.   His compassion on their misery was such as caused him to bring away by stealth five or six of the said prisoners, which served only to exasperate the minds of the Spaniards.   For soon after they sent the rest of the prisoners to the chief city of the island, there to work and toil about the fortifications which then were making, forcing them to bring and carry stones and all sorts of materials belonging thereto.   These being finished, the Governor transported them to Havana, where they employed them in like manner, in fortifying that city.   Here they caused them to work in the day-time, and by night they shut them up as close prisoners, fearing lest they should enterprize upon the city.   For of such attempts the Spaniards had had divers proofs on other occasions, which afforded them sufficient cause to use them after that manner.

Afterwards at several times, wherein ships arrived there from New Spain, they transported them by degrees into Europe, and landed them at the city of Cadiz.   But

notwithstanding this care of the Spaniards to disperse
them, they soon after met almost all together in France,
and resolved among themselves to return again to
Tortuga with the first opportunity should proffer. To
this effect, they assisted one another very lovingly with
what necessaries they could spare, according to every
one's condition : so that in a short while the greatest
part of those Pirates had nested themselves again at
Tortuga, their common place of rendezvous. Here,
some time after, they equipped again a new fleet, to revenge their former misfortunes on the Spaniards, under
the conduct of one Le Sieur Maintenon, a Frenchman
by nation. With this fleet he arrived at the Island of
Trinidad, situated between the Isle of Tobago and the
neighbouring coasts of Paria. This island they sacked,
and afterwards put to the ransom of ten thousand pieces
of eight. Hence they departed, with design to take and
pillage the city of Caracas, situated over against the
Island of Curaçoa, belonging to the Hollanders.

CHAPTER X.

A relation of what encounters lately happened at the Islands of Cayana and Tobago, between the Count de Estres, Admiral of France, in America, and the Heer Jacob Binkes, Vice-Admiral of the United Provinces, in the same parts.

It is a thing already known to the greatest part of Europe that the Prince of Courland began to establish a colony in the Island of Tobago. As also, that somewhile after, his people, for want of timely recruits from their own country, abandoned the said island, leaving it to the first that should come and possess it. Thus it fell into the hands of the Heers Adrian and Cornelius Lampsius, natives of the city of Flushing, in the province of Zeeland. For being arrived at the said Island of Tobago, in the year 1654, they undertook to fortify it, by command of their sovereigns, the States-General. Hereupon they built a goodly castle, in a convenient situation, capable of hindering the assaults of any enemies that might enterprize upon the island.

The strength of this castle was afterwards sufficiently tried by Monsieur de Estres, as I shall presently relate, after I have first told you what happened before at Cayana, in the year 1676. This year the States-General of the United Provinces sent their Vice-Admiral, Jacob Binkes, to the Island of Cayana, then in possession of the French, to retake the said island, and hereby restore it to the dominions of the United Provinces aforementioned. With these orders he set forth from Holland, on the 16th day of March in the said year, his fleet consisting of seven men-of-war, one fireship and five other

small vessels of less account. This fleet arrived at
Cayana the 4th day of the month of May next following.
Immediately after their arrival, the Heer Binkes landed
nine hundred men, who, approaching the castle, summoned
the Governor to surrender, at their discretion. His
answer was: He thought of nothing less than surrendering, but that he and his people were resolved to defend
themselves, even to the utmost of their endeavours.
The Heer Binkes having received this answer, presently
commanded his troops to attack the castle on both sides
at once. The assault was very furious. But at length,
the French being few in number and overwhelmed with
the multitude of their enemies, surrendered both their
arms and the castle. In it were found thirty-seven
pieces of cannon. The Governor, who was named
Monsieur Lesi, together with two priests, were sent into
Holland. The Heer Binkes lost in the combat fourteen
men only, and had twenty two wounded.

The King of France no sooner understood this success
than he sent in the month of October following the
Count de Estres, to retake the said island from the
Hollanders. He arrived there in the month of December, with a squadron of men-of-war, all very well
equipped and provided. Being come on his voyage as
far as the river called Aperovaco, he met there with a
small vessel of Nantes, which had set forth from the said
Island of Cayana but a fortnight before. This ship gave
him intelligence of the present state and condition,
wherein he might be certain to find the Hollanders at
Cayana. They told him there were three hundred men
in the castle; that all about it they had fixed strong
palisades, or empalements; and that within the castle
were mounted twenty-six pieces of cannon.

Monsieur de Estres, being enabled with this intelligence to take his own measures, proceeded on his voyage,
and arrived at a port of the said island, three leagues
distant from the castle. Here he landed eight hundred

men, whom he divided into two several parties. The one he placed under the conduct of the Count de Blinac, and the other he gave to Monsieur de St. Faucher. On board the fleet he left Monsieur Gabaret, with divers other principal troops, which he thought not fit or necessary to be landed. As soon as the men were set on shore, the fleet weighed anchor, and sailed very slowly towards the castle, while the soldiers marched by land. These could not travel otherwise than by night, by reason of the excessive heat of the sun and intolerable exhalations of the earth, which here is very sulphurous, and consequently no better than a smoky and stinking oven.

On the 19th day of the said month the Count de Estres sent Monsieur de Lesi (who had been Governor of the island, as was said before),demanding of them, to deliver the castle to the obedience of the King, his master, and to him in his sovereign's name. But those who were within resolved not to deliver themselves up, but at the expense of their lives and blood, which answer they sent to Monsieur de Estres. Hereupon the French, the following night, assaulted and stormed the castle on seven several sides thereof all at once. The defendants, having performed their obligation very stoutly, and fought with as much valour as was possible, were as last forced to surrender. Within the castle were found thirty-eight persons dead, besides many others that were wounded. All the prisoners were transported into France, where they were used with great hardship.

Monsieur de Estres, having put all things in good order at the Isle of Cayana, departed thence for that of Martinique. Being arrived at the said island, he was told that the Heer Binkes was at that present at the Island of Tobago, and his fleet lay at anchor in the bay. Having received this intelligence, Monsieur de Estres made no long stay there, but set sail again, steering his course directly for Tobago. No sooner was he come near the island than Vice-Admiral Binkes sent his land-forces, together with a good number of mariners, on shore, to manage and defend the artillery that was there. These forces were commanded by the Captains Van der Graef, Van Dongen and Ciavone, who laboured very hard all that night in raising certain batteries and filling up the palisades, or empalements, of the fortress called Sterreschans.

Two days after, the French fleet came to an anchor in the Bay of Palmit, and immediately, with the help of eighteen boats, they landed all their men. The Heer Binkes, perceiving the French to appear upon the hills, gave orders to burn all the houses that were near the castle, to the intent the French might have no place to shelter themselves thereabouts. On the 23rd day of February, Monsieur de Estres sent a drum over to the Hollanders, to demand the surrender of the fort, which was absolutely denied. In this posture of affairs things continued until the 3rd of March. On this day the French fleet came with full sail, and engaged the Dutch fleet. The Heer Binkes presently encountered them, and the dispute was very hot on both sides. In the meanwhile the land-forces belonging to the French being sheltered by the thickness of the woods, advanced to-wards the castle, and began to storm it very briskly, with more than ordinary force, but were repulsed by the Dutch with such vigor as caused them after three distinct attacks to retire, with the loss of above one hundred and fifty men, and two hundred wounded. These they carried off, or rather dragged away, with no small difficulty, by reason of their disorderly retreat.

All this while the two fleets continued the combat, and fought very desperately, until on both sides some ships were consumed between Vulcan and Neptune. Of this number was Monsieur de Estres' own ship, mounted with twenty-seven guns of prodigious bigness, besides other pieces of lesser port. The battle continued from break of day until the evening. A little before which time, Monsieur de Estres quitted the bay with the rest of his ships, unto the Hollanders, excepting only two, which were stranded under sail, as having gone too high within the port. Finally, the victory remained on the side of the Hollanders, howbeit with the loss of several of their ships that were burnt.

Monsieur de Estres finding himself under the shame of the loss of this victory, and that he could expect no advantage for that present, over the Island of Tobago, set sail from those quarters the 18th day of March, and arrived the 21st day of June next following at the port of Brest in France. Having given an account of these transactions to his most Christian Majesty, he was pleased to command him to undertake again the enterprize of Tobago. To this effect, he gave orders for eight great men-of-war to be equipped with all speed, together with eight others of smaller account : with all which vessels he sent again Monsieur de Estres into America the same year. He set sail from the said port of Brest on the 3rd day of October following, and arrived the 1st of December at the Island of Barbados. Afterwards, having received some recruits from the Isle of Martinique, he sent beforehand to review the Island of Tobago, and consider the condition thereof. This being done, he weighed anchor and set sail directly for the said island, where he arrived the 7th day of the said month of December with all his fleet.

Immediately after his arrival he landed five hundred men, under the conduct of Monsieur de Blinac, Governor of the French islands in America. These were followed soon after by one thousand more. The 9th day of the said month they approached within six hundred paces of a certain post called Le Cort, where they landed all the artillery designed for this enterprize. On the 10th day Monsieur de Estres went in person to take a view of the castle, and demanded of the Heer Binkes, by a messenger, the surrender thereof, which was generously denied. The next day the French began to advance towards the castle, and on the 12th of the said month, the Dutch from within began to fire at them with great perseverance. The French made a beginning to their attack by casting fire-balls into the castle with main violence. The very third ball that was cast in happened to fall in the path-way that led to the store-house, where the powder and ammunition was kept, belonging to the castle. In this path was much powder scattered up and down, through the negligence of those that carried it to and fro for the necessary supplies of the defendants. By this means the powder took fire in the path, and thence ran in a moment as far as the store-house above mentioned, so that suddenly both the store-house was blown up, and with it Vice-Admiral Binkes himself, then Governor of the island, and all his officers. Only Captain Van Dongen remained alive. This mischance being perceived by the French, they instantly ran with five hundred men, and possessed themselves of the castle. Here they found three hundred men alive, whom they took prisoners, and transported into France. Monsieur de Estres after this commanded the castle to be demolished, together with other posts that might serve for any defence, as also all the houses standing upon the island. This being done, he departed thence the 27th day of the said month of December, and arrived again in France, after a prosperous voyage.

PART IV.

Containing the dangerous voyage and bold assaults
of Captain Bartholomew Sharp and others,
performed in the South Sea, for
the space of two years, etc.

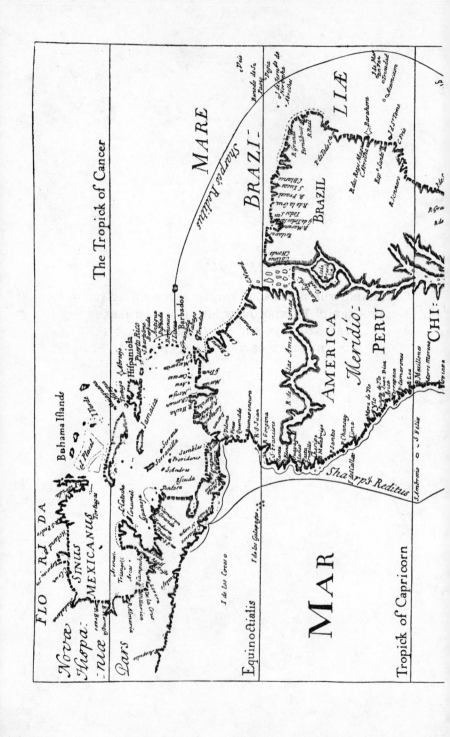

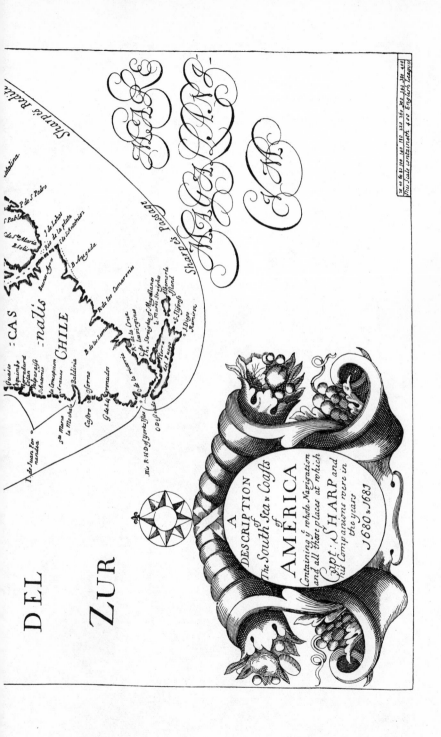

THE BUCCANEERS OF AMERICA.

PART IV.

CHAPTER I.

Captain Coxon, Sawkins, Sharp and others set forth in a fleet towards the province of Darien, upon the continent of America. Their designs to pillage and plunder in those parts. Number of their ships, and strength of their forces by sea and land.

AT a place called Boca del Toro was the general rendezvous of the fleet, which lately had taken and sacked Porto Bello the second time; that rich place having been taken once before, under the conduct of Sir Henry Morgan, as is related above. At this place also were two other vessels; the one belonging to Captain Peter Harris, and the other to Captain Richard Sawkins; both Englishmen and privateers. Here therefore a report was made to the fleet of a peace concluded between the Spaniards and the Indians of the land of Darien, who for the most part wage incessant wars against one another. Also, that since the conclusion of the said peace, they had been already tried, and found very faithful to Captain Bournano, a French commander, in an attempt on a certain place called Chepo, near the South Sea. Further, that the Indians had promised to conduct him to a great and very rich place, named Toca-mora: upon which he had likewise promised them to return in three months time with more ships and men. Hereupon we all agreed to go and visit the said place, and thus dispersed ourselves into several coves (by the Spaniards called *cúèvas*, or hollow creeks under the coasts), there to careen and fit our vessels for that purpose. In this place, Boca del Toro, we found plenty of fat tortoises, the pleasantest meat in the world. When we had refitted our vessels, we met at an island, called by us the Water-key; and this was then our strength, as follows :

	Tons	Guns	Men
Captain Coxon in a ship of .	80	8	97
Captain Harris . . .	150	25	107
Captain Bournano . .	90	6	86
Captain Sawkins . . .	16	1	35
Captain Sharp . . .	25	2	40
Captain Cook . . .	35	0	43
Captain Alleston . . .	18	0	24
Captain Row . . .	20	0	25
Captain Macket . . .	14	0	20

We sailed thence March 23rd, 1679, and in our way touched at the islands called Samballas. These are certain islands reaching eight leagues in extent, and lying fourteen leagues westward of the river of Darien. Being here at anchor, many of the Indians, both men and women, came to see us. Some brought plantains, others other fruits and venison, to exchange with us for beads, needles, knives, or any trifling bauble whereof they stand in need. But what they most chiefly covet are axes and hatchets to fell timber with. The men here go almost naked. They wear as an ornament in their noses a golden or silver plate, in shape like a half-moon, which, when they drink they hold up with one hand, while they lift the cup with the other. They paint themselves sometimes with streaks of black ; as the women do in like manner with red. These have in their noses a pretty thick ring of gold or silver ; and for cloth-

ing they cover themselves with a blanket. They are
generally well-featured women : among them I saw
several fairer than the fairest of Europe, with hair like
the finest flax. Of these it is reported, they can see far
better in the dark than in the light.

These Indians misliked our design for Tocamora, and
dissuaded us from it, asserting it would prove too tedious
a march, and the way so mountainous, and uninhabited
that it would be extremely difficult to get provisions for
our men. Withal they proffered to guide us, undescried,
within a few leagues of the city of Panama, in case we
were pleased to go thither ; where we could not choose
but ourselves know we should not fail of making a good
voyage. Upon these and other reasons which they gave
us, we concluded to desist from the journey of Tocamora,
and to proceed to Panama. Having taken these resolutions, Captain Bournano and Captain Row's vessels
separated from us, as being all French, and not willing
to go to Panama, they declaring themselves generally
against a long march by land. Thus we left them at
the Samballas. Thence an Indian captain or chief commander, named Andrœas, conducted us to another island,
called by the English the Golden Island, situated somewhat to the westward of the mouth of the great river of
Darien. At this island we met, being in all seven sail,
on April 3rd, 1680.

Here at the Golden Island, the Indians gave us notice
of a town called Santa Maria, situated on a great river,
which bears the same name, and which runs into the
South Sea by the Gulf of San Miguèl. In the town was
kept a garrison of four hundred soldiers ; and from this
place much gold was carried to Panama, which was
gathered from the mountains thereabouts. In case we
should not find sufficient booty there, we might thence
proceed by sea to Panama, where we could not easily fail
of our designs. This motion of the Indians we liked so
well, that we landed three hundred and thirty-one men,

on April 5th, 1680, leaving Captains Alleston and Macket with a party of seamen to guard our ships in our absence with which we intended to return home.

The men that were landed had each of them three or four cakes of bread (called by the English dough-boys) for their provision of victuals; and for drink, the rivers afforded enough. At the time of our landing Captain Sharp was very faint and weak, having had a great fit of sickness lately, from which he had scarcely recovered. Our several companies that marched were distinguished as follows. First, Captain Bartholomew Sharp with his company had a red flag, with a bunch of white and green ribbons. The second division led by Captain Richard Sawkins, with his men had a red flag striped with yellow. The third and fourth, led by Captain Peter Harris, had two green flags, his company being divided into two several divisions. The fifth and sixth, led by Captain John Coxon, who had some of Alleston's and Mackett's men joined to his, made two divisions or companies, and had each of them a red flag. The seventh was led by Captain Edmund Cook with red colours striped with yellow, with a hand and sword for his device. All or most of them, were armed with fuzee, pistol and hanger.

CHAPTER II.

They march towards the town of Santa Maria with design to take it. The Indian King of Darien meets them by the way. Difficulties of this march, with other occurrences till they arrive at the place.

BEING landed on the coast of Darien, and divided into companies, as was mentioned in the preceding chapter, we began our march towards Santa Maria, the Indians serving us for guides in that unknown country. Thus we marched at first through a small skirt of a wood, and then over a bay almost a league in length. After that, we went two leagues directly up a woody valley, where we saw here and there an old plantation, and had a very good path to march in. There we came to the side of a river, which in most places was dry, and built us houses, or rather huts, to lodge in.

To this place came to us another Indian, who was a chief commander and a man of great parts, named Captain Antonio. This Indian officer encouraged us very much to undertake the journey to Santa Maria, and promised to be our leader, saying he would go along with us now, but that his child lay very sick. However, he was assured it would die by the next day, and then he would most certainly follow and overtake us. Withal, he desired we would not lie in the grass for fear of monstrous adders, which are very frequent in those places. Breaking some of the stones that lay in the river, we found them shine with sparks of gold. These stones are driven down from the neighbouring mountains

in time of floods. This day four of our men tired, and
returned to the ships. So we remained in all 327 men,
with six Indians to conduct us. That night some
showers of rain fell.

The next day of our march we mounted a very steep
hill, and on the other side at the foot thereof we rested
on the bank of a river, which Captain Andrœas told us
ran into the South Sea, being the same river on which
the town of Santa Maria was situated. Hence we continued our march until noon, and then ascended another
mountain very much higher than the former. Here we
ran much danger oftentimes and in many places, the
mountain being so perpendicular, and the path so narrow,
that but one man at a time could pass. We arrived by
the dark of the evening to the other side of the mountain, and lodged again by the side of the same river,
having marched that day, according to our reckoning,
about eighteen miles. This night likewise some rain
fell.

The next morning being April 7th, we marched all
along the river aforementioned, crossing it often, almost
at every half-mile, sometimes up to the knees and at
other times up to the middle, in a very swift current.
About noon we came to a place where we found some
Indian houses. These were very large and neat: the
sides were built with cabbage-trees, and the roofs of
wild canes, thatched with palmetto royal, but far neater
than ours at Jamaica. They had many divisions into
rooms, though no ascent by stairs into chambers. At
this place were four of these houses together, that is,
within a stone's throw one of another, each of them having a large plantain walk before it. At the distance of
half a mile from this place lived the king or chief captain
of these Indians of Darien, who came to visit us in royal
robes, with his queen and family. His crown was made
of small white reeds, which were curiously woven, having
no other top than its lining, which was of red silk.

Round about the middle of it was a thin plate of gold, more than two inches broad, laced behind ; whence did stick two or three ostrich feathers. About this plate went also a row of golden beads, which were bigger than ordinary peas ; underneath which the red lining of the crown was seen. In his nose he wore a large plate of gold in the form of a half moon, and in each ear a great golden ring, nearly four inches in diameter, with a round thin plate of gold of the same breadth, having a small hole in the centre, by which it hung to the ring. He was covered with a thin white cotton robe, reaching to the small of his legs, and round its bottom a fringe of the same, three inches deep. So that by the length of this robe, our sight was impeded, that we could see no higher than his naked ankles. In his hand he had a long bright lance, as sharp as any knife. With him he had three sons, each of them having a white robe, and their lances in their hands, but standing bare-headed before him ; as also were eight or nine persons more of his retinue, or guard. His queen wore a red blanket, which was closely girt about her waist, and another that came loosely over her head and shoulders, like our old-fashioned striped hangings. She had a young child in her arms, and two daughters walked by her, both marriageable, with their faces almost covered with stripes or streaks of red, and almost laden about their neck and arms with small beads of several colours. These Indian women of the province of Darien, are generally very free, airy and brisk ; yet withal very modest, and cautious in their husbands' presence, of whose jealousy they stand in fear. With these Indians we made an exchange, or had a truck, as it is called, for knives, pins, needles, or any other such like trifles ; but in our dealing with them we found them to be very cunning. Here we rested ourselves for the space of one day, and withal chose Captain Sawkins to lead the For-lorn, to whom, for that purpose, we gave the choice of fourscore men. The king ordered us each man to have three plantains, with sugar-canes to suck, by way of a present. But when these were consumed, if we could not truck we must have starved, for the king himself did not refuse to deal for his plantains. This sort of fruit is first reduced to mash, then laid between leaves of the same tree, and so used with water ; after which preparation they call it Miscelaw.

On April 9th, we continued our march along the banks of the river abovementioned, finding on our way, here and there a house. The owners of the said houses would most commonly stand at the door, and give, as we passed by, to every one of us, either a ripe plantain, or some sweet cassava-root. Some of them would count us by dropping a grain of corn for each man that passed before them ; for they know no greater number, nor can count no farther than twenty. That night we arrived at three great Indian houses, where we took up our lodgings, the weather being clear and serene all night.

The next day Captain Sharp, Captain Coxon, and Captain Cook, with about threescore and ten of our men, embarked themselves in fourteen canoes upon the river, to glide down the stream. Among this number I also embarked, and we had in our company our Indian Captain Andrœas, of whom mention was made above, and two Indians more in each canoe, to pilot or guide us down the river. But if we had been tired whilst travelling by land before, certainly we were in a worse condition now in our canoes. For at the distance of almost every stone's cast, we were constrained to quit and get out of our boats, and haul them over either sands or rocks, and at other times over trees that lay across and filled up the river so that they hindered our navigation ; yea, several times over the very points of land itself. That very night we built ourselves huts for shelter upon the riverside, and rested our wearied limbs until next morning.

This being come, we prosecuted our journey all day long with the same fatigue and toil, as we had done the day before. At night came a tiger and looked on us for some while, but we did not dare to fire at the animal, fearing we should be descried by the sound of our fuzees ; the Spaniards, as we were told, not being at any great distance from that place.

But the next day, which was April 12th, our pain and labour was rather doubled than diminished; not only for the difficulties of the way, which were intolerable, but chiefly for the absence of our main body of men, from whom we had parted the day before. For now hearing no news of them, we grew extremely jealous of the Indians and their councils, suspecting a design of those people thus to divide our forces, and then by cutting us off, to betray us to the Spaniards our implacable enemies. That night we rested ourselves by building huts, as we had done, and as has been mentioned before.

On Tuesday morning, the next ensuing day, we continued our navigation down the river, and arrived at a beachy point of land, at which place another arm joins the same river. Here as we understood, the Indians of Darien did usually rendezvous, whensoever they drew up in a body, with intention to fight their ancient enemies, the Spaniards. Here also we made a halt, or waited for the rest of our forces and company, the Indians having now sent to seek them, as being themselves not a little concerned at our dissatisfaction and jealousies. In the afternoon our companions came up with us, and were hugely glad to see us, they having been in no less fear for us than we had been at the same time for them. We remained and rested there that night also, with design to fit our arms for action, which now, as we were told, was near at hand.

We departed thence early the next morning, which was the last day of our march, having in all now the number of threescore and eight canoes, wherein were embarked 327 of us Englishmen, and 50 Indians, who served us for guides. To the point abovementioned the Indians had hitherto guided our canoes with long poles or sticks ; but now we made ourselves oars and paddles to row with, thus to make what speed we could. Thus we rowed with all haste imaginable, and upon the river we happened to meet two or three Indian canoes that were laden with plantains. About midnight we arrived and landed at the distance of half a mile, more or less, from the town of Santa Maria, whither our march was all along intended. The place where we landed was deeply muddy, insomuch that we were constrained to lay our paddles on the mud to wade upon, and withal lift ourselves up by the boughs of the trees to support our bodies from sinking. Afterwards we were forced to cut our way through the woods for some space, where we took up our lodgings for that night, for fear of being discovered by the enemy, to whom we were so near.

CHAPTER III.

They take the town of Santa Maria with no loss of men, and but small booty of what they fought for. Description of the place, country and river adjacent. They resolve to go and plunder for the second time the city of Panama.

THE next morning, which was Thursday, April 15th, about break of day, we heard from the town a small arm discharged, and after that a drum beating *à travailler*. With this we were roused from our sleep, and taking up our arms we put ourselves in order and marched towards the town. As soon as we came out of the woods into the open ground, we were descried by the Spaniards, who had received intelligence before-hand of our coming, and were prepared to receive us, having already conveyed away all their treasure of gold, and sent it to Panama. They ran immediately into a large palisaded fort, having each pale or post twelve feet high, and began to fire very briskly at us as we came. But our vanguard ran up to the place, and pulling down two or three of their palisades, entered the fort incontinently, and made themselves masters thereof. In this action not fifty of our men had come up before the fort was taken, and on our side only two were wounded, and not one killed. Notwithstanding within the place were found two hundred and threescore men, besides which number two hundred others were said to be absent, having gone up into the country to the mines to fetch down gold, or rather to convey away what was already in the town. This golden treasure comes down another

branch of this river to Santa Maria, from the neighbouring mountains, where are thought to be the richest mines
of the Indies, or, at least, of all these parts of the western
world. Of the Spaniards we killed in the assault twenty-
six, and wounded to the number of sixteen more. But
their governor, their priest, and all, or most of their chief
men, made their escape by flight.

Having taken the fort, we expected to find here a considerable town belonging to it. But it proved to be
only some wild houses made of cane, the place being
chiefly a garrison designed to keep in subjection the
Indians, who bear a mortal hatred towards, and are often
apt to rebel against, the Spaniards. But bad as the
place was, our fortune was much worse. For we came
only three days too late to meet with three hundred
weight of gold, which was carried thence to Panama in a
bark, that is sent thence twice or thrice every year, to
fetch the gold brought to Santa Maria from the mountains. This river called by the name of the town,
is hereabouts twice as broad as the river Thames at
London, and flows above three score miles upwards,
rising to the height of two fathom and a half at the town
itself. As soon as we had taken the place, the Indians
who belonged to our company, and had served us for
guides, came up to the town. For whilst they heard the
noise of the guns, they were in great consternation, and
dared not approach the palisades, but hid themselves
closely in a small hollow, so that the bullets, while we
were fighting, flew over their heads.

Here we found and redeemed the eldest daughter of
the King of Darien, of whom we made mention above.
She had, as it should seem, been forced away from her
father's house by one of the garrison (which rape had
hugely incensed him against the Spaniards) and was
with child by him. After the fight the Indians destroyed
as many of the Spaniards as we had done in the assault,
by taking them into the adjoining woods, and there

stabbing them to death with their lances. But so soon as we learnt of this barbarous cruelty, we hindered them from taking any more out of the fort, where we confined them every one prisoners. Captain Sawkins, with a small party of ten more, put himself into a canoe, and went down the river, to pursue and stop, if it were possible, those that had escaped, for they were the chief people of the town and garrison. But now, our great expectations of taking a huge booty of gold at this place being totally vanished, we were unwilling to have come so far for nothing, or to go back empty-handed, especially considering what vast riches were to be had at no great distance. Hereupon, we resolved to go to Panama, which place, if we could take, we were assured we should get treasure enough to satisfy our hungry appetite for gold and riches, that city being the receptacle of all the plate, jewels, and gold that is dug out of the mines of all Potosi and Peru. For this purpose therefore, and to please the humours of some of our company, we made choice of Captain Coxon as our general or commander-in-chief. Before our departure, we sent back what small booty we had taken here by some prisoners, under the charge of twelve of our men to convey it to the ships.

Thus we prepared to go forward on that dangerous enterprise of Panama. But the Indians who had conducted us having got from us what knives, scissors, axes, needles and beads they could, would not stay any longer, but all, or the greater part of them, returned to their home. Which notwithstanding, the king himself, Captain Andrœas, Captain Antonio, the king's son, called by the Spaniards Bonete de Oro, or King Golden-cap, as also his kinsman, would not be persuaded by their falling off to leave us, but resolved to go to Panama, out of the desire they had to see that place taken and sacked. Yea, the king promised, if there should be occasion, to join fifty thousand men to our forces. Besides which promises, we had also another very considerable encouragement to undertake this journey. For the Spaniard who had forced away the king's daughter, as was mentioned above, fearing lest we should leave him to the mercy of the Indians, who would have but little on him, having shown themselves so cruel to the rest of his companions, for the safety of his life had promised to lead us, not only into the town, but even to the very bedchamber door of the governor of Panama, and that we should take him by the hand and seize both him and the whole city, before we should be discovered by the Spaniards, either before or after our arrival.

CHAPTER IV.

The Buccaneers leave the town of Santa Maria, and proceed by sea to take Panama. Extreme difficulties, with sundry accidents and dangers of that voyage.

HAVING been in possession of the town of Santa Maria only the space of two days, we departed thence on Saturday, April 17th, 1680. We all embarked in thirty-five canoes, and a periagua, which we had taken here lying at anchor before the town. Thus we sailed or rather rowed down the river in quest of the South Sea, upon which Panama is seated, towards the Gulf of Belona, whereat we were to disembogue into that ocean. Our prisoners, the Spaniards, begged very earnestly that they might be permitted to go with us, and not be left to the mercy of the Indians, who would show them no favour, and whose cruelty they so much feared. But we had much ado to find a sufficient number of boats for ourselves, the Indians that left us having taken with them, either by consent or stealth, so many canoes. Yet notwithstanding this they found soon after either bark logs, or old canoes, and by that means shifted so well for their lives, as to come along with us. Before our departure we burnt both the fort, the church and the town, which was done at the request of the king, he being extremely incensed against it.

Among these canoes it was my misfortune to have one that was very heavy, and consequently sluggish. By this means we were left behind the rest a little way, there being only four men besides myself, that were embarked

therein.   As the tide fell, it left several shoals of sand
naked, and hence, we not knowing of the true channel,
amongst such a variety of streams, happened to steer within a shoal, for above two miles, before we perceived our
error.   Hereupon, we were forced to lay by until high
water came, for to row in such heavy boats against
the tide is totally impossible.   As soon as the tide began
to turn, we rowed away in prosecution of our voyage,
and withal made what haste we could, but all our endeavours were in vain, for we neither could find nor
overtake our companions.   Thus at about ten o'clock
at night, the tide being low, we stuck up an oar in the
river, and slept by turns in our canoe, several showers of
rain falling all the night long, which pierced us to the
skin.

But the next morning, no sooner had day come than
we rowed away down the river as before, in pursuit of our
people.   Having gone about the space of two leagues,
we were so fortunate as to overtake them.   For they had
lain that night at an Indian hut, or *embarcadero*, that is
to say landing place, and had been taking in water till
then.   Being arrived at the place they told us that we
must not omit to fill our jars there with water, otherwise
we should meet with none in the space of six days' time.
Hereupon we went every one of us the distance of a
quarter of a mile from the *embarcadero*, to a little pond,
to fill our water in calabashes, making what haste we
could back to our canoe.   But when we returned, we
found not one of our men, they all being departed and
already got out of sight.   Such is the procedure of these
wild men that they care not in the least whom they lose
of their company, or leave behind.   We were now more
troubled in our minds than before, fearing lest we should
fall into the same misfortune we had so lately overcome.

Hereupon we rowed after them, as fast as we possibly
could, but all in vain.   For here are found such huge
numbers of islands, greater and lesser, as also keys about

the mouth of the river, that it was not difficult for us, who were unacquainted with the river, to lose ourselves a second time amongst them. Yet notwithstanding, though with much trouble and toil, we found at last that mouth of the river, that is called by the Spaniards Boca chica, or the Little Mouth. But as it happened, it was now young flood, and the stream ran very violently against us ; so that though we were not above a stone's cast from the said mouth, and this was within a league broad, yet we could not by any means come near it. Hence we were forced to put ashore, which we did accordingly, until high-water. We hauled our canoe close by the bushes, and when we got out, we fastened our rope to a tree, which the tide had almost covered, for it flows here nearly four fathom deep.

As soon as the tide began to turn, we rowed away from there to an island, distant about a league and a half from the mouth of the river, in the Gulf of San Miguel. Here in the gulf it went very hard with us, whensoever any wave dashed against the sides of our canoe, for it was nearly twenty feet in length, and yet not quite one foot and a half in breadth where it was at the broadest, so that we had only just room enough to sit down in her, and a little water would easily have both filled and overwhelmed us. At the island aforesaid, we took up our resting-place for that night, though it was, from the loss of our company, and the great dangers we were in, the sorrowfullest night that until then, I had ever experienced in my whole life. For it rained impetuously all night long, insomuch that we were wet from head to foot and had not one dry thread about us ; neither, through the violence of the rain, were we able to keep any fire burning wherewith to warm or dry ourselves. The tide ebbs here a good half-mile from the mark of high-water, and leaves bare wonderfully high and sharp-pointed rocks. We passed this heavy and tedious night without one minute of sleep, being all very sorrowful to see ourselves so far and remote from the rest of our companions, as also totally destitute of all human comfort; for a vast sea surrounded us on one side, and the mighty power of our enemies, the Spaniards, on the other. Neither could we descry at any hand the least thing to relieve us, all that we could see being the wide sea, high mountains and rocks; while we ourselves were confined to an egg-shell, instead of a boat, without so much as a few clothes to defend us from the injuries of the weather. For at that time none of us had a shoe to our feet. We searched the whole key to see if we could find any water, but found none.

CHAPTER V.

Shipwreck of Mr. Ringrose, the author of this narrative. He is taken by the Spaniards and miraculously by them preserved. Several other accidents and disasters which befel him after the loss of his companions till he found them again. Description of the Gulf of Vallona.

ON Monday, April 19th, at break of day, we hauled our canoe into the water again, and departing from the island aforementioned : wet and cold as we were, we rowed away towards the Punta de San Lorenzo, or Point St. Lawrence. In our way we met with several islands which lie straggling thereabouts. But now we were again so hard put to it, by the smallness of our vessel, and being in an open sea, that it had become the work of one man, yea sometimes of two, to cast out the water, which came in on all sides of our canoe. After struggling for some time with these difficulties, as we came near one of those islands, a heavy sea overturned our boat, by which means we were all forced to swim for our lives. But we soon got to the shore, and to the same place our canoe came tumbling after us. Our arms were very fast lashed to the inside of the boat, and our locks were as well cased and waxed down as was possible ; so were also our cartouche boxes and powder-horns. But all our bread and fresh water was utterly spoilt and lost.

Our canoe being tumbled on shore by the force of the waves, our first business was to take out and clear our arms. This we had scarcely done, when we saw another canoe fall into the same misfortune at a little distance to leeward of us, amongst a great number of rocks that bounded the island.   The persons that were cast away proved to be six Spaniards of the garrison of Santa Maria, who had found an old canoe, and had followed us to escape the cruelty of the Indians.   They presently came to us, and made us a fire which being done, we got our meat and broiled it on the coals, and all of us ate amicably together.   But we stood in great need of water, or other drink to our victuals, not knowing in the least where to get any.   Our canoe was thrown up by the waves to the edge of the water, and there was no great fear of its splitting, being full six inches in thickness, on the sides thereof.   But that in which the Spaniards came, split itself against the rocks, being old and slender, into an hundred pieces.   Though we were thus shipwrecked and driven ashore, as I have related, yet otherwise, and at other times, is this Gulf of San Miguel a mere mill-pond for smoothness of water.

My company was now altogether for returning, and proceeding no farther, but rather for living amongst the Indians, in case we could not reach the ships we had left behind us in the Northern Sea.   But with much ado I prevailed with them to go forward, at least one day longer, and in case we found not our people the next day, that then I would be willing to do anything which they should think fit.   Thus we spent two or three hours of the day in consulting about our affairs, and withal keeping a man to watch and look out on all sides, for fear of any surprisal by the Indians, or other enemies. About the time that we were come to a conclusion in our debates, our watchman by chance spied an Indian ; who, as soon as he saw us, ran into the woods.   I sent immediately two of my company after him, who overtook him, and found that he was one of our friendly Indians.   Thus he led them to a place not far distant, where seven more of his company were, with a great canoe which they had brought with them.   They came to the place where I was with the rest of my company, and seemed to be glad to meet us on that island. I asked them by signs for the main body of our company, and they gave me to understand, that if we would go with them in their canoe, which was much bigger than ours, we should be up with the party by the next morning. This news, as may easily be supposed, not a little rejoiced our hearts.

Presently after this friendly invitation, they asked who the other six men were, whom they saw in our company, for they easily perceived us not to be all of one and the same coat and *lingua.* We told them they were *Wankers,* which is the name they commonly give to the Spaniards in their own language. Their next question was, if they should kill those Spaniards? but I answered them, No, by no means, I would not consent to have it done. With which answer they seemed to be satisfied for the present. But a little while after, my back being turned, my company thinking that they should thereby oblige the Indians, beckoned to them to kill the Spaniards. With this, the poor creatures perceiving the danger that threatened them, made a sad shriek and outcry, and I came in time to save all their lives. But withal, I was forced to give way and consent that they should have one of them for to make their slave. Hereupon I gave the canoe that I came in to the five Spaniards remaining, and bid them get away and shift for their lives, lest those cruel Indians should not keep their word, and they should run the same danger again they had so lately escaped. Having sent them away whilst I rested myself here, I took a survey of this gulf, and the mouth of the river, which I finished the same day, and do here present to the view of the reader.

But now, thanks be to God, joining company with those Indians, we got into a very large canoe, which for its bigness, was better able to carry twenty men, than our own that we had brought to carry five. The

Indians had also fitted a very good sail to the said
canoe ; so that having now a fresh and strong gale of
wind, we set sail from thence, and made therewith brave
way, to the infinite joy and comfort of our hearts, seeing
ourselves so well accommodated, and so happily rid of the
miseries we but lately had endured.   We had now a

A Description of Laguna
or Gulf of Ballona

smooth and easy passage, after such tedious and labour-
some pains as we had sustained in coming so far since
we left Santa Maria.   Under the point of St. Lawrence,
mentioned above, is a very great rippling of the sea,
occasioned by a strong current which runs hereabouts,
and which often almost filled our boat with its dashes,
as we sailed.   This evening, after our departure from the

island where we were cast away, it rained vehemently
for several hours, and the night proved to be very dark.
About nine o'clock that night we descried two fires on
the shore of the continent, over against us. These
fires were no sooner perceived by the Indians of our
canoe, than they began to shout for joy and cry out,
Captain Antonio, Captain Andrœas, the names of their
Indian captains and leaders ; and to affirm they were
assured those fires were made by their companions.
Hence they made for the shore towards those fires, as
fast as they could drive. But so soon as our canoe came
among the breakers near the shore, there came out
from the woods about threescore Spaniards with clubs
and other arms, and laying hold of our canoe on both
sides thereof, hauled it out of the water quite dry. So
that by this means we were all suddenly taken and made
their prisoners. I laid hold of my gun, thinking to
make some defence for myself, but all was in vain, for
they suddenly seized me between four or five of them
and hindered me from action. Meanwhile our Indians
leaped overboard, and got away very nimbly into the
woods ; my companions standing amazed at what had
happened, and the manner of our surprisal. I asked
them presently if any of them could speak either French
or English ; but they answered, No. Hereupon as well
as I could, I discoursed to some of them, who were more
intelligent than the rest, in Latin, and by degrees came
to understand their condition. These were Spaniards
who had been turned ashore here by our English party,
who left them upon this coast, lest by carrying them
nearer to Panama any of them should make their escape
and discover our march towards that city. They had me
presently after I was taken into a small hut which they
had built, covered with boughs, and made there great
shouts for joy, because they had taken us, designing in
their minds to use us very severely for coming into those
parts, and especially for taking and plundering their town

of Santa Maria. But while the captain of those Spaniards was examining me, in came the poor Spaniard that was come along with us, and reported how kind I had been to him, and the rest of his companions, by saving their lives from the cruelty of the Indians.

The captain having heard him, arose from his seat immediately and embraced me, saying, that we Englishmen were very friendly enemies, and good people, but that the Indians were very rogues, and a treacherous nation. Withal, he desired me to sit down by him, and to eat part of such victuals as our companions had left them when they were turned ashore. Then he told me, that for the kindness I had showed to his countrymen, he gave us all our lives and liberties, which otherwise he would certainly have taken from us. And though he could scarcely be persuaded in his mind to spare the Indians' lives, yet for my sake he pardoned them all, and I should have them with me in case I could find them. Thus he bid me likewise take my canoe, and go in God's name, saying withal, he wished us as fortunate as we were generous. Hereupon I took my leave of him, after some little stay, though he invited me to tarry all night with him. I searched out, and at last found my Indians, who for fear had hid themselves in the bushes adjoining to the neighbouring woods where they lay concealed. Having found them, the captain led me very civilly down to the canoe, and bidding my companions and the Indians get in after me; as they at first hauled us ashore, so now again they pushed us off to sea, by a sudden and strange vicissitude of fortune. All that night it rained very hard, as was mentioned above; neither durst we put ashore any more at any place, it being all along such, as by mariners is commonly called an iron coast.

The next morning being come, we sailed, and paddled, or rowed, till about ten o'clock. At which time we espied a canoe making towards us with all speed imaginable.

Being come up with us, and in view, it proved to be of our own English Company, who mistaking our canoe for a Spanish periagua, was coming in all haste to attack us. We were infinitely glad to meet them, and they presently conducted us to the rest of our company, who were at that instant coming from a deep bay which lay behind a high point of rocks, where they had lain at anchor all that night and morning. We were all mutually rejoiced to see one another again, they having given both me and my companions up for lost.

CHAPTER VI.

The Buccaneers prosecute their voyage, till they come within sight of Panama. They take several barks and prisoners by the way. Are descried by the Spaniards before their arrival. They order the Indians to kill the prisoners.

FROM the place where we rejoined our English forces, we all made our way towards a high hummock of land, as it appeared at a distance, but was nothing else than an island seven leagues distant from the bay afore-mentioned. On the highest part of this island the Spaniards keep a watch or look-out (for so it is termed by the seamen) for fear of pirates or other enemies. That evening we arrived at the island, and being landed, went up a very steep place, till we came to a little hut where the watchman lodged. We took by surprisal the old man who watched in the place, but happened not to see us, till we were got into his plantain walk before the lodge. He told us in his examination, that we were not as yet descried by the Spaniards of Panama or any others that he knew, which relation of the old fellow much encouraged us to go forwards with our design of surprising that rich city. This place, if I took its name rightly, is called Farol de Plantanos, or in English, Plantain-watch.

Here, not long before it was dark that evening, a certain bark came to an anchor at the outward side of the island, which instantly was descried by us. Hereupon we speedily manned out two canoes, who went under the shore and surprised the said boat. Having examined the persons that were on board, we found she had been absent the space of eight days from Panama, and had landed soldiers at a point of land not far distant from this island, with intention to fight and curb certain Indians and negroes, who had done much hurt in the country thereabouts. The bark being taken, most of our men endeavoured to get into her, but more especially those who had the lesser canoes. Thus there embarked thereon to the number of one hundred and thirty-seven of our company, together with that sea-artist, and valiant commander, Captain Bartholomew Sharp. With him went also on board Captain Cook, whom we mentioned at the beginning of this history. The remaining part of that night we lay at the quay of the said island, expecting to prosecute our voyage the next day.

Morning being come, I changed my canoe and embarked myself on another, which, though it was something lesser than the former, yet was furnished with better company. Departing from the island, we rowed all day long over shoal water, at the distance of about a league from land, having sometimes not above four foot water, and white ground. In the afternoon we descried a bark at sea, and instantly gave her chase. But the canoe wherein was Captain Harris happened to come up the first with her, who after a sharp dispute took her. Being taken, we put on board the said bark thirty men. But the wind would not suffer the other bark, in chasing, to come up with us. This pursuit of the vessel did so far hinder us in our voyage, and divide us asunder, that night soon coming on, we lost one another, and could no longer keep in a body together. Hereupon we laid our canoe ashore, to take up our rest for that night at the distance of two miles, more or less, from high-water mark, and about four leagues to leeward of the island of Chepillo, to which place our course was then directed.

The next morning, as soon as the water began to float us, we rowed away for the fore-mentioned island Chepillo, where by assignation our general rendezvous

was to be. On our way as we went, we spied another
bark under sail, as we had done the day before. Captain
Coxon's canoe was now the first that came up with this
vessel. But a young breeze freshening at that instant,
she got away from him after the first onset, killing in the
said canoe one Mr. Bull, and wounding two others. We
presently conjectured that this bark would get before
us to Panama, and give intelligence of our coming to
those of the town ; all which happened as we had foreseen. It was two o'clock in the afternoon before all
our canoes could come together, and join one another
as it was assigned at Chepillo. We took at that island
fourteen prisoners, between Negros and Mulattos ; also
great store of plantains and good water, together with
two fat hogs. But now believing that ere this we had
been already descried at Panama by the bark afore-mentioned, we resolved among ourselves to waste no time,
but to hasten away from the said island, to the intent we
might at least be able to surprise and take their shipping,
and by that means make ourselves masters of those seas,
in case we could not get the town which now we judged
almost impossible to be done. At Chepillo we took also
a periagua, which we found at anchor before the island,
and presently we put some men on board her. Our stay
here was only of few hours, so that about four o'clock in
the evening, which now was coming on, we rowed away,
designing to reach Panama before the next morning, to
which place we had now only seven leagues to go, it
being no farther distant from Chepillo. But before we
departed from the said island, it was judged convenient
by our commanders, for certain reasons which I could
not dive into, to rid their hands of the prisoners which
we had taken. And hereupon orders were given unto
our Indians, who they knew would perform them very
willingly, to fight, or rather to murder and slay the said
prisoners upon the shore, and that in view of the whole
fleet. This they instantly went about to do, being glad

of this opportunity to revenge their hatred against their enemies, though in cold blood. But the prisoners, although they had no arms wherewith to defend themselves, forced their way through those barbarous Indians, in spite of their lances, bows and arrows, and got into the woods of the island, only one man of them being killed. We rowed all night long, though many showers of rain ceased not to fall.

CHAPTER VII.

They arrive within sight of Panama. Are encountered by three small men-of-war. They fight them with only sixty-eight men, and utterly defeat them, taking two of the said vessels. Description of that bloody fight. They take several ships at the Isle of Perico before Panama.

THE next morning, which was on April 23rd, 1680, that day being dedicated to St. George, our Patron of England, we came before sunrise within view of the city of Panama, which makes a pleasant show to the vessels that are at sea from off the shore. Soon after we saw also the ships belonging to the said city which lay at anchor at an island called Perico, distant only two leagues from Panama. On the aforesaid island are to be seen several storehouses which are built there, to receive the goods delivered out of the ships. At that time there rode at anchor at Perico five great ships, and three pretty big barks, called Barcos de là Armadilla, or little men-of-war; the word *Armadilla* signifying a *Little Fleet*. These had been suddenly manned with design to fight us, and prevent any further attempts we should make upon the city or coasts of those seas. As soon as they spied us, they instantly weighed anchor, and got under sail, coming directly to meet us whom they expected very shortly, according to the intelligence they had received of our coming. Our two periaguas being heavy could not row so fast as we that were in the canoes, and hence we were got pretty far before them. In our five canoes (for so many we were now in company) we had only thirty-six men, in a very unfit condition to fight, being tired with so much rowing, and so few in number, in comparison with the enemy that came against us. They sailed towards us directly before the wind, insomuch that we feared lest they should run us down before it. Hereupon we rowed up into the wind's eye, as the seamen term it, and got close to windward of them. While we were doing this, our lesser periaguas, in which were thirty-two or more of our company, came up with us. So that we were in all sixty-eight[1] men that were engaged in the fight of that day, the king himself, who was in the periagua aforementioned, being one of our number. In the vessel that was admiral of these three small men-of-war, were fourscore and six Biscayners, who have the repute of being the best mariners, and also the best soldiers amongst the Spaniards. These were all volunteers, who came designedly to show their valour, under the command of Don Jacinto de Barahona, who was High Admiral of those seas. In the second were seventy-seven negroes, who were commanded by an old and stout Spaniard, a native of Andalusia in Spain, named Don Francisco de Peralta. In the third and last were sixty-five Mestizos, or Mulattos, or Tawnymores, commanded by Don Diego de Carabaxal. So that in all they made the number of two hundred and twenty-eight men. The commanders had strict orders given them, and their resolution was to give quarter to none of the pirates or buccaneers. But such bloody commands as these seldom or never do happen to prosper.

---

[1] There seems to be some confusion as to the number of buccaneers who took part in this action. Ringrose no doubt states accurately the number of canoes and men engaged, but fails to account for the absence of the greater portion. On April 14th the numbers are precisely stated as three hundred and twenty-seven English and fifty Indians, yet on the 23rd only sixty-eight men are said to have joined in the engagement with the Spaniards. Another account gives the force of the pirates as a little under two hundred. It is evident that Sharp and his company were absent, for they are described as being away in the bark in search of water, rejoining on the 25th.

The canoe of Captain Sawkins, and also that wherein I was, were much to leeward of the rest. So that the ship of Don Diego de Carabaxal came between us two, and fired presently on me to windward, and on him to leeward, wounding with these broadsides, four men in his canoe, and one in that I was in ; but he paid so dear for his passage between us, that he was not very quick in coming about again and making the same way. For we killed with our first volley of shot, several of his men upon the decks. Thus we also got to windward, as the rest were before. At this time the Admiral of the *Armadilla*, or *Little Fleet*, came up with us suddenly, scarce giving us time to charge, and thinking to pass by us all, with as little or less damage as the first of his ships had done. But as it happened it fell out much worse with him, for we were so fortunate as to kill the man at the helm, so that his ship ran into the wind, and her sails lay a-back, as is usually said in marinery. By this means we had time to come all up under his stern, and firing continually into his vessel, we killed as many as came to the helm, besides which slaughter we cut asunder his main sheet and brace with our shot. At this time the third vessel, in which Captain Peralta was, was coming up to the aid of their general. Hereupon Captain Sawkins, who had changed his canoe, and was gone into the periagua, left the Admiral to us four canoes (for his own was quite disabled) and met the said Peralta. Between him and Captain Sawkins the dispute, or fight, was very hot, lying board on board together, and both giving and receiving death unto each other as fast as they could charge. While we were thus engaged, the first ship tacked about, and came up to relieve the Admiral. But we perceiving that, and foreseeing how hard it would go with us if we should be beaten from the Admiral's stern, determined to prevent his design. Hereupon two of our canoes, to wit, Captain Springer's and my own, stood off to meet him. He made up directly towards the Admiral, who stood upon the quarter-deck, waving to him with a handkerchief so to do. But we engaged him so closely, in the middle of his way, that had he not given us the helm, and made away from us, we had certainly been on board him. We killed so many of them, that the vessel had scarce men enough left alive, or unwounded, to carry her off. Yet the wind now blowing fresh, they made shift to get away from us, and hereby saved their lives.

The vessel which was to relieve the Admiral being thus put to flight, we came about again upon the Admiral, and all together gave a loud halloo, which was answered by our men in the periagua, though at a distance from us. At that time we came so close under the stern of the Admiral, that we wedged up the rudder; and withal, killed both the Admiral himself and the chief pilot of his ship, so that now they were almost quite disabled and disheartened likewise, seeing what a bloody massacre we had made among them with our shot. Hereupon, two-thirds of their men being killed, and many others wounded, they cried for quarter, which had several times been offered unto them, and as stoutly denied until then. Captain Coxon entered on board the Admiral, and took with him Captain Harris, who had been shot through both his legs, as he boldly adventured up along the side of the ship. This vessel being thus taken, we put on board her also all the rest of our wounded men, and instantly manned two of our canoes to go and aid Captain Sawkins, who now had been three times beaten from on board by Peralta, such valiant defence had he made. And indeed, to give our enemies their due, no men in the world did ever act more bravely than these Spaniards.

Thus coming up close under Peralta's side, we gave him a full volley of shot, and expected to have the like return from him again, but on a sudden we saw his men blown up, that were abaft the mast ; some of them falling on the deck, and others into the sea. This disaster was no sooner perceived by their valiant Captain Peralta, than he leaped overboard, and in spite of all our shot, got several of them into the ship again, though he was much burnt in both his hands himself. But as one misfortune seldom comes alone, whilst he was recovering these men to reinforce his ship withal, and renew the fight, another jar of powder took fire forward, and blew up several others upon the forecastle. Among this smoke, and under cover thereof, Captain Sawkins laid them on board and took the ship. Soon after they were taken, I went on board Captain Peralta, to see what condition they were in, and indeed such a miserable sight I never saw in my life, for not one man there was found, but was either killed, desperately wounded, or horribly burnt with powder, insomuch, that their black skins were turned white in several places, the powder having torn it from their flesh and bones. Having compassionated their misery, I went afterwards on board the Admiral, to observe likewise the condition of his ship and men. Here I saw what did much astonish me, and will scarcely be believed by others than ourselves who saw it. There were found on board this ship but twenty-five men alive, whose number before the fight had been fourscore and six, as was said above. So that threescore and one, out of so small a number, were destroyed in the battle. But what is more, of these twenty-five men only eight were able to bear arms, all the rest being desperately wounded, and by their wounds totally disabled to make any resistance, or defend themselves. Their blood ran down the decks in whole streams, and scarce one place in the ship was found that was free from blood.

Having possessed ourselves of these two *Armadilla* vessels, or *little men-of-war*, Captain Sawkins asked the prisoners how many men there might be on board the greatest ship that we could see, lying in the harbour of the island of Perico above-mentioned, as also in the others that were something smaller. Captain Peralta hearing these questions, dissuaded him as much as he could from attempting them, saying that in the biggest alone there were three hundred and fifty men, and that he would find the rest too well provided for defence against his small number. But one of his men, who lay a-dying upon the deck, contradicted him as he was speaking, and told Captain Sawkins there was not one man on board any of those ships that were in view; for they had all been taken out of them to fight us in these three vessels called the *Armadilla*, or *Little Fleet*. To this relation we gave credit, as proceeding from a dying man; and steering our course to the island, we went on board them, and found, as he had said, not one person there. The biggest ship of these, which was called *La Santissima Trinidad*, or the *Blessed Trinity*, they had set on fire, made a hole in her, and loosened her foresail, but we quenched the fire with all speed, and stopped the leak. This being done, we put our wounded men on board her, and thus constituted her for the time being our hospital.

Having surveyed our own loss and damages, we found that eighteen of our men had been killed in the fight, and twenty-two were wounded. These three captains against whom we fought, were esteemed by the Spaniards to be the valiantest in all the South Seas. Neither was this reputation undeservedly conferred upon them, as may easily be inferred from the relation we have given of this bloody engagement. As the third ship was running away from the fight, she met with two more that were coming out to their assistance, but gave them so little encouragement that they returned back, and dared not engage us. We began the fight about half an hour after sunrise, and by noon had finished the battle, and quite overcome them. Captain Peralta, while he was our prisoner, would often break out in admiration of our valour, and say, " Surely we Englishmen were the valiantest men in the whole world, who designed always to fight open, whilst all other nations invented all the ways imaginable to barricade themselves, and fight as close as they could." And yet, notwithstanding, we killed more of our enemies than they of us.

Two days after our engagement, we buried Captain Peter Harris, a brave and stout soldier, and a valiant Englishman, born in the county of Kent, whose death we very much lamented. He died of the wounds he received in the battle, and besides him only one man more ; all the rest of our wounded men recovered. Being now come before Panama, I here inquired of Don Francisco de Peralta, our prisoner, many things concerning the state and condition of this city, and the neighbouring country, and he satisfied me in manner following.

CHAPTER VIII.

Description of the state and condition of Panama, and the parts adjacent. What vessels they took while they blocked up the said Port. Captain Coxon with seventy more returns home. Sawkins is chosen in chief.

THE famous city of Panama is situated in the latitude of nine degrees north. It stands in a deep bay, belonging to the South Sea. It is in form round, excepting only that part where it runs along the sea-side. Formerly it stood four miles more to the east, when it was taken by Sir Henry Morgan, as is related in the " History of the Buccaneers." But then being burnt, and three times more since that time by casualty, they removed it to the place where it now stands. Yet notwithstanding, there are some poor people still inhabiting the old town, and the cathedral church is still kept there, the beautiful building whereof makes a fair show at a distance, like that of St. Paul's in London. This new city of which I now speak, is much bigger than the old one, and is built for the most part of brick, the rest being of stone, and tiled. As for the churches belonging thereto, they are not as yet finished. These are eight in number, whereof the chief is called Santa Maria. The extent of the city comprehends better than a mile and a half in length, and above a mile in breadth. The houses for the most part are three stories in height. It is well walled round about, with two gates belonging thereto, excepting only where a creek comes into the city, the which at high-water lets in barks, to furnish the inhabitants with all sorts of provisions and other necessaries.

Here are always three hundred of the King's soldiers to garrison the city; besides which number, their militia, of all colours, are one thousand one hundred. But at the time that we arrived there, most of their soldiers were out of town, insomuch, that our coming put the rest into great consternation, they having had but one night's notice of our being in those seas. Hence we were induced to believe, that had we gone ashore, instead of fighting their ships, we had certainly rendered ourselves masters of the place; especially considering, that all their chief men were on board the Admiral; I mean, such as were undoubtedly the best soldiers. Round about the city, for the space of seven leagues, more or less, all the adjacent country is Savanna, as they call it in the Spanish language, that is to say, plain and level ground, as smooth as a sheet, for this is the signification of the word Savanna. Only here and there is to be seen a small spot of woody land, and everywhere this level ground is full of *vacadas* or *beef stations*,[1] where whole droves of cows and oxen are kept, which serve as well as so many look-outs or watch towers, to descry if an enemy is approaching by land. The ground whereon the city stands, is very damp and moist, which renders the place of bad repute for the concern of health. The water is also very full of worms, and these are much prejudicial to shipping; which is the cause that the King's ships lie always at Lima, the capital city of Peru, unless when they come down to Panama to bring the King's plate, which is only at such times as the fleet of *galleons* comes from Old Spain to fetch and convey it thither. Here in one night after our arrival, we found worms of three-quarters of an inch in length, both in our bed-clothes and other apparel.

At the Island of Perico above-mentioned we seized in all five ships; of these, the first and biggest was named,

---

[1] The word in the text is *stantions*, evidently the Spanish word *estancia*. The Australian term *station* has been substituted.

as was said before, the *Trinidad*, and was a great ship, of the burden of four hundred tons. Her lading consisted of wine, sugar, sweetmeats (whereof the Spaniards in those hot countries make infinite use), skins, and soap. The second ship was of about three hundred tons burden, and not above half laden with bars of iron, which is one of the richest commodities that are brought into the South Sea. This vessel we burnt with the lading in her, because the Spaniards pretended not to want that commodity, and therefore would not redeem it. The third was laden with sugar, being of the burden of one hundred and fourscore tons, more or less. This vessel was given to be under the command of Captain Cook. The fourth was an old ship of sixty tons burden, which was laden with flour of meal. This ship we likewise burnt with her lading ; esteeming both bottom and cargo, at that time, to be useless to us. The fifth was a ship of fifty tons, which, with a periagua, Captain Coxon took along with him when he left us.

Within two or three days after our arrival at Panama, Captain Coxon being much dissatisfied with some reflections which had been made upon him by our company, determined to leave us, and return back to our ships in the Northern Seas, by the same way he came thither. Unto this effect, he persuaded several of our company, who sided most with him, and had had the chief hand in his election, to fall off from us, and bear him company in his journey or march, overland. The main cause of those reflections was his backwardness in the last engagement with the *Armadilla*, concerning which point some sticked not to defame, or brand, him with the note of cowardice. He drew off with him threescore and ten of our men, who all returned back with him in the ship and periagua above-mentioned, towards the mouth of the river of Santa Maria. In his company also went back the Indian King, Captain Antonio, and Don Andrœas, who, being old, desired to be excused from staying any longer with us. However, the King desired we would not be less vigorous in annoying their enemy and ours, the Spaniards, than if he were personally present with us. And to the intent we might see how faithfully he intended to deal with us, he at the same time recommended both his son and nephew to the care of Captain Sawkins, who was now our newly-chosen General or Commander-in-Chief, in the absence of Captain Sharp. The two *Armadilla* ships which we took in the engagement we burnt also, saving no other thing of them both but their rigging and sails. With them also we burnt a small bark, which came into the port laden with fowls and poultry.

On Sunday, which was April 25th, Captain Sharp with his bark and company came in and joined us again. His absence was occasioned by want of water, which forced him to bear up to the King's Islands. Being there, he found a new bark, which he at once took, and burnt his old one. This vessel did sail excellently well. Within a day or two after the arrival of Captain Sharp, came in likewise the people of Captain Harris, who were still absent. These had also taken another bark, and cut down the masts of their old one by the board, and thus without masts or sails turned away the prisoners they had taken in her. The next day we took in like manner another bark, which arrived from Nata, being laden with fowls, as before. In this bark we turned away all the meanest of the prisoners we had on board us.

Having continued before Panama for the space of ten days, being employed in the affairs afore-mentioned, on May 2nd we weighed from the Island of Perico, and stood off to another island, distant two leagues farther from thence, called Tavoga. On this island stands a town which bears the same name, and consists of a hundred houses, more or less. The people of the town had all fled on seeing our vessels arrive. While we were

here, some of our men being drunk on shore, happened
to set fire to one of the houses, the which consumed
twelve houses more before any could get ashore to quench
it. To this island came several Spanish merchants
from Panama, and sold us what commodities we needed,
buying also of us much of the goods we had taken in
their own vessels. They gave us likewise two hundred
pieces of eight for each negro we could spare them, of
such as were our prisoners. From this island we could
easily see all the vessels that went out, or came into the
Port of Panama ; and here we took likewise several barks
that were laden with fowls.

Eight days after our arrival at Tavoga, we took a ship
that was coming from Truxillo, and bound for Panama.
In this vessel we found two thousand jars of wine, fifty
jars of gunpowder, and fifty-one thousand pieces of eight.
This money had been sent from that city, to pay the
soldiers belonging to the garrison of Panama. From the
said prize we had information given us, that there was
another ship coming from Lima with one hundred thousand pieces of eight more ; which ship was to sail ten or
twelve days after them, and which they said could not
be long before she arrived at Panama. Within two
days after this intelligence we took also another ship
laden with flour from Truxillo, belonging to certain
Indians, inhabitants of the same place, or thereabouts.
This prize confirmed what the first had told us of that
rich ship, and said, as the others had done before, that
she would be there in the space of eight or ten days.

Whilst we lay at Tavoga, the president, that is to say,
the Governor of Panama, sent a message by some merchants to us, to know what we came for into those parts.
To this message Captain Sawkins made answer, "That
we came to assist the King of Darien, who was the true
Lord of Panama and all the country thereabouts. And
that since we were come so far, there was no reason but
that we should have some satisfaction. So that if he

pleased to send us five hundred pieces of eight for each man, and one thousand for each commander, and not any farther to annoy the Indians, but suffer them to use their own power and liberty, as became the true and natural lords of the country, that then we would desist from all further hostilities, and go away peaceably; otherwise that we should stay there, and get what we could, causing to them what damage was possible." By the merchants also that went and came to Panama, we understood, there lived then as Bishop of Panama one who had been formerly Bishop of Santa Martha, and who was prisoner to Captain Sawkins, when he took the said place about four or five years past. The Captain having received this intelligence, sent two loaves of sugar to the bishop as a present. On the next day the merchant who carried them, returning to Tavoga, brought to the Captain a gold ring for a retaliation of said present. And withal, he brought a message to Captain Sawkins from the President above-mentioned, to know farther of him, since we were Englishmen, "from whom we had our commission, and to whom he ought to complain for the damages we had already done them?" To this message Captain Sawkins sent back for answer, "That as yet all his company were not come together; but that when they were come up we would come and visit him at Panama, and bring our commissions on the muzzles of our guns, at which time he should read them as plain as the flame of gunpowder could make them."

At this Island of Tavoga, Captain Sawkins would fain have stayed longer, to wait for the rich ship above-mentioned, that was coming from Peru; but our men were so importunate for fresh victuals, that no reason could rule them, nor their own interest persuade them to anything that might conduce to this purpose. Hereupon, on May 15th we weighed anchor, and sailed thence to the Island of Otoque. Being arrived there, we lay by it while our boat went ashore and fetched off fowls and hogs and other things necessary for sustenance. Here at Otoque I finished a draught, from point Garachine, to the bay of Panama, etc. Of this I may dare to affirm, that it is in general more correct and true than any the Spaniards have themselves, for which cause I have here inserted it, for the satisfaction of those that are curious in such things.

From Otoque we sailed to the island of Cayboa, which is a place very famous for the pearl fishery thereabouts, and is at the distance of eight leagues from another place called Puebla Nueva, on the mainland. In our way to this island we lost two of our barks, the one whereof had fifteen men in her, and the other seven. Being arrived, we cast anchor at the said island.

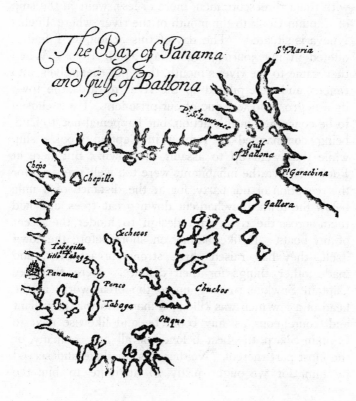

CHAPTER IX.

Captain Sawkins, chief commander of the Buccaneers, is killed before Puebla Nueva. They are repulsed from the said place. Captain Sharp chosen to be their leader. Many more of their company leave them and return home overland.

WHILE we lay at anchor before Cayboa, our two chief commanders, Captain Sawkins and Captain Sharp, taking with them threescore men, more or less, went in the ship of Captain Cook to the mouth of the river where Puebla Nueva is situated. The day of this action, as I find it quoted in my journal, was May 22nd, 1679. When they came to the river's mouth, they put themselves into canoes, and were piloted up the river towards the town by a negro, who was one of our prisoners. I was chosen to be concerned in this action, but happened not to land, being commanded to remain in Captain Cook's ship while they went up to assault the town. But here at Puebla Nueva the inhabitants were too well prepared for the reception of our party, for at the distance of a mile below the town, they had cut down great trees, and laid them across the river, with design to hinder the ascent of any boats. In like manner on shore before the town itself, they had raised three strong breastworks, and made other things for their defence. Here therefore Captain Sawkins running up to the breastworks at the head of a few men was killed ; a man who was as valiant and courageous as any could be, and likewise next to Captain Sharp, the best beloved of all our company, or the most part thereof. Neither was this love undeserved by him, for we ought justly to attribute to him the greatest honour we gained in our engagement before Panama, with the Spanish *Armadilla*, or *Little Fleet*, especially, considering that as has been said above, Captain Sharp was by accident absent at the time of that great and bloody fight.

We that remained behind on board the ship of Captain Cook carried her within the mouth of the river of Puebla Nueva, and entered close by the east shore, which here is crowned with a round hill. Here within two stone's cast of shore, we had four fathom water. Within the point opens a very large and fine river, which falls from a sandy bay, at a small distance from thence. But as we were getting in, being strangers to the place, we unwittingly ran our ship aground, nigh to a rock which lies on the westward shore : for the true channel of the said river is nearer to the east than the west shore. With Captain Sawkins, in the unfortunate assault of this place, there died two men more, and three were wounded in the retreat, which they performed to the canoes in pretty good order. On their way down the river, Captain Sharp took a ship, whose lading consisted of indigo, otto, manteca, or butter, and pitch, and likewise burnt two vessels more, as being of no value. With this he returned on board our ships, much troubled in his mind, and grieved for the loss of so bold and brave a partner in his adventures as Sawkins had constantly shown himself to be. His death was much lamented, and occasioned another party of our men to mutiny, and leave us, returning overland, as Captain Coxon and his company had done before.

Three days after the death of Captain Sawkins, Captain Sharp, who was now Commander-in-Chief, gave the ship which he had taken in the river of Puebla Nueva, which was of the burden of one hundred tons, more or less, to Captain Cook, to command and sail in. Ordering withal that the old vessel which he had, should go with those men that designed to leave us ; their mutiny and our distraction being now grown very high. Hereupon Captain Sharp coming on board La Trinidad, the greatest of our ships, asked our men in full council, who of them were willing to go or stay, and prosecute the design Captain Sawkins had undertaken, which was to remain in the South Sea, and there to make a complete voyage ; after which, he intended to go home round about America, through the Straits of Magellan. He added withal, that he did not as yet fear, or doubt in the least, but to make each man who should stay with him, worth one thousand pounds, by the fruits he hoped to reap of that voyage. All those who had remained after the departure of Captain Coxon, for love of Captain Sawkins, and only to be in his company and under his conduct, thinking thereby to make their fortunes, would stay no longer, but pressed to depart. Among this number I acknowledge myself to have been one, being totally desirous in my mind, to quit those hazardous adventures, and return homewards with those who were now going to leave us. Yet being much afraid and averse to trust myself among wild Indians any farther, I chose rather to stay, though unwilling, and venture on that long and dangerous voyage. Besides which danger of the Indians, I considered that the rains were now already up, and it would be hard passing so many gullies, which of necessity would then be full of water, and consequently create more than one single peril to the undertakers of that journey. Yet notwithstanding, sixty-three men of our company were resolved to encounter all these hardships, and to depart from us. Hereunto they took their leave of us, and returned homewards, taking with them the Indian king's son, and the rest of the Indians for their guides overland.[1] They had, as was said above,

---

[1] There is again much want of precision in reckoning the number of buccaneers who finally stayed with Captain Sharp. Ringrose does not give the figures, but from another account it would appear that one hundred and forty-six in all remained to accompany Sharp in his voyage.

the ship wherein Captain Cook sailed to carry them, and out of our provisions as much as would serve for treble their number.

Thus on the last day of May they departed, leaving us employed about taking in water and cutting down wood at the island of Cayboa afore-mentioned, where this mutiny happened. Here we caught very good tortoises and red deer. We killed also alligators of a very large size, some of them being above twenty feet in length. But we could not find but that they were very fearful of a man, and would fly from us very hastily when we hunted them. This island lies S.S.E. from the mouth of the river above-mentioned. On the south-east side of the island is a shoal or spit of sand, which stretches itself the space of a quarter of a league into the sea. Here therefore, just within this shoal, we anchored in fourteen fathom water. The island on this side thereof makes two great bays, in the first of which we watered, at a certain pond not distant above the cast of a stone from the bay. In this pond, as I was washing myself, and standing under a mançanilla tree, a small shower of rain happened to fall on the tree, and from thence dropped on my skin. These drops caused me to break out all over my body into red spots, of which I was not well for the space of a week after. Here I ate very large oysters, the biggest that ever I ate in my life, insomuch that I was forced to cut them into four pieces, each quarter of them being a good mouthful.

Three days after the departure of the mutineers, Captain Sharp ordered us to burn the ship that they hitherto had sailed in, only out of design to make use of the iron-work belonging to the said vessel. Withal, we put all the flour that was her lading into the last prize, taken in the river of Puebla Nueva, and Captain Cook, as was said before, was ordered to command her. But the men belonging to his company would not sail any longer under his command. Hereupon he quitted his vessel and came on board our Admiral, the great ship above-mentioned, called *La Trinidad*, determining to rule over such unruly company no longer. In his place was put one, whose name was John Cox, an inhabitant of New England, who forced kindred, as was thought, upon Captain Sharp, out of old acquaintance, in this conjuncture of time, only to advance himself. Thus he was made, as it were, Vice-Admiral to Captain Sharp. The next day three of our prisoners, *viz.* an Indian, who was Captain of a ship, and two mulattos, ran away from us, and made their escape.

After this it was thought convenient to send Captain Peralta prisoner in the Admiral, on board the ship of Mr. Cox. This was done to the intent he might not hinder the endeavours of Captain Juan, who was commander of the money-ship we took, as was mentioned at the island of Tavoga. For this man had now promised to do great things for us, by piloting and conducting us to several places of great riches, but more especially to Guayaquil, where he said we might lay down our silver, and lade our vessels with gold. This design was undertaken by Captain Sawkins, and had not the head-strongness of his men brought him to the island of Cayboa, where he lost his life, he had certainly effected it before now. That night we had such thunder and lightning as I never had heard before in all my life. Our prisoners told us that in these parts it very often causes great damages both by sea and land. And my opinion led me to believe that our mainmast received some damage on this occasion. The rainy season being now entered, the wind for the most part was at N.W. though not without some calms.

CHAPTER X.

They depart from the Island of Càyboa to the Isle of Gorgona, where they careen their vessels. Description of this Isle. They resolve to go and plunder Arica, leaving their design of Guayaquil.

HAVING got in all things necessary for navigation, we were now in readiness to depart, on Sunday, June 6th, 1680. That day some rain fell, which now was very frequent in all places. About five o'clock in the evening we set sail from the island of Cayboa, with a small breeze, the wind being at S.S.W. Our course was E.S. by E. and S.E. having all night a very small, or little wind. The same calmness of weather continued all the next day, insomuch, that we lay and drove only as the current horsed us to N.W.

Little better than a calm we had also the third day of our navigation. Meanwhile a current drove us to the westward. About sunrising we descried Quicara, which at that time bore N.W. by W. from us at the distance of five leagues, more or less. With the rising of the sun an easy gale of wind sprung up, so that at noon we had altered our bearing, which was then N. by E. being six leagues distant, and appearing thus, as is underneath demonstrated.

QUICARA.   LAT. 7 DEG. 4°. N.

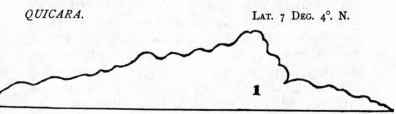

These are two several islands, whereof the least is to the southward of the other. The land is a low table land these islands being more than three leagues in length. About six o'clock that evening, we were nigh ten leagues distant W.S.W. from them. Much like the former weather we had the fourth day of our sailing, with little wind in the forenoon, and rather less than more in the afternoon. I judged about the middle of the day, we were at the distance of twenty leagues S.S.W. from the said islands.

Thursday, June 10th, we had very small and variable winds. This day I reckoned that we had made hitherto a S. by E. way, and a S. by W. from our departure; being driven by a current, according to the observation I made, into lat. 6° 30″.

This day we saw many tortoises floating upon the sea. Hereupon we hoisted out our boat, and came to one of them, who offered not to stir until she was struck, and even then not to sink to the bottom, but rather to swim away. The sea hereabouts is very full of several sorts of fish, as dolphins, bonitos, albicores, mullets, and old wives, etc., which came swimming about our ship in whole shoals. The next day, which was Friday, we had likewise very little wind, which was no more than we had all Thursday night, with some showers of rain. That day we had an observation which was lat. 6° N. In the evening a fresh wind came up at S.W., our course being S.S.E. On Saturday we had in like manner, about seven in the morning, a fresh breeze at S. So we stood W.S.W. with cloudy weather, and several showers of rain. This day our Spanish prisoners informed us we must not expect any settled wind until we came within the latitude of three degrees, for all along the western shore of these seas there is little wind, which is the cause that those ships that go from Acapulco to the islands called de las Philipinas, do coast along the shore of California, until they get into the height of forty-five degrees, yea, sometimes of fifty degrees latitude. As the wind varied, so we tacked several times, thereby to make the best of our way that was possible to the southward.

As our prisoners had informed us, so we found it by experience. For on the next day, which was Sunday, June 13th, we had very little wind, and most commonly none, for the space of twenty-four hours. That day we tried the current of the sea, and found it very strong to the eastward. The same day we had much rain, and in the afternoon a small breeze at W., and W.S.W., but mostly at W. Yet notwithstanding all this calmness of weather, the next day in the morning very early, by a sudden gale of wind which arose, we made shift to split our main top-sail. We had all the night before and that day, continual and incessant showers of rain, and made a S.W. and by S. way; seeing all along as we went a multitude of dolphins, bonitos, and several other sorts of fish floating upon the seas, whereof in the afternoon we caught many, the weather being now changed from stormy to calm again; insomuch that we could fish as we sailed along, or rather as we lay tumbling in the calm.

Tuesday, June 15th, the morning continued calm as the day before; and this day also we saw multitudes of fish of several sorts, whereof we caught some for our table as we were wont to do. By an observation which was made this day, we found ourselves to be now in lat. 4° 21'. At this time the course of our navigation and our whole design, was to go and careen our vessels at the islands commonly called by the Spaniards, de los Galapagos, that is to say, of the Tortoises, being so denominated from the infinite number of those animals swarming and breeding thereabouts. These islands are situated under the equinoctical line, at the distance of a hundred leagues more or less from the main continent of America, in the South Sea. In the afternoon of this day we had a small breeze to push us forwards.

June 16th being Wednesday, we made our way this

day, and for the four and twenty hours last past, E.S.E.
with much rain, which ceased not to fall, as in all this
voyage, since our departure from Cayboa.   This day
likewise we caught several dolphins, and other sorts of
fish, but in the evening we had again a fresh breeze at
S. by W. our course being, as was just now said, E.S.E.

The next day, which was June 17th, about five in the
morning, we descried land, which appeared all along to
be very low, and likewise full of creeks and bays.   We
instantly asked our pilot what land that was before us?
but he replied, he knew it not.   Hereupon, being doubtful of our condition, we called Mr. Cox on board us, who
brought Captain Peralta with him.   This gentleman
being asked, presently told us the land we saw was the
land of Barbacoa, being almost a wild country all over.
Withal, he informed us, that to leeward of us, at the distance of ten leagues, or thereabouts, did lie an island
called by the name of Gorgona, the which island, he said,
the Spaniards did shun, and very seldom come nigh to,
by reason of the incessant and continual rains there falling, scarce one day in the year being dry at that place.
Captain Sharp having heard this information of Captain
Peralta, judged the said island might be the fittest place
for our company to careen at, considering, that if the
Spaniards did not frequent it, we might in all probability lie there undescried, and our enemies the Spaniards,
in the meantime might think, that we were gone out of
those seas.   At this time it was, that I seriously repented
my staying in the South Seas, and that I did not return
homewards in company of them that went before us.
For I knew, and could easily perceive, that by these
delays the Spaniards would gain time and be able to send
advice of our coming to every port all along the coast,
so that we should be prevented in all, or most of our
attempts and designs wheresoever we came.   But those
of our company, who had got money by the former prizes
of this voyage, over swayed the others who had lost all

their booty at gaming. Thus we bore away for the island aforesaid of Gorgona, and at the distance of six leagues and a half, at S.W.I. observed it to make the appearance following.

GORGONA. LAT. I. 0°. N.

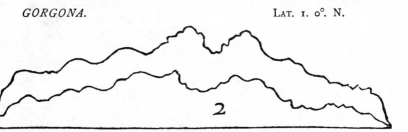

2

On the mainland over against this island of Gorgona, we were told by our prisoners, that up a great laguna, or lake, is seated an Indian town, where they have great quantity of sand grains of gold. Moreover, that five days' journey up a river, belonging to the said laguna, do dwell four Spanish superintendents, who have each of them the charge of overseeing fifty or sixty Indians, who are employed in gathering that gold which slips from the chief collectors, or finders thereof. These are at least threescore and ten, or fourscore Spaniards, with a great number of slaves belonging to them, who dwell higher up than these four superintendents, at a distance of twenty-five or thirty days' journey on the said river. That once every year, at a certain season, there comes a vessel from Lima, the capital city of Peru, to fetch the gold that here is gathered, and to bring to these people such necessaries as they want. By land it is nothing less than six weeks travel from thence to Lima.

The mainland to windward of this island is very low, and full of rivers. All along the coast it rains most desperately. The island is only four leagues distant from the continent. While we lay at it, I took the whole circumference thereof, which is according to what is here underneath described.

Captain Sharp gave to this island the name of Sharp's Isle, by reason we careened at this place. We anchored on the south side of the island, at the mouth of a very fine river, which there disgorges itself into the sea. There belong to this island about thirty rivers and rivulets, which all fall from the rocks on the several sides of the island. The whole circumference thereof is about three leagues and a half, being all high and mountainous land, excepting only on that side where we cast anchor. Here therefore we moored our ship in the depth of eighteen or twenty fathom water, and begun to unrig the vessel. But we were four or five days space before we could get our sails dry, so as to be able to take them from the yards, there falling a shower of rain almost every hour of the day and night. The mainland to the east of the island, and so stretching northward, is extremely high and towering, and perpetually clouded, excepting only at the rising of the sun, at which time the tops of those hills are clear. From the south side of this island where we anchored, as was said above, we could see the lowland of the main, at least a point thereof which lies nearest to the island. The appearance it makes, is as it were of trees growing out of the water.

Friday, July 2nd, as we were heaving down our ship, our mainmast happened to crack. Hereupon our carpenters were constrained to cut out large fishes, and fish it, as the usual terms of that art do name the thing.

On the next day after the mischance of our mainmast, we killed a snake which had fourteen inches in circumference, and eleven feet in length. About the distance of a league from this island runs a ledge of rocks, over which the water continually breaks; the ledge being about two miles, more or less in length. Had we anchored but half a mile more northerly, we had ridden in much smoother water; for here where we were, the wind came in upon us in violent gusts. While we were there, from June 30th to July 3rd, we had dry weather, which was esteemed as a rarity by the Spaniards, our prisoners. And every day we saw whales and grampuses, who would often come and drive under our ship. We fired at them several times, but our bullets rebounded from their bodies. Our choice and best provisions here, were Indian conies, monkeys, snakes, oysters, conchs, periwinkles, and a few small turtle, with some other sorts of good fish. Here in like manner we caught a sloth, a beast well deserving that name, given it by the Spaniards, by whom it is called *pereza*, from the Latin word *pigritia*.

At this island died Josephe Gabriel, a Spaniard, born in Chili, who was to have been our pilot to Panama. He was the same man who had stolen and married the Indian king's daughter, as was mentioned above. He had all along been very true and faithful to us, in discovering several plots and conspiracies among our prisoners, either to get away or destroy us. His death was occasioned by a calenture, or malignant fever, which killed him after three days' sickness, having lain two days senseless. During the time of our stay at this island, we lengthened our topsails, and got up topgallant masts ; we made two staysails, and refitted our ship very well. But we wanted provisions extremely, as having nothing considerable of any sort, but flour and water. Being almost ready to depart, Captain Sharp, our commander, gave us to understand he had changed his resolution concerning the design of going to Guayaquil, for he thought it would be in vain to go thither considering that in all this time we must of necessity have been descried before now. Yet notwithstanding he himself before had persuaded us to stay. Being very doubtful among ourselves what course we should take, a certain old man, who had long time sailed among the Spaniards, told us he could carry us to a place called Arica, to which town, he said, all the plate was brought down from Potosi, Chiquisaca, and several other places within the land, where it was dug out of the mountains and mines, and that he doubted not, but that we might get there of purchase at least two thousand pounds every man. For all the plate of the South Sea lay there, as it were, in store, being deposited at the said place until such time as the ships did fetch it away. Being moved with these reasons, and having deliberated thereupon, we resolved in the end to go to the said place. At this island of Gorgona aforementioned, we likewise took down our round-house coach, and all the high carved work belonging to the stern of the ship, for when we took her from the Spaniards before Panama, she was high as any third-rate ship in England.

CHAPTER XI.

The Buccaneers depart from the Isle of Gorgona, with design to plunder Arica. They lose one another by the way. They touch at the Isle of Plate, or Drake's Isle, where they meet again. Description of this Isle. Some memoirs of Sir Francis Drake. An acconnt of this voyage, and the coasts all along. They sail as far in a fortnight, as the Spaniards usually do in three months.

ON Sunday, July 25th, in the afternoon, all things being now in readiness for our departure, we set sail, and stood away from the island of Gorgona, or Sharp's Isle, with a small breeze which served us at N.W. But as the sun went down that day, so our breeze died away by degrees. Yet already we could begin to experiment, that our ship sailed much better, since the taking down of her round house, and the other alterations which we made in her.

The next day about two o'clock in the morning we had a land breeze to help us, which lasted for the space of six hours, more or less. So that at noon we found ourselves to be five leagues and a half distant to the south west from Gorgona. This day the Spaniards, our prisoners, told us, in common discourse, that in most part of this lowland coast they find threescore fathom water. In the afternoon we had a very strong land breeze : meanwhile we continued making short trips off and in. That night we had much rain for the greatest part of the night, which occasioned the next morning, being the third day of our navigation, to be very cloudy until ten o'clock. About that hour it cleared up, and then we saw the island of Gorgona at E.N.E. being distant about twelve leagues more or less from us. We had the wind all this day at S.W. where it continued, seldom varying above two points of the compass to the westwards. Night being come, about two o'clock, Captain Sharp ordered me to speak to Captain Cox, and bid him go about and stand off from the shore, for he feared less Cox should come too nigh to it. But he replied, he knew well that he might stand in until two o'clock. The next day very early in the morning, we saw him not, the morning being cloudy and stark calm. Yet notwithstanding at eight o'clock it cleared up, and neither then could we see him. Hence we concluded, and so it proved, that we had lost him in the obscurity of the night, through his obstinacy in standing in too long, and not coming about when we spoke to him. Thus our Admiral's ship was left alone, and we had not the company of Captain Cox any longer in this voyage, till we arrived at the Isle of Plate, where we had the good fortune to find him again, as shall be mentioned hereafter. The weather being clear this morning, we could see Gorgona, at a distance of at least fifteen or sixteen leagues to the E.N.E. All this day it continued calm, till about four in the afternoon, at which time we had a W.S.W. wind, which continued to blow all that night

Thursday, July 29th, 1679. This day the wind continued pretty fresh all day long. About four in the afternoon we came within sight of the island del Gallo, which I guessed to be nigh twenty-eight leagues distant from that of Gorgona, the place of our departure S.W. It is about nine leagues distant E. from the main. So that the island with the mainland S.W. from it appears thus.

GALLO.   Lat. 2. 12. N.

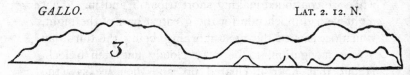

All this day the weather continued clear, and the wind W.S.W.

The next day, July 30th, the wind blew very fresh
and brisk; insomuch, that we were in some fear for
the heads of our low masts, being very sensible that
they were but weak. About three or four in the afternoon, we saw another island, six or seven leagues distant from Gallo, called Gorgonilla. At E. by S. from
us it made the appearance which I have here adjoined.
All the mainland hereabouts lies very low and flat, and
is in very many places overflowed and drowned every
high-water.

GORGONILLA.

On Saturday July 31st in the morning, the island del
Gallo, at E.N.E. being distant about eight leagues, gave
us this appearance.

GALLO, Another Prospect thereof.

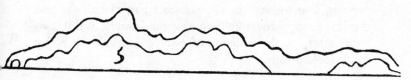

The point of Mangroves is a low and level point, running out S.S.W. This day, and the night before it, we
lost by our computation three leagues of our way, which
I believe happened because we stood out too far from
the land, having stood off all night long.

August 1st, which was Sunday, we had a very fresh
wind at W.S.W. This was joined also with several
small showers of rain which fell that day. In the meanwhile we got pretty well to windward with it, by making
small trips to and fro, which we performed most commonly, by standing in three glasses, and as many out.

The next day, August 2nd, in the morning, we came up into the highland of Santiago, where begins the highland of this coast. We kept at the distance of ten leagues from it, making continual short trips, as was mentioned before. The next day likewise we continued to do the same. But the weather was cloudy, and for the most part full of rain.

Wednesday, August 4th, we continued still turning in the wind's eye, as we had done for two days before. This day in the afternoon we discovered three hills at E.N.E. of our ship. These hills make the land of San Matteo, which gives this following appearance:

SAN MATTEO.

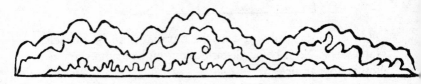

All the coast along hereabouts is highland. That evening also we saw the cape of San Francisco. At first this cape appeared like two several islands. But two hours after, at the distance of twelve leagues, at S. by W. it looked thus.

CAPE OF SAN FRANCISCO.

Thursday, August 5th, we being then about the cape, it looked very like to Beachy Head in England. It is full of white cliffs on all sides. The land turns off here to E. of S., and makes a large and deep bay, the circumference whereof is full of pleasant hills. In the bight of the bay are two high and rocky islands, which represent exactly two ships with their sails full. We were now come out of the rainy countries, into a pleasant and fair region, where we had for the most part a clear sky, and dry weather. Only now and then we could here find a small mist, which soon would vanish away. In the meanwhile, every night a great dew used to fall, which supplied the defect of rain.

The two next days following, we continued plying to windward with fair weather, nothing else remarkable happening in them which might deserve any notice to be taken thereof.

On Sunday, August 8th, we came close under a wild and mountainous country. This day likewise we saw Cape Passao, at the distance of ten leagues more or less to windward of us. Ever since we came on this side Mangrove point, we had observed a windward current did run all along as we sailed. Under shore the land is full of white cliffs and groves, lower towards the pitch of the cape.

The next day we had both a fair day and a fresh wind to help us on our voyage. We observed that Cape Passao makes three points, between which are two bays. The leeward-most of the two, is of the length of three leagues, and the other of four. Adjoining to the bays is seen a pleasant valley. Our prisoners informed us, that northward of these capes live certain Indians, who sell maize, and other provisions to any ships that happen to come in there. The Cape itself is a continuous cliff, covered with several sorts of shrubs and low bushes. Under these cliffs lies a sandy bay of the depth of forty feet. The Spaniards say, that the wind is always here between the S.S.W. and W.S.W. The cape represents with much likeliness the brow of an alligator or cayman. At S. Cape Passao appears thus:

CAPE PASSAO. LAT. I. 30. S.

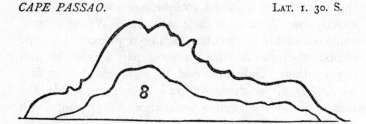

Tuesday, August 10th. This morning the sky was so thick and hazy, that we could not see the highland ; though it were just before us, and not altogether two leagues distant from us. But as soon as it cleared up, we stood in towards the land, until we came within a mile of the shore. Here having sounded, we found seven fathom and a half of water, under which was a light and clayey ground. The coast all along is very mountainous, and likewise full of high and towering cliffs. When we sounded, the tide was almost at low-water. Here it ebbs and flows nearly four fathom perpendicular. From this cape the land runs along S.E. for the space of three or four leagues, with huge highland cliffs, like those of Calais over against England. Being past this cape, the highland S. from us is Cape St. Lawrence.

August 11th, we found ourselves N.N.W. from Monte de Christo, a very high and round hill. Thence to windward is seen a very pleasant country, with spots here and there of woody land ; which causes the country all over, to look like so many enclosures of ripe cornfields. To leeward of the said hill, the land is all high and hilly, with white cliffs at the sea-side. The coast runs S.W. till it reaches to a point of land, within which is the port of Manta, as it is called. This port of Manta is nothing else than a settlement of Spaniards and Indians together where ships that want provisions call in, and are furnished with several necessaries. About six or seven leagues to windward of this port is Cape St. Lawrence, butting out into the sea, being in form like the top of a

church. Monte de Christo gives this appearance at
sea :

MONTE DE CHRISTO.   LAT. 50. S.

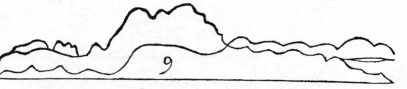

The cape rises higher and higher from the port of
Manta. As we sailed along we saw multitudes of grampuses every day ; also water-snakes of divers colours.
Both the Spaniards and Indians are very fearful of these
snakes, believing there is no cure for their bitings. At
the distance of eight leagues, or thereabouts, to leeward
of Cape St. Lawrence, it appears thus :

CAPE ST. LAWRENCE.   LAT. 55. S.

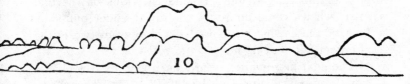

This day before night we came within sight of Manta.
Here we saw the houses of the town belonging to the
port, which were not above twenty or thirty Indian houses,
lying under the windward and the mount. We were not
willing to be descried by the inhabitants of the said place,
and stood off to sea again.

On Thursday, August 12th, in the morning, we saw
the island of Plate at S.W. at the distance of five leagues
more or less. It appeared to us to be an even land.
Having made this island, we resolved to go thither and refit our rigging, and get some goats which there run wild
up and down the country. For, as was said before, at
this time we had no other provision than flour and water.

The island itself is indifferent highland and off at sea looks thus, as is here described :

ISLE OF PLATE.   Lat. 2. 42. S.

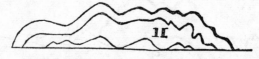

But the highland of Cape Passao, of which we have spoken before, at the distance of fifteen leagues to N., gives in several hummocks this appearance :

HIGHLAND OF CAPE PASSAO.

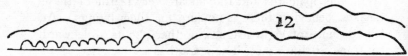

The land of Cape St. Lawrence is all white cliffs ; the head of the cape running N. and S. This day several great whales came up to us, and dived under our ship. One of these whales followed our ship, from two in the afternoon till dark night.

The next morning very early, at about six o'clock, we came under the aforesaid Isle of Plate, and here unexpectedly, to our great joy, we found at anchor the ship of Captain Cox, with his whole company, whom we had lost at sea for the space of a whole fortnight before. We found they had reached this island, and had been there at anchor four days before us, being now just ready to depart thence. At about seven we came to anchor, and then the other vessel sent us a live tortoise, and a goat to feast upon that day, telling us withal, of great store of tortoises to be found ashore upon the bays, and of much fish to be caught hereabouts. The island is very steep on all sides, insomuch, that there is landing only on the N.E. side thereof, where is a gully, nigh to which we anchored in twelve fathom water. Here at the dis-

tance of a furlong, or little more from the shore as you
go to land, you will see on the left hill a cross still standing, there erected in former times. No trees are to be
found on the whole island, but only low shrubs, on which
the goats feed, which cattle is here very numerous. The
shore is bold and hard, neither is there any water to be
found upon it, excepting only on the S.W. side of the
island, where it cannot be come at, lying so much enclosed
by the rocks, and too great a sea hindering the approach
to it in boats.

This island received its name from Sir Francis Drake
and his famous actions, for here it is reported by tradition
that he made the dividend, or sharing of that quantity of
plate which he took in the *Armada* of this sea, distribut-
ing it to each man of his company by whole bowls full.
The Spaniards affirm to this day that he took at that
time twelve score tons of plate, and sixteen bowls of
coined money a man, his number then being forty-five
men in all. Insomuch that they were forced to heave
much of it overboard, because his ship could not carry it
all. Hence was this island called by the Spaniards themselves the Isle of Plate, from this great dividend, and by
us Drake's Isle.

All along as we sailed, we found the Spanish pilots to
be very ignorant of the coasts. But they plead thus much
for their ignorance, that the merchants, their employers,
either of Mexico, Lima, Panama, or other parts, will not
entrust one penny worth of goods on that man's vessel
that corks her, for fear she should miscarry. Here our
prisoners told us likewise, that in the time of Oliver
Cromwell, or the commonwealth of England, a certain
ship was fitted out of Lima with seventy brass guns,
having on board her no less than thirty millions of dollars,
or pieces of eight, all which vast sum of money was given
by the merchants of Lima, and sent as a present to our
gracious king (or rather his father) who now reigneth, to
supply him in his exile and distress, but that this great

and rich ship was lost by keeping along the shore in the
Bay of Manta above-mentioned, or thereabouts.   What
truth there may be in this history, I cannot easily tell,
at least, it seems to me as scarce deserving any credit.

At this island we took out of Mr. Cox's ship the old
Moor (for of that nation he was), who pretended he
would be our pilot to Arica.   This was done, lest we
should have the misfortune of losing the company of
Cox's vessel, as we had done before, our ship being the
biggest in burden, and having the greatest number of
men.   Captain Peralta admired oftentimes that we were
got so far to windward in so little space of time ;
whereas they had been, he said, many times three or four
months in reaching to this distance from our departure.
Their long and tedious voyages, he added, were occasioned by their keeping at too great a distance from the
shore.   Moreover, he told us, that had we gone to the
islands of Galapagos, as we were once determined to
do, we had met in that voyage with many calms, and
such currents, that many ships have by them been lost
and never heard of to this day.   This island of Plate is
about two leagues in length, and very full of both deep
and dangerous bays, as also such as we call gullies in
these parts.   The circumference and description of the
said island is exactly thus :

We caught at this island and salted, good number of

goats and tortoises. One man standing here on a little
bay in one day turned seventeen tortoises ; besides which
number our mosquito strikers brought us in several more.
Captain Sharp, our commander, showed himself very ingenious in striking them, he performing it as well as the
tortoise strikers themselves. For these creatures here are
so little fearful, that they offer not to sink from the fishermen, but lie still until such time as they are struck. But
we found that the tortoises on this side were not so large,
nor so sweet to the taste, as those on the north side of
the island. Of goats we have taken, killed, and salted,
above a hundred in a day, and that without any labour.
While we stayed here, we made a square maintopsail yard.
We cut also six feet off our bowsprit, and three feet more
off our head. Most of the time that we remained here,
we had hazy weather. Only now and then the sun would
happen to break out, and then to shine so hot that it
burnt the skin off the necks of several of our men. As
for me, my lips were burnt in such a manner that they
were not well in a whole week afterwards.

CHAPTER XII.

Captain Sharp and his company depart from the Isle of Plate, in prosecution of their voyage towards Arica. They take two Spanish vessels by the way, and learn intelligence from the enemy. Eight of their company destroyed at the Isle of Gallo. Tediousness of this voyage, and great hardships they endured. Description of the coast all along, and their sailings.

HAVING taken in at the Isle of Plate what provisions and other necessaries we could get, we set sail thence on Tuesday, August 17th, 1679, in prosecution of our voyage and designs above-mentioned, to take and plunder the vastly rich town of Arica. This day we sailed so well, and the same we did for several others afterwards, that we were forced to lie by several times, besides reefing our topsails, to keep our other ship company, lest we should lose her again.

The next morning about break of day, we found ourselves to be at the distance of seven or eight leagues to the westward of the island whence we had departed, standing W. by S. with a S. by W. wind. About noon that day we had laid the land. After dinner the wind came at S.S.W. at which time we were forced to stay more than once for the other vessel belonging to our company.

On the following day we continued in like manner a west course all the day long. Sometimes this day the wind would change, but then in a quarter of an hour it would return to S.S.W. again. Hereabouts where we now were, we observed great ripplings of the sea.

August 20th, yesterday in the afternoon about six o'clock, we stood in S.E., but all night and all this day, we had very small winds. We found still that we gained very much on the small ship, which did not a little both perplex and hinder us in our course.

The next day likewise we stood in S.E. by S. though with very little wind, which sometimes varied, as was mentioned above. That day I finished two quadrants, each of which were two feet and a half radius. Here we had in like manner, as has been mentioned on other days of our sailings, very many dolphins, and other sorts of fish swimming about our ship.

On the morning following, we saw again the island of Plate at N.E. of our ship, giving us this appearance at that distance of prospect:

ISLE OF PLATE.

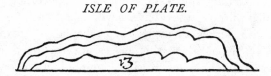

The same day at the distance of six leagues more or less from the said island, we saw another island, called Solango. This isle lies close in by the mainland. In the evening we observed it to bear E.N.E. from us. Our course was S.E. by S. and the wind at S.W. by S. This day likewise we found that our lesser ship was still a great hindrance to our sailing, being forced to lie by, and stay for her two or three hours every day. We found likewise, that the farther from shore we were, the less wind we had all along, and that under the shore we were always sure of a fresh gale, though not so favourable to us as we could wish it to be. Hitherto we had used to stand off forty leagues, and yet notwithstanding, in the space of six days, we had not got above ten leagues on our voyage, from the place of our departure.

August 23rd, this day the wind was S.W. by S. and S.S.W. In the morning we stood off. The island of Solango, at N.E. by N. appears thus:

ISLE OF SOLANGO.

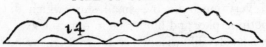

At S. by W. and about six leagues distance from us, we descried a long and even hill. I took it to be an island, and conjectured it might be at least eight leagues distant from the continent. But afterwards we found it was a point of land joining to the main, and is called Point St. Helena, being continued by a piece of land which lies low, and in several places is almost drowned from sight, so that it cannot be seen at two leagues distance. In this lowland the Spaniards have conveniences for making pitch, tar, salt, and some other things, for which purpose they have several houses here, and a friar, who serves them as their chaplain. From the island of Solango, to this place, are reckoned eleven leagues, more or less. The land is hereabouts indifferent high, and is likewise full of bays. We had this day very little wind to help us in our voyage, excepting what blasts came now and then in snatches. These sometimes would prove pretty fair to us, and allow us for some little while a south course. But our chief course was S.E. by S. The point of St. Helena at S. half E., and at about six leagues distance, gives exactly this appearance as follows:

PUNTA DE SANTA HELENA.

Here we found no great current of the sea to move anyway. At the isle of Plata, afore described, the sea ebbs and flows nearly thirteen feet perpendicular. About four leagues to leeward of this point is a deep bay, having a key at the mouth of it, which takes up the

better part of its width. In the deepest part of the bay
on shore, we saw a great smoke, which was at a village
belonging to the bay, to which place the people were
removed from the point above-mentioned. This afternoon we had a small westerly wind, our course being
S.S.W. Hereabouts it is all along a very bold shore.
At three o'clock in the afternoon, we tacked about to
clear the point. Being now a little way without the
point, we spied a sail, which we conceived to be a bark.
Hereupon we hoisted out our canoe, and sent in pursuit
of her, which made directly for the shore. But the
sail proved to be nothing else than a pair of bark-logs,[1]
which arriving on shore, the men spread their sail on
the sand of the bay to dry. At the same time there
came down on the shore an Indian on horseback, who
hallooed to our canoe, which had followed the logs.
But our men fearing to discover who we were, in case
they went too near the shore, left the design and returned
back to us. In these parts the Indians have no canoes,
nor any wood indeed that may be thought fit to make
them of. Had we been descried by these poor people,
they would in all probability have been very fearful of
us. But they offered not to stir, which gave us to understand they knew us not. We could perceive from the
ship a great path leading to the hills, so that we believed this place to be a look-out, or watch-place, for
the security of Guayaquil. Between four and five we
doubled the point, and then we descried the Point
Chandy, at the distance of six leagues S.S.E. from this
point. At first sight it seemed like to a long island,
but withal, lower than that of St. Helena.

Tuesday, August 24th, at noon we took the other ship,
wherein Captain Cox sailed in tow, she being every day

---

[1] This is no doubt the native craft *Balsa* still used in the vicinity.
It is a raft bearing one or two large sails and provided with sliding keels
in the shape of large planks drawn up or let down according to circumstances. Perhaps the earliest example of the use of sliding keels.

a greater hindrance than before to our voyage. Thus, about three in the afternoon we lost sight of land, in standing over for Cape Blanco. Here we found a strong current to move to the S.W. The wind was at S.W. by S., our course being S. by E. At the upper end of this gulf, which is framed by the two capes aforementioned, stands the city of Guayaquil, being a very rich place, and the *embarcadero* or sea-port to the great city of Quito. To this place likewise, many of the merchants of Lima do usually send the money they design for Old Spain in barks, and by that means save the custom that otherwise they would pay to the king by carrying it on board the fleet. Hither comes much gold from Quito, and very good and strong broadcloth, together with images for the use of the churches, and several other things of considerable value. But more especially cacao-nut, whereof chocolate is made, which is supposed here to be the best in the whole universe. The town of Guayaquil consists of about one hundred and fifty great houses, and twice as many little ones. This was the town to which Captain Sawkins intended to make his voyage, as was mentioned above. When ships of greater burden come into this gulf, they anchor outside Lapina, and then put their lading into lesser vessels to carry it to the town. Towards the evening of this day, a small breeze sprang up, varying from point to point, after which, about nine o'clock at night, we tacked about, and stood off to sea, W. by N.

As soon as we had tacked, we happened to spy a sail N.N.E. from us. Hereupon we instantly cast off our other vessel which we had in tow, and stood round about after them. We came very near to the vessel before the people saw us, by reason of the darkness of the night. As soon as they spied us, they immediately clapped on a wind, and sailed very well before us; insomuch, that it was a pretty while before we could come up with them, and within call. We hailed them in

Spanish, by means of an Indian prisoner, and commanded them to lower their top-sails. They answered they would soon make us to lower our own. Hereupon, we fired several guns at them, and they as thick at us again with their Harquebuses. Thus they fought us for the space of half an hour or more, and would have done it longer, had we not killed the man at the helm, after which, none of the rest dared to be so hardy as to take his place. With another of our shot we cut in pieces and disabled their main-top halliards. Hereupon they cried out for quarter, which we gave them, and entered their ship. Being possessed of the vessel, we found in her five and thirty men, of which number twenty-four were natives of Old Spain. They had one and thirty fire-arms on board the ship, for their defence. They had only fought us, as they declared afterwards, out of bravado, having promised on shore so to do, in case they met us at sea. The captain of this vessel was a person of quality, and his brother, since the death of Don Jacinto de Barabona, killed by us in the engagement before Panama, was now made admiral of the sea armada. With him we took also in this bark, five or six other persons of quality. They did us in this fight, though short, very great damage in our rigging, by cutting it in pieces, besides which, they wounded two of our men, and a third man was wounded by the negligence of one of our own men, occasioned by a pistol which went off unadvisedly. About eleven o'clock this night we stood off to the west.

The next morning about break of day, we hoisted out our canoe, and went aboard the bark which we had taken the night before. We transported on board our own ship more of the prisoners taken in the said vessel, and began to examine them, to learn what intelligence we could from them. The captain of the vessel, who was a very civil and meek gentleman, satisfied our desires in this point very exactly, saying to us: *Gentlemen, I am now your prisoner at war by the over-ruling providence of fortune; and moreover, am very well satisfied that no money whatsoever can procure my ransom, at least for the present at your hands. Hence I am persuaded, it is not my interest to tell you a lie, which if I do, I desire you to punish me as severely as you shall think fit. We heard of your taking and destroying our Armadilla, and other ships at Panama, about six weeks after that engagement, by two several barks which arrived here from thence. But they could not inform us whether you designed to come any farther to the southward; but rather, desired we would send them speedily all the help by sea that we could. Hereupon, we sent the noise and rumour of your being in these seas, by land to Lima, desiring they would expedite what succours they could send to join with ours. We had at that time in our harbour two or three great ships, but all of them very unfit to sail. For this reason at Lima, the Viceroy of Peru pressed three great merchant ships, into the biggest of which he put fourteen brass guns, into the second, ten, and in the other, six. To these he added two barks, and put seven hundred and fifty soldiers on board them all. Of this number of men they landed eightscore at Point St. Helena; all the rest being carried down to Panama, with design to fight you there. Besides these forces, two other men of war, bigger than the afore-mentioned, are still lying at Lima, and fitting out there in all speed to follow and pursue you. One of these men of war is equipped with thirty-six brass guns, and the other with thirty. These ships, beside their complement of seamen, have four hundred soldiers added to them by the Viceroy. Another man of war belonging to this number, and lesser than the afore-mentioned, is called the Patache. This ship consists of twenty-four guns, and was sent to Arica to fetch the King's plate thence. But the Viceroy, having received intelligence of your exploits at Panama, sent for this ship back from thence with such haste, that they came away and left the money behind them. Hence the Patache now lies at the Port of Callao, ready to sail on the first*

occasion, or news of your arrival thereabouts, they having
for this purpose sent to all parts very strict orders to keep
a good look-out on all sides, and all places along the coasts.
Since this, from Manta, they sent us word that they
had seen two ships at sea pass by that place. And from
the Goat Key also we heard that the Indians had seen
you, and that they were assured, one of your vessels was
the ship called la Trinidad, which you had taken before
Panama, as being a ship very well known in these seas.
Hence we concluded that your design was to ply, and make
your voyage thereabouts. Now this bark, wherein you
took us prisoners, being bound for Panama, the Governor
of Guayaquil sent us out before her departure, if possible,
to discover you, which if we did, we were to run the bark
on shore and get away, or else to fight you with these
soldiers and firearms that you see. As soon as we heard
of your being in these seas, we built two forts, the one of
six guns, and the other of four, for the defence of the
town. At the last muster taken in the town of Guayaquil
we had there eight hundred and fifty men, of all colours;
but when we came out, we left only two hundred men that
were actually under arms. Thus ended the relation of
that worthy gentleman. About noon that day we un-
rigged the bark which we had taken, and after so doing
sunk her. Then we stood S.S.E., and afterwards S. by
W. and S.S.W. That evening we saw point St. Helena
at N. half E., at the distance of nine leagues, more or less.

The next day, being August 26th, in the morning we
stood S. That day we cried out all our pillage, and
found that it amounted to 3,276 pieces of eight, which
was accordingly divided by shares amongst us. We also
punished a friar, who was chaplain to the bark afore-mentioned, and shot him upon the deck, casting him overboard before he was dead. Such cruelties, though I
abhorred very much in my heart, yet here was I forced
to hold my tongue and contradict them not, as having
not authority to oversway them. At ten o'clock this

morning we saw land again, and the pilot said we were
sixteen leagues to leeward of Cabo Blanco. Hereupon
we stood off, and on, close under the shore, which all
appeared to be barren land.

The morning following we had very little wind, so that
we advanced but slowly all that day. To windward of
us we could perceive the continent to be all high land,
being whitish clay, full of white cliffs. This morning,
in common discourse, our prisoners confessed to us, and
acknowledged the destruction of one of our little barks,
which we lost on our way to the Island of Cayboa. They
stood away, as it appeared by their information, for the
Goat Key, thinking to find us there, as having heard
Captain Sawkins say that he would go thither. On their
way they happened to fall in with the island of Gallo,
and understanding its weakness by their Indian pilot,
they ventured on shore, and took the place, carrying
away three white women in their company. But after a
small time of cruising, they returned again to the aforesaid island, where they stayed two or three days, after
which they went out to sea again. Within three or four
days they came to a little key four leagues distant from
this isle. But whilst they had been out and in thus
several times, one of their prisoners made his escape to
the mainland, and brought off thence fifty men with fire-
arms. These, placing themselves in ambush, at the first
volley killed six of the seven men that belonged to the
bark. The other man that was left, took quarter of
the enemy, and he it was that discovered to them our
design upon the town of Guayaquil. By an observation
which we made this day, we found ourselves to be in
lat. 3° 50″. At this time, our prisoners told us, there
was an embargo laid on all the Spanish ships, commanding them not to stir out of the ports, for fear of their
falling into our hands at sea.

Saturday, August 28th. This morning we took out
all the water, and most part of the flour that was in

Captain Cox's vessel. The people in like manner came on board our ship. Having done this, we made a hole in the vessel, and left her to sink, with a small old canoe at her stern. To leeward of Manta, a league from shore, in eighteen fathom water, there runs a great current outwards. About eleven in the forenoon we weighed anchor, with a wind at W.N.W. turning it out. Our number now in all being reckoned, we found ourselves to be one hundred and forty men, two boys, and fifty-five prisoners, being all now in one and the same bottom. This day we got six or seven leagues in the wind's eye.

All the day following we had a very strong S.S.W. wind, insomuch that we were forced to sail with two reefs in our main-top sail, and one also in our fore-top sail. Here Captain Peralta told us that the first place which the Spaniards settled in these parts, after Panama, was Tumbes, a place that now was to leeward of us, in this gulf where we now were. That there a priest went ashore with a cross in his hand, while ten thousand Indians stood gazing at him. Being landed on the strand, there came out of the woods two lions ; and he laid the cross gently on their backs, and they instantly fell down and worshipped it : and moreover, that two tigers following them, did the same ; whereby these animals gave to the Indians to understand the excellency of the Christian religion, which they soon after embraced. About four in the evening we came abreast the cape, which is the highest part of all. The land hereabouts appeared to be barren and rocky. At three leagues distance east from us, the cape showed thus :

Cape BLANCO.

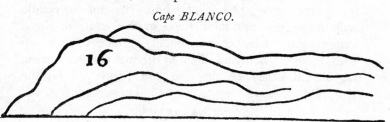

Were it not for a windward current which runs under the shore hereabouts, it were totally impossible for any ships to get about this cape, there being such a great current to leeward in the offing. In the last bark which we took, of which we spoke in this chapter, we made prisoner one Nicolas Moreno, a Spaniard by nation, and who was esteemed to be a very good pilot of the South Sea. This man did not cease continually to praise our ship for her sailing, and especially for the alterations we had made in her. As we went along, we observed many bays to lie between this cape and Point Parina, of which we shall soon make mention hereafter.

In the night the wind came about to S.S.E. and we had a very stiff gale of it. So that by break of day the next morning, we found ourselves to be about five leagues distant to windward of the cape afore mentioned. The land hereabouts makes three or four several bays, and grows lower and lower the nearer we came to Punta Parina. This point looks at first sight like two islands. Between four and five of the clock that evening we were W. from the said point.

The next day likewise, being the last day of August, the wind still continued S.S.E. as it had done the whole day before. This day we thought it convenient to stand farther out to sea, for fear of being descried at Paita, which now was not very far distant from us. The morning proved to be hazy—but about eleven we spied a sail, which stood then just as we did E. by S. Coming nearer to it, by degrees we found her to be nothing else than a pair of bark logs[1] under a sail, which were going that way. Our pilot advised us not to meddle with those logs, nor mind them in the least, for it was very doubtful whether we should be able to come up with them or not, and then by giving chase to them, we should easily be descried and known to be the English pirates, as they called us. These bark logs sail

---

[1] See note on p. 345.

excellently well for the most part, and some of them are
of such a size that they will carry two hundred and fifty
packs of meal from the valleys to Panama, without wetting any of it.   This day, by an observation made, we
found ourselves to be in lat. 4° 55′ S ; point Parina at
N.E. by E. and at the distance of six leagues, more or
less, gives this following appearance :

Punta PARINA.

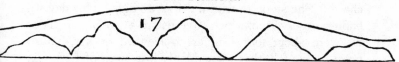

At the same time La Silla de Paita bore from us S.E.
by E. being distant only seven or eight leagues.   It had
the form of a high mountain, and appeared thus to us :

La Silla de PAITA.

The town of Paita itself is situated in a deep bay,
about two leagues to leeward of this hill.   It serves for
an *Embarcadero*, or port town, to another great place
which is distant thence about thirteen leagues higher in
the country, and is called Piura, seated in a very barren
country.

On Wednesday, September 1st, our course was S. by
W.   The midnight before this day we had a landwind
that sprang up.   In the afternoon La Silla de Paita, at
the distance of seven leagues, at E. by N. appeared thus :

La Silla de PIATA.

All along hereabouts is nothing but barren land, as was said before; likewise, for three or four days last past, we observed along the coasts many seals.

That night as we sailed we saw something that appeared to us to be as it were a light. And the next morning we spied a sail, whence we judged the light had come. The vessel was at the distance of six leagues from us, in the wind's eye, and thereupon we gave her chase. She stood to windward as we did. This day we had an observation, which gave us lat. 5° 30′ S. At night we were about four leagues to leeward of her, but so great a mist fell, that we suddenly lost sight of her. At this time the weather was as cold with us as in England in November. Every time we went about with our ship the other did the like. Our pilot told us that this ship set forth from Guayaquil eleven days before they were taken, and that she was laden with rigging, woollen and cotton cloth, and other manufactures, made at Quito. Moreover, that he had heard that they had spent a mast and had put into Paita to refit it.

The night following they showed us several lights through their negligence, which they ought not to have done, for by that means we steered directly after them. The next morning she was more than three leagues in the wind's eye distant from us. Had they suspected us, it could not be doubted, but they would have made away towards the land, but they seemed not to fly nor stir for our chase. The land here all along is level, and not very high. The weather was hazy, so that at about eleven o'clock that morning we lost sight of her. At this time we had been for the space of a whole week, at an allowance of only two draughts of water each day, so scarce were provisions with us. That afternoon we saw the vessel again, and at night we were not full two leagues distant from her, and not more than half a league to leeward. We made short trips all the night long.

On Saturday, September 4th, about break of day,

we saw the ship again, at the distance of a league, more or less, and not above a mile to windward of us. They stood out as soon as they espied us, and we stood directly after them. Having pursued them for several hours, about four of the clock in the afternoon, we came up within the distance of half our small arms shot, to windward of them. Hereupon they, perceiving who we were, presently lowered all their sails at once, and we cast dice among ourselves for the first entrance. The lot fell to larboard; so that twenty men belonging to that watch entered her. In the vessel were found fifty packs of cacao-nut, such as chocolate is made of, many packs of raw silk, Indian cloth, and thread stockings; these things being the principal part of her cargo. We stood out S.W. by S. all the night following.

The next day being come, we transported on board our ship the chief part of her lading. In her hold we found some rigging, as had been told us by Nicholas Moreno, our pilot, taken in the former vessel off of Guayaquil, but the greatest part of the hold was full of timber. We took out of her also some Osnaburgs, of which we made top-gallant sails, as shall be said hereafter. It was now nineteen days, as they told us, since they had set sail from Guayaquil, and then they had only heard there of our exploits before Panama, but did not so much as think of our coming so far to the southward, which did not give them the least suspicion of us, though they had seen us for the space of two or three days before at sea, and always steering after them, otherwise they had made for the land, and endeavoured to escape our hands.

The next morning, likewise, we continued to take in the remaining part of what goods we desired out of our prize. When we had done we sent most of our prisoners on board the said vessel, and left only their foremast standing, all the rest being cut down by the board. We gave them a foresail to sail withal, all their own water, and some of our flour to serve them for provisions, and thus we turned them away, as not caring to be troubled or encumbered with too many of their company. Notwithstanding we detained still several of the chief of our prisoners. Such were Don Thomas de Argandona, who was commander of the vessel taken before Guayaquil, Don Christoval, and Don Baltazar, both gentlemen of quality, taken with him, Captain Peralta, Captain Juan Moreno, the pilot, and twelve slaves, of whom we intended to make good use, to do the drudgery of our ship. At this time I reckoned that we were about the distance of thirty-five leagues, little more or less, from land, moreover, by an observation made this day, we found lat. 7° 1′ S. Our plunder being over, and our prize turned away, we sold both chests, boxes, and several other things at the mast, by the voice of a crier.

On the following day we stood S.S.W. and S.W. by S. all day long. That day one of our company died, named Robert Montgomery, the same man who was shot by the negligence of one of our own men with a pistol through the leg at the taking of the vessel before Guayaquil, as was mentioned above. We had an observation also this day, by which we now found lat. 7° 26′ S. On the same day likewise we made a dividend, and shared all the booty taken in the last prize. This being done, we hoisted into our ship the launch which we had taken in her, as being useful to us. All these days last past it was observed that we had every morning a dark cloud in the sky, the which in the North Sea would certainly foretell a storm, but here it always blew over.

Wednesday, September 8th, in the morning, we threw our dead man above-mentioned into the sea, and gave him three French volleys for his funeral ceremony. In the night before this day, we saw a light belonging to some vessel at sea, but we stood away from it, as not desiring to see any more sails to hinder us in our voyage towards Arica, whither now we were designed. This light was undoubtedly from some ship to leeward of us, but on the next morning we could descry no sail. Here I judged we had made a S.W. by S. way from Paita, and by an observation found 8° 00′ S.

CHAPTER XIII.

A continuation of their long and tedious voyage to Arica, with a description of the coasts and sailings thereunto. Great hardship they endured for want of water and other provisions. They are descried at Arica, and dare not land there ; the country being all in arms before them. They retire from thence, and go to Puerto de Hilo, close by Arica. Here they land, take the town with little or no loss on their side, refresh themselves with provisions ; but in the end are cheated by the Spaniards, and forced shamefully to retreat from thence.

On September 9th we continued still to make a S.W. by S. way, as we had done the day before. By a clear and exact observation, taken the same day, we found now lat. 8° 12′ S. All the twenty-four hours last past afforded us but little wind, so that we advanced but little on our voyage and were forced to tack about every four or five hours.

The next day, by another observation taken, we found then lat. 9° 00′ S. Now the weather was much warmer than before, and with this warmth we had small and misty rains that frequently fell. That evening a strong breeze came up at S.E. by E.

The night following likewise we had a very great dew that fell, and a fresh wind continued to blow. At this time we were all hard at work to make small sails of the Osnaburgs we had taken in the last prize, as being much more convenient for their lightness. The next morning being Saturday, September 11th, we lay by to mend our rigging. These last twenty-four hours we had made a S. by W. way. And now we had an observation that gave us lat. 10° 9′ S. I supposed this day that we were west from Cosmey, about the distance of eighty-nine leagues and a half.

September 12th. This day we reckoned a S.S.W. way, and that we had made thirty-four leagues and three-quarters, or thereabouts. Also that all our westing from Paita was eighty-four leagues, We supposed ourselves now to be in lat. 11° 40′ S. But the weather being hazy no observation could be made.

September 13th. Yesterday in the afternoon we had a great eclipse of the sun, which lasted from one o'clock till three after dinner. From this eclipse I then took the true judgment of our longitude from the Canary Islands, and found myself to be 285° 35′, in lat. 11° 45′ S. The wind was now so fresh that we took in our top-sails, making a great way under our courses and sprit-sail.

September 14th we had a cloudy morning, which continued so all the first part thereof. About eight it cleared up, and then we set our fore-topsail and, about noon, our main-topsail likewise. This was observable, that all this great wind precedent did not make anything of a great sea. We reckoned this day that we had run by a S.W. by W. way, twenty-six leagues and two-thirds.

The next day, in like manner, we had close weather, such as the former morning. Our reckoning was twenty-four leagues and two-thirds, by a S.W. by W. way. But, by observation made, I found myself to be 23° S. of my reckoning, as being in the lat. of 15° 17′ S.

On the 16th we had but small and variable winds. For the twenty-four hours last past we reckoned twenty-four leagues and two-thirds, by a S.W. by S. way. By observation we had lat. 16° 41′. That evening we had a gale at E.S.E. which forced us to hand our top-sails.

The 17th likewise, we had many gusts of wind at several times, forcing us to hand our top-sails often. But in the forenoon we set them with a fresh gale at E.S.E. My reckoning this day was thirty-one leagues, by a S.S.W. way. All day long we stood by our top-sails.

On the 18th we made a S. by W. way. We reckoned ourselves to be in lat. 19° 33′ S. The weather was hazy, and the wind began to die this day by degrees.

The next day, being the 19th, we had very small wind. I reckoned thirteen leagues and a half, by a S.W. by S. way, and our whole westing from Paita to be 164 leagues in lat. 20° 06′ S. All the afternoon we had a calm, with drizzling rain.

Monday, September 20th. Last night we saw the clouds, which are so famous among the mariners Magellan of these southern seas. The least of these clouds was about the bigness of a man's hat. After this sight the morning was very clear. We had run at noon at E.S.E. thirteen leagues and a half, and, by an observation then made, we found lat. 20° 15′ S. This day the wind began to freshen at W. by S. Yet, notwithstanding, we had a very smooth sea.

But on the next morning, the wind came about to S.W. and yet slackened by degrees. At four this morning it came to S. by E., and at ten the same day, to S.E by S. We had this day a clear observation, and by it lat. 20° 25′ S. We stood now E. by N. with the wind at S.E.

September 22nd. This morning the wind was at E.S.E. By a clear observation we found lat. 19° 30′ S. Likewise on a N.E. by E. way, . . . and two leagues and two-thirds.

September 23rd. We had a fresh wind and a high sea. This morning early the wind was at E. and about ten at E.N.E. From a clear observation we found our latitude to be 20° 35′ S. The way we made was S. by W. That morning we happened to split our sprit-sail.

Next morning the wind was variable and inconstant, and the weather but hazy. We reckoned a S. by E. way ; this day we bent a new main-topsail, the old one serving for a fore-topsail. In the afternoon we had but little wind, whereupon we lowered our top-sails, having, in like manner, a very smooth sea.

The following day, likewise, brought us calm and warm weather, which occasioned us to set up our shrouds both fore and aft. An observation taken this day afforded us lat. 21° 57′. That evening we bent a sprit-sail.

On September 26th an observation gave us lat. 22° 05′ S. At noon we had a breeze at N.N.E., our course being E.S.E. In the afternoon we set up a larboard top-sail studding-sail. In the evening the wind came about at N. pretty fresh.

The next day we had a smooth sea, and took in four studding-sails. For yesterday in the afternoon we had put out, besides that above mentioned, another studding-sail, and two main studding-sails more. This day we had by observation 22° 45′ S., having made by an E.S.E. way, thirty-five leagues and a half. Our whole meridian difference sixty-eight leagues and a half.

September 28th. All the forenoon we had very little wind, and yet withal a great southern sea. By observation we had lat. 22° 40′ S.

September 29th. All the night past we had much wind, with three or four fierce showers of rain. This was the first that we could call rain, ever since we left Cape Francisco above-mentioned, This day our allowance was shortened, and reduced to three pints and a half of water, and one cake of boiled bread to each man for a day. An observation this day gave us lat. 21° 59′ S. by a N.E. by E. way.

On September 30th we had a cloudy day, and the wind very variable, the morning being fresh. Our way was N.E. half N. wherein we made eighteen leagues.

October 1st. All the night past and this day we had a cloudy sky, and not much wind. We made a N.E. by E. way, and by it seventeen leagues and two miles. This day we began at two pints and a half of water for a day.

The 2nd, we made a E.N.E. way, and by it twenty-six leagues, more or less. Our observation this day gave us lat. 20° 29′ S. I reckoned now that we were ten leagues and a half to E. of our meridian, the port of Paita, so that henceforward our departure was eastward. The wind was this day at S.E. by S.

On the 3rd we had both a cloudy morning, a high sea, and drizzling weather. An observation which we had this day, gave us lat. 19° 45′ S. In the afternoon the wind blew so fresh that we were forced to hand our top-sails and sprit-sail.

The 4th, likewise, we had a high sea and a cold wind. At break of day we set our top-sails. An observation made afforded us lat. 19° 8′ S. Here we supposed ourselves fifty-nine leagues D.M.

The 5th, we had still a great sea, and sharp and cold winds, forcing us to our low sails. By a N.E. by E. way, we reckoned this day twenty-six leagues and a half.

But on the 6th we had great gusts of wind. Insomuch, that this morning our ring-bolts gave way, which held our main-stay, and had like to have brought our main-mast by the board. Hereupon we ran three or four glasses west before the wind. By an observation we found lat. 19° 4′ S.

On October 7th the wind had somewhat fallen. We had both a cloudy day and variable winds.

The 8th of the said month we had again a smooth sea, and small whiffling winds. This morning we saw a huge shoal of fish, two or three water-snakes, and several seals.

On the next day we had in like manner a very smooth sea, and withal a cloudy day. Our course was E.

October 10th. We had likewise a cloudy day, with small and variable winds, and what is consequent to these, a smooth sea. Our way was S. by E. This day we spied floating upon the sea several tufts of sea-grass, which gave us good hopes that we were nct far from shore. In the afternoon we had a N.E. by E. wind that sprang up ; the night was very cold and cloudy.

On the 11th we had a fresh wind at S.E. and E.S.E. together with a cloudy day, such as we had experienced for several days before. We reckoned this day thirty-two leagues by a N.E. by E. way. Here our pilot told us that the sky is always hazy near the shore upon these coasts where we now were.

On October 12th we had a clear day, and N.E. way.

The 13th we had but little wind. This day we saw a whale, which we took for an infallible token that we were not far distant from land, which now we hoped to see in a few days. We made an E.S.E. way, and by it we reckoned nineteen leagues. All the evening was very calm.

Thursday, October 14th, we had both a calm and close day until the afternoon. Then the weather became very hot and clear. This day we saw several land-fowls, being but small birds, concerning which our pilot said, that they use to appear about one or two days' sail from the land. Our reckoning was eleven leagues by an E.S.E. way. In the evening of this day we thought that we had seen land, but it proved to be nothing else than a fog bank.

October 15th. Both the night past and this day, was very clear. We made an observation this day, which gave us lat. 18° 00′ S.

The 16th. Last night and this day were contrary to the former, both cloudy. Our way was N.E. by E. whereof we reckoned thirteen leagues.

Sunday, October 17th, the wind blew very fresh, our course being E.N.E. About five that morning we saw land, but the weather was so hazy, that at first we could scarce perceive whether it was land or not. It was distant from us about eight leagues, and appeared as a high and round hill, being in form like a sugar-loaf. We saw land afterwards all along to the S.E. by E. from it. In the evening, we being then within five leagues of the shore, the land appeared very high and steep.

October 18th. All the night last past we stood off to sea with a fresh wind. This morning we could just see

land at N.N.E.   We reckoned a S.E. by E. way, and
by observation we found lat. 17° 17' S.

Tuesday, October 19th.   We had very cloudy weather,
finding what our pilot had told us to be very true concerning the haziness of this shore.   We saw all along as
we went very high land, covered with clouds; insomuch
that we could not see its top.

On Wednesday, the next day, we had likewise cloudy
weather, and for the most part calm.   The same weather
being very cloudy, as before, continued in like manner
on Thursday.

Friday, October 22nd.   This morning we saw the
land plain before us.   Our pilot being asked what land
that was, answered, it was the Point of Hilo.   At N.N.E.
and about six or seven leagues distance it appeared thus
to us :

Punta de HILO.   Lat. 18° 4' S.

There is every morning and evening a brightness over
the point, which lasted for two or three hours, being
caused by the reflection of the sun on the barren land, as
it is supposed.   This day we had but little wind, and the
huge want of water we were now under, occasioned much
disturbance among our men.   As for my part, I must
acknowledge I could not sleep all night long through the
greatness of my drought.   We could willingly have
landed here to seek for water, but the fear of being discovered and making ourselves known, hindered us from
so doing.   Thus we unanimously resolved to endure our
thirst for a little longer.   Hereabouts is a small current
that runs under the shore.   This morning we had but
little wind at S., our course being E.S.E.   The point

at the distance of five leagues N.E. looks on the following side thus :

Punta de HILO.

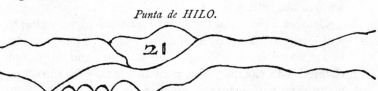

Our wind continued to blow not above six hours each day. We reckoned the difference of our meridian to be this day, one hundred and eighty leagues. Very great was our affliction now for want of water, we having but half a pint a day to our allowance.

October 23rd. This day we were forced to spare one measure of water, thereby to make it hold out the longer, so scarce it became with us. At three this afternoon the point looked thus :

Punta de HILO.   *Mora de SAMA.*

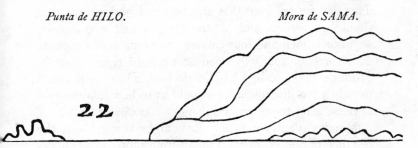

Here the point looks like an island, and Mora de Sama to the southward thereof, gives this appearance :

Mora de SAMA.

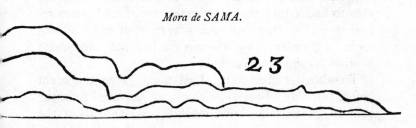

At about nine o'clock at night we had a land wind, and with it we stood S.E. by S., but all the night after we had but little wind.

October 24th. All the night past we had very cloudy and dark weather, with mizzling rain. The morning being come it cleared up, but all the land appeared covered with clouds. Yet, notwithstanding, in the afternoon it gave us again this appearance :

Mora de SAMA.   Lat. 18° 29′ S.

Under the hill of Mora de Sama are eighteen or nineteen white cliffs which appear in the form thus described. This day we resolved that one hundred and twelve men should go ashore, and, at about eight this evening, we sent our launch and four canoes, with four score men, to take three or four fishermen at a certain river, close by Mora de Sama, called El Rio de Juan Diaz, with intent to gain what intelligence we could as to how affairs stood at present on the coast and country thereabouts.

Monday, October 25th. Last night being about the distance of one league and a half from shore, we sounded, and found forty-five fathom water, with a hard ground at the bottom. This morning our people and canoes, that were sent to take the fishermen, returned, not being able to find either their houses or the river. They reported withal, they had had a very fresh wind all the night long under shore, whereas we had not one breath of wind all night on board.

Tuesday, October 26th. Last night being the night before this day, about six o'clock, we departed from the ship to go to take Arica, resolving to land about the distance of a league to windward of the town. We were about six leagues distant from the town when we left our ship, whereby we were forced to row all night, that we might reach the place of our landing before day. Towards morning the canoes left the launch, which they had had all night in tow, and wherein I was, and made all the speed they possibly could for the shore, with design to land before the launch could arrive. But being come nigh the place where we designed to land, they found, to our great sorrow and vexation, that we were descried, and that all along the shore, and through the country they had certain news of our arrival. Yet, notwithstanding our discovery, we would have landed, if we could by any means have found a place to do it in. But the sea ran so high, and with such a force against the rocks, that our boats must needs have each been staved into one thousand pieces, and we in great danger of wetting our arms, if we should adventure to go on shore. The bay all round, and likewise the tops of the hills, was possessed by several parties of horse which seemed to be gathered there by a general alarm through the whole country, and they waited only for our landing, with design to make a strong opposition against us. They fired a gun at us, but we made them no answer, but rather returned to our ship, giving over this enterprise until a fairer opportunity. The hill of Arica is very white, being occasioned by the dung of multitudes of fowls that nest themselves in the hollow thereof. To leeward of the said hill lies a small island, at the distance of a mile, more or less, from the shore. About half a league from that island we could perceive six ships to ride at anchor, four of which had their yards taken down from their masts, but the other two seemed to be ready to sail. We asked our pilot concerning these ships, and he told us that one of them was mounted with six guns, and the other with only four. Being disappointed of our expectations at Arica, we now resolved to bear away thence to the village of Hilo, there to take in water and other provisions, as also to learn what intelligence we could obtain. All that night we lay under a calm.

On October 27th, in the morning, we found ourselves to be about a league to windward of Mora de Sama. Yet, notwithstanding, the weather was quite calm, and we only drove with the current to leeward. The land between Hilo and Mora de Sama forms two several bays, and the coast runs along N.W. and S.E. as may appear by the following demonstration. Over the land we could see from our ship, as we drifted, the coming or rising of a very high land, at a great distance far up in the country.

October 28th. The night before this day we sent away our four canoes with fifty men in them, to seize and plunder the town of Hilo. All that day was very calm, as the day before.

The next morning, about break of day, a fair breeze sprang up, with which we lay right in with the port. About one in the afternoon we anchored, and the port lies thus, as is here described :

Port of HILO.

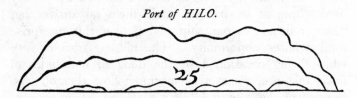

We cast anchor at the distance of two miles from the village, and then we perceived two flags, which our men had put out, having taken the town, and set up our English colours. The Spaniards were retreated to the hills, and there had done the same. Being come to an anchor, our Commander, Captain Sharp, sent a canoe on board of us, and ordered that all the men our ship could spare, should come ashore. Withal they told us, that

those of our party that landed the morning before, were
met by some horsemen on the shore, who only exchanged
some few vollies of shot with our men, but were soon
put to flight. That hereupon our forces had marched
directly to the town, where the Spaniards expecting we
should have landed at first, had made a breastwork, thirty
paces long, of clay and banks of sand. Here, in a small
skirmish, we happened to kill an Indian, who told us before he died, that they had received news of our coming
nine days ago, from Lima, and but one day before from
Arica. Having taken the town, we found therein great
quantity of pitch, tar, oil, wine and flour, with several
other sorts of provisions. We endeavoured to keep as
good a watch as the Spaniards did on the hills, fearing
lest they should suddenly make an attempt to destroy us.

On the next day, October 30th, we chose out threescore men of them who were the fittest to march, from
among the rest, and ordered them to go up and search
the valley adjoining and belonging to the town. We
found the said valley to be very pleasant, being all over
set with fig, olive, orange, lemon, and lime-trees, with
many other fruits agreeable to the palate. About four
miles up, within the valley, we came to a great sugar-
work, or *Ingenio d'azucar*, as it is called by the
Spaniards, where we found great store of sugar, oil, and
molasses, but most of the sugar the owners had hidden
from us in the cane itself. As we marched up the valley,
the Spaniards marched along the hills, and observed our
motion. From the tops of the hills they often tumbled
down great stones upon us, but with great care we endeavoured to escape those dangers, and the report of our
gun would suddenly cause them all to hide their heads.
From this house, I mean the sugar-work above-mentioned, Mr. Cox, myself, and one Cannis, a Dutchman
(who was then our interpreter), went to the Spaniards
with a flag of truce. They met us very civilly, and
promised to give us fourscore beeves as ransom of the

sugar-work, upon condition that it should not be spoilt nor demolished. We agreed with them, that they should be delivered to us at the port, next day at noon. Hereupon Captain Sharp, in the evening, sent down to the port twenty men, with strict orders that our forces there should offer no violence to those that brought down the beeves.

Sunday, October 31st. This day being employed in casting up some accounts belonging to our navigation, I reckoned that Hilo was to the eastward of Paita, one hundred and eighty seven leagues. This morning the captain of the Spaniards came to our commander, Captain Sharp, with a flag of truce, and told him that sixteen beeves were already sent down to the port, and that the rest should certainly be there the next morning. Hereupon we were ordered to prepare ourselves to retreat, and march back to the port, and there embark ourselves on board our ship. My advice was to the contrary, that we should rather leave twenty men behind to keep the house of the sugar-work, and that others should possess themselves of the hills, thereby to clear them of the Spaniards and their look-out. But my counsel not being regarded, each man took away what burden of sugar he pleased, and thus we returned to our vessel. Being come there, we found no beeves had been brought down at all, which occasioned us much to suspect some double dealing would in the latter end be found in this case.

The next morning, November 1st, our captain went to the top of the hills afore-mentioned, and spoke with the Spaniards themselves, concerning the performance of their agreement. The Spaniards made answer that the cattle would certainly come down this night, but in case they did not, that the master or owner of the sugar-work had now returned from Potosi, and we might go up and treat with him, and make, if we pleased, a new bargain for the preservation of his house and goods, it

being his interest, more than theirs, to save it from being
demolished. With this answer our men returned to us,
and we decided to wait until the next day for the delivery
of the beeves.

On the following day about eight in the morning, there
came in to us a flag of truce from the enemy, telling us,
that the winds were so high, that they could not drive
the cattle, otherwise they had been delivered before now.
But withal, that by noon we should in no manner fail to
have them brought to us. Noon being come, and no
cattle appearing, we, now having filled our water, and
finished other concerns, resolved to be revenged on the
enemy, and do them what mischief we could, at least, by
setting fire to the sugar-work. Hereupon, threescore men
of us marched up the valley, and burnt both the house,
the canes, and the mill belonging to the *ingenio.* We
broke likewise the coppers, coggs, and multitudes of great
jars of oil that we found in the house. This being done,
we brought away more sugar, and returned to the port
over the hills or mountains ; the which we found to be
very pleasant, smooth, and level after once we had ascended them. It fell out very fortunately to us that we
returned back this way, for otherwise our men at the sea-
side had inevitably been cut off and torn in pieces by the
enemy, they being at that time dispersed and straggling
up and down in parties of two and three. For from the
hills we spied coming from the northward of the bay,
above three hundred horsemen, all riding at full speed
towards our men, who had not as yet descried them, and
little thought of any such danger from the enemy so nigh
at hand. Being alarmed with this sight, we threw down
what sugar we had, and ran incontinently to meet them,
thereby to give our other men time to rally, and put themselves into a posture of defence. We being in good rank
and order, fairly proffered them battle upon the bay, but as
we advanced to meet them, they retired and rode towards
the mountains to surround us, and take the rocks from us

if they possibly could.   Hereupon, perceiving their intentions, we returned back and possessed ourselves of the
said rocks, and also of the lower town, as the Spaniards
themselves did of the upper town (at the distance of half
a mile from the lower), the hills and the woods adjoining
thereunto.   The horsemen being now in possession of
these quarters, we could perceive, as far as we could see,
more and more men resort to them, so that their forces
increased hourly to considerable numbers.   We fired one
at another as long as we could reach, and the day would
permit.   But in the meanwhile we observed, that several
of them rode to the watch-hill, and looked out often to
the sea-board.   This gave us occasion to fear, that they
had more strength and forces coming that way, which
they expected every minute.   Hereupon, lest we should
speed worse than we had done before, we resolved to
embark silently in the dark of the night, and go off from
the coast where we had been so early descried, and the
enemy was so much prepared against us.   We carried off
a great chest of sugar, whereof we shared seven pound
weight and a half each man ; thirty jars of oil, and great
plenty of all sorts of garden herbs, roots, and most excellent fruit.

A Description of Hilo

Valley of Hilo

upper Hilo

Rocks

Hilo next the Sea

The Creek

The point of Hilo

Rocks

Mooring place

CHAPTER XIV.

The Buccaneers depart from the Port of Hilo, and sail to that of Coquimbo. They are descried before their arrival. Notwithstanding they land: are encountered by the Spaniards, and put them to flight. They take, plunder, and fire the City of la Serena. A description thereof. A Stratagem of the Spaniards in endeavouring to fire their ship, discovered and prevented. They are deceived again by the Spaniards, and forced to retire from Coquimbo, without any ransom for the City, or considerable pillage. They release several of their chief Prisoners.

THE next morning (being Wednesday, November 3rd, 1679), about seven o'clock, we set sail from Hilo, standing directly off to sea, with a small land-wind. Upon the shore we could not discover this morning, above fifty men of our enemies forces, which caused us to suspect the rest were run away from their colours, and had deserted in the dark of the night. If this were so we were equally afraid of each other, and as we quitted the land, being jealous of their multitudes, so they abandoned their stations for fear of our encounters. All the while we lay in the port of Hilo, we had a fresh wind, but now being come out thence, we found it was almost stark calm. Hereabouts runs a great sea all along this coast, as we experimented at Arica; insomuch that there is no landing except under the favour of some rock or other.

November 4th, in the morning, we saw the port of Hilo at E.N.E. at the distance of nine leagues more or less, from the land. The white sand gives a bright reflection over the land, which we could see after we had lost sight of the land itself.

The next day to this, we had an indifferent fresh wind at S.S.E. We reckoned a S.W. half W. way, and by it, that we had made twenty leagues. The day was very fair and sunshiny, and the sea very smooth.

November 6th. We had a clear night the last past, and the day proved very fair and clear, like the former. We reckoned by a S.W. by W. way, about twenty-one leagues. In the afternoon it was almost stark calm.

On the following day we had in like manner very little wind, no more than the last twenty-four hours. We were now about this time many of us very much troubled and diseased with the scurvy. It proceeded as we judged, from the great hardship and want of provisions which we had endured for several months past, as having had only bread and water, as was mentioned above. Only at Hilo we killed a mule, which gave to those who would eat of the flesh a very good meal, as we esteemed it, the Spaniards having swept away with them all other provisions of flesh. But there we had plundered some small quantity of good chocolate, whereof the Spaniards make infinite use. So that now we had each morning a dish of that pleasant liquor, containing almost a pint.

Next day likewise we had very little wind, as before. We made an observation this day, and found lat. 20° 05′ S.

November 9th we had still very little wind, and that variable. We took almost every hour an observation, and found ourselves to be in lat. 20° 18′ S.

The 10th we had in like manner but little wind, as for so many days before. We observed an E.S.E current, or nearest to it, to run hereabouts. This day we saw the homing of a very high land, which we much admired, for at this time I conceived we could not be less than thirty-five or forty leagues distant from land. We supposed it to be Mora Tarapaca. That day we set up our shrouds.

Upon the 11th an indifferent gale of wind sprang up

at S.W by S., by which we made twenty-five leagues and one third. We had now a great S.S.W. sea. In the night the wind we found, came one or two points from the land. This morning we saw the like homing of land, whereby we were made sensible that it was no land which we had seen the day before.

On the 12th we had several mists of rain, with windy weather. We made by a S.S.W. half S. way, twenty-five leagues and one third. We had likewise a great and rolling S.S.W. sea, as the day before.

The 13th of the said month we had both cloudy and misty weather. We made a S.S.W. and one quarter S. way by which we ran fifty leagues.

But the next day, fair and clear weather came about again. We had likewise an easy gale of wind, by which we made a S.W. way, and advanced twenty-two leagues and a half.

On November 15th, we had also clear weather, and an indifferent gale of wind. Our way was S.W. by W., by which we reckoned eighteen leagues. Likewise that our westing from Hilo, whence we had set forth, was one hundred and fourteen leagues and one third. By observation we found lat. 23° 25′. I took now the declination-table used and made by the cosmographer of Lima.

Tuesday, November 16th. Last night we had a shower or two of rain. By observation, we found lat. 23° 35′ S.

The 17th we made a S.W. by W. half S. way. By observation we found lat. 23° 46′ S. with very little wind.

The 18th upon a S.W. by W. way, we made twenty-one leagues. By observation we found lat. 24° 20′ S.

Friday, November 19th, 1680. This morning about an hour before day, we observed a comet to appear a degree N. from the bright in Libra. The body thereof seemed dull, and its tail extended itself eighteen or twenty degrees in length, being of a pale colour, and pointing directly N.N.W. Our prisoners hereupon reported to us that the Spaniards had seen very strange sights, both at Lima, the capital city of Peru, Guayaquil, and other places, much about the time of our coming into the South Seas. I reckoned this day we had run twenty leagues by a S.W. way.

The day following the appearance of the comet, we had many storms of wind at S.S.E. and E.S.E. Our reckoning by a S.W. by W. way, was twenty-two leagues.

Sunday, November 21st, we had likewise many gusts of wind, such as the day before, with frequent showers of rain. The wind varied, to and fro, according as the clouds drew it here and there. We reckoned a S.S.W. way, and by it twenty-one leagues and a half. In all, W. from Hilo, we judged ourselves to be one hundred and seventy-eight leagues and two thirds. We had this day a great S.W. Sea, and cloudy weather. I supposed our latitude to be 26° 53′ S.

November 22nd we had in like manner cloudy weather, and now but little wind. We reckoned a S. way, and fifty one leagues.

The 23rd we had very little wind, all the storm, after the appearance of the comet, being now quite allayed. We reckoned we had made a S.E. by E. way. By observation, found lat. 27° 46′ S.

Wednesday, November 24th. All the last twenty-four hours we had a N.W. wind. Our way was S.E. half. S. by which we reckoned thirty-one leagues and one third.

The 25th. Last night the wind blew at W.S.W. but this morning it came about again at N.W. as the day before. Our reckoning this day was a S.E. and one quarter E. way, twenty-nine leagues and one third. Lat., by observation, 39° 57′ S. Our difference of meridian 135⅓.

November 26th. In the night the wind started to S.S.W., but this day at noon we had little better than a calm. I reckoned an E.S.E. half E. way, and by it twenty-three leagues.

Saturday 27th. Yesterday in the evening the wind

came to S. I reckoned an E., and something S. way, and by that, twenty-three leagues, as the day before this.

November 28th. All the last twenty-four hours we enjoyed a fresh wind at S.S.E. having a high S.W. sea. Our reckoning was an E. by N. and half N. way, and withal twenty-four leagues. By observation, lat. 30° 16′ S. and meridian distance eighty-eight leagues. At noon the wind came at S. half E.

On the 29th we had a very great S.W. sea; and withal cloudy weather. My reckoning was by an E. one third S. way, twenty leagues and one third. This day we happened to see two or three great fowls flying in the air, concerning which our pilot told us, that they used to appear seventy or eighty leagues off from the island, called Juan Fernandez. The day before this, Captain Peralta, our prisoner, was taken very frantic, his distemper being occasioned, as we thought, through too much hardship and melancholy. Notwithstanding, this present day he became indifferent well again.

The following day we had likewise cloudy weather. We made, according to our account, an E. half N. way, and by it sixteen leagues and two thirds. Our meridian difference fifty-two leagues.

December 1st. We had hazy weather, and withal an indifferent good wind at S., yea, sometimes S. by W. Our way was E. by S. by which we reckoned twenty-two leagues. The night before this day, we sailed over white water like banks, of a mile in length, or more. But these banks, upon examination, we found to be only great shoals of anchovies.

On December 2nd, very early in the morning, we espied land, which appeared to be very high. About noon this day we were six leagues distance from it. All the preceding night we had so much wind that we were forced to make use only of a pair of courses. By an observation made this day, we found lat. 30° 35′ S. We went away largely, driving better than nine leagues every watch. With this wind we made all the sail we possibly could, designing by this means to get into Coquimbo, upon which coast we now were, before night. But the wind was so high, that sometimes we were forced to lower all our sail, it blowing now a mere fret of wind. Towards the evening it abated by degrees, insomuch, that at midnight it was stark calm again. At that time we hoisted out our launch and canoes, and putting into them one hundred men, we rowed away from the ship, with design to take by surprisal a considerable city, situated nigh to the coast, called by the Spaniards, la Ciudad de la Serena.

Friday, December 3rd, 1679. When we departed from the ship, we had above two leagues, more or less, to row to the shore. But as it happened, the launch (wherein I was) rowed so heavily in comparison to the canoes, that we could not keep pace with the said boats. For this reason, and no other, it was broad day before we got to a certain store-house, situated upon the shore ; the which we found our men had passed by in the dark of the night, without perceiving it. They being landed, immediately marched away from their canoes, towards the city aforementioned of la Serena, but they had not proceeded far on their march, when they found, to the great sorrow and chagrin of us all, that we were discovered here also, as we had been at the other two places before, to wit, Arica and Hilo. For as they marched in a body together, being but thirty-five men in all, who were all those that were landed out of the canoes, they were suddenly encountered and engaged by a whole troop of an hundred Spanish horse. We that were behind hearing the noise of the dispute, followed them at their heels, and made all the haste we possibly could to come up to their relief. But before we could reach the place of battle, they had already routed the Spaniards, and forced them to fly away towards the town.

Notwithstanding this rout given to the horse, they

rallied again, at a distance of about a mile from that place, and seemed as if they did wait for us, and would engage us anew. But as soon as all our forces were come together, whereof we could make but fourscore and eight men in all, the rest being left behind to guard the boats, we marched towards them and offered them battle. As we came nigh to them we clearly found they designed no such thing, for they instantly retired and rode away before us, keeping out of the reach of our guns. We followed them as they rode, being led by them designedly clear out of the road that went to the town, that we might not reach nor find it so soon. In this engagement with the horse, our company had killed three of their chief men, and wounded four more, killing also four of their horses. When we found that we had been led by this stratagem of the enemy out of the way of the town, we left the bay, and crossed over the green fields to find it; wading oftentimes over several branches of water, which there serve to enclose each plot of ground. Upon this march we came to several houses, but found them all empty, and swept clean both of inhabitants and provisions. We saw likewise several horses and other heads of cattle in the fields, as we went along towards the City. This place of la Serena our pilot had reported to us to be but a small town, but being arrived there, we found in it no fewer than seven great churches and one chapel belonging thereto. Four of these churches were monasteries or convents, and each church had its organ for the performance of divine service. Several of the houses had their orchards of fruit, and gardens, belonging to them, both houses and gardens being as well and as neatly furnished as those in England. In these gardens we found strawberries as big as walnuts, and very delicious to the taste. In a word, everything in this city of la Serena, was most excellent and delicate, and far beyond what we could expect in so remote a place. The town was inhabited by all sorts of tradesmen, and besides

them, had its merchants, some of which were accounted
to be very rich.

The inhabitants of la Serena, upon our approach and
discovery, were all fled, carrying with them whatever
was most precious of their goods and jewels, or less cum-
bersome to them.   Much of their valuable things they
had likewise concealed or buried, having had time since
we were first discovered, so to do.   Besides, they had
had warning enough to beware of us, sent them over
land from Arica, and several other places where we had
landed or been descried at sea.   Notwithstanding, we
took in the town one friar, and two Chilenos, or Spaniards, natives of the Kingdom of Chile, which adjoins
that of Peru, towards the Straits of Magellan.   These
prisoners related to us, that the Spaniards, when they
heard of our coming, had killed most of the Chilian
slaves, fearing lest they should run or revolt from them
to us.   Moreover, that we had been descried from their
coasts four days before our arrival, or descent upon
land ; all which time they had employed in carrying
away their plate and goods.   To this information they
added, that for their defence they had received a supply
of sixty men from Arica.   Having taken possession of
the town, that evening there came a Negro to us, running away from the Spaniards.   He likewise informed
us, that when we were before Panama, we had taken a
Negro, who was esteemed to be the best pilot in all the
South Sea, but more especially for this place and all the
coasts of Coquimbo.   Moreover, that if the Spaniards
had not sent all the Negroes belonging to this city
farther up into the country, out of our reach and com-
munication, they would all undoubtedly have revolted
to us.

That night about midnight our boatswain, accompanied
by forty men, and having a Chilian for their guide, went
out of the town some miles within the country, with
design to find out the places where the Spaniards lay con-

1 St Francis
2 St Domingo
3 St Peter
4 St Iohn y^e Cathedrall
5 St Aysune
6 St Mary
7 St Phillip
8 S.S.^tSaviours
9 Governours Seat
10 Scriveners house
11 Market place
12 Hospitall
13 Entrance from y^e Sea

The Citty of la Serena   Altitude 30. d.   00. South.

383

cealed, and had hid their goods and plate. But before they came, the Spaniards had received intelligence thereof from some secret spies they had in the town, and both the men and their women were all fled to places that were more occult and remote. So that by this search, they only found an old Indian woman and three children, but no gold nor plate, nor yet any other prisoners. This morning our ship came to an anchor, by the store-house above-mentioned, named Tortuga, at the distance of a furlong from shore, in seven fathom water. While we were quartered in the town, I took this following ground-plate thereof.

The next morning, being Saturday, December 4th, there came into the town a flag of truce from the enemy. Their message was to proffer a ransom for the town to preserve it from burning ; for now they began to fear we would set fire to it, as having found no considerable booty or pillage therein. The captains, or chief commanders of both sides, met about this point, and agreed betwixt them for the sum of 95,000 pieces of eight to be the price of the whole ransom. In the afternoon of this day, I was sent down to the bay of Coquimbo, with a party of twenty men, to carry thither both goods taken in the town, and provisions for the ship. It is two leagues and a half from the town to the port ; one league on the bay, the rest being a very great road, which leads from the bay to the city. The Spaniards promised that the ransom should be collected and paid in by the next day. This day also there died one of our Negro slaves on board the ship.

The following day in the morning, I returned back to the town, with the men I had brought down the day before. Only six of them I left behind, to look after our canoes at the end of the bay. When I came up into the city, I found that the Spaniards had broken their promise, and had not brought in the ransom they had agreed for ; but had begged more time until to-morrow

at eight in the forenoon.   This evening another party of
our men went down to the ship, to carry goods, such
as we had pillaged in the town.   Moreover, that night
about nine o'clock, happened an earthquake, which we
were very sensible of, as we were all together in the
church of San Juan, where our chief rendezvous and
Corps du Garde was kept.   In the night the Spaniards
opened a sluice, and let the water run in streams about
the town, with intent either to overflow it, and thereby
force us out of the place, or at least that they might the
easier quench the flame, in case we should fire the town.

On the next morning we set fire to the town, perceiving it to be overflowed, and that the Spaniards had not
performed, or rather that they never designed to perform
their promise.   We fired, as nigh as we could, every house
in the whole town, to the intent it might be totally
reduced to ashes.   Thus we departed from la Serena,
carrying with us what plunder we could find, having sent
two parties before, loaded with goods to the ship, as
was mentioned above.   As we marched down to the
bay, we beat up an ambuscade of two hundred and fifty
horse, which lay by the way in private, with an intent to
fall on our men, in case we had sent down any other party
again with goods to the ship.   When we came to the
sea-side, being half way to our ship, we received advice
that the Spaniards had endeavoured, by an unusual
stratagem, to burn our ship, and by these means destroy
us all.   They acted thus : They blew up a horse's hide
like a bladder, and upon this float a man ventured to
swim from shore, and come under the stern of our ship.
Being arrived there, he crammed oakum and brimstone,
and other combustible matter, between the rudder and the
stern-post.   Having done this, he fired it with a match,
so that in a small time, our rudder was on fire, and all
the ship in a smoke.   Our men both alarmed and amazed
with this smoke, ran up and down the ship, suspecting the
prisoners to have fired the vessel, thereby to get their

liberty and seek our destruction.   At last they found out where the fire was, and had the good fortune to quench it before its going too far.   As soon as they had put it out, they sent the boat ashore, and found both the hide afore-mentioned, and the match burning at both ends, whereby they became acquainted with the whole matter. When we came to the store-house on the shore-side, we set at liberty the friar, our prisoner, and another gentleman who was become our hostage for the performance of the ransom.   Moreover, when we came aboard, we sent away and set at liberty Captain Peralta, Don Thomas de Argandona, Don Baltazar, Don Christoval, Captain Juan, the Pilot's Mate, the old Moor, and several others of our chief prisoners.   To this release of our prisoners we were moved, partly because we knew not well what to do with them, and partly because we feared lest by the example of this stratagem, they should plot our destruction in earnest, and by the help of so many men, especially persons of quality, be able to go through with it.

CHAPTER XV.

The Buccaneers depart from Coquimbo for the Isle of Juan Fernandez. An exact account of this voyage. Misery they endure, and great dangers they escape very narrowly there. They mutiny among themselves, and choose Watling to be their chief commander. Description of the island. Three Spanish men-of-war meet with the buccaneers, at the said island; but these outbrave them on the one side, and give them the slip on the other.

BEING all embarked again, as was mentioned in the preceding chapter, the next morning, which was Tuesday, December 7th, twenty of us were sent ashore to observe the motion of the enemy. We went to the look-out, or watch-hill, but could learn nothing thence. Hereupon about noon we returned on board the ship, and at two in the afternoon we weighed anchor and set sail, directing our course for the Isle of Juan Fernandez, not far distant from the coast of Coquimbo. At night we were five leagues distant thence at N.W. by N. The southermost island of those which are called De los Paxaros, or the Islands of Birds, was then N.N.W. from us. Before our departure, I took this draft of the bay of Coquimo and city of La Serena.

December 8th we had but very little wind and a leeward current here, which we perceived did heave us to the Northward. The afore-mentioned island, de los Paxaros, at three in the afternoon, bore N.E. of us. At the dis-

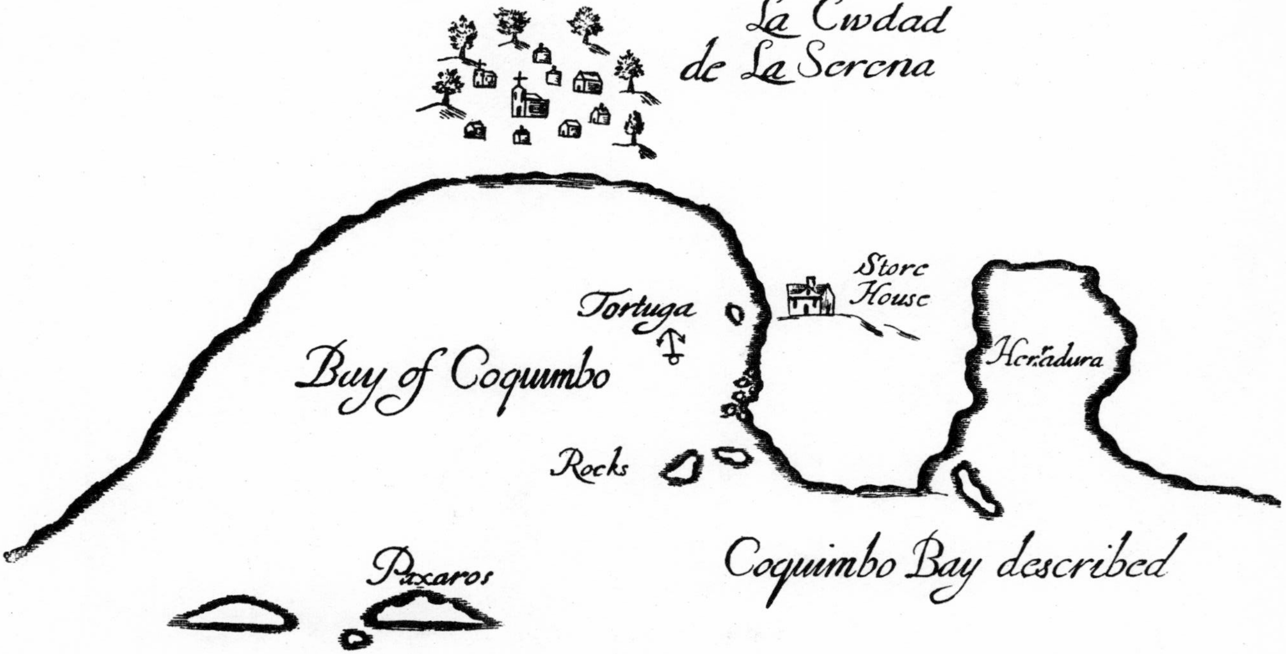

La Cuidad de La Serena

Store House

Herradura

Tortuga

Rocks

Bay of Coquimbo

Pizaros

Coquimbo Bay described

tance of three leagues, more or less, it appeared thus :—

Isle de los PAXAROS.

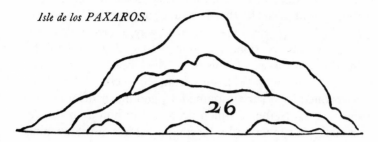

It is distant from the main continent four leagues, and from the next island of the same name, about two. The mainland is extremely high and mountainous hereabouts. At evening we were west from the said island five leagues. About eight or nine leagues to windward of Coquimbo are certain white cliffs, which appear from the shore to those that are off at sea.

On December 9th, we had likewise but little wind, as the day before. I supposed myself this day to be about thirteen leagues W. from the island above-mentioned. The weather was cloudy, with mizzling rain, so that no observation could be taken. However, this day it was thought convenient to put us to an allowance of water ; for we had taken in little or none at Coquimbo. The same weather, or very like it, we had the next day, being the tenth ; that is to say, stark calm and cloudy.

On December 11th, we had some small rain in the forepart of the day. But in the afternoon it cleared up, so that the weather was very hot. We had still but little wind.

The next day, December 12th, we had very fair weather, and by a clear observation made this day, we found lat. 30° 06′ S.

December 13th. By a W.S.W. way, we made forty-two leagues. By observation we found lat. 30° 45′ S. D.M. four leagues and two thirds.

On the 14th in the morning, we had a handsome shower of rain, which continued for some while. Then, about eight o'clock, there sprang up a S.S.W. breeze. My reckoning was by an E.S.E. way, fourteen leagues. And by observation, we found this day 30° 30′ S. In the afternoon of this day, died one of our men, whose name was William Cammock. His disease was occasioned by a surfeit, gained by too much drinking on shore at La Serena ; which produced in him a *calenture*, or malignant fever and a hiccough. Thus in the evening we buried him in the sea, according to the usual custom of mariners, giving him three French vollies for his funeral.

The following day, we had an indifferent fresh wind on both tacks. Our way was W.S.W., and by it we reckoned thirty-four leagues. So likewise by an observation we had lat. 30° 42′ S. All the afternoon blew a S. by W. wind very fresh, with a short topping S.W. sea.

But on the next ensuing day, we had no small breeze, but rather hard gusts of wind. These grew so high, that they forced us to take in our top-sails. We made a S.W. half S. way, and forty-five leagues.

On the 17th we had likewise high winds, and withal a S.W. sea. Our way W. by S. By observation this day, lat. 30° 51′ S. In the afternoon we had a S.S.E. wind, our course being S.W.

December 18th. This day we had the same high winds as before, at S.S.E. We reckoned by a W.S.W. way forty-five leagues. At noon the wind was somewhat fallen, and then we had some rain.

The 19th we had both cloudy and windy weather. My reckoning was a S.W. by S. way, and hereupon fifty-eight miles. Yesterday we were assured by our pilot that we were now in the meridian of the island of Juan Fernandez, whither our course was directed for the present. What occasioned him to be so positive in his assertion, was the seeing of those great birds, of which we made mention in the foregoing chapter.

On the 20th, we had cloudy weather in the morning on both tacks. We made a S.W. and half S. way, and by it fifty-two leagues. By observation this day, lat. 32° 20′ S. D.M. one hundred and twenty-three leagues.

The next day likewise we had cloudy weather ; yet by observation we found a W. way. On the 22nd by observation we found an E. way proved.

Thursday, December 23rd. All the night past we had a fresh wind. But in the morning, from top-mast head, we descried a hummock of land. In the evening we saw it again. We found afterwards that what we had seen was the westernmost island of Juan Fernandez ; which is nothing but a mere rock, there being no riding, nor scarce landing, near to it.

Friday, December 24th. This morning we could descry the island of Juan Fernandez itself S. by E., it being at sixteen leagues distance when we saw it yesterday. At seven this morning the island stood E., the wind being N.W. or by N. At eight the same morning the island, at the distance of five leagues, little more or less, appeared thus :

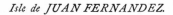

Isle de JUAN FERNANDEZ.

Here my observation was that I could see neither fowl nor fish near this island ; both which things are usually to be seen about other islands. Having told my observation to our pilot, he gave me for answer, that he had made many voyages by this island, and yet never saw either fowl or fish any more than I. Our reckoning this day was an E.S.E. way, and hereby thirty-six leagues. By observation, lat. 33° 30′ S.

Saturday, December 25th. Yesterday in the afternoon, at three o'clock, we saw the other island, making two or three hummocks of land. This morning we were about eight leagues distant from it, the island bearing E.S.E. from us. At eight the same morning we were right abreast with it. Here therefore are two islands together, the biggest whereof is three leagues and a half in length, nearest N.W. and S.E., the other, and lesser, is almost one league, and no more in circumference. At ten o'clock we sent off from the ship one of our canoes, to seek for the best landing and anchoring for our vessel. As we approached, both islands seemed to us nothing but one entire heap of rocks. That which lies more to the N. is the highest, though we could not now see the tops thereof, for the clouds which covered it. In most places it is so steep that it becomes almost perpendicular.

This day being Christmas-day, we gave in the morning early three vollies of shot for solemnization of that great festival. I reckoned an E. by S. way. By a clear observation from the middle of the island, lat. 33° 45′ S., and M.D. ninety-nine leagues. In the evening of this day, we came to an anchor at the south end of the island, in a stately bay that we found there, but which lies open from the S, to the S.E. winds. We anchored in eleven fathom water, and at the distance of only one furlong from the shore. Here we saw multitudes of seals covering the bay everywhere, insomuch that we were forced to kill them to set our feet on shore.

Sunday, December 26th. This day we sent a canoe to see if we could find any riding secure from the southerly winds; these being the most constant winds that blow on these coasts. The canoe being gone, our commander sent likewise what men we could spare on shore, to drive goats, whereof there is great plenty in this

island. They caught and killed that day to the number
of threescore, or thereabouts. The canoe returning to
the ship made report that there was good riding in
another bay, situate on the North side of the island, in
fourteen fathom water, and not above one quarter of a
mile from the shore. Moreover that there was much
wood to be had, whereas in the place where we had first
anchored, not one stick of wood nor tuft of grass was to
be found.

The next day, being the 27th, between two and four
o'clock in the morning, we had a tempest of violent winds
and fierce showers of rain. The same day we got in two
hundred jars of water, bringing them the full distance of
a league from the place of our riding. In the meanwhile,
others were employed to catch goats, as they had done
the day before.

On the 28th of the said month, in the morning, I went
with ten more of our company and two canoes, to fetch
water from the land. Being come thither, and having
filled our jars, we could not get back to the ship, by
reason of a southerly wind that blew from off the ocean,
and hindered our return. Thus we were forced to lie
still in a water-hole, and wait till the winds were over for
a safer opportunity. Meanwhile, the violence of the
wind increasing, our ship was forced to get under sail,
and make away, not without danger of being forced
ashore. Hereupon she sailed out of the harbour, to seek
another place of anchoring. At noon I ventured out, to
try if I could follow the ship, but was forced in again by
the wind and a raging sea. Thus we lay still for some
while longer, till the evening came on. This being come,
we ventured out again both canoes together; but the
winds were then so high, that we were forced to throw
all our jars of water overboard to lighten our boats,
otherwise we had inevitably perished. I ought to bless
and praise God Almighty for this deliverance; for in all
human reason, the least wave of that tempest must have

sunk us. Notwithstanding, we came that night to our place or harbour, where we expected to have found our ship (called False Wild Harbour) but found her not. Hereupon, not knowing what to do, we went ashore, and hauled up our canoes dry. Having done this, we ascended higher within the island, along a gulley, for the space of half a mile, there to clear ourselves of the noise and company of the seals, which were very troublesome on the shore. Here we kindled a fire, dried our clothes, and rested ourselves all night, though with extremely hungry bellies, having eaten very little or nothing all the day before. In the sides of the hill, under which we lay, we observed many holes like coney-holes. These holes are the nests and roosting-places of multitudes of birds that breed in this island, called by the Spaniards Pardelas. One of these birds, as we lay drying and warming ourselves, fell down into our fire.

The next morning being come, very early before sunrise, we went farther to the northward, to seek for our ship, which we feared we had lost. But we were not gone far, when we soon spied her at sea. Hereupon we passed a point of land, and entered a certain bay, which was about a mile deep, and not above half a league over. Into this bay we put, and instantly made a fire, thereby to show the ship whereabouts we were. Here we found good watering and wooding close to the shore. In this bay also we saw another sort of amphibious animal, which I imagined to be the same that by some authors is called a Sea-Lion.[1] These animals are six times bigger than seals. Their heads are like that of a lion, and they have four fins not unlike a tortoise. The hinder parts of these creatures are much like fins, but are drawn after them, being useless upon the shore. They roared as if they had been lions, and were full of a certain short and thick hair, which was of a mouse colour ; but that of the young ones was somewhat lighter.

[1] Or walrus.

The old ones of these sea-lions are between twelve and fourteen feet long, and about eleven or twelve feet in circumference. A seal is very easily killed, as we often experimented, but two of our men with great stones could not kill one of these animals.

That day in the afternoon there came a canoe from on board the ship with provisions for us, they fearing lest we should be starved. In like manner the launch came with men to cut wood. They told us that the ship came to an anchor in the other bay, but that within half an hour the cable broke, and they were forced to leave their anchor behind them and get out to sea again. Night being come, we made our beds of fern, whereof there is huge plenty upon this island; together with great multitudes of trees like our English box, which bear a sort of green berries, smelling like pimento, or pepper. All this day the ship was forced to ply off at sea, not being able to get in.

December 30th. The morning of this day we employed in filling water and cutting down wood. But in the afternoon, eight of us eleven went aboard the ship, all in one and the same canoe, sending her ashore again with provisions for the men that were there. This day in like manner we could not get into the harbour, for no sooner the ship came within the parts of land but the wind, coming out of the bay, blew us clear out again. Thus we were forced to ply out all that night and great part of the following day.

On the next day, having overcome all difficulties and many dangers, we came to an anchor in the afternoon, in fifteen fathom water, at the distance of a cable's length from shore. Here it was observable that we were forced to keep men ashore on purpose to beat off the seals, while our men filled water at the sea-side, at high-water mark, for the seals covet hugely to lie in fresh water. About this island fish is so plentiful that, in less than one hour's time, two men caught enough for our whole company.

Saturday, January 1st, 1681. This day we put up a new main-top, larger than the old one, and we caught cray-fish that were bigger than our English lobsters.

The next day, being January 2nd, died a chief man of our company, whose name was John Hilliard. This man, until our weighing anchor from the port of Coquimbo, had been our Master all the space of this voyage. But from that time we chose John Cox for the starboard, and John Fall for the larboard watch. The disease whereof he died was the dropsy. That evening we buried our dead companion, and gave him a volley for his funeral, according to the usual custom.

On January 3rd we had terrible gusts of wind from the shore every hour. This day our pilot told us that many years ago a certain ship was cast away upon this island, and only one man saved, who lived alone upon the island five years before any ship came this way to carry him off. The island has excellent land in many valleys belonging thereunto. This day likewise we fetched our anchor which we left in the other bay when the ship broke her cable.

Tuesday, January 4th, 1681. This day we had such terrible flaws of wind, that the cable of our ship broke, and we had undoubtedly been on shore had not the other held us fast. At last it came home and we drove outward. By the way it caught hold of a rock, and held some time, but at last we hauled it up, and the wind came with so much violence that the waves flew as high as our main-top, and made all the water of a foam.

January 5th, the same huge gusts of wind continued all the night last past, notwithstanding which this day at noon it was brave and calm. But in the morning the anchor of our ship gave way again, and we drove to the eastward more than half a mile; till at last we happened to fasten again in sixty fathom water. Here in this bay, where we rode at anchor, did run a violent current, sometimes into and at other times out of the bay, so that all was uncertain with us. But our greatest discomfort was, that our men were all in a mutiny against each other, and much divided among themselves, some of them being for going home towards England, or our foreign plantations, and that round about America through the Straits of Magellan, as Captain Sawkins had designed to do ; others of them being for staying longer, and searching farther into those seas, till such time as they had got more money. This day at noon our anchor drove again ; whereupon to secure ourselves from that dangerous place, we sailed thence into the West bay, anchored there in twenty-five fathom water ; and moored our ship one quarter of a mile from shore.

On Thursday, January 6th, our differences being now grown to a great height, the mutineers made a new election of another person to be our chief captain and commander, by virtue whereof they deposed Captain Sharp, whom they protested they would obey no longer. They chose therefore one of our company, whose name was John Watling, to command in chief, he having been an old privateer, and gained the esteem of being a stout seaman. The election being made, all the rest were forced to give their assent to it, and Captain Sharp gave over his command, whereupon they immediately made articles with Watling, and signed them.

The following day, being the 7th, we burnt and tallowed the starboard side of our ship. In this bay where we now anchored, we found a cross cut in the bark of a tree, and several letters besides. Hereupon, in another tree up the gulley, I engraved the two first letters of my name, with a cross over them. This day likewise William Cook, servant to Captain Edmund Cook, being searched, we found a paper with all our names written in it, which it was suspected he designed to have given to the Spanish prisoners. For these reasons this evening our Captain thought it convenient to put him in irons, which was accordingly done. The next day we finished the other side of our ship.

Sunday, January 9th. This day was the first Sunday that ever we kept by command and common consent, since the loss and death of our valiant commander, Captain Sawkins. This generous-spirited man threw the dice overboard, finding them in use on the said day.

January 10th. This day the weather was very clear and settled again. We caught every day in the bay where we now were great plenty of fish ; and I saw the same day a shoal of fish a mile and more long.

On the next day, being the 11th, we filled our water and carried our wood on board the ship. Moreover, our two canoes went to the other side of the island to catch goats, for on the barren side thereof are found and caught the best ; and by land it is impossible to go from one side of the island to the other.

Wednesday, January 12th. This morning our canoes returned from catching goats, firing guns as they came towards us to give us warning. Being come on board, they told us they had espied three sail of ships, which they conceived to be men-of-war, coming about the island. Within half an hour after this notice given by our boats, the ships came in sight to leeward of the island. Hereupon we immediately slipped our cables and put to sea, taking all our men on board that were ashore at that time. Only one, William, a Mosquito Indian, was then left behind on the island, because he could not be found at this our sudden departure.[1] Upon the Island of Juan Fernandez grow certain trees that are called by the name of bilby-trees. The tops of these trees are excellent cabbage, and of them is made the same use that we do of cabbage in England. Here fish abound in such quantity, that on the surface of the water

[1] From this statement and the subsequent remark of the Spanish pilot it is clear that Alexander Selkirk was not the first nor the only solitary who had inhabited this Island.

I have taken fish with a bare and naked hook, that is to say unbaited. Much fish is taken here of the weight of twenty pounds ; the smallest that is taken in the bay being almost two pound weight. Very good timber for building of houses and other uses is likewise found upon the island. It is distant from the main continent ninety-five leagues, or thereabouts, being situate in 33° 40′ S. The plats of the island lie N.W. and S.E.

Being got out of the bay we stood off to sea, and kept to windward as close as we could. The biggest of these Spanish men-of-war, for such they proved to be, was of the burden of eight hundred tons, and was called *El Santo Christo*, being mounted with twelve guns. The second, named *San Francisco*, was of the port of six hundred tons, and had ten guns. The third was of the carriage of three hundred and fifty tons, whose name I have forgot. As soon as they saw us, they instantly put out their bloody flags, and we, to show them that we were not as yet daunted, did the same with ours. We kept close under the wind, and were, to confess the truth, very unwilling to fight them, by reason they kept all in a knot together, and we could not single out any one of them, or separate him from the rest. Especially considering that our present commander Watling had showed himself at their appearance to be faint-hearted. As for the Spaniards themselves, they might have easily come to us, since we lay by several times ; but undoubtedly they were cowardly given, and peradventure as unwilling to engage us as we were to engage them.

The following day, being January 13th, in the morning we could descry one of the fore-mentioned men-of-war under the leeward side of the island; and we believed that the rest were at anchor thereabouts. At W. by S. and at the distance of seven leagues the island appeared thus :

Isle of JUAN FERNANDEZ.   Lat. 33° 40 S.

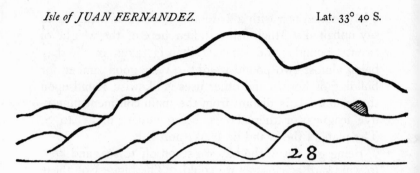

At noon that day we stood towards the island, making as if that we intended to be in with them. But in the afternoon our commander propounded the question to us, whether we were willing now that the fleet was to windward, to bear away from them? To this we all agreed with one consent. And hereupon, night being come, with a fresh wind at S.S.E. we stood away N.E. by N., and thus gave them handsomely the slip, after having outbraved them that day and the day before.

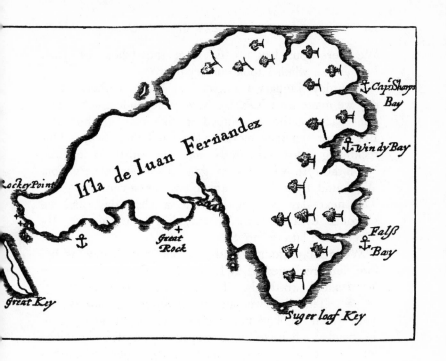

CHAPTER XVI.

*The Buccaneers depart from the Isle of Juan Fernandez to that of
Iquique. Here they take several prisoners, and learn intelligence of the posture of affairs at Arica. Cruelty committed
upon one of the said prisoners, who had rightly informed
them. They attempt Arica the second time, and take the
town, but are beaten out of it again before they could plunder,
with great loss of men, many of them being killed, wounded,
and made prisoners. Captain Watling, their chief Commander, is killed in this attack, and Captain Sharp presently
chosen again, who leads them off, and through mountains of
difficulties, makes a bold retreat to the ship.*

HAVING bid our enemies adieu, after the manner as was
said in the precedent chapter, the next morning, being
January 14th, we bore N.E. We reckoned this day a
N.N.E. one quarter S. way, and by it thirty leagues.

We were four leagues E. from the Island of Juan Fernandez, when I took our departure.

Saturday, January 15th, we had hazy weather. This day we made by a N.E. by N. way eleven leagues. The same hazy weather continued in like manner the 16th. But about ten that morning the wind died away. Our reckoning was a N.E. by N. way, and thirty-six leagues.

On the 17th we had a soft gale, and a clear observation. We found by it lat. 28° 47′ S. easting seventy leagues. The next day we had likewise a clear day, and we reckoned by a N.E. by N. way, thirty-one leagues. By observation lat. 27° 29′ S.

Wednesday, January 19th, we had a clear day, as before, and reckoned a N.E. by N. way, and thirty-five leagues and two thirds. By observation we took lat. 25° 00′ S. This day we put up our top-gallant masts and sails, which we had taken down at the island of Juan Fernandez, when we thought to have gone directly thence for the Straits of Magellan. But now our resolutions were changed, and our course was bent for Arica, that rich place, the second time, to try what good we could do upon it by another attempt, in order to make all our fortunes there. In the evening of this day we saw land at a great distance.

January 20th, about midnight, we had a small land-wind that sprang up and reached us. At break of day we could descry land again, at the distance of nine or ten leagues, more or less. This day was very hot and calm, easting ninety-two leagues.

On the 21st, we had very little wind, and all along as we went we could descry high land, and that barren. We sailed N. by E, and N.N.E. along the coast of the continent.

The next day being Saturday, January 22nd, we had very hot weather. This day we sailed N. and N. by E. and looked out continually for the island of Iquique, which our pilot told us was hereabouts. We kept at a just distance from land, for fear of being descried by the enemy.

On the following day, Sunday, 23rd, we sailed in like manner N.N.E. along the coast, which seems to be very full of bays hereabouts. By observation this day we took lat. 21° 49′ S.

Monday, January 24th. This day we had an indifferent gale of wind, and we stood N. and by E. the wind being S.S.E. By observation, lat. 21° 02′ S. Our whole easting, I reckoned to be ninety-two leagues and a half. In the afternoon of this day Captain Watling, our commander, and twenty-five men more departed from the ship in two canoes, with design to seek for and take the island of Iquique, and there to gain intelligence of the posture of affairs at Arica. We were at the distance of twelve leagues from shore, when they went away from the ship.

The next day by a clear observation, lat. 20° 40′ S. At four in the afternoon this day, one of our canoes returned, bringing word that they could not find the island, though they had searched for it very diligently. At night came the other, being brought back by a wrong sign given us by the first canoe. This second canoe had landed upon the continent, and there found a track, which they followed for some little space. Here they met a dead whale, with whose bones the Spaniards had built a hut, and set up a cross. There lay also many pieces of broken jars. They observed likewise that hereabouts upon the coast were many bays, good landings, and anchoring for ships. That evening, about seven o'clock, a fresh gang departed from the ship to seek for the same island, while we lay becalmed all night, driving about a league to leeward.

Wednesday, January 26th, we had extremely hot weather. This day the Spanish pilot told us that on the continent over against us, and at the distance of a very little way within the land, are many rich mines of silver,

but that the Spaniards dared not open them for fear of
an invasion from some foreign enemy or other. We
sailed N., at the distance of about two leagues from
shore. At noon by observation, found lat. 20° 21′ S.
At four o'clock we saw a smoke made by our men, close
by a white cliff, which proved to be the island. Hereupon we immediately sent away another canoe with
more men, to supply them in their attempts. But in the
meanwhile the first canoe, which had departed the evening before this day, came aboard, bringing with them four
prisoners, two old white men and two Indians.

The other canoe, which set out last, brought back
molasses, fish, and two jars of wine. To windward of
the said island is a small village of eighteen or twenty
houses, having a small chapel near it, built of stone, and
for adornment thereof, it is stuck full of hides or the skins
of seals. They found about fifty people in this hamlet,
but the greatest part of them made their escape at the
arrival of the canoe. To this island frequently come
barks from Arica, which city is not far distant, to fetch
clay, and they have already transported away a considerable part thereof. The poor Indians, inhabitants or
natives of this island, are forced to bring all the fresh
water they use the full distance of eleven leagues, that is
to say, from a river, named Camarones, which lies to
leeward of the island. The barque wherein they used to
bring it, was gone for water when our men landed upon
the place. The island all over is white, but the bowels
thereof are of a reddish sort of earth. From the shore
is seen here a great path which leads over the mountains
into the country. The Indians of this island eat much
and often a sort of leaves that are of a taste much like
our bay-leaves in England, insomuch that their teeth are
dyed a green colour by the continual use of it.[1]   The

---

[1] This is no doubt the famous coca or cuca, erythroxylon coca (the
betel of South America), and universally in request by the Indian population of the West Coast of South America. It is a shrub which grows

inhabitants go stark naked, and are very robust and strong people ; yet notwithstanding they live more like beasts than men.

Thursday, January 27th. This morning on board the ship we examined one of the old men, who were taken prisoners upon the island the day before. But finding him in many lies, as we thought, concerning Arica, our commander ordered him to be shot to death, which was accordingly done. Our old commander, Captain Sharp, was much troubled in his mind and dissatisfied at this cruel and rash proceeding ; whereupon he opposed it as much as he could. But seeing he could not prevail, he took water and washed his hands, saying, "Gentlemen, I am clear of the blood of this old man ; and I will warrant you a hot day for this piece of cruelty, whenever we come to fight at Arica." These words were found at the latter end of this expedition of Arica to contain a true and certain prophesy, as shall be related hereafter.

The other old man being under examination, informed us that the island of Iquique afore-mentioned belonged to the Governor of Arica, who was proprietor thereof ; and that he allowed these men a little wine and other necessaries, to live upon for their sustenance. That he himself had the superintendence of forty or fifty of the governor's slaves, who caught fish and dried it, for the profit of the said governor ; and he sold it afterwards to the inland towns, and reaped a considerable benefit thereby. That by a letter received from Arica eight days ago, they understood there was then in the harbour of Arica three ships from Chile, and one bark. That they had raised there a fortification mounted with twelve copper guns. But that when we were there before, they had conveyed

to the height of six or eight feet. The leaves stripped of their stalks, with the addition of a little unslaked lime (or of the ashes of the quinoa plant, chenopodium quinoa) are chewed like betel. It has a warm pungent taste, is a powerful nervous stimulant, and is also said to be a remedy for rheumatic affections. From the plant is also obtained the alkaloid cocaine well known in modern medicine.

out of the town to the neighbouring stations all their plate, gold and jewels, burying it there in the ground and concealing it after several manners and ways, which whether it were now returned or not, he could not easily tell. That there were two great places, the one at ten, the other at twenty-five leagues distance from Arica, at which towns lay all their strength and treasure. That the day before had passed a post to declare our having been at Coquimbo. That the embargo laid on all vessels going northward was now taken off; so that a free passage was allowed them. That by land it was impossible to go hence to Arica in less than four or five days, forasmuch as they must carry water for themselves and horses for the whole journey. And lastly, that those arms that were brought from Lima to Arica, as was mentioned above, were now carried away to Buenos Ayres. All these things pleased us mighty well to hear. But, however, Captain Sharp was still much dissatisfied, because we had shot the old man. For he had given us information to the full, and with all manner of truth, how that Arica was greatly fortified, and much more than before ; but our misfortune was that we took his information to be all contrary to the truth.

The leaves of which we made mention above are brought down to this island in whole bales, and then distributed to the Indians by a short allowance given to each man. This day we had very hot weather, and a S.W. sea. By observation we found lat. 20° 13′ S. Besides the things above-mentioned, our prisoners informed us that at Arica the Spaniards had built a breastwork round about the town, and one also in every street, that in case one end of the town were taken, they might be able to defend the other. We stood off and on for the greatest part of this day. In the afternoon we were eight leagues and a half distant from shore, with a fresh wind. That morning, moreover, we took the bark that was at the river of Camarones, to fill water for the island.

Friday, January 28th. Last night about midnight we left the ship, and embarked ourselves in the bark aforementioned, the launch, and four canoes, with design to take Arica by surprise. We rowed and sailed all night, making in for the shore.

Saturday, January 29th. About break of day we got under shore, and there hid ourselves among the rocks for all the day long, fearing lest we should be descried by the enemy, before we came to Arica. At this time we were about five leagues to southward of Arica, near Quebrada de San Vitor, a place so-called upon that coast. Night being come, we rowed away from there.

Sunday, January 30th, 1680. This day (being the day that is consecrated in our English Calendar, to the Martyrdom of our glorious King Charles the First) in the morning about sun-rise, we landed amongst some rocks at some distance of four miles, more or less, to the southward from Arica. We put on shore ninety-two men in all, the rest remaining in the boats, to keep and defend them from being surprised by the enemy, with the intent we might leave behind us a safe retreat, in case of necessity. To these men we left strict orders, that if we made one smoke from the town, or adjoining fields, they should come after us towards the harbour of Arica with one canoe ; but in case we made two, that they should bring all away, leaving only fifteen men in the boats. As we marched from our landing-place towards the town, we mounted a very steep hill, and saw thence no men nor forces of the enemy ; which caused us to hope we were not as yet descried, and that we should utterly surprise them. But when we were come about half of the way to the town, we spied three horsemen, who mounted the look-out hill ; and seeing us upon our march, they rode down full speed towards the city, to give notice of our approach. Our commander Watling chose out forty of our number, to attack the fort, and sent us away first thitherwards, the rest being designed for the town. We that were appointed for the fort had ten hand grenades among us when we gave the assault, and with them, as well as with our other arms, we attacked the castle, and exchanged several shot with our enemies. But at last, seeing our main body in danger of being overborne with the number of our enemies, we gave over that attempt on the fort, and ran down in all haste to the valley, to help and assist them in the fight. Here the battle was very desperate, and they killed three, and wounded two more of our men from their out-works, before we could gain upon them. But our rage increasing with our wounds, we still advanced, and at last beat the enemy out of all, and filled every street in the city with dead bodies. The enemy made several retreats to several places, from one breastwork to another; and we had not a sufficient number of men wherewith to man all places taken. Insomuch, that we had no sooner beat them out of one place, than they came another way, and manned it again with new forces and fresh men.

We took in every place where we vanquished the enemy, great number of prisoners, more indeed than peradventure we ought to have done or knew well what to do with; they being too many for such a small body as ours was to manage. These prisoners informed us that we had been descried no less than three days before, from the island of Iquique, whereby they were in expectation of our arrival every hour, knowing we still had a design to make a second attempt upon that place. That into the city were come four hundred soldiers from Lima, who, besides their own, had brought seven hundred arms for the use of the country-people; and that in the town they had six hundred armed men, and in the fort three hundred.

Being now in possession of the city, or the greatest part thereof, we sent to the fort, commanding them to surrender, but they would not vouchsafe to send us any answer. Hereupon we advanced towards it, and gave it a second attack, wherein we persisted very vigorously for a long time. Not being able to carry it, we got upon the top of a house that stood near it, and from there fired down into the fort, killing many of their men and wounding them at our ease and pleasure. But while we were busied in this attack, the rest of the enemy's forces had taken again several posts of the town, and began to surround us in great numbers, with design to cut us off. Hereupon we were constrained to desist the second time as before, from assaulting the fort, and make head against them. This we no sooner had done than, their numbers and vigour increasing every moment, we found ourselves to be overpowered, and consequently we thought it convenient to retreat to the place where our wounded men were, under the hands of our surgeons, that is to say, our Hospital. At this time our new commander, Captain Watling, both our quartermasters and a great many others of our men were killed, besides those that were wounded and disabled. So that now the enemy rallying against us and beating us from place to place, we were in a very distracted condition, and in more likelihood to perish every man than escape the bloodiness of that day. Now we found the words of Captain Sharp to bear a true prophesy, being all very sensible that we had had a day too hot for us, after that cruel heat in killing and murdering in cold blood the old Mestizo Indian whom we had taken prisoner at Iquique, as before was mentioned.

Being surrounded with difficulties on all sides, and in great disorder, having no head or leader to give orders for what was to be done, we were glad to turn our eyes to our good and old commander, Captain Bartholomew Sharp, and beg of him very earnestly to commiserate our condition and carry us off. It was a great while that we were reiterating our supplications to him, before he would take any notice of our request in this point, so much was he displeased with the former mutiny of our people against him, all which had been occasioned by the

instigation of Mr. Cook.   But Sharp is a man of an undaunted courage, and of an excellent conduct, not fearing
in the least to look an insulting enemy in the face, and a
person that knows both the theory and practical parts of
navigation as well as most do.   Hereupon, at our request
and earnest petition, he took upon him the command-in-
chief again, and began to distribute his orders for our
safety.   He would have brought off our surgeons, but
that they had been drinking while we assaulted the fort,
and thus would not come with us when they were called.
They killed and took of our number twenty-eight men ;
eighteen more that we brought off were desperately
wounded.   At this time we were extremely faint for
want of water and victuals, whereof we had had none
all that day.   Moreover, we were almost choked with the
dust of the town ; this being so much raised by the work
that their great guns had made that we could scarcely
see each other.   They beat us out of the town, and then
followed us into the Savannas, or open fields, still charging us as fast as they could.   But when they saw that we
rallied again, resolving to die one by another, they then
ran from us into the town, and sheltered themselves
under their breastworks.   Thus we retreated in as good
order as we could possibly observe in that confusion.
But their horsemen followed us as we retired, and fired
at us all the way, though they would not come within
reach of our guns ; for their own reached farther than
ours, and out-shot us more than one third.   We took the
seaside for our greater security ; which, when the enemy
saw, they betook themselves to the hills, rolling down
great stones and whole rocks to destroy us.   In the meanwhile those of the town examined our surgeons, and other
men whom they had made prisoners.   These gave them
our signs that we had left to our boats that were behind
us, so that they immediately blew up two smokes, which
were perceived by the canoes.   This was the greatest of
our dangers.   For had we not come at the instant that

we did to the seaside, our boats had been gone, they being already under sail ; and we had inevitably perished every man. Thus we put off from the shore, and got on board about ten o'clock at night ; having been involved in a continual and bloody fight with the enemy all that day long.

CHAPTER XVII.

A description of the Bay of Arica. They sail hence to the Port of Guasco, where they get provisions. A draft of the said port. They land again at Hilo to revenge the former affronts, and take what they could find.

HAVING ended our attempt at Arica, the next day, being January the last, we plied to and fro in sight of the port, to see if they would send out the three ships we had seen in the harbour to fight us. For upon them we hoped to revenge the defeat and disappointment we had received at the town the day before. But our expectations in this point also were frustrated, for not one of those vessels offered to stir.

The houses of this town of Arica are not above eleven feet high, being built of earth, and not of brick or timber. The town itself is four-square in figure, and at one corner stands the Castle, which may easily be commanded even with small arms from the hill which lies close to it. This place is the Embarcadero, or port town of all the mineral towns that lie hereabouts, and hence is fetched all the plate that is carried to Lima, the head city of Peru. I took the bay of Arica as it appeared to me.

On Tuesday, February 1st, we had a clear observation, and by it we found lat. 19° 06′ S. This day we shared the old remains of our plate, taken in some of our former booties. Our shares amounted only to thirty-seven pieces of eight to each man.

N.B.—*Here I would have my reader take notice that from this day forward I kept no constant Diary or Journal, as I had done before, at least for some consider-*

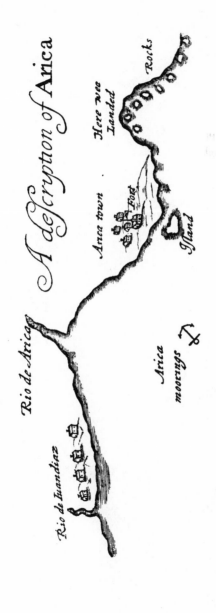

A description of Arica

Rio de Aricae

Rio de Juandiaz

Here wea landed

Rocks

Arica town

Fort

Island

Arica moorings

able space of time, as you see hereafter; my disease and sickness at sea being the occasion of intermitting what I had never failed to do in all the course of this voyage till now. Only some few memorandums, as my weakness gave leave, I now and then committed to paper, which I shall give you as I find them, towards a continuance of this history. Thus :—

Monday, February 14th. This night between eleven and twelve o'clock died on board our ship William Cook, who was the servant afore-mentioned to Captain Edmund Cook, of whom likewise mention has been often made in this Journal.

February 16th, 1680. This day we found ourselves to be in lat. 27° 30′ S. We had a constant breeze at S.E. and S.S.E. till we got about two hundred leagues from land. Then, at the eclipse of the moon, we had a calm for two or three days ; and then a breeze at N. for the space of two days ; after which we had a calm again for two or three days more.

March 1st. By observation, lat. 34° 01′ S. At this time begins the dirty weather in these seas. We lay under a pair of courses, the wind being at S.E. and E.S.E. with a very great sea at S.S.E.

March 3rd. All hands were called up, and a council held ; wherein considering it was now dirty weather and late in the year, we bore up the helm and resolved to go to the main for water, and thence to leeward, and so march overland towards home, or at least to the North Sea. But God directed us from following this resolution, as you shall hear hereafter. We being thus determined that day, we stood N.E. with a strong wind at S.E. and E.S.E.

On March 5th died our Coquimbo Indian. The seventh we had a West-wind, our course being E. by N. The eighth of the said month we were put to an allowance, having only one cake of bread a day. March 10th, we had a strong South-wind.

On March 12th we fell in with the main-land, somewhat to leeward of Coquimbo.   Within the island of
Paxaros are double lands, in whose valleys are fires for the
melting of copper, with which metal these hills abound.
Off to sea-board it is a rocky land, and within it is sandy.
About the distance of eight leagues to leeward is a rocky
point with several keys or rocks about it.   About one
half mile to leeward of this point turns in the port of
Guasco.   Right against the anchoring are three rocks,
close under the shore.

Being arrived here, we landed on shore threescore
men of our company, with design to get provisions, and
anything else that we could purchase.   The people of the
country all ran away as soon as they saw us.   There was
building on shore in this port a fire bark of sixteen or
eighteen tons burden, with a cock-boat belonging to it.
We took one Indian prisoner, and with him went up the
space of six or seven miles into the country to an Indian
town of threescore or fourscore houses.   Thence we came
back to the church, which is distant four miles from the
seaside, and lodged there all night.   Here are multitudes
of good sheep and goats in the country adjoining this
port, and it is watered with an excellent fresh-water
river ; but the getting of the water is very difficult, the
banks being very high or otherwise inaccessible.   However, we made a shift to get in five hundred jars of water.
Furthermore, we brought away one hundred and twenty
sheep and fourscore goats, with which stock we victualled
our vessel for a while.   As for oxen, they had driven
them away farther up into the country.   The jurisdiction
of Guasco itself is governed by a Tenente, or Deputy-
Governor and a Friar, and is in subjection to the city of
La Serena above-mentioned, being a dependence upon
it.   Here grows corn, peas, beans and several other
sorts of grain ; and for fruits this place is not inferior to
Coquimbo.   Here we found likewise a mill to grind corn,
and about two hundred bushels thereof ready ground ;

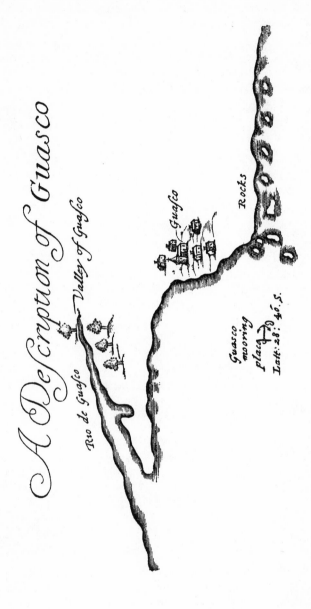

A Description of Guasco

Rio de Guasco

Valley of Guasco

Guasco

Rocks

Guasco mooring place

Lat: 28: 46. S.

which we conveyed on board our ship. Every house of
any account has branches of water running through its
yards or courts. The inhabitants had hidden their wine
and other best things, as plate and jewels, having descried
us at sea before our landing: so that our booty here,
besides provisions, was inconsiderable. However, we
caught some few fowls, and eat five or six sheep and likewise a great hog, which tasted very like our English
pork. The hills are all barren, so that the country which
bears fruit is only an excellent valley, being four times
as broad as that of Hilo above-mentioned. These people
of Guasco serve the town of Coquimbo with many sorts
of provisions. We gave the Indian whom we had taken
his liberty, and I took the port of Guasco.

Tuesday, March 15th, 1680. This morning we departed from the port of Guasco afore-mentioned, with
very little wind, having done nothing considerable there,
excepting only the taking in the few provisions above-
related. We were bent therefore to seek greater matters,
having experienced but ill success in most of our attempts
hitherto. On March 20th, Moro de Horse, being high
doubled land, and at E. by N. appeared thus to us, in
lat. 24° S.

Moro de Horse.   Lat. 24° S.

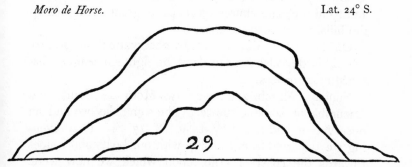

29

At N., and at the distance of ten leagues, more or
less, we saw the great and high hill of Moro Moreno,
being so called from its colour. It is a dark hill, but

much higher and bigger than the other afore-mentioned,
and appears like an island, thus :

Moro Moreno.   Lat. 23° 30′ S.

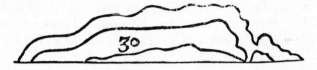

We had now very dark weather all along the coast.
On March 21st, we were W. from the bay of Mexil-
lones.   The point of this bay one league upwards represents exactly a sugar-loaf.

March 22nd.   This day our boat and canoes went
from the ship, well manned, to find the river Loa.
They went also about two leagues to leeward of it, to a
fishing village, but could find no place fit for landing ;
whereupon they returned without doing anything.   The
next day another canoe of our company went out upon
the same exploit, but found the same success.   Yet notwithstanding, here Sir Francis Drake watered, and built
a church, as we were told by our pilot.   This church is
now standing on the seaside by the river, whose mouth
is now dry.   There are several huts to windward of it ;
and from the said church or chapel a great path goes up
the hills, which leads to Pica.

On Thursday, March 24th, by observation, lat. 20° 10′
S.   This day also we saw land, at eighteen leagues distance more or less.

Sunday, March 27th, we saw Mora de Sama, and
Lacumba at some distance.   The same day we had an
observation, and found by it lat. 18° 17′ S.   That evening we departed from the ship with our boats and canoes
towards the coast of Hilo, upon which we now were.
We landed and took the village of Hilo undescried, they
scarce suspecting we could have any design upon that
place the second time.   We caught the friar who was

chaplain to the town and most of the inhabitants asleep, making them prisoners of war. Here we heard a flying report, that five thousand English had lately taken Panama the second time, and kept it. But this rumour, as it should seem, proved to be a falsity. At this time the river came out, and was overflowed, it being near the time of the freshes. Here the prisoners told us, that in Arica ten of our men were still alive, whereof three were surgeons, all the rest being dead of their wounds. The Spaniards sent word to Hilo, that we had killed seventy men and wounded three times as many of their forces. Here the inhabitants said that of forty-five men sent to the relief of Arica from hence, there came home but only two alive. We filled what water we pleased here, but a small boat that we brought from Guasco broke loose from us, and was staved to pieces on the rocks. Here we took eighteen jars of wine, and good store of new figs. On Tuesday following we went up to the sugar-work, mentioned in our former expedition against Hilo, and found all fruits just ripe and fit for eating. There we laded seven mules downwards with molasses and sugar. The inhabitants told us, moreover, that those who came to fight us when we were here the first time, were most of them boys, and had only fifty firearms amongst them, they being commanded by an English gentleman who is married at Arequipa. Likewise that the owner of the sugar-work afore-mentioned was now engaged in a suit-at-law against the town of Hilo, pretending it was not the English who robbed him and spoilt his *Ingenio*, when we were there before, but the townsmen themselves. This day in the evening we sailed from Hilo with dark weather and little wind, which continued for several days afterwards.

CHAPTER XVIII.

They depart from the Port of Hilo to the Gulf of Nicoya, where they take down their decks and mend the sailing of their ship. Forty-seven of their companions leave them, and go home over land. A description of the Gulf of Nicoya. They take two barks and some prisoners there. Several other remarks belonging to this voyage.

From the time that we set sail from the port of Hilo, until Sunday, April 10th, 1681, nothing happened to us that might be accounted remarkable; neither did I take any notes all this while, by reason of my indisposition afore-mentioned. This day we could hear distinctly the breaking of the seas on the shore, but could see no land, the weather being extremely dark and hazy. Notwithstanding, about noon it cleared up, and we found ourselves to be in the bay called de Malabrigo. The land in this bay runs due E. and W. By an observation made, we found this day 6° 35′ S. We saw from here the leeward island of Lobos, or Seals, being nothing but a rocky and scraggy place. On the S.W. side thereof is a red hill, which is a place about the said island, which the Indian fishermen much frequent. It is situated in lat. 6° 15′ S. This day likewise in the evening we saw the point called Aguja.

On Saturday, April 16th, we came within a league distance of the west-end of the island of Plate, above described. The next day to this, being Sunday, April 17th, 1681, our mutineers broke out again into an open dissension, they having been much dissatisfied all along the course of this voyage, but more especially since our unfortunate fight at Arica, and never entirely reconciled to us since they chose Captain Watling, and deposed Sharp at the isle of Juan Fernandez, as was related above. Nothing now could appease them, nor serve their turn, but a separation from the rest of the company, and a departure from us. Hereupon this day they departed from the ship, to the number of forty-seven men, all in company together, with design to go over land by the same way they came into those seas. The rest who remained behind, did fully resolve, and faithfully promise to each other, they would stick close together. They took five slaves in their company, to guide and do them other service in that journey.[1] This day we had lat. 1° 30′ S. We sailed N.N.W. before the wind.

The next day after their departure, being April 18th, we began to go to work about taking down one of our upper decks, thereby to cause our ship still to mend her sailing. We now made a N.W. by N. way, by observation, lat. 25° N., the wind being at S.W.

On April 19th we made a N.W. by N. way. By observation, lat. 2° 45′ N. In the afternoon we had cloudy weather. The following day likewise we made the same way, and by it seventy miles, according to my reckoning.

On the 21st in the morning we had some small showers of rain, and but little wind. We saw some turtle upon the surface of the water, and great quantity of fish. We caught twenty-six small dolphins. By a N.W. by N. way, we reckoned this day forty miles.

April 22nd. This day we caught seven large dolphins and one bonito. We saw likewise whole multitudes of turtle swimming upon the water, and took five of them.

[1] This party, among whom were William Dampier and Lionel Wafer, proceeded in boats to the Gulf of San Miguel, where they landed and crossed the Isthmus. Dampier published in the first volume of his voyages a short account of Sharp's expedition, and of their return across the Isthmus to the West Indies. Wafer being accidently injured on the land passage remained some months with the Indians of Darien, and afterwards published his experiences among them.

By observation, lat. 5° 28′ N. Hereabouts runs a great and strong current. This day we lowered the quarter deck of our ship, and made it even to the upper deck.

The following day we had but small wind, and yet great showers of rain. Hereupon every man saved water for himself, and a great quantity was saved for the whole company. In the morning of this day we caught eight bonitos, and in the evening ten more.

On April 24th we had both cloudy and rainy weather. By observation, lat. 7° 37′ N. M.D. ninety-two leagues. This morning we caught forty bonitos, and in the evening thirty more. In the afternoon we stood N., the wind being at S.W. by S.

Monday, April 25th. All the night before this day we had huge gusts of wind and rain. At break of day we were close in with land, which upon examination proved to be the island of Cano. To westward thereof is very high land. About noon this day it cleared up, and we had lat. 8° 34′ N. In the evening we sent a canoe to search the island. In it they found good water, and even ground, but withal, an open road. At night we stood off the first watch, and the last we had a land wind.

The next day following, at daylight we stood in, and about noon we came to an anchor at the east side of the island afore-mentioned, which is not in breadth above one league. In the afternoon we removed from our former anchoring place, and anchored again within shot of the N.E. point of the island. In this place grows great number of cacao trees, all over the greatest part of the isle. On the north side thereof are many rivulets of good water to be found in sandy bays. We saw moreover some good hogs on shore, whereof we killed one, and two pigs. Here are great numbers of turtle-doves, and huge store of fish, but withal, very shy to be caught. To northward of the island it looks thus :

Isla DEL CANO. Lat. 8° 45′ N.

April 27th, we had some rain and wind the forepart of the day, but the afternoon was fair. The next day in like manner we had great quantity of rain. On Saturday, the 30th, about seven o'clock in the morning, we weighed anchor from the aforesaid island with little wind, and stood N.W. That day fell much rain, with great thunder and lightning.

Monday, May 2nd. This day we observed and found lat. 9° N. The coast all along appeared to us very high and mountainous, and scarce six hours did pass but we had thunder, lightning, and rain ; the like continued for the two days following, wherein we had nothing but almost continual thunder and rain.

On May 5th we had an indifferent fair day, and that evening we were right off of the Gulf of Nicoya.

Friday, May 6th. This morning we saw the cape very plain before us. N. by E. from it, are certain keys at eight leagues distance, close under the main. We steered N.N.W. towards the biggest of them, at whose E.S.E. side are two or three small rocks. The main eastward is fine savanna, or plain and even land, through which goes a very great road, which is to be seen from the sea. At noon the port of Caldero, commonly called Puerto Caldero, bore N. from us. At which time the ebb forced us to sound in the middle of the gulf, where we found fourteen fathom water. After this we anchored nearer to the eastern keys, in nineteen fathom, where we had oozy ground.

Saturday, May 7th. The night before this day was very fair all night long. In the morning we went in a canoe, being several in company, to seek for a place to lay our ship in. Amongst the islands along the shore, we found many brave holes, but little or no water in them, which caused us to dislike what we had found. On one of the said islands we happened to find a hat, and many empty jars of water, which showed us that some people had been lately there. About eight in the evening our ship weighed anchor at young flood, and about three in the afternoon we anchored again in six fathom water.

Sunday, May 8th, 1681. The night before this day, we had much rain, with thunder and lightning. The morning being come, our commander, Captain Sharp, departed from the ship in two canoes, with twenty-two men in his company, out of design to surprise any vessels or people they could meet hereabouts. In the meanwhile, in the evening we drove up with the tide (there being no wind) in the ship, for the space of two or three leagues higher, till we found but three fathom at high water. Here we backed astern. At this time we saw one of our canoes coming off from the island, that was ahead of us (which was named Chira) calling for more men and arms, and saying there were two ships to be seen higher up the gulf. Hereupon eight of us went away with them ashore, whereof two joined the party afore-mentioned, and the six remaining were appointed to guard the prisoners they had taken. To these we showed ourselves very kind, as finding that they were very sensible of the cruelties of the Spaniards towards them and their whole nation. Here we found eight or nine houses, and a small chapel standing. These people have been in former times a considerable and great nation, but are now almost destroyed and extinguished by the Spaniards. We ascended a creek of the sea for a league, or thereabouts, and took two barks by surprisal, which were the two sail they had told us of before. One of these barks was the same we had taken before at

Panama, of which I made mention at the beginning of this history.

On Monday following this day, we weighed anchor with our barks, and drove down the creek, with the tide at ebb, towards our ship. The prisoners that we had taken here, informed us, that when we were to westward in these seas before, there lay one hundred men at the port of Santa Maria. That our men who left us at the island of Cayboa, as was mentioned above, met the other bark that we lost at sea, as we were sailing thither, and thus all went over land together. That in the North Seas, near Porto Bello, they had taken a good ship, and that for this cause, ever since the Spaniards had kept at the mouth of the river of Santa Maria, three Armadilla barks, to stop and hinder others from going that way. On Monday night our captain, with twenty-four men, went from the ship into another creek, and there took several prisoners, among whom was a shipwright and his men, who were judged able to do us good service in the altering of our ship; these carpenters being there actually building two great ships for the Spaniards. Having taken these men, they made a float of timber to bring down the tools and instruments they were working withal. Here it happened that they put several tools, and some quantity of iron-work, into a dory, to be conveyed down the river with the float. But this dory sank by the way, being overladen with iron, and one of our company, by name John Alexander, a Scotchman, was unfortunately drowned by this means.

On Thursday following, May 12th, we sent a canoe from the ship, and found the dory that had been sunk. That evening likewise drove down the body of our drowned man afore-mentioned. Hereupon we took him up, and on Friday morning following threw him overboard, giving him three French vollies for his customary ceremony. Both this day and the day before, we fetched water from a point near the houses, on the island of Chira afore-mentioned. From the ship also we sent away a Spanish merchant, whom we had taken among the prisoners, to fetch a certain number of beeves, that might serve for a ransom of the new bark taken here. This day the weather was fair, but on Sunday following it rained from morning until night.

On Monday, May 16th, we began to work all hands together on our ship. On Tuesday an Indian boy named Peter ran away from us. He belonged to Captain Sawkins, and waited on him as his servant. On Wednesday died an Indian slave, whose name was Salvador. On Thursday we heard thirty or forty guns fired on the main, which caused us to think that these would also turn to Hilo beeves. On Friday we caught cockles, which were as large as both our fists. At night there fell such dreadful rain, with thunder, lightning, and wind, that for the space of two hours the air was as light as day; the thunder not ceasing all the while. On Sunday we continued to work; the night before which day we had more thunder, lightning, and rain.

Wednesday, May 25th. This day we finished our great piece of work, viz. the taking down the deck of our ship. Besides which, the length of every mast was shortened, and all was now served and rigged. Insomuch that it would seem incredible to strangers, could they but see how much work we performed in the space of a fortnight or less. The same day likewise we set at liberty our Spanish carpenters, who had been very serviceable to us all this while, the old pilot, the old Spaniard taken at the isle of Iquique, and several others of our Spanish prisoners and slaves. To these people, but chiefly to the Spanish carpenters as a reward for their good service, we gave the new bark which we had taken at this place. But the old bark we thought fit to keep, and sail in our company, as we did, putting into her for this purpose six of our own men and two slaves. The next day we fell down as low as Vanero, a place so called

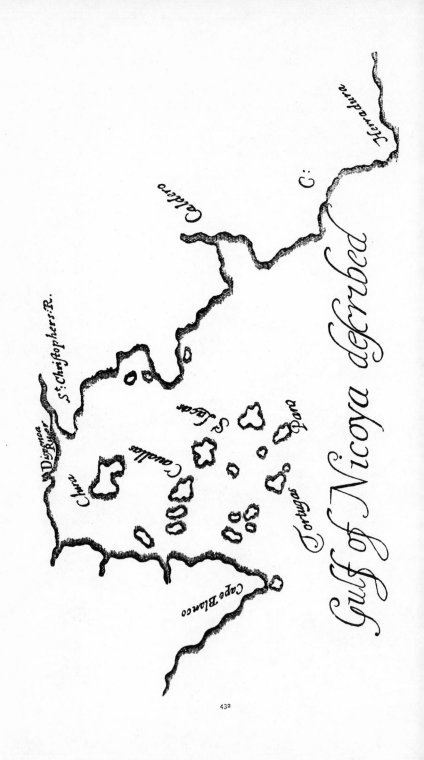

Gulf of Nicoya described

Henadura

C:

Caldero

S:Christophers:R.

Dispenoa Rivers

Chira

Cavallos

S:Lucar

Para

Tortugas

Cape Blanco

hereabouts, and would have sailed away again that very evening, but that our tackle gave way in hoisting our anchor, whereby we lay still. In the Gulf of Nicoya we experienced most commonly a fresh breeze, and at night a land wind.

Friday, May 27th. This day likewise we drove down with the tide as low as Cavallo, another place so named in the gulf. Here we stayed and watered that day ; and here one Cannis Marcy, our interpreter, ran away from us.

On May 28th in the morning we sailed from thence, and came within twenty-nine leagues of that rich and rocky shore. Yet notwithstanding we had but seven fathom water. Here I saw this day a white porpoise. Behind this island is a town called New Cape Blanco. At Puerto Caldero above-mentioned is but one storehouse to be seen. We came to an anchor in the depth of seven fathom water, at the distance of a league from shore, and caught five turtle.

May 29th. This day we saw Cape Blanco. Both this day and the day following we continued tacking out of the gulf, against a south wind. Here I took the ensuing demonstration of the Gulf of Nicoya, which, for the use of the reader, I have hereunto annexed.

CHAPTER XIX.

They depart from the Gulf of Nicoya to Golfo Dulce, where they careen their vessel. An account of their sailings along the coast. Also a description of Golfo Dulce. The Spaniards force the Indians of Darien to a peace, by a stratagem contrived in the name of the English.

WEDNESDAY, June 1st, 1681. This day we had very fair weather, and yet but little wind. Hereupon the tide, or current, drove us to the westward of Cape Blanco. Off this Cape, and at the distance of two miles within the sea, is situate a naked and nothing but barren quay. At E. by N., and at four leagues distance, Cape Blanco gave us this appearance :

Cabo BLANCO.   Lat. 9° 30′ N.

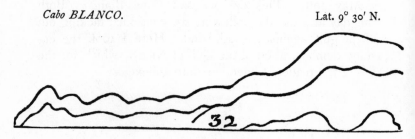

The coast here along runs N.W. half W., and grows lower and lower towards Cape Guyones. This cape at seven leagues distance, and at N.W. by N., appeared thus to us :

Cabo de GUYONES.   Lat. 10° 00′ N.

At first sight the cape appeared very like two islands. The latter part of this day was cloudy, which hindered much our prospect.

June 2nd. This morning we saw land, which appeared like several keys to us at N.W. by N., and at seven leagues distance. It was the land of Puerto de Velas, and appeared thus :

Puerto de VELAS.

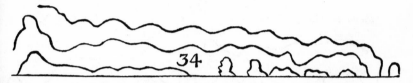

This evening our captain called us together, and asked our opinions concerning the course we ought to steer. Having discussed the points by him proposed amongst us, we all resolved to bear up for Golfo Dulce, and there careen our vessels. This being done, we concluded to go from thence to the cape, and cruise thereabouts under the equinoctial. We observed this day that our bark taken at the gulf of Nicoya sailed much better than our ship.

Friday, June 3rd. The night before this day was very fair, and we had a fresh wind, our course being S.E. This morning we saw no land. In the evening the wind came about at S.S.W. and S.W. by S.

June 4th. This day we stood E. and E. by N., the wind being W. and W. by N. In the evening we stood N.E., and descried land at the distance of twenty-four leagues, more or less, from Cape Blanco.

Sunday, June 5th. Last night we lay by for all, or the greater part thereof. This morning we saw the island of Cano above described, which bore E.S.E. from us. We saw likewise multitudes of fish, but they would not bite. Also water-snakes of divers colours.

June 6th. All last night we had rain, and with it but little wind, yea, scarce enough to carry us clear off from the island afore-mentioned. Towards morning we had a fresh wind at N.N.W. So then we stood out S. until morning, and this being come, we stood N.E. by E. The land runs from Punta Mala to Golfo Dulce, and Punta Borrica, E.S.E. half S. At nine leagues distance we laid the island of Cano. Punta Borrica at the same distance, or thereabouts, looks thus :

Punta Borrica.   Lat. 8 oo' N.

The west end of Golfo Dulce is very high land, and a high rock lies close off it. Besides which, two other rocks lie farther out ; the outermost of which is a mile distant from the shore. The east side is also high, but breaks into small points and bays, growing lower and lower to Punta Borrica. We came about a mile within the mouth of the gulf, then anchored in eight fathom and a half water. The mouth of the gulf is almost three leagues over.

The next day, being June 7th, we weighed anchor again at young flood, and got about two leagues higher. At evening we came again to anchor in seven fathom and a half water. It rained this day until eight o'clock, more like the pouring down of water from the clouds, than the usual falling of drops.

Wednesday, June 8th, at daybreak we weighed anchor again, with a fresh sea-breeze. The higher up we went, the deeper we found the gulf, and at last no ground even with thirty fathom of line. This day we sent our canoe away to seek water and a good place to lay our ship in. Having landed, they found one Indian and two boys, which they made prisoners and brought aboard ; we used them very kindly, giving them victuals and clothes, for they had no other than the bark of a tree to cover their nakedness withal. Being examined, they informed us that a Spanish priest had been amongst them, and had made peace with their nation, ordering them strictly not to come near any ship nor vessel that had red colours ; forasmuch as that they were Englishmen, and would certainly kill them. Being asked where now the priest was, they answered that he was gone to a great Spanish town, which was distant thence four sleeps up in the country. After this the Indian left the two boys, his children, with us, and went to fetch more Indians to us, from a plantain-walk or grove, situated by a river a league off, or thereabouts. We came to an anchor in a bay close by one of the Indian quays, where two fresh rivers were within a stone's throw of each other, in twenty-seven fathom and a half water, and at a cable's length from the mark of low water. The Indians whom our prisoner went to seek, came to us several times, selling to us honey, plantains, and other necessaries that we usually bought of them, or trucked for with other things. We also made use of their bark logs in tallowing our ship, in which concern they did us good service. Their darts are headed with iron as sharp as any razor.

Here one of the prisoners which we took at the gulf of Nicoya, informed us by what means, or rather stratagem of war, the Spaniards had forced a peace upon the Indians of the province of Darien, since our departure thence. The manner was as follows : A certain Frenchman who ran from us at the island of Taboga to the Spaniards, was sent by them in a ship to the river's mouth, which disembogueth from that province into the South Sea. Being arrived there, he went ashore by himself in a canoe, and told the Indians that the English who had passed that way, were come back from their adventures in the South Sea. Withal, he asked them, if

they would not be so kind and friendly to the Englishmen, as to come aboard and conduct them on shore.
The poor deceived Indians were very joyful to understand this good news, and thus forty of the chief men
among them went on board the Spanish vessel, and
were immediately carried prisoners of war to Panama.
Here they were forced to conclude a peace, though upon
terms very disadvantageous to them, before they could
obtain their liberty.

These poor and miserable Indians of Golfo Dulce,
would come every day into our company, and eat and
drink very familiarly with us all the time we were there.
We laid our ship on ground, but the water did not ebb
low enough to see her keel.   Whilst we were careening
our vessel, we built a house upon the shore, both to
lodge and eat in, and every day we caught plenty of good
fish.   On Sunday, June 12th, the work of careening our
ship going on in due order, we came to cleanse our hold,
and here on a sudden, both myself and several others
were struck totally blind with the filth and nastiness of
the said place.   Yet soon after we recovered our sight
again without any other help than the benefit of the fresh
and open air, which dissipated those malignant vapours
that had oppressed our eyes.   On June 14th, we had a
great and fierce tornado, with which our cable broke, and
had it not then happened to be high water at that instant,
we had been lost inevitably.   However, we had the
good fortune to shore her up again, and by that means
secure ourselves from farther danger.   On June 21st we
weighed anchor again, and went a league higher than the
former place.   Here we watered, and in the meanwhile
left men below to cut wood.

Thursday, June 23rd.   This day ran away from us
two negroes ; the name of one of them was Hernando ;
who was taken with Don Thomas de Argandona on
the coast of Guayaquil, as was mentioned above.   The
other was named Silvestre, having been taken at the

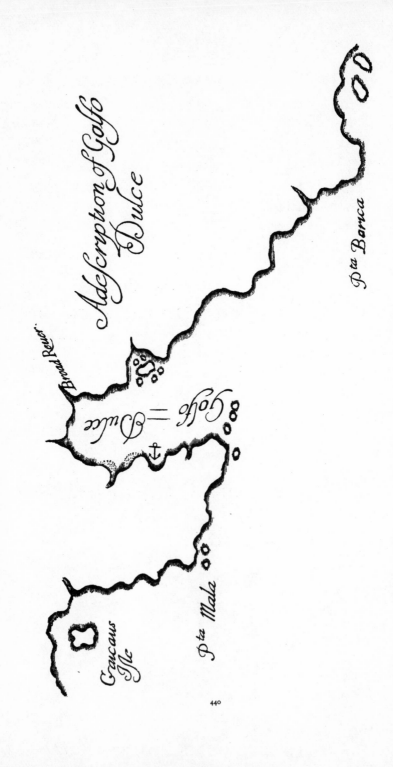

A description of Golfo Dulce

Broad Reuer.

Golfo = Dulce

P.ta Barica

P.ta Mala

Garcaius Ile

town of Hilo. Following the example of these afore-
mentioned, on Monday, June 27th, that is, four days
after, two more of our prisoners endeavoured to make
their escape, both of them slaves. One of these was
named Francisco, who was a negro, and had been taken
in the cacao-ship mentioned before. The name of the
other was also Francisco, and he was an Indian born,
who was taken before Panama. Their attempts to escape
succeeded not, for we caught them both again before
they got on shore. On Tuesday following I went to sail
up and down the gulf, in the little bark belonging to our
ship ; and having viewed all places, took this description
of Golfo Dulce here inserted. Our captain gave this
gulf the name of King Charles, his Harbour.

CHAPTER XX.

*They depart from Golfo Dulce, to go and cruise under the
Equinoctial. Here they take a rich Spanish vessel with
37,000 Pieces of Eight, besides plate and other goods. They
take also a Packet-boat bound from Panama to Lima. An
account of their sailings and the coasts along.*

OUR vessel being now careened, and all things in a
readiness for our departure, on Tuesday, June 28th, in
the afternoon, we weighed anchor to go to sea again,
turning out towards the mouth of Golfo Dulce. Our
design was to cruise under the equinoctial, as had been
concluded upon before, thereby to get what purchase we
could by sea, seeing the greatest part of our attempts
on land had proved hitherto very unsuccessful to us.

Wednesday, June 29th. Both the night last past and
this day we had rainy weather. About three in the
afternoon a fresh gale sprang up at S.W. and S.S.W.,
our course being S.E. and S.E. by S. At five this
evening the gulf bore N.W. by W., seven leagues distant, and Punta Borrica three leagues and a half distant.

Thursday, June 30th. All night past we enjoyed a
fresh gale at S.S.W. We sailed in the bark (where I
was) better than the man-of-war, for so we called the
Trinity vessel, notwithstanding that she was newly
cleansed and tallowed. This day we had hazy weather,
and I reckoned myself from Punta Borrica S.S.E. eighteen leagues and a half.

July 1st, 1681. Last night we had two or three
tornados. I reckoned this day a S.S.E. way, and by a
clear observation found lat. 6° 10′ N. We saw great
quantities of fish as we sailed this day.

July 2nd. We made a S.E. way, and our reckoning was

64 by it. By observation I found lat. 5° 20′ N. At noon the same day we had a fresh gale at S.W., with some rain.

July 3rd. We had hazy weather. We made a S.E. by S. way, and 37.

Monday, July 4th. The night just past was windy, with rain, which forced us to hand our top sails. Our reckoning this day was a S.E. way, and a hundred miles.

July 5th. We had a clear night, and, withal, a fresh gale. By this we made a S.E. way. Our latitude this day gave us 2° 20′ N. This morning we saw land southward of us, lying in low hummocks. It was the point, so called, of Manglares.

Wednesday, July 6th. We turned up along shore, and by observation took this day lat. 2° 02′ N. Hereabouts with every new moon is experienced a windward current. In the evening of this day we were close in with low land. We had windy weather and a great sea.

Thursday, July 7th. This day by observation we found lat. 01° 48′ N. In the evening of the said day we lost sight of the said ship.

The next day, being July 8th, we saw the ship again. whose loss began to create some concern in our minds. This day we made very high land all along as we went. And the port, or rather bay, of San Mateo, or St. Matthew, appeared to us like several islands.

Saturday, July 9th. This morning we stood fair in with the port of Tucames. Off the highest part of the land there seems to lie a key. At the north-east point of the port it appears exactly thus :

Puerto de Tucames.

This day at noon we had a clear observation, which gave us lat. 01° 22′ N.

Sunday, July 10th. Last night we stood off to sea, thereby to keep clear of the shore. This day observation showed us lat. 01° 31′ N. About noon the same day we happened to spy a sail, to which immediately we gave chase. We bore up one point of the compass, thereby to hinder her lasking away; but notwithstanding in the evening lost sight of her again. However, our great ship got up with her, and at about eight o'clock at night made her a prize. She proved to be the same ship, named San Pedro, which we had taken the last year, being then bound from Truxillo to Panama, and laden with wine, gunpowder, and pieces of eight, whereof mention was made in its due place. Thus this same bottom became doubly fortunate to us, being twice taken by us in the space of fourteen months. For she had on board her now twenty-one thousand pieces of eight, in eight chests, and in bags sixteen thousand more, besides plate.

Monday and Tuesday, the 11th and 12th of the said month, we made in for the shore. Our prize was so deeply laden, that she seemed to be buried in the water. She had forty men on board her, besides some merchants and friars. On Tuesday an observation gave us lat. 1° 20′ N.

Wednesday, July 13th. This day we dared not adventure into the bay of San Mateo, because we saw some Indians, who had made a great fire on shore, which, as we judged, was designedly done to give intelligence of our arrival. Hereupon we bore away for the river of Santiago, six leagues distant, more or less, from the bay afore-mentioned, to the north-east. Thursday, Friday, and Saturday of the said week, we spent in taking out what parcels of cacao-nut we thought fit from on board the prize, which was chiefly laden with the said commodity. This being done, we cut down the mainmast by the board, and gave them only their main-sail, and thus turning the ship loose, sent away in her all our old slaves, for the good service they had done us, taking new ones from the prize in their room. One only we still detained, who was Francisco, the negro that attempted to run away by swimming ashore, as was mentioned above.

Sunday, July 17th. This day we went from the ship, and found the river of Santiago above-mentioned. At the mouth of this river we stayed Monday and Tuesday following to take in water, which we now much wanted. On the sides of the river we found good store of plantains. Our fresh water we fetched the distance of four miles up the river. We saw several Indians, but could not speak with them they were so shy of us, being forewarned by the Spaniards not to come near us.

On Wednesday, July 20th, we shared our plunder among ourselves, or rather this day made part of the dividend of what we had taken, the rest being reserved to another day. Our prisoners being examined, informed us that the Spaniards had taken up our anchors and cables which we left behind us at the isle of Juan Fernandez. Also that they had surprised the Mosquito Indian that we left behind us there on shore, by the light of a fire which he made in the night upon the isle.

Tuesday, July 21st. All the last four-and-twenty hours we stood off and on. The next day we shared the rest of our things taken in the prize, as also the money that was in the bags; the rest we laid up to divide upon another occasion, especially after such time as we were got through the Straits of Magellan. Our dividend amounted to the sum of 234 pieces of eight to each man. Our prisoners informed us this day that a new Viceroy of Peru was arrived at Panama, and that he dared not adventure up to Lima in a ship of twenty-five guns that was at Panama, for fear of meeting with us at sea, but had chosen rather to wait until the Armada came down from Lima to safeguard and conduct him thither.

July 23rd we had a fresh breeze at S.W., and the next day a clear observation, which gave us only latitude 14′ N. This day Cape San Francisco at N.E. appeared thus to us:

Cabo de San Francisco.

Monday, July 25th. This day we observed latitude 01° 20′ S., and we had a south-west wind.

July 26th. This morning we had a very great dew fallen in the night last past. The weather in like manner was very close.

On Wednesday, July 27th, Cape Passao, at S.S.W. and at six leagues distance, appeared thus:

Cabo Passao.

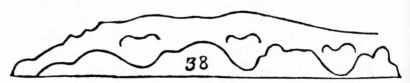

The same morning about seven o'clock we spied a sail E.S.E. from us, under the shore. We presently gave her close chase, as eagerly as we could, and about noon came up with her. But several of the people belonging to her were already got on shore, whereby they made their escape from being taken our prisoners. These were chiefly a friar, who was either a passenger or chaplain to the vessel, and five negroes. She proved to be a Barco d'Aviso, or Packet boat, that was going with letters from Panama to Lima. In this bark we took among other prisoners two white women who were passengers to the same place. Both these and the rest of the prisoners told us, they had heard at Panama that we were all gone out of these seas homewards over land, and that made them adventure now up towards Lima, otherwise they had not come. This day and the Thursday following, we spent in taking out of the packet-boat what we could find in her, which all were things of no considerable value, they having scarce brought any thing with them but the packet. They told us, moreover, that the new Viceroy of Peru, of whom we made mention above, was setting forth from Panama under the conduct of three sail of ships, the one of sixteen, the other of eight, and the third of six guns. That a general peace was all over Europe, excepting only that the English had wars with the Algerines by sea, and the Spaniards by land. Having got what we could out of the prisoners and the vessel, we gave them their liberty, and sent them away in the same bark, as being desirous not to encumber ourselves with more than we could well manage. That night we stood out to sea all night long, most of our men being fuddled.

CHAPTER XXI.

They take another Spanish ship richly laden under the equinoctial.
They make several dividends of their booty among themselves.
They arrive at the Isle of Plate, where they are in danger of
being all massacred by their slaves and prisoners. Their de-
parture thence for the port and bay of Paita, with design to
plunder the said place.

THE next morning after we had turned away the packet-
boat afore-mentioned, the weather being very close, we
spied another sail creeping close under our lee. This
vessel looked mighty big; so that we thought she had
been one of their chief men-of-war, who was sent to surprise or destroy us. Notwithstanding, our brave commander, Captain Sharp, resolved to fight her, and either
to take the said vessel, though never so big, or that she
should take us. To this effect, coming nearer to her, we
easily perceived she was a merchant-ship of great bulk,
as most of your Spanish vessels are, and very deeply
laden. Being up with them, those within her fired three
or four guns at us first, thinking to make their party
good against us. But we answered them briskly, with
a continual volley of small arms, so that they soon ran
down into the hold, and surrendered, crying aloud for
quarter. As it should seem we had killed in that volley
their captain and one seaman, and also wounded their
boatswain; which loss of their commander daunted them
so suddenly, he being a man of good repute in those
seas. Captain Sharp, with twelve more of our company,
entered her the first. In this vessel I saw the most
beautiful woman that I ever saw in all the South Sea.

The name of the captain of this vessel was Don Diego Lopez, and the ship was called El Santo Rosario, or the Holy Rosary. The men we found on board her were about the number of forty, more or less.

Having examined our prisoners, they informed us that the day before they set sail from El Callao from which port they were going towards Panama, our men whom they had taken prisoners at Arica were brought into that place, and very civilly entertained there by all sorts of people, but more especially by the women. That one of our surgeons, whom we suspected to be Mr. Bullock, was left behind, and remained still at Arica.

We lay at anchor from Friday, July 29th, which was the day we took this prize, until Wednesday following, at the same place under Cape Passao as we anchored before. Here we sank the bark that we had taken at the Gulf of Nicoya, being willing to make use of what rigging she had, and also to contract our number of men. In the meanwhile we took out of the prize much plate, and some money ready coined, besides six hundred and twenty jars of wine and brandy, and other things. Thus, leaving only the foremast standing in the said vessel, we turned her away, as we had done the others before, together with all the prisoners in her, giving them their liberty not to be encumbered with them, being desirous to spare our provisions as much as we could. We detained only one man, named Francisco, who was a Biscayner, because he reported himself to be the best pilot of those seas. This being done, we shared all the plate and linen taken in our prize, and weighed thence, standing S.S.E. with a fresh wind that sprang up.

Friday, August 4th. This day we shared the ready money taken in the Rosario, our last prize. Our dividend came to ninety-four pieces of eight each man. Cape Passao, under which all these prizes were taken, at N.E. appears thus :

Cabo Passao.

The land runs S.E. and is for five leagues together to windward of this cape, all mountainous and high land.

The next day, being August 5th, we completed our dividends, sharing this day all our odd money, ready-coined, and plate, with some other things.

Saturday, August 6th. This day perusing some letters taken in the last prize, I understood by them that the Spaniards had taken prisoner one of the last party of our men that left us. Also, that they were forced to fight all their way over land as they went, both against the Spaniards and the Indians, these having made peace with the Spaniards since our departure, as was mentioned above. That our Englishmen had killed, amongst other Spaniards, the brother of Captain Assientos, and Captain Alonso, an officer so-named. Moreover, that ten sail of privateers were coming out of the North Sea, with intent to march over-land into the South Sea, as we had done before, but that they were prevented, being forced back by the great rains that fell near the islands called Samballas.

On August 7th we had very fair weather, notwithstanding some strong winds from shore, and also a strong current to leeward. This ran so fierce against us the next day, August 8th, that in the space of the last four and twenty hours we lost three leagues.

Tuesday, August 9th, we saw the port and town of Manta ; this being nothing but sixteen or seventeen straggling houses, with a large and high brick church belonging to it. What we got in the day by the help of the wind, we lost in the night by the current. The same fortune we had the next day, for we still gained no way all this while.

Thursday, August 11th. All last night we had but little wind; this day we had a violent current to windward, as before, with some gusts of wind. However, by the help of these we made shift to get to windward of the isle of Plate.

August 12th, in the morning, we came to an anchor at the aforesaid isle. We sent our boat ashore with men, as we had done formerly, to kill goats, but we found them to be extremely shy and fugitive, compared with what they were the last year. Here it was that our quarter-master, James Chappel, and myself fought a duel together on shore. In the evening of this day, our slaves agreed among themselves, and plotted to cut us all in pieces, not giving quarter to any, when we should be buried in sleep. They conceived this night afforded them the fittest opportunity, by reason that we were all in drink. But they were discovered to our commander by one of their own companions, and one of them named Santiago, whom we brought from Iquique, leapt overboard; who, notwithstanding, was shot in the water by our captain, and thus punished for his treason. The rest laid the fault on that slave, and so it passed, we being not willing to enquire any farther into the matter, having terrified them with the death of their companion. We lay at this isle until Tuesday following, and in the meanwhile gave our vessel a pair of boots and tops, being very merry all the while with the wine and brandy we had taken in the prize.

On Tuesday, August 16th, in the afternoon, we weighed thence with a S.W. wind. The island at N.W. from us, gave us this following appearance:

Isle de la Plata.

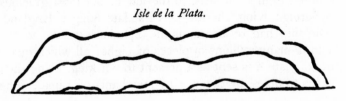

Wednesday, August 17th, the island at E., this morning and at two leagues and an half distance appeared thus :

Island of Plate.

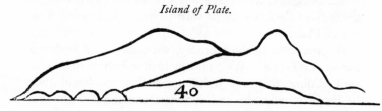

All the day long until the evening we had a leeward current, but then I could not perceive any.

Thursday, August 18th. This morning we were to windward of the island of Solango. In the night before we had continual misty rain. At noon the aforesaid island bore N. by E. of us, and at three leagues distance appeared thus :

Isle de Solango.

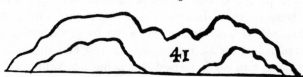

About three leagues from Solango are two rocks, called Los Ahorcados. They appear both high and black to the view, Besides this N.N.E. from Point St. Helena is a high rock, which to windward thereof runs shoaling for the space of half a mile under water. It is distant about eight leagues, more or less, from the said point, and is called Chanduy. At this place, and upon this rock, was lost the ship afore-mentioned, that was ordered from these seas, to the aid of our most gracious Sovereign, King Charles the First, late King of England. Said ship had on board, as the Spaniards relate, to the sum of many millions of pieces of eight ; all which quantity of plate was sent as a present to our king, being then in his troubles, by the worthy merchants of Lima. The rock afore-mentioned lies about two leagues distant from the mainland.

August 19th. This day our pilot told us that since we were to windward a certain ship that was coming from Lima, bound for Guayaquil, ran ashore on Santa Clara, losing there in money to the value of one hundred thousand pieces of eight ; which otherwise, peradventure, we might very fortunately have met with. Moreover, that the Viceroy of Peru had beheaded their great Admiral Ponce, for not coming to fight and destroy us, while we were at Gorgona. This evening we saw point St. Helena, at the distance of ten leagues to S.S.E. from us.

August 20th. This day we had both misty and cold weather. In the afternoon we saw Point St. Helena, at N.E. by N. and at seven leagues distance more or less.

On Sunday, August 21st, we had a fair and clear day. I reckoned myself this day to be about twenty-five leagues to the southward of St. Helena.

August 22nd. This morning about two o'clock we came close in with the shore. We found ourselves to leeward of a certain point called Punta de Mero, which is nothing else than a barren and rocky point. Here runs an eddy current under the shore.

Tuesday, August 23rd. This day in the morning we had but little wind. At noon it blew fresh again. We made all day but short trips, and reefed topsails.

Wednesday, August 24th. This morning a great dew fell. At noon we were W. from Cape Blanco. We found by observation lat. 4° 13′ S. We resolved now to bear up for Paita, and take it by surprise if possible, thereby to provide ourselves with many necessaries that we wanted.

CHAPTER XXII.

They arrive at Paita, where they are disappointed of their expecta-
tions, as not daring to land, seeing all the country alarmed
before them. They bear away for the Strait of Magellan.
Description of the bay and port of Paita, and Colan. An ac-
count of their Sailings towards the Strait afore-mentioned.

THURSDAY, August 25th. The night before this day, we
stood off to sea for fear of the shore, and lest we should
be descried from the coast of Paita, to which we were
now pretty nigh. About noon this day we began to
stand in again, and saw the homing of the land, though
with hazy weather. The next day, being August 26th,
we had cold winds, great dews, and dry weather.

Saturday, August 27th. All this day, but more especially in the morning, we had many fogs. In the afternoon we saw la Silla de Paita at W.S.W. being about
five leagues distant from it.

Sunday, August 28th. Last night about ten o'clock
we were close into land, at the distance of half a league
more or less to leeward of the island of Lobos. We
continued our course all that night, and about break of
day found ourselves close under Pena Horadada, a high
and steep rock so-called. From hence we sailed with a
landwind, and sent away from the ship two canoes well
manned and armed, with good hopes to have taken the
town of Paita undescried. But as it should seem, they
had already received news of our coming, or being upon
that coast, and also had received supplies of forces that
were sent them from the city of Piura, distant thence
twelve leagues up country. These supplies consisted

chiefly of three companies of horse and foot, all of them
being armed with fire-arms. Besides this, they had made
a breast-work along the seaside for the defence of the
town, and the great church which lies at the outermost
part of the town. From these places, as also from a hill
that covers the town, they fired at our men, who were
innocently rowing towards shore with their canoes. This
preposterous firing was the preservation of our people,
for had the Spaniards permitted our men to come ashore,
they had assuredly destroyed them every man. But fear
always hinders that nation of victory, at least in most of
our attempts.

Our men perceiving themselves to be discovered, and
the enemy prepared for their reception, hereupon retreated, and came on board the ship again without
attempting to land, or do anything else in relation to the
taking of the place. We judged there could not be less
than one hundred and fifty fire-arms, and four times as
many lances upon the shore, all in readiness to hinder
our people from landing. Within the town our pilot told
us, there might be one hundred and fifty families.

Being disappointed of our expectations at Paita we
stood down the bay towards Colan. This is another
town so called, and which exceeds Paita three times.
It is chiefly inhabited by fishermen, and thence they
send fish to most inland towns of Peru ; and also serve
Paita with water from the river Colan, not far distant
from the town. It is two leagues more or less from the
town of Paita afore-mentioned to Colan, and thence to
the river, one league, although the houses of Colan do
reach almost to the river. The town of Colan itself is
only inhabited by Indians, and these are all rich ; because they will be paid in ready money for everything
they do for the Spaniards. But the town of Paita is
chiefly inhabited by Spaniards, though there be also some
Indians ; but the Spaniards do not suffer the Indians to
be any great gainers, or grow rich under them.

About ten o'clock a young breeze sprang up, and with that we stood away W., and W. by S. Within a little while it blew so fresh, that we were forced to reef our topsails, the weather being very dark and hazy. I took the port of Paita, and bay of Colan, as they lay exactly situated (see map on next page).

Monday, August 29th. All our hopes of doing any further good upon the coasts of the South Sea being now frustrated, seeing we were descried before our arrival wherever we came, we resolved unanimously to quit all other attempts, and bear away for the Strait of Magellan in order to return homewards either for England or some of our plantations in the West Indies. This day we had a great dew, and I reckoned myself W. S.W. from Paita thirteen leagues and a half, with very little wind. So we stood E.

The next day, August 30th, we had misty weather. We made a W.S.W. way, and by it five leagues and one third. In the afternoon of this day, the wind freshened again, having been but little before, and we stood E.S.E.

The last day of August we had very fair weather. I believed now that the wind was settled at S.E. and S.S.E. We made a S.S.W. way, and twenty-one leagues and two thirds.

September 1st. Last night was very cloudy, but withal we had a fresh gale. Our reckoning was a S.W. by S. way, and that we had made sixteen leagues and two thirds.

September 2nd. We reckoned a S.W. way, and by it twenty-six leagues and two thirds. This day we had an observation, and found lat. 7° 40′ S.

September 3rd brought us both cloudy and misty weather. We made a W.S.W. way, and fourteen leagues.

September 4th. This day the wind was at E.S.E. and sometimes E. coming in many flaws. We had a

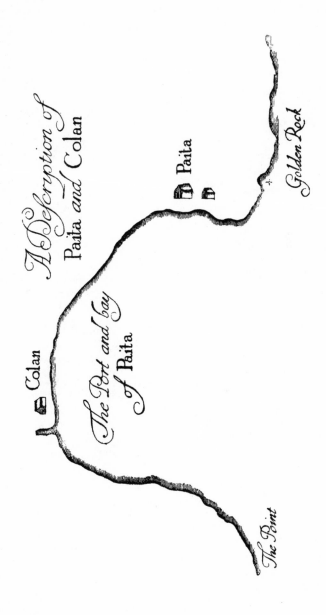

A Description of
Paita and Colan

Colan

The Port and bay
of Paita

The Point

Paita

Golden Rock

457

S.W. by S. way, and reckoned twenty-three leagues and
two thirds.   We had a great sea from S.

Monday, September 5th, we had great winds, and a
high and short sea.   Our way was S.S.W. and half W.
by which we reckoned twenty-eight leagues and two
thirds of a league.

September 6th, we had a very fresh wind at S.E. by
E. with an indifferent smooth sea.   By observation we
found this day latitude 12° oo′ S.   We made a S.W.
by S. way, and twenty-eight leagues and one third.

Wednesday, September 7th, we had a very fresh wind.
We reckoned a S.W. by S. way, and thirty-six leagues.
We observed latitude 13° 24′ S.   We make now for each
mess a plum pudding of salt water and wine lees.

On the eighth we enjoyed a fresh gale of wind,
though with hazy weather.   Our reckoning was a S.W.
by S. way, and hereby twenty-five leagues, and one third
of a league.

September 9th, we made a S.W. by S. way, and
twenty-one leagues and a third.   In the afternoon the
wind came about something more S., allowing us a S.W.
course.

Saturday, September 10th.   All last night past and
this morning the wind was very fresh at E.   Our way
was S.S.W. and by our reckoning thirty-five leagues and
one third.   The weather now was warm.   An observation this day gave us latitude 16° 40′ S.

September 11th we had whiffling winds.   A S.W.
half S. way, and thereby twelve leagues and two thirds.
By an observation we found 17° 10′ S.   Now we had a
very great sea, so that we took in our sprit sail.

September 12th.   All the night before this day we
were under a pair of courses, yet this morning we heaved
out main topsail.   We made a W.S.W. way, and seventeen leagues and one third.   By observation we found
lat. 17° 30′ S.

The 13th.   During last night we had huge and great

storms of wind. In the morning our goose head gave
way, so that at about noon we were forced to lie by till
four in the afternoon to mend it. Our course was S.W.
half W. and our reckoning twenty-nine leagues, and two
thirds of a league. Lat. by observation 18° 12′ S.

Wednesday, September 14th. This day we had very
hazy weather. We made a S.S.W. way, and twenty
leagues.

September 15th. This day likewise we had a S.S.W.
way, and reckoned twenty-three leagues and one half.
Our observation taken this day gave us 20° 09′ S.

On September 16th we had a clear day, a S.W. half
S. way, and made sixteen leagues and two thirds. We
found by observation, lat. 20° 48′ S.

The 17th. Last night was very calm. Also this day,
it being a full moon. We reckoned a S.W. way, and
only by reason of the calmness of the weather nine leagues
and one third of a league,   We had an observation which
afforded us 21° 08′ S. lat.

Sunday, September 18th. Last night a wind sprang
up at S.S.E. which the morning of this day freshened at
S.E. We made a W.S.W. way, and by it eighteen
leagues. Moreover, this day we had a clear observation
that showed us lat. 21° 30′ S.

September 19th. All last night we had a very fresh
wind, but this morning it came about to E. by S. and
E.S.E. with hazy weather. I reckoned a S.W. by S.
way, and twenty-two leagues.

September 20th. This day gave us a fresh wind, hazy
weather, a S. by W. way, and hereupon twenty-three
leagues and one third.

September 21st. This day also the fresh gale continued, with cloudy, and sometimes misty weather. Our
reckoning showed us a S. by W. way as the day before,
and by it twenty-eight leagues and one third. By an
observation made, we found lat. 25° 15′ S.

Thursday, September 22nd. This day we had a very

fresh wind. We reckoned a S. half W. way, and by that twenty-nine leagues and two thirds. An observation taken gave us lat. 26° 42′ S. We observed this day a N.E. sea, which seemed very strange to us.

The next day we had several showers of small rain. My reckoning was a S. by W. way; and thereupon twenty-six leagues. We found by observation lat. 27° 57′ S.

September 24th. We had hazy weather, and the wind not so fresh at E.S.E., with a smooth sea. We made a S.S.W. way half westerly, and twenty-three leagues and two thirds. This day also an observation gave us lat. 28° 57′ S. I reckoned now that we were distant from Paita 302 leagues and two thirds.

Sunday, September 25th. This day we had not much wind, and hazy weather. At noon the wind came E., then E.N.E. and then again N.E. by E. We reckoned a S. by E. way, half E. and 55.

Monday 26th. We had hazy weather and a fresh wind at N.E. We reckoned a S.E. half S. way, and twenty-four leagues. In the afternoon we experienced a N.N.E. sea, and then soon after a N.N.E. wind. After this a N. wind, and that but very little.

September 27th. All the night before this day we had a fresh wind at N.N.E. About eight this morning, it came about again to N.N.W. We made a S.E. by S. way, and thirty-eight leagues. By observation I found lat. 32° 30′ S. Now we enjoyed a very smooth sea, and fair weather.

Wednesday, September 28th. In the night past a very fresh wind at N.N.W. and N.W. At break of day we had a wind at . . . heaving us aback at once. At noon again the wind was at S.W. our course being S.E. This morning we took down our top gallant masts. We made a S.E. by E. way, and on this road twenty-seven leagues and two thirds. By observation, lat. 33° 16′ S., a S.W. sea.

On the 29th we had very windy and hazy weather, with some rain now and then. All last night we handed our maintop sail. We made a S.E. by E. way, and thirty-two leagues and two thirds. We had a S.W. sea and wind.

Friday, September 30th. This day we had fresh winds between S.W. and W. We reckoned a S.E. half S. way, and thereupon forty-four leagues. By observation we found lat. 35° 54′ S.

October 1st. The wind this day was not very fresh, but varying. My reckoning was a S.E. half S. way, and twenty-four leagues. An observation gave us 36° 50′ S. This day I finished another quadrant, being the third I finished in this voyage. We had a S.W. sea, with showers of rain and gusts of wind.

Sunday, October 2nd. The wind this day was hanging between W.N.W., and N.W. by N. We made a S.E. by S. way, and thirty-three leagues and two thirds. By observation we found 38° 14′ S. About noon we had a fresh wind at N.W. and S.W.

October 3rd. Last night in the forepart thereof was clear, but the latter was rainy. The wind very fresh at N.W. by N., but this day we had little wind, and cloudy weather, a S.W. by W. wind, and a S.E. by S. way, by which we reckoned thirty-three leagues and one third.

October 4th. We had a clear night and very fresh wind. We reckoned a S.E. by S. way, and thereby forty-three leagues. By observation, lat. 41° 34′ S. This day also fell several showers of rain.

October 5th. We had a windy night, and a clear day. We reckoned a S.S.E. half E. way, and forty-four leagues and two thirds. By observation, lat. 43° 26′ S. The weather now was very windy, causing a huge tempestuous sea. The wind at N.W. and N.W. by N. blowing very high.

October 6th. This day the wind was still at N.W.

and yet not so fresh as it was yesterday, the weather very foggy and misty. As for the wind it came in gusts, so that we were forced to hand our topsails, and spritsail. We reckoned a S.E. half S. way, and thereby forty-three leagues and one third. The seas now were not so high as for some days past. In the evening we scudded away under our fore course.

Friday, October 7th. Last night was very cloudy, and this day both dark and foggy weather with small rain. We made a S.E. way, and thirty leagues and two thirds. A fresh wind at N.N.W. and N.W. We keep still under a fore course, not so much for the freshness of the wind, as the closeness of the weather.

October 8th. We had a clear night the night before this day, and a strong gale; insomuch that this day we were forced to take in our foresail, and loosen our mizzen, which was soon blown to pieces. Our eldest seamen said that they were never in the like storm of wind before, the sea was all in a foam. In the evening it dulled a little. We made a S.E. half E. way, and eighteen leagues, with very dark weather.

Sunday, October 9th. All the past night we had a furious W.N.W. wind. We set our sail a drough, and so drove to the southward very much, and almost incredibly if an observation had not happened, which gave us lat. 48° 15′ S. We had a very stiff gale at W.N.W. with a great sea from W. which met with a S.S.W. sea as great as it. Now the weather was very cold, and we had one or two frosty mornings. Yesterday in the afternoon we had a very great storm of hail. At noon we bent another mizzen.

Monday, October 10th. This day brought us a fresh wind at N.W. and N.N.W. We made a S.E. half E. way, and by it forty-four leagues. By observation we found lat 49° 41′ S. I reckoned myself now to be east from Paita sixty-nine leagues and a half.

Tuesday Oct. 11th. Last night we had a small time

calm. This day was both cloudy and rainy weather
The wind at S.W. and S.S.W. so furious, that at ten
o'clock this morning we scudded under a main sail. At
noon we lowered our fore yard while we sailed. We
made a S.E. by E. way, and thirty leagues.

CHAPTER XXIII.

The Buccaneers arrive at a place incognito, to which they give the name of the Duke of York's Islands. A description of the said islands, and of the gulf, or lagoon, wherein they lie, so far as it was searched. They remain there many days by stress of weather, not without great danger of being lost. An account of some other remarkable things that happened there.

WEDNESDAY, October 12th. All the night before this day we had many high winds. I reckoned an E.S.E. way, and twenty leagues; for our vessel drove at a great rate. Moreover, we were in lat. 50° 50' S., so that our easting from Paita by my account ought to be one hundred and one leagues, or thereabouts.

This morning about two hours before day, we happened by great accident to spy land. It was the great mercy of God, which had always attended us in this voyage, that saved us from perishing at this time, for we were close ashore before we saw it; and our foreyard, which we most needed on this occasion, was taken down. The land we had seen was very high and towering; and here appeared to be many islands scattered up and down. We steered in with what caution we could, between them and the main, and at last, God be praised, arrived at a place or rather bay, where we perceived ourselves to be land-locked, and, as we thought, pretty safe from the danger of those tempestuous seas. From hence we sent away our canoe to sound and search the fittest place for anchoring. At this time one of our men, named Henry

Shergall, as he was going into our sprit-sail top, happened to fall into the water, and was drowned before any help could be had, though we endeavoured it as much as we possibly could. This incident several of our company interpreted as a bad omen of the place, which proved not so, through the providence of the Almighty, though many dangers were not wanting here to us, as I shall relate.

We came to an anchor in the depth of forty fathom, more or less, and yet at no greater distance than a stone's cast from shore. The water where we anchored was very smooth, and the high lands round about all covered with snow. Having considered the time of the year, and all other circumstances, we resolved, that in case we could find a sufficient stock of provisions here, we would stay longer, that is, until summer came, or something more, before we prosecuted our intended voyage homewards through the Straits of Magellan; which now we began to be careful how to find. That day of our anchoring in this bay, we shot six or eight brave geese, and some smaller fowl besides. Here we found also many hundreds of mussel-banks; all which were very plentifully stocked with that kind of fish. We buried our dead man on the shore, giving him several vollies for his funeral-rites, according to the custom. In the night of this day our anchor came home, so that we were forced to let go a grappling to secure ourselves. But still every flaw of wind drove us. Hereupon we set our sprit-sail, and ran about a mile into another bay, where we let go another anchor, and thus anchored again. The first anchor, which was also the biggest in our ship, we lost by this accident, the cable being cut by the rocks. To these islands afore-mentioned our captain gave the name of His Royal Highness the Duke of York's Islands.

Thursday, October 13th. This day we began to moor

our ship, she driving as we easily could perceive with every flaw of wind that blew. The tide flows here full seven feet up and down. We moored our vessel into a rocky point, being a key whereof there are many in the circumference of this bay. The ground of the bottom of the said bay we found was hard and sandy, being here and there rocky. This evening we brought on board great store of limpets, of which we made a kettle of broth that contained more than all our company could eat.

On Friday, October 14th, we killed several geese, as also many of another sort of fowl like an eagle, but having a bigger beak, with their nostrils rising from the top of the middle of their beak by a hand trunk. This fowl lives on fish, but we saw none. Yesterday in the evening there fell a great sleet of snow on the hills round about the bay, but none where we were at anchor. Moreover, this day in the evening we caught limpets in great quantity, being three times as many as we could eat. Our men in ranging the keys for game, found grass plaited above a fathom long, and a knot tied at the end thereof. In like manner on other keys they found mussels and limpet shells. From these things we presently concluded that these countries were inhabited, and that some Indians or others were to be found hereabouts.

Saturday, October 15th. Last night we had much rain, with large hailstones. About midnight the wind came to north with such great fury that the tree to which our cable was fastened on shore gave way, and came up by the roots. All those gusts of wind were mixed with violent storms of rain and hail. Thus we fastened again to other trees. But here it happened that our ship coming up to the shore, our rudder touched, and thereupon broke our goose-neck. Great was now our ex-, tremity, and greater it will be, if God send not better weather. Scarce a minute now passed without flaws of wind and rain.

Sunday, October 16th. Last night was rainy, as before. About nine o'clock our biggest hawser gave way and broke. All this day likewise we had rain, with several showers of hail, and but little wind to W. of N.

Monday, October 17th. All last night, until five this morning, it ceased not to rain. Then until ten it snowed. On the hills it snowed all the night long. This day we hunted on the shore many tracks of people hereabouts, but could find none hitherto, they having fled and concealed themselves for fear of us, as we supposed.

October 18th. In the past night we had much rain and hail. But the day was very clear. Hereupon we made an observation, which gave us lat. 50° 40′ S. Moreover, this day we had pretty warm weather.

October 19th. Both clear and frosty last night. This day was hazy, and somewhat windy from the north quarter. Every day we had plenty of limpets and mussels of a very large size.

October 20th. Last night was rainy, and this day windy, with very great gusts of wind at N.N.W. until the afternoon. Then we had wind at N.W., being very fresh and in gusts.

October 21st. All the past night was tempestuous, with huge gusts of wind and showers of hail. Yesterday in the evening we carried a cable ashore, and fastened it to a tree. This being done, at midnight our biggest cable broke in the middle. Towards morning we had much snow. In the day, great gusts of wind with large hailstones ; and also great plenty of limpets.

October 22nd. Last night we had strange gusts of wind from N.W., together with much hail and rain. This day we killed a penguin ; and also began to carry water on board.

October 23rd. All the last twenty-four hours we had much rain. The wind was but little at W. and W.S.W.

October 24th. All this time until noon nothing but rain. At that time it held up fair for the space of half an hour, or thereabouts, and then it rained again all the rest of the day.

October 25th. All this while we had not one minute fair. Towards evening it held up from raining, but the weather was cloudy, and withal much warmer than when we came hither at first.

Wednesday, October 26th. All the past night, and this forenoon, we had fair weather. But afternoon it rained again. We found cockles like those we have in England.

Thursday, October 27th. Last night we had much rain, with very great gusts of wind, lasting for the whole space thereof. Yet notwithstanding, this day proved to be the fairest that we ever had since we came into this place. In the evening of this day our canoe, which was gone to search the adjacent places for Indians, or what else they could find, returned to the ship, with a dory at her stern. They had gone, as it should seem, beyond the old bay where we first anchored, and thereabouts happened to meet with this dory. In it were three Indians, who perceiving themselves near being taken, leaped overboard to make their escape. Our men in pursuing them unadvisedly shot one of them dead. A second, being a woman, escaped their hands. But the third, who was a lusty boy about eighteen years of age, was taken, and him they brought on board the ship. He was covered only with a seal's skin, having no other clothing about him. His eyes squinted, and his hair was cut pretty short. In the middle of the dory they had a fire burning, either for dressing victuals or some other use. The dory itself was built sharp at both ends, and flat bottomed. They had a net to catch penguins, and a club like our bandies, called by them a tomahawk. His language we could not understand, but he pointed up the lagoon, giving us to understand that there were more people thereabouts. This was confirmed by our men, who also said they had seen more. They had darts to throw against an enemy, pointed with wood.

On the next day, being October 28th, in the evening our canoe went from the ship again to seek for more Indians. They went into several lagoons, and searched them narrowly. But they could find nothing but two or three huts, all the natives being fled before our arrival. In the evening they returned to the ship, bringing with them very large limpets, and also mussels which were six inches and a half long. Our Indian prisoner could open these mussels with his fingers, which our men could not so readily do with their knives. Both the night past and this day we had very fair weather.

On the 29th we had in like manner a very fair day, and also a smooth wind at S.S.E. Our Indian this day pointed to us that there were men in this country, or not far off from here, with great beards. He appeared to us by his actions to be very innocent and foolish. But by his carriage I was also persuaded that he was a man-eater. This day likewise we caught limpets enough to suffice us for the morrow.

Sunday, October 30th. This day was fair, and there blew a small S.S.E. wind. In the morning we sent a canoe over to the eastward shore, to seek either for provisions or Indians. I myself could not go as I desired, being, with two or three more, at that time very much tormented with the gripes. I am persuaded that this place where we now were, is not so great an island as some hydrographers lay it down, but rather an archipelago of smaller islands. We saw this day many penguins, but they were so shy that we could not come near them. They paddle on the water with their wings very fast, but their bodies are too heavy to be carried by the said wings. The sun now made the weather very warm, insomuch that the snow melted apace.

October 31st. Both last night and this day were very fair. At noon our canoe returned from the eastern shore, bringing word that they had found several good bays and harbours, that were deep even close to the shore ; only that there lay in them several sunken rocks, which we had also where we were. But these rocks are not dangerous to shipping, by reason that they have weeds which lie two fathoms in circumference about them. This morning blew a small wind at N.N.E.

November 1st. This day was also fair, and we had a small wind as before, at N.N.E.

November 2nd. Last night I took the polar distance of the South star of the cock's foot, and found it to be 28° 25′. I observed also the two Magellan clouds, of which I made mention in this Journal before, and found them to be as follows, viz., the lesser 14° 05′, and the greater 14° 25′. The morning of this day we hoisted on end our top-masts, and also brought too a maintop-sail and fore-sail, and finished our filling all the water we needed. At the same time the wind hung easterly ; and I was still much tormented with the gripes as before.

November 3rd. This morning we hung our rudder, the greatest piece of work we had to do, after those violent storms above-mentioned. In the afternoon we hauled in our two biggest hawsers, and also our biggest cable from the shore. For the last three days we had a very great and dark fog between us and the eastward shore. We had now very little wind in the cove where we were, but abroad at sea there blew at the same time a stiff gale at S.S.E. Moreover, we could perceive now, the stormy weather being blown over, much small fry of fish about the ship, whereof we could see none, as was mentioned before. This day we had a very clear and calm evening.

November 4th. Both all last night and this day we had very calm weather. And this morning a small breeze sprang up at N. and N.N.E., which afterwards wheeled about to S. and S.S.E. This morning we hoisted our main and fore-yards; and likewise fetched off from the shore our other hawser and cable, into eleven fathom water. Our resolutions were now changed for a departure, in order to seek the mouth of the Straits of Magellan, seeing that we could not winter here for want of provisions, which we could not find either on the continent or about these islands afore-mentioned. The weather now was very warm, or rather hot, and the birds sung as sweetly as those in England. We saw here both thrushes and blackbirds, and many other sorts of those that are usually seen in our own country.

Saturday, November 5th. This morning brought us a wind at N.N.E. hereupon; we warped to a rocky point, thereby to get out of the cove where we lay. For our anchor came home to us as we were carrying our warp out. At this time a second breeze came up very fresh in our stern; so that we took the opportunity thereof, and went away before it. By noon this day we hoisted in our canoes, and also turned away loose to the sea our Indian dory. As for the Indian boy whom we had taken in said dory we kept him still prisoner, and called him Orson. Our cove at our departure from this place looked thus, as I took then the description thereof. When we were come out into the channel, the weather grew dead calm. Only now and then we had a small breeze, sometimes from one quarter and then from another. By this slackness of wind we observed that the current hoisted us to the southward. On the east side of this lagoon we perceived the Indians make a great smoke at our departure.

A description of his Royal Highnesses Isles

Salt Ness

The Cave

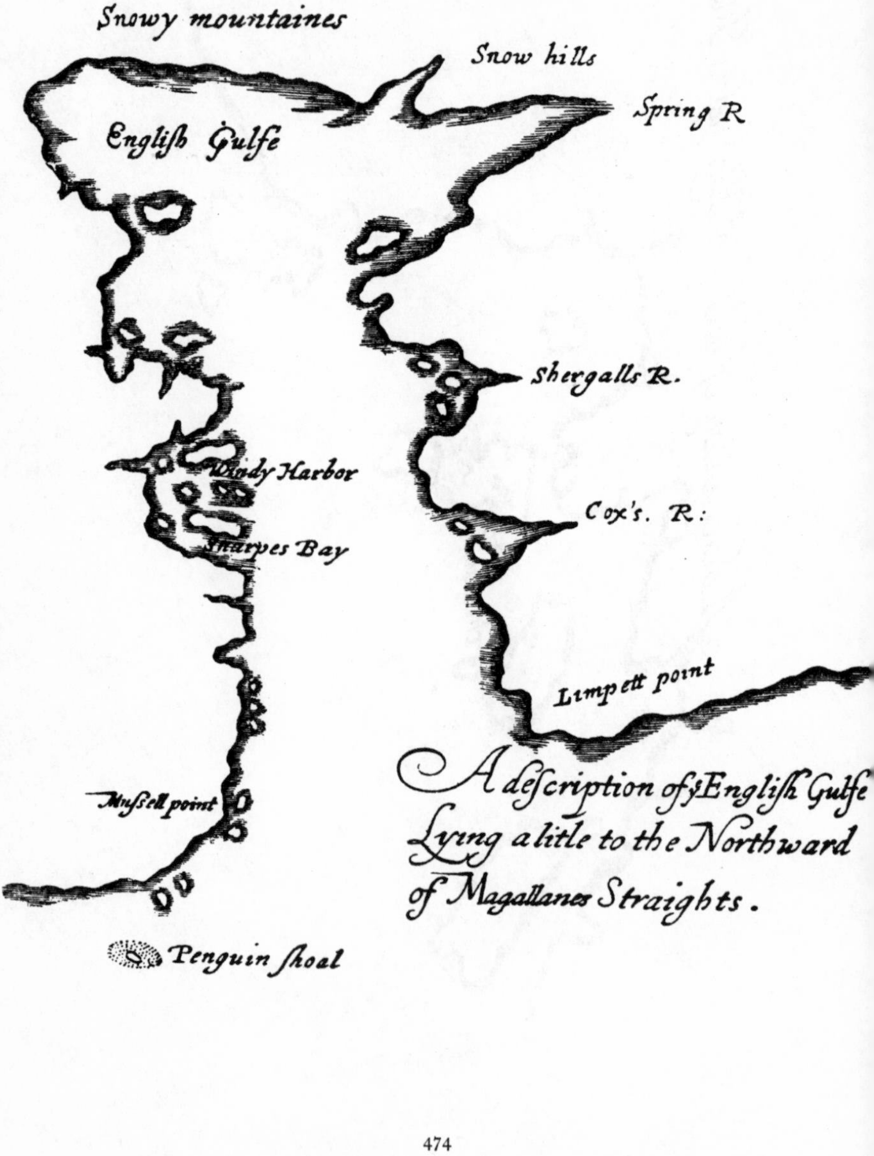

Snowy mountaines

Snow hills

Spring R

English Gulfe

Shergalls R.

Cox's. R:

Windy Harbor

Sharpes Bay

Limpett point

Mussell point

A description of ye English Gulfe
Lying a litle to the Northward
of Magallanes Straights.

Penguin shoal

474

We had a very fair day till six in the evening ; when we got without the mouth of the gulf, it blew so hard, that in an hour it forced us to hand our top-sails. Having now a fit gale at N.W. and N.N.W., we stood S.W. by W. to clear ourselves of some breaks which lie four leagues from the gulf's mouth at S. and S.S.E. Hereabouts we saw many reefs and rocks, which occasioned us to stand close hauled. I have drawn here and given to my reader so much as I have seen of the gulf itself ; the rest must be completed in due time by them that have greater opportunities of making a farther search into it than I had at the time of our stay here under such tempestuous weather as I have described, and the distemper which hung upon me at the same time.

The Duke of York's Island is probably situated near the S. part of the island of Madre de Dios, and English Gulf is the Brazo de la Concepcion a little to the N. of Magellan's Straits on the Pacific side.

CHAPTER XXIV.

They depart from the English Gulf in quest of the Straits of Magellan which they cannot find. They return home by an unknown way, never navigated before.

SUNDAY, November 6th. This morning we had lost the sight of land, so that we could see it no more. All the last night, and this day, we were under our two courses and sprit-sail. The weather this day was hazy. My reckoning was a S.W. half S. way, and by it twenty-one leagues. We had now an indifferently high sea, and a fresh wind at N.N.W.

November 7th. Last night was both rainy and foggy, but in the morning it cleared up. The wind for the most part was at W. and W.N.W. But at noon it came about at W.S.W. Our reckoning was a S.W. by S. way, and by it twenty leagues. We found by observation lat. 52° 03′. We now steered away S.S.E., the wind being at that time at W.S.W. In the evening of this day I found a variation of the needle to N.E. to the number of 15° or better. I was still troubled with the gripes as I had been before.

November 8th. Last night was fair. About midnight the wind came to N.N.W. At the break of day, we all were persuaded that we had seen land, but at noon we saw that it was none, but only a cloud. The wind was now at N. My reckoning was a S.E. half E. way, and thirty-two leagues and one third. We had an observation that gave us 53° 27′ S. The whole day was very fine and warm, and we saw great numbers of fowls and seals.

November 9th. Yesterday in the evening the weather

was cloudy. Hereupon we lay by under a main course. After midnight we sailed East, and E. by N., with a fresh wind at W.N.W. and not any great sea. The day itself was cloudy, and toward noon we had some rain. So at two in the afternoon we lay by under a main course, the wind being fresh at N.W. I reckoned an E.N.E. way, and thereby twenty-eight leagues.

Thursday, November 10th. All last night we lay under a main course, with a mere fret of wind at N.W. and N.N.W. Day being come, the wind rather increased ; insomuch that about noon our sail blew to pieces. Hereupon we were forced to lower the yard, and unbend the sail, lying for a little while under a mizzen. But that also soon gave way : so that all the rest of this day we lay a hull in very dark weather, foggy and windy, with a huge sea, which oftentimes rolled over us. In the afternoon it seemed to abate for some space of time ; but soon after it blew worse than before, which compelled us to lower our foreyard.

November 10th. All last night we had furious windy and tempestuous weather, from the points of N.W. and N.N.W., together with seas higher and higher. In the evening we set our mizzen. At which time the sun appeared very watery ; but the wind now abated by degrees and the seas also.

November 12th. This morning little wind was stirring, but only some rain fell. About ten it cleared up, by observation, lat. 55° 25′. The sea was now much fallen, and a fresh wind sprung up at W. and W.S.W. We experienced also a very great current to the S.W. In the afternoon of this day we set our sails again, resolving now unanimously to make for the Straits of St. Vincent, otherwise called the Straits of Fernando de Magellan. We had a fresh wind at W.N.W., our course being S.S.E. under our spritsail, foresail, and foretopsail. This day we saw many fishes, or rather fowls, who had heads like Muscovy ducks, as also two feet like them.

They had two fins like the fore-fins of turtles : white breasts and bellies, their beak and eyes being red. They are full of feathers on their bodies, and their hinder parts are like those of a seal, wherewith they cut the water. The Spaniard calls these fowls *paxaros ninos.* They weigh most commonly about six or seven pounds, being about one foot, a little more or less, in length. Our commander, Captain Sharp, had so much dexterity as to strike two of them. In the evening we set also our mainsail ; the wind now coming to S. of W.

Sunday, November 13th. All last night we had a fresh wind between S.W. and W.N.W. with sometimes mists of small rain. In the evening we enjoyed a fine leading gale at W.N.W. together with both clear and wholesome weather. We made a S.E. way, and by it forty-two leagues and two thirds. This day an observation gave us lat. 56° 55′ S. We still experienced a great S.W. current. In the afternoon of this day we steered E.S.E. and in the evening had whiffling winds.

November 14th. Both last night and this morning we had cloudy weather. About eight it cleared up. My reckoning was a S.E. by E. way, and by it thirty-two leagues. Our observation gave us lat. 57° 50′ S. This day we could perceive land, and at noon were due W. from it. In the evening we stood E. by S.

November 15th. All the past night was very cloudy. We judged now that we should be close in with the land we had seen the day before, but the morning being come we could see none. In the night much snow fell, and in the day we had great sleets thereof, the weather being very cold and cloudy. I reckoned an E.S.E. way, and hereby twenty-nine leagues and two thirds, moreover, that our lat. was 58° 25′ S. The wind was now so fresh at N., that we were forced to lie under our two courses and spritsail.

November 16th. Most of this time we had still rain and snow, but now no night at all, though the weather was dark. The wind was various, but from midnight before this day the wind was at S.E. and S.S.E. We now lay E.N.E. I reckoned a N.E. by E. way, and twenty-three leagues. About four in the afternoon two of our fore shrouds' bolts broke, but were presently mended. This afternoon also we saw a very large whale. In the evening we handed in our foretop sail, and lay under our pair of courses and sprit sail, the evening being very clear.

November 17th. In the past night there was a very hard frost. At four this morning we saw two or three islands of ice at the distance of two or three leagues to the S. of us. Soon after this, we saw several others, the biggest of them being at least two leagues round. By observation, lat. 58° 23′ S. We had now a vehement current to the S. At noon I saw many others of these islands of ice afore-mentioned, of which some were so long that we could scarce see the end of them, and extended about ten or twelve fathom above water. The weather in the meanwhile was very clear, and the wind cold.[1] I found variation of the needle eighteen degrees to the N.E.

November 18th. All last night was very fair. I must call it night ; for otherwise it was not dark at all. The sea was very smooth, and the wind at N. and N.N.W. I reckoned a N.E. by N. way, and by the same twenty-two leagues. At ten it grew dead calm, which held all the afternoon of this day. But at night we had a wind again at N. and N. by E.

November 19th. This day was cloudy with snow, and a frosty night preceding it. The wind now was so fresh at N. that we were forced to take in our topsails, and lie all day under our courses and spritsail. We made by an E.S.E. way eighteen leagues and two thirds.

November 20th. We had a cloudy night, together

---

[1] It is impossible to ascertain precisely when they doubled the Horn, but probably about this date.

with mizzling rain and snow. This morning fell so great a fog, that we could not see from stem to stern of our ship. From ten o'clock last night we had also calm, and very cold weather. But what was worse than all this, we were now kept to a very short allowance of our sorry victuals, our provisions growing very scanty with us. About ten this morning we had a very small breeze at N. Several of our men were not able to endure the cold, so fierce it was, whereby they were forced to lie and keep themselves as close as they could. We made an E. way, and by the same sixteen leagues. This day at noon I reckoned myself to be E. from the gulf, whence we last departed, two hundred and five leagues and two thirds.

Monday, November 21st. Last evening we caught a small and white land fowl, and saw two or three more ; and also this morning. This sight afforded us good hopes we were not far distant from some coast or other, yet none could we see in all this long and tedious voyage. In the night past we had a calm, and all this morning a great fog with much snow and rain. We reckoned an E. by N. way, and ten leagues. At one in the afternoon we had a fresh gale that sprang up at E., and at E. by N.

November 22nd. Most part of this day was calm. In the meanwhile we could observe our ship to drive E. My reckoning was an E.N.E. way, and thereby thirteen leagues and one third. At one in the afternoon we had a small gale at W.S.W., our course being N.N.E. and N.E. by N.

November 23rd. This day we had a gale at N.W. and freshening still more and more ; so that we were forced to take in our topsails and spritsail. The wind was not a settled gale, but often varied from point to point. At noon it came at N.E. and our course was then N.N.W. By a N. way we reckoned sixteen leagues.

November 24th. Both last night and this morning was foggy weather, with some calms between-times. But at eight in the morning the sun broke out, though not-withstanding the day was not clear. By a N.N.E. way we reckoned fifteen leagues. This morning the wind came about to E., and by noon it was again at N.E. We had a clear evening and a fresh gale.

November 25th. All last night we had a fresh wind at E. and E.N.E., insomuch, that at eight in the morning we took in our topsails. But at noon the wind was not so fresh as it had been before. I reckoned a N.N.W. half W. way, and by the same twenty leagues.

November 26th. Last night the wind was not alto-gether so fresh as before; but this morning it was again very high. The weather was both dark and cloudy, and brought now and then rain and snow. We made a N.N.E. way, and hereby thirty leagues. The wind all along E. by S. and E.S.E. In the evening we had fair weather again. We experienced for the last ten days a great Western sea, and saw in the same time several seals.

Sunday, November 27th. All the past night we en-joyed a fresh gale and clear weather. I reckoned thirty-six leagues by a N.E. by N. way. By observation, lat. 52° 48′ S. And I judged myself to be E. from the gulf two hundred and eighty-five leagues. In the evening of this day we had a very exact sight of the sun, and found above 30° variation of the needle: whence ought to be concluded that it is very difficult to direct a course of navigation in these parts. For in the space of only twenty-five leagues sailing we have experienced eight or nine degrees difference of variation, by a good Dutch azimuth compass.

November 28th. All last night we had a fresh wind at E.S.E. Towards morning we had but little wind, all the day being hazy weather. This day we saw a whole flight of land fowls, of which sort we killed one before, as was mentioned above. This sight gave us occasion to believe that, neither then nor at this present.

were we far distant from land, and yet we descried none in the residue of this whole voyage. We made by a N.N.E. way thirty-three leagues. Yesterday in the evening we set a new spritsail, and about three this morning we also set our main sail. At one in the afternoon the wind came about N.E. and N.N.E. which in the evening blew very fresh, with cloudy weather.

November 29th. The night proved very cloudy, and the wind blew very fresh at E.N.E. and N.E. by E. This morning it was at E., with both snow and hail. Towards noon the weather cleared up, and we found by an observation taken lat. 49° 45′ S. Our reckoning was a N. way, and thirty leagues. This day we had a short E. sea, and withal a very cold evening. I took the sun, and hereby I found variation 26° 30′ to the N. E. This night the wind came about W. and W.N.W., continuing so all the night.

November 30th. This day the wind was N. and N.N.E., with some clouds hovering in the sky. At this time we had already almost four hours of night. The morning of this day was very fair and clear. Hereupon, to give myself satisfaction in the point, fearing the truth of Spanish books, I worked the true amplitude of the sun, and found his variation to be 26° 25′ to the N.E., being very conformable to what I had both read and experimented before. Hereabouts also we experienced a current to N. Moreover, this day we saw much rockweed, which renewed our hopes once more of seeing land. We reckoned a N.E. way, and by the same twenty-two leagues. By an observation made we found lat. 48° 53′ S. This day also we saw several of those fowl-fish afore described called *paxaros-ninos*, and these of a larger size than any we had seen before. In the afternoon the wind came about at N.N.E. whereby we stood N.W. by W., with a fresh gale and smooth water. The weather now began to grow warmer than hitherto, and the evening of this day was clear.

Tuesday, December 1st. The latter part of last night was very cloudy, and also sometimes rainy. About midnight we had a furious and violent tornado, forcing us in a moment to hand in our topsails. At five in the morning we set them again, and at eleven we had another tornado, forcing us to hand our topsails the second time. We made a N.N.E. two thirds E. way, and thereby thirteen leagues and two thirds. The afternoon of this stormy day proved very fair, and the wind came to W.S.W., our course being N.E. by N. In the evening the wind freshened, with cloudy weather.

December 2nd. Last night we experienced a very furious whirlwind, which, notwithstanding, it pleased God, did pass about the length of our ship, to W. of us. However, we handed in our topsails, and hauled up our lowsails, in the brails. After the whirlwind came a fresh storm of large hail stones, in the night, and several tornados ; but, God be thanked, they all came large of our ship. We now made great way under a forecourse and spritsail. At four o'clock this morning our foresail split, whereby we were forced to lower our foreyard. At half an hour aften ten we hoisted it again with a furious S.W. wind. We made a N.E. by E. way, and by the same forty-seven leagues and a half. By observation we now had lat. 46° 54' S. We reefed our foresail in consequence of the violence of the wind. But in the evening this rather increased, and we had a very great sea. Our standing rigging, through the fury of this gale, gave way in several places, but was soon mended again.

December 3rd. The wind all last night was very fresh, with several flaws both of wind and rain at S.W. and S.W. by S. We enjoyed now very warm weather. This morning we set our foretop sail. Our reckoning gave us a N.E. half E. way and forty-five leagues. We found lat. by observation 45° 28' S. This day at noon a large shoal of young porpoises came about our ship, and played up and down.

December 4th.   All last night we had a fresh gale at
W.S.W.   The night was clear, only that now and then
we had a small cloud affording some rain.   In the morning from four o'clock till eight it rained ; but then it
cleared up again, with a S.W. wind and a very smooth
sea.   We made by a N.E. one quarter N. way, thirty-
nine leagues.   By observation we found lat. 44° 01′ S.
At noon the wind came to S.S.W., our course then being
N.N.E.   This day we agreed among ourselves, having
the consent of our commander, to share the eight chests
of money, which as yet were remaining unshared.   Yesterday in the evening we let out the reef of our foresail,
and hoisted up our foreyard.   This evening I found
variation 17° N.E.

Monday, December 5th.   All last night a clear night,
and this a fair day, with a fresh wind at S.S.W.   We
reckoned a N.E. 5° N. way, and by the same forty-two
leagues.   An observation gave us lat. 42° 29′ S.   This
afternoon we shared of the chests above-mentioned three
hundred pieces of eight each man.   I now reckoned
myself to be E from my departure four hundred and
seventy-one leagues and one third.   At night again we
shared twenty-two pieces-of-eight more to each.

December 6th.   We had a clear starlight night the
last, and a fair morning this day, with a fresh gale at S.W.
At noon we took in our foretop sail.   We reckoned
a N.E. half N. way, and hereby fifty leagues and two
thirds.   An observation taken afforded us 40° 31′ S.
This evening was cloudy.

December 7th.   The night was both windy and cloudy.
At one in the morning we took in our topsails, and at
three handed our spritsail, and so we scudded away before the wind, which now was very fresh at West.   This
morning a gust of wind came and tore our mainsail into
a hundred pieces, which made us put away before the
wind, till we could provide for that accident.   My reckoning was a N.E. three quarters E. way, and by the same

thirty-three leagues. By observation we found lat. 39°
37' S. We had now a great sea, and a fresh wind.
At three in the afternoon we set another foresail, the first
being blown to pieces. Moreover, at the same time, we
furled our spritsail. At five the wind came at W.S.W.
with very bad weather. This day our worthy commander,
Captain Sharp, had very certain intelligence given him,
that on Christmas Day, which was now at hand, the
company, or at least a great part thereof, had a design to
shoot him ; he having appointed that day some time since
to be merry. Hereupon he made us share the wine
amongst us, being persuaded they would scarce attempt
any such thing in their sobriety. The wine we shared
fell out to three jars to each mess. That night the wind
increased.

December 8th. Last night was both cloudy and
windy, the wind often varying between N.W. and S.W.
This morning it varied between W. and N.W. by W.
About noon this day we brought a new mainsail to the
yard, but did not set it then, because there blew too
much wind. I reckoned a N.E. half N. way, and by
the same thirty leagues. By observation, lat. 38° 29' S.
In the afternoon we had one or two squalls of wind and
rain ; but the violence of both fell astern of us. In the
evening it blew again very hard. I observed this day
the rising and setting of the sun, and found the exact
variation to be 12° 15' N.E.

December 9th. The night was starry, but withal
very windy. About the break of day the wind came to
N.W., and at seven we set our foretop sail, and stood
N.N.E. with not much wind. We made since our last
reckoning a N.E. quarter E. way, and twenty-nine
leagues. We found by observation lat. 37° 30' S. The
sea was much fallen, but our ship now began to complain
of several leaks, through our tedious and long voyage.
This afternoon we hoisted up our mainyard and set up
backstays and main swifter, whose ring-bolt gave way

but was mended. In the evening of this day we had but little wind.

December 10th. The night was very clear, but till ten o'clock this forenoon we had no wind. Then a small breeze sprang up at N. and N. by E. We made an E.N.E. one third N. way, and hereby twenty-one leagues. An observation gave us lat. 37° 01′ S. In the afternoon of this day our chief surgeon cut off the foot of a negro boy, which was perished with cold. Now it was like to be bad weather again. Hereupon we furled our topsails, and lay under a pair of courses. But in the evening we lay under a foresail and mizzen, with misty weather.

Sunday, December 11th. All last night we had a fresh wind at N. and sometimes at N.N.W. The weather was very cloudy with drizzling rain. We made an E. way, and thereby twenty-five leagues. This day brought a great sea. About ten in the morning one of our main shrouds gave way. In the evening fell some small rain.

December 12th. All last night we had misty rain and but little wind; yea, in the morning a perfect calm. At noon came up a small gale at E.S.E. and S.E., bringing with it cloudy weather. We reckoned a N.E. by E. way, and by the same eighteen leagues. Yesterday died the negro boy whose leg was cut off by our surgeon, as was mentioned the day before. This afternoon also died another negro, somewhat bigger than the former, named Chepillo. The boy's name was Beafero. All this evening but small wind.

December 13th. All night the wind was at E.S.E., our course being N.N.E. At three in the morning it came about at S.S.W. and at nine at E. by N. I reckoned a N.E. by N. way, and fifteen leagues. The weather was hazy. In the afternoon the wind was at N.E. our course being N.N.W. We enjoyed now a very smooth sea, and saw multitudes of grampuses, whales and porpoises every day as we sailed along.

December 14th. Last evening was cloudy, as also

the night foggy. Hereupon we took in our topsails. At half an hour after three this morning, we stood N.E. the wind being then at N.N.W. At five we put out our topsails again. At seven of the morning we saw a turtle floating upon the sea. We reckoned a N.N.E. way. This day's observation afforded us 34° 32′ S. At this time we had very hot weather, and great dews in the night. My whole easting I reckoned to be now six hundred and seventy-seven leagues and one third.

December 15th. Last night was fine with a great dew. The wind in the interim was between N. and N.W. I reckoned a N.E. half E. way, and by the same thirty-one leagues. We had an observation that gave us lat. 33° 46′ S. At noon the wind came about at N.N.W. our course being N.E. We had this day a very clear evening, and at the same time a fresh wind.

December 16th. We had a fair night and wind at N.N.W. and N.W. by N. This morning I took the sun at its rising, and found N.E. variation 20° 30′. My reckoning was a N.N.E. way, and thirty-six leagues and one third. By observation I found lat. 32° 09′ S. At noon this day the wind came about to N.W.

December 17th. Most part of last night the wind was at N.W. as before. But towards morning a fine and easy gale sprang up at W.N.W. This morning we saw several dolphins playing upon the sea, which made us hope they would at last befriend us and suddenly show us some land or other. We reckoned a N.E. by N. one third N. way, and by the same twenty-five leagues. An observation gave us lat. 31° 04′. A fair evening.

December 18th. We had a clear night, together with a smooth gale at N.W., which this morning was at W. by S. We had now a smooth sea for several days past. Our reckoning was twenty-five leagues, by a N.E. by N. way. By observation we perceived lat. 29° 48′ S.

December 19th. A clear night and a fresh breeze at S.S.W. and S.W. by E., lasting until nine in the morn-

ing.　Then sprang up a wind at S.E. by E.　I reckoned
this day a N.N.E. half E. way, and upon the same thirty
leagues.　By observation, lat. 28° 29′ S.　The day was
very fair, and a smooth sea, with weather that was very
hot.　My whole easting I reckoned now to be seven
hundred and sixty leagues.　This evening I found variation 02° 50′ N.E.

CHAPTER XXV.

The Buccaneers continue their navigation, without seeing any land, till they arrive at the Caribbean Islands in the West Indies. They give away their ship to some of their companions that were poor, and disperse for several countries. The author of this Journal arrives in England.

DECEMBER 20th, 1681. The night before this day was somewhat cloudy, but the weather was fair and the wind but little. At noon the wind came about N. by E., our course being W.N.W. We made a N.N.W. way, and thereby as I reckoned twenty two leagues. By an observation made we took lat. 27° 25′ S. The evening of this day was cloudy, and now and then there fell a shower of rain.

December 21st. At eight o'clock last night the wind came N.W. by N., but with such dark weather that we were forced to take in our top-sails. The night was somewhat rainy, and the weather this morning calm and rainy. About ten we had a small breeze at N.W. We reckoned a N. by E. way, and by the same sixteen leagues. The afternoon of this day was calm and still.

December 22nd. We had a fair and clear night which produced this day a smooth sea and extremely hot weather, and very little wind near the sun ; so that no observation was made.

December 23rd. The night was very fair. At midnight, or thereabouts, a fresh gale sprang up at S.E. and E.S.E., which sometime was E. This freshened by degrees. We had in the day very hot and clear weather. By a N. way I reckoned fifteen leagues.

December 24th. Last night we had both a fresh gale and a clear night. The wind was at E. by S. We reckoned a N.E. by E. way, and by it thirty-one leagues.

Sunday, December 25th. This day being Christmas day, for celebration of that great festival we killed yesterday in the evening a sow. This sow we had brought from the Gulf of Nicoya, being then a sucking pig of three weeks old, more or less, but now weighed about fourscore and ten pounds. With this hog's flesh we made our Christmas dinner, being the only flesh we had eaten ever since we turned away our prizes under the equinoctial, and left the island of Plata. We had this day several flaws of wind and some rain; but the weather otherwise was pretty clear. I reckoned a N. by E. way, and thirty-three leagues by the same. It was now also extremely hot weather, as we signified before.

December 26th. We had this day several gusts of wind, which forced us to stand by our top-sails. Yet were they but very short, and all the rest of the while we enjoyed an indifferent fresh gale at E. and E. by S. We reckoned a N. by E. way, and twenty-eight leagues.

December 27th. We had fair weather, and a fresh wind at E. and E. by S. I reckoned a N. by E. way, and upon the same thirty-two leagues. The evening of this day was cloudy.

December 28th. Last night was cloudy, with a fresh wind. We reckoned a N.E. way, and by the same forty-six leagues. We found by observation, lat. 15° 30′ S. My whole easting I reckoned this day to be eight hundred and twenty-five leagues. Now we saw much flying fish, with some dolphins, bonitos, and albicores; but they will not take the hook.

December 29th. All last night was cloudy, with a fresh wind between E. and E.S.E. The weather all the afternoon was hazy. I reckoned a N. by E. way, and hereupon forty leagues and one third. In the afternoon we had a S.E. by E. wind, which blew very fresh. The evening was clear. At sunset I found variation to N.W. 04° 19'.

December 30th. Last night was cloudy. Towards morning the wind came about at E. At six it came E.S.E. and at ten to S.E. by S. We made a N. by E. way, and forty-three leagues. By observation, lat. 11° 03' S. The evening of this day was clear.

December 31st. We had a cloudy night, but the morning was hazy. We came now to a strict allowance of only three good pints of water each day. We made a N. by E. way, lat. by observation 08° 55' S. In the afternoon we had an E.S.E. and S.E. by E. wind. My whole easting I reckoned now to be eight hundred and eighty four leagues and one third. At noon we stood away N.W.

Sunday, January 1st, 1682. All last night was cloudy, as this day also, with some showers of rain. We made a N.W. one eighth N. way, and forty leagues. In the afternoon came about a fresh wind at S.E. and E.S.E.

January 2nd. The weather this day was both dull and cloudy. We reckoned a N.W. one quarter N. way, and by the same thirty-two leagues. By observation, lat. 06° 06' S. The wind came pretty fresh at S.E.

January 3rd. We had several squalls of wind, and some rain. But withal a fresh wind at S.E. and E.S.E. Our reckoning was a N.W. one quarter N. way, and thirty-four leagues. The afternoon was clear, but the evening cloudy.

January 4th. All last night was very cloudy, but this forenoon it cleared up. Yesterday we put abroad our maintop-sail, studding-sails, but took them in at night. At four this morning we set our larboard studding-sail, and before noon fitted up top-gallant masts and yards. We made a N.W. way, and by it forty leagues and two thirds. By observation, lat. 03° 09' S. This afternoon also we set our topgallant-sail, being forced to make out all its running rigging. The wind was pretty fresh at S.E. and S.E. by E.

January 5th. Most part of the past night was clear and starlight, though with some rain towards the morning. This being come, we put out our top-gallant sail, and both our top-sail, studding-sails. At noon likewise we put up our fore-top-gallant mast and yard. We caught an albicore this day, weighing about one hundred and twenty pounds. The wind was at S.E. by S. and S.S.E. We made a N.W. way, and reckoned thereby thirty-five leagues. By observation, lat. 02° 03′ S. We had now mighty hot weather.

January 6th. Yesterday in the evening we caught another albicore, which weighed only eight or nine pounds. We made a N.W. way, and reckoned thirty-five leagues as before. By observation, lat. 00° 49′ S. The evening of this day was very clear.

January 7th. The wind was variable between S.S.E. and S.S.W., though not altogether so fresh as before. Our reckoning was a N.W. one quarter N. way, and thirty-six leagues by the same. This day an observation gave us lat. 00° 32′ N. of the equinoctial, which now we had passed again. In the afternoon of this day we caught another albicore, which weighed more than the first we took, that is, between one hundred and thirty-five and one hundred and forty pounds. But little wind stirring this afternoon.

January 8th. Last evening we had little better than a calm. At nine this morning we had a fresh wind at S.S.E. with dark weather, so that we thought it convenient to take in our maintop-sail. But at noon we set it again, and also our larboard top-studding-sail, with both top-gallant sails. We made a N.W. way, and by it thirty-four leagues. By observation, lat. 01° 55′ N. We had now extremely hot weather, and a very small allowance of water.

January 9th. Last night we took in top-sails all

night, the wind then whiffling between S. and W. We had notwithstanding for the most part very little wind. The morning of this day was rainy, and thereupon with good diligence we saved a bumpkin of water. There was now a great rippling sea, rising very high ; and it is reported that sometimes and somewhere hereabouts is to be seen an enchanted island ; which others say, and dare assert, that they have sailed over. I reckoned a N.W. by N. one quarter N. way, and twenty-five leagues. This afternoon we had very dark and calm weather, looking as if we should have much rain. Now, reckoning up my meridian, I found myself E. from my departure seven hundred and two leagues. In the evening we had very rainy weather and a cockling sea.

January 10th. All last night was cloudy. About midnight sprang up a small breeze varying all round the compass. At five this morning we had a breeze at S.E. and a very clear sky, which afterwards continued to freshen, with the same clearness as before. We made a N.W. by N. one quarter N. way, and by the same two leagues and two thirds. By clear observation, lat. 03° 16′ N. At four this evening the wind was at E.S.E., the weather being violent hot ; insomuch that our allowance of water was tedious to us for its shortness. At the same time we had an indifferent smooth sea from the E.

January 11th. All last night we had little or no wind. But about two in the morning the wind freshened again at E.N.E., and brought both a clear and hot day. We made twenty-three leagues by a N.W. one quarter W. way. This day's observation gave us lat. 04° 06′ N. In the afternoon we had a shower of rain, and afterwards a fresh wind at E.N.E. But the evening grew dull.

January 12th. Last night we had two or three squalls of wind, and some showers of rain. In the meanwhile the wind blew fresh at N.E. and N.E. by E., as it also continued to do in the day. I reckoned a N.W. way, and forty-four leagues and one third. Our observation this day gave us 05° 49′ N. Yesterday and to-day we set our maintop sail. Now I could not find much variation of the needle.

January 13th. We had a fresh gale all last night, but more northerly than before ; for now it was N.E. by N. We reckoned a W.N.W. way, and thereupon —— leagues and two-thirds. An observation showed, lat. 06° 41′ N. We had a N.N.E. sea and very clear weather.

January 14th. We had a clear night, and a fresh wind at E.N.E. We made a N.W. one fifth W. way, and thirty-eight leagues. By observation, lat. 07° 46′ N. We had a smooth sea ; and now we were come to only three horns of water a day, which made in all but a quart allowance for each man. The evening was clear, and we had a fresh wind.

Sunday, January 15th. Last night was clear, and the wind fresh at E.N.E., and again at N.E. by E. very fresh. At about eleven o'clock at night there died one of our companions, named William Stephens. It was commonly believed that he poisoned himself with mançanilla in Golfo Dulce, for he never had been in health since that time. This forenoon was cloudy. We reckoned forty-four leagues and a N.W. way. An observation gave us this day 09° 18′ N. All last night we kept out our top-gallant sails. We saw hereabouts many flying fish, being very large in size. This morning also we threw overboard our dead man, and gave him two French vollies and one English one. I found now again very small variation.

January 16th. We had a clear night, and a very fresh wind at N.E. and E.N.E., with a long, homing sea. My reckoning was a N.W. one seventh W. way, and thereby forty-eight leagues and one-third. The observation made this day gave us lat. 10° 48′ N. I reckoned myself now E. from my departure five hundred and fifty-three leagues. We had a very cloudy evening.

January 17th. All last night we enjoyed a fresh wind, and so this day also, at N.E. by N. We made a N.W. half W. way, and thereupon forty-seven leagues and one-third. By observation we found lat. 12° 19' N. We had now a long north sea. At noon this day we steered away N.N.W. The day was very hot, but the night both cool and dewy.

January 18th. All last night was both cloudy and windy. At six this morning our sprit sail topmast broke. I reckoned a W.N.W. way, and forty-eight leagues by the same. We found by observation, lat. 13° 12' N. At noon we steered away W., the wind being at N.E. fresh, with a clear evening.

January 19th. We had a clear night, and a fresh wind at E.N.E., which sometimes came in pushes. Our reckoning was a W. half S. way, and by the same forty-six leagues. We found by observation lat. 13° 01' N. Yesterday in the evening we put up a new sprit sail topmast; with a fine, smooth gale at N.E. by E.

January 20th. Last night was clear, and not very fresh, but at daybreak it freshened again. Last night we saw a great shoal of fish; whereof we caught none, by reason the porpoises frightened them from us, as they ofttimes had done before. Yesterday in the evening also we saw a man-of-war fowl, and that gave us good hopes we should e'er long see land. These hopes, and the great desires we had to end our voyage, gave us occasion this day to put in, or stake down, each man of our company a piece of eight for a reward to him that should first discover land. We reckoned a W. one-sixth N. way, and by it thirty-eight leagues. An observation gave us this day lat. 13° 11' N. The wind was at N.E. and E.N.E. This day we passed over many ripplings, and also saw many multitudes of fish; but the porpoises did always hinder us from having any good of them.

January 21st. We made a W. way, and reckoned forty-seven leagues. By observation we found lat. 13°

07′ N. The wind was at E.N.E., and thence came a long sea. The evening was very clear.

January 22nd. We had a fair and a clear day, the wind being at E. We reckoned a W. by N. one-third W. way, and forty leagues. An observation showed us lat. 13° 17′ N. We had a clear evening, and a fresh wind at E.N.E.

January 23rd. This day was both clear and hot, with a fresh wind at E.N.E. My reckoning was a W. way, and forty-six leagues. Our observation this day afforded us lat. 13° 15′ N. In the evening we had some rain.

January 24th. This day brought us likewise clear weather, such as the day before. I reckoned a W. way, and forty leagues and one-third. By observation we found lat. 13° 12′ N. The afternoon was cloudy, and had some rain, the wind freshening at E.N.E. and at E. by N. I reckoned now that I was E. from my departure three hundred and eleven leagues. We had a cloudy evening.

January 25th. Both last night and this morning the weather was cloudy. This morning we saw several tropical birds of divers sorts. Our reckoning was a W. three-quarters N. way, and forty-three leagues. We found by observation lat. 13° 29′ N. This afternoon we saw a booby flying close aboard the horizon. The weather was hazy. But now we began to look out sharp on all sides for land, expecting to see it every minute. I reckoned myself to be E. of my departure two hundred and sixty-eight leagues.

January 26th. Last night was indifferent clear. Yet notwithstanding, this morning we had a smart shower of rain, and it was very windy. Hereupon we furled our sprit sail, the weather being very hazy to W. We reckoned a W. way, and thereby forty-six leagues and one-third. By observation, lat. 13° 17′ N. At noon this day we had a very fierce tornado and rain together ; but a clear afternoon. We had a high E.N.E. sea, and saw multitudes of flying-fish, and amongst these, two or three boobies. The evening was hazy.

January 27th. All last night we had a fresh wind, and clear weather. This morning our foretop mast back-stay gave way, and at daybreak the star-board sheet of our foretop sail broke. We had several tornadoes this day, and dark weather. Our reckoning was a W. way, and forty-eight leagues by the same. We had a clear evening and a dark night. This day also a certain bird, called a noddy, came on board us, which we took for a certain token that we were not now very far from land.

Saturday, January 28th. We had a very clear night. About an hour before day one of our company happened to descry land, which proved to be the Island of Barbados, at S.S.W. from us, and at two leagues and a half distance, more or less. Hereupon we clapped on a wind, N. and by W. At daybreak we were only four leagues distant from Chalky Mount, at which time we stood S.W. by S. As we sailed we saw several ships at anchor in Spikes Road. Soon after a shallop passed by, between us and the shore, but would not come within call of us. Hereupon we stood in, within a mile of the shore, and made a wiff to a pinnace which we saw coming out of the road afore-mentioned. She came close aboard us, and as it should seem, was the barge of one of his Majesty's frigates, the *Richmond*, then lying at the Bridge-town at anchor. They told us of peace at home, but would not come on board us, though often invited thereto. Neither dared we be so bold as to put in there at Barbados ; for hearing of a frigate lying there, we feared lest the said frigate should seize us for privateers, and for having acted in all our voyage without commission. Thus we stood away thence for the Island of Antigua.

Here I cannot easily express the infinite joy we were possessed with this day to see our own countrymen again. They told us that a ship, which we saw in the offing to leeward of the island, was a Bristol-man, and an interloper; but we feared that same vessel to be the frigate afore-mentioned. I reckoned a way of twenty-five leagues, so that I was now by my account to eastward of my departure one hundred and fifty-one leagues. Now we stood N. by W., and by observation found lat. 13° 17' N., we being then N.W. from the body of the island of Barbados between seven and eight leagues. This afternoon we freed the negro who was our shoemaker by trade, giving him his liberty for the good service he had done us in all the course of this voyage. We gave also to our good commander, Captain Sharp, a mulatto boy, as a free gift of the whole company, to wait upon him, in token of the respect we all were owing to him, for the safety of our conduct through so many dangerous adventures. This being done, we shared some small parcels of money, that had not as yet been touched of our former prizes; and this dividend amounted to twenty-four pieces-of-eight each man.

At one o'clock this day from our fore-yard we descried the island of St. Lucia, being one of the Western Islands, not far distant from that of Barbados. I had omitted to tell a passage which happened in our ship, on Thursday last, which was the 26th day of this month, and just two days before we made the island of Barbados. On that day, therefore, a little Spanish shock-dog, which we had found in our last wine-prize, taken under the equinoctial and had kept alive till now, was sold at the mast by public cry for forty pieces-of-eight, his owner saying that all he could get for him should be spent upon the company at a public merriment. Our commander, Captain Sharp, bought the dog, with intention to eat him, in case we did not see land very soon. This money, therefore, with one hundred pieces-of-eight more, which our boatswain, carpenter, and quartermaster had refused to take at this last dividend, for some quarrel they had against the sharers thereof, was all laid up in store till we

came to land, with the intent of spending it ashore, at a
common feast or drinking bout. At sunset the island
of St. Lucia bore W.S.W. from us, and was at ten
leagues distance. Also the island of Martinique bore
N.W. by W. of us at twelve or thirteen leagues distance.
We had this day a very clear evening.

Sunday, January 29th. We had a clear night and a
fresh wind at E. by N. and at E.N.E. Our reckoning
was a N.N.W. half W. way, and hereby forty-six leagues.
By observation we took lat. 15° 46′ N. At noon this
day we saw the island named La Desirade, or the Desired Island, which then bore N.W. from us, and seemed
to be at eight leagues distance, more or less. At six
o'clock in the evening we saw likewise Mariegalante,
another of the Caribbee Islands, at S.W. by W. from us,
and that of Guadaloupe, streaking itself in several hummocks of land, both W. and N. ; as also La Desirade
above-mentioned at S.E., which from there shows like
table-land, and at each end has a low point running
out. At six this evening it was W.S.W., and at five
or six leagues distance from us. At the same time we
saw the island of Montserrat, at a great distance from
our ship, and making three round hummocks close together. This evening likewise we caught an albicore of
twenty pound weight.

Monday, January 30th. We had a fair night all the
last past, and a fresh wind. Hereupon, all night we
hauled up our main sail in brails, standing at the same
time N. by W., with the wind at E.N.E. At midnight
we stood N.W. At three in the morning we lay by until
five. Then we stood away W.N.W. until six, and at that
hour we stood W. At eight o'clock we saw the island of
Antigua, called by us Antego, to the S. of us, making
three round hummocks of land, and a long high hill to
N. Hereupon we stood W.S.W. for it. At noon we
found lat. 17° N., the island being then just W. from us.

We came about to the S. of the island, and sent a

canoe on shore to get tobacco and other necessaries that we wanted, as also to ask leave of the Governor to come into the port. The gentry of the place and common people were very willing and desirous to receive us. But on Wednesday, February 1st, the governor flatly denied us entry ; at which all the gentry were much grieved, and showed themselves very kind to us.[1] Hereupon we agreed among ourselves to give away, and leave the ship to them of our company who had no money left of all their purchase in this voyage, having lost it all at play ; and then to divide ourselves into two ships, which were now bound for England. Thus I myself and thirteen more of our company went on board Captain Robert Porteen's ship, called the *Lisbon Merchant*, and set sail from Antigua on February 11th, and landed at Dartmouth in England, March 26th, anno 1682.

[1] Sharp and others were tried in England on their return, at the instance of the Spanish Ambassador, for piracy in the South Seas, but escaped.   On the charge of taking the *Rosario* and killing her captain it was successfully pleaded in defence that as the Spaniards fired first the pirates were justified in defending themselves.   Three of the same crew were tried at Jamaica, of whom one was hanged on his plea of guilty, the other two being acquitted in default of evidence.

INDEX.

Abelcose tree, 27.
Acajou, 8, 25.
Achioc, 251.
Acoma tree, 25.
Agreements among the Bucca-
    neers, 40, 41, 189.
Aguja Point, 424.
Alcatraces, 19.
Alleston, Capt., 276.
Alexander, J., drowned, 429.
Alligator—see Crocodile.
Aloes, 7, 25.
Alta Gracia, 17.
Anana, 8.
Andrœas, Capt., 277, 287, 313.
Antigua, arrival, 499.
Antonio, Capt., 279, 287, 313.
Apricot, 23.
Argandona, Don T. de, 356, 387.
Arica, xxiii., 366; attack on, 409–
    412; map, 415.
Arrows, Indian, 245, 247.
Articles—see Agreements.
Aso Pueblo d', 18.

B.

Bachelors' Delight, xl.
Bacones, 8.
Ballona Gulf, 289, 296.
Balsa, 345, 352.
Baltazar, Don, 356, 357.
Banana, 44; wine, 66.
Baptism, crossing line by French,
    2, 4; by Dutch, 3.
Barbacoa, 326.
Barahona, Don J. de, 305.
Barbados, 497.

Bark log—see Balsa.
Barracoa, 131.
Basco ⎫ Michael de, 84.
Basque ⎭
Bayame, 131.
Belona—see Ballona.
Bête rouge, 27.
Bilby tree, 400.
Binkes, Jacob, 265; Cayana, 267;
    Tobago, 270; death, 272.
Bitumen, 107.
Blanco, Cape, 346, 351, 434.
Bleevelt Bay, 246.
Bliniac, Comte de, 269, 271.
Boar, 8; dog, 34.
Boca del Dragon, 243; del Toro,
    239, 275.
Borrica Point, 434.
Boucan, xxiv., xxvi.
Bournano, Capt., 275, 276.
Brasiliano, Roche, origin, 69;
    exploits, 70–72.
Brazil wood, 25.
Brethren of coast—see Bucca-
    neers.
British Honduras, xxvi., xxvii.
Brodeley, Capt., 198.
Buccaneers, derivation, xxi.,
    xxv.; mode of fighting,
    xxix.; causes of decay, xxxi.;
    partners, xxvii., 59, 62; ori-
    gin and customs, 39; hunt-
    ers, 40; planters, 41; piracy,
    54; provisions, 58; agree-
    ments, xxvii., 59, 62; shares,
    60; wounds, 62, 189.
Bull, Mr., 302.
Bullock, Mr., 447.
Bustos, Don A. de, 174.

C.

Cabbage palm, 21 ; paper, *ib.*; Juan Fernandez, 400.
Cabreros, 39.
Caçadores de moscas, 29.
Calarodes, 174.
Caldero, 427.
Camarones River, 406.
Cammock, Wm., 392.
Campeche, xxxiii., 74; wood, 110.
Campo, Don E. de, 124 ; letter, 168.
Candle wood, 7.
Cannis, 369.
Cano, I., 427.
Canoes, 25.
Carabaxal, Don D. de, 305.
Caracas, 266.
Caramite tree, 24.
Carasoles, 8.
Carpenter birds ⎱ 38.
Carpinteros ⎰
Cassava, 43.
Cassia, 25.
Cattle, 38.
Cayana, 267 ; taken, 269.
Cayboa, 317 ; mutiny, 321.
Cayman—*see* Crocodile.
Cayos, 132.
Cazeres, F. de, 128.
Cedars, 25.
Celebes, xlii.
Centipedes, 29.
Chagre, 198 ; defence, 199–202.
Chandelle, Bois de, 7.
Chandy Point, 305.
Chapelet palm, 22.
Chappel, Jas, 449.
Chepillo, 301.
Chepo, 275.
China root, 7.
Christoval, Don, 356, 357.
Ciavone, Capt., 270.
Citrons, 20.
Coca, 406–8.
Cochinillas, 28.
Colan, 457.
Coma, 49.
Comana, 181.
Commissions, 53.
Comrades, 40.

Cook, Capt. E., 276, 301, 319, 321, 399.
Cook, Wm., 399 ; died, 417.
Coquimbo, 385 ; map, 389.
Corrientes, Cape, 131.
Cow, sea, 243.
Cowley, xliv.
Cox, Capt. John, 322, 338, 369, 398.
Coxon, Capt., xxxix., 276, 287, 302.
Crab, 9 ; lemon, 20.
Crickets, 28.
Crocodiles, 30, 32, 256, 321.
Crows, 39.
Cuba, 131.
Curaçoa, 259.
Cygnet, The, xl., xli., xlii.

D.

Dampier, W., xxxix., xl., 425.
Darien Indians, 276 ; king, 279 ; king's daughter, 286.
Date tree, 20, 21.
Davis, John, xl.–xliii.; Nicaragua, 74; St. Augustine, 76
Desirade, La, 499.
Dog, 34–37; sale of, 498.
Donna Maria, Cape, 19.
Drake's Isle—*see* Plata.
Duke of York Isles, 466, 473.
Dulce Gulf, 436, 440.

E.

Elemi gum, 7, 25.
English Gulf, 475.
Espada Point, 19.
Espinosa—*see* Prickle palm.
    „   Don—*see* Campo.
Espiritu Santo, 131.
Esquemeling, John, birth, xliv., li.; voyage, 1; sold, 14; pirate, 15.
Estancias, 312.
Estreès, Comte d', Cayana, 268, 270 ; Tobago, 272.

F.

Faisanes, 246.
Fall, John, 398.

False Wild Harbour, 396.
Faral de Plantanos, 300.
Fire-flies, 28 ; ship, 170.
Fly, species, 27, 28 ; catcher, 29.
François, Pierre, 62–64.
Frank palm, 21.
French in Hispaniola, manners, 39 ; planters revolt, 46 ; quarrel with English, 138 ; with Morgan, 150–153.
Friar killed, 349.

G.

Gabaret, Msr., 269.
Gabriel, Josephe, 329.
Galapagos, xli.
Gallo, 332 ; surprise, 350.
Galeno, Capt. J., 128.
Galleon, Panama, 226.
Genipa-tree ink, 24.
Genoese factory, Panama, 224.
Gibraltar, 89 ; L'Ollonais, 93–98 ; Morgan, 159–166.
Gimbes, 46.
Glow-worm—*see* Fire-flies.
Goat-keeper bird, 39 ; key, 350.
Goave, St. J. de, 18.
Godolphin treaty, xlvii.
Gold mine, 112; Darien, xl., 279; Gorgona, 327.
Golden Island, 277.
Gorgona, 326–7–8, 331.
Gorgonilla, 333.
Gracias a Dios, Cape, 249.
Grammont, xxxviii.
Granada, xliii.
Grand, Pierre le, 54–56.
Grillones—*see* Crickets.
Grogniet, Capt., xli.–xliii.
Guanadillas, 260.
Guarda costas, xxiii.
Guasco, 418, 420.
Guayaquil, xl., xlii., xliii., 346; action, *ib.*
Guaiacum, 7, 18, 25.
Guines agudos, 44.
Gum Elemi—*see* Elemi.
Guyones, Cape, 432.
Guzman, Don J. P. de, 124.

H.

Hacha, Rio de la, 186.
Hansel, Capt., 181.
Harris, Capt. Peter, 275–6, 301 ; killed, 310.
Havana, La, 131.
Hilliard, John, 398.
Hilo, 364; taken, 368–372 ; map, 374 ; retaken, 422.
Hispaniola, 16 ; French in, 46 ; Dutch, 47 ; rebellion, 48.
Honduras, British, xxvi., xxvii.
Horadada Peña, 454.
Horn, Cape, 479.
Horses, 37.
Horse, Mors de, 454.

I.

Indians' treatment, 36 ; Maracaibo tree-dwellers, 88 ; Yucatan, 108 ; infant marriage, 109 ; Las Pertas, 113 ; cannibals, 44 ; Boca del Toro, 239 ; del Drago, 243 ; Gracias a Dios, 249 ; Darien, 276, 437 ; Mosquito, 341 ; Dulce, 438 ; Duke of York Isles, 469.
Indigo, 46.
Ink—*see* Genipa.
Iquique, 405–407.

J.

Jamaica, 257, 259.
Juan Fernandez, xxxix., xl., 393; mutiny, 399 ; action, 401.
Juan Diaz, Rio de, 366.

K.

Katalina, Sª, xxxiv.
Kidnappers, 49.
King of Darien, 279, 286, 313.
    „   Charles' Harbour, 441.
Knight, Capt. W., xli., xlii.

L.

Lacumba, 422.
Lady, Spanish, 230, 235.

Lampsius, Adr. and Corn., Tobago, 267.
Lapina, 346.
Latanier palm, 22.
Lavelia, xlii.
Lemons—*see* Limes.
Leon, xli.
L'Escayer, xli.
Lesi, Msr., Cayana, 268.
Lexa, Rio, xli.
Leyva, Don J. R. de, 128.
Lignum Sanctum—*see* Guaiacum.
Lima merchant's ship, 339; fleet, 348.
Limes, 20.
Lisbon merchant, The, 498.
Lobos, Cape, 19.
Logwood, 110; cutters, xxvi.
L'Ollonais, origin, 79; wrecked, 80; De los Cayos, 81; Maracaibo, 86–93; Gibraltar, 93–98; cruelties, 92, 103; P° Cavallo, 102; takes ship, 111; left by men, 113; death, 116.
Lopez, Don D., 449.

M.

Macket, Capt., 276.
Macoa, 106.
Madre de Dios, 475.
Magellan clouds, 360, 471; straits, 475.
Magniot, 8.
Maintenon, Lieut., 266.
Maiz, 43.
Malabrigo Bay, 424.
Mamayn } 8.
Mammee }
Mançanilla } 25, 321, 494.
Manchineel }
Mandioca, 43.
Manglares, 443.
Mansvelt, 74, 121, 122.
Manta, 336, 450.
Mapou, 25.
Maracaibo, 86; L'Ollonais, 91; Morgan, 157.
Marcy, C., 369, 433
Mariegalante, 499.
Martinique, 499.
Mata Ricos, 131.

Merida, 89.
Mestizos, 18.
Millipedes, 29.
Mindanao, xlii.
Miracle, 357.
Mirick, 44.
Miscelaw, 282.
Monkey, 246.
Montbars, xxxiv.
Monte de Christo, 336.
Montgomery, Robt., 356.
Montserrat, 499.
Moreno, Juan, 352, 356, 357.
Moreno, Moro, 424.
Mosquito Indians, 341.

N.

Nata, 314.
Negroes, Mosquito, 250, 254.
Nevis, xxxiii.
New Cape Blanco, 433.
Nicaragua, xxxiii., xli., 74.
Nicoya Gulf, xl., 427, 433.
Nicholas, The, xl.
Nicobar Islands, xlii.

O.

Ocoa, 153.
Ogeron, Msr., Tortuga, 13, 35; Curaçoa, 260, 261; Porto Rico, 264; Trinidad, 266.
Old man killed, 407.
Old Providence, xxxiv.
Otoque, 316.

P.

Paita, 353, 454; map, 457.
Palm, 21; wine, 22.
Palmetto, 8.
Panama, 122; Morgan, 208; Coxon, 304; action, 305; Sawkins, 316; map, 317.
Paper-palm, 21.
Paquayes, 8.
Pardelas, 396.
Parina, 352.
Parrots, 38.
Partners—*see* Buccaneers.
Passao Cape, 335, 338, 446, 447.
Passeur, Msr. Le, 11.

Patache, The, 348.
Pearls, Rancherias, 63; Cayboa, 317.
Peralta, Don F. de, 305, 322, 326, 356, 379.
Perico, 304, 313.
Perlas, Las, Indians, 113.
Pheasants, 246.
Picard, Pierre le, 112.
Pigeons, 8, 39.
Pilot, Maracaibo, 173; Gabriel, 329; Moreno, 352.
Pine-apple, 8.
Pintadas, 38.
Pirate—*see* Buccaneers.
Pitch Lake, 117.
Place, Msr. de la, 79.
Plata, Isle de la, xxiii., xxiv., 337-343; mutiny, 425, 487; plot, 452.
Plate, ditto.
Ponce, Admiral, 453.
Porto Bello, 141, 143, 145.
   „ Rico, Ogeron, 264.
Portugues, Bart., 65.
Potato, 8, 43.
Prickle palm, 23.
Providence, Old, xxxiv.; New, xxxv.
Puerto del Principe, 134; Marrano, 131.
Puis, A. de, 86.

Q.

Quebrada, 409.
Quibo, xxxi., xxxiii.
Quicara, 323.
Quito, 346.

R.

Racoven, 115.
Rancherias, 63.
Raqueltes, 105.
Ravens—*see* Crows.
Revenge, The, xli.
Richmond, The, 497.
Ringrose, Basil, xlii., xliv., 293, 297, 298; Hilo, 369; Coquimbo, 385.
Rojados—*see* Bête rouge.
Rosary Palm, 22.

Rosario, The, 448, 500.
Row, Capt., 276.

S.

St. Catherine, Mansvelt, 74; Morgan, 191.
St. Christopher ⎫ 9.
   „ Kitts ⎭
   „ Faucher, 269.
   „ Helena Point, 344.
   „ Laurence, 293, 336.
   „ Lucia, 498.
   „ Nicholas, 19.
Sama, Mora de, 365.
Samana, Cape, 19.
Samballas, 110, 276.
Sanchez, Don S., 159.
Sandal wood, 7.
Sand fly, 27.
San Domingo, 16.
   „ Francisco, 334, 448.
   „ Mateo, 334, 443.
   „ Miguel Gulf, 277, 291.
   „ Pedro, 444.
   „ Rosario, xl., 448.
Santa Cruz, 131.
   „ Maria, 131, 277, 285.
Santiago, 17, 131, 334; River 445.
Saunders wood, 7.
Savona, 17, 155.
Sawkins, Capt. R., xxxix., 276, 306, 314; President of Panama, 310; killed, 318; dice, 400.
Scolopendria, 29.
Scorpions, 29.
Scot, Lewis, 74.
Sea cow—*see* Manati.
   „ lions—*see* Walrus.
Seals, 397.
Selkirk, 400.
Serena, La, 380, 386; map, 384.
Servants—*see* Slaves.
Sharp, Capt. Bart., xxxix., xl., 276, 301, 314, 318; Hilo, 370, 390, 411; Chira, 428, 485, 498, 500.
Sharp's Island—*see* Gorgona.
Shergall, H., 466.
Silver, xl.

Simon, Sieur, 122.
Slaves, cruelty to, 50.
Sloth, 329.
Snakes, 28, 337.
Solango, 344, 452.
Sourdis, Chev., 2.
Spider, 29, 156.
Sprenger, Capt., 306.
Stevens, Will., 494.
Sugar, 42 ; works, 369.
Swan, Capt., xl.

T.

Tarapaca, Mora, 376.
Tavoga, 314.
Tiburon, 10.
Timor, xlii.
Tobacco, 41, 45.
Tobago, 267, 272.
Tocamora, 275.
Torongas—*see* Limes.
Tortoise, 17, 29, 61, 106, 324.
    341.
Tortuga, 6, 9, 10, 13.
Townley, Capt., xli., xlii., xliii.
Trinidad town, 131 ; island, 266.
    „   La Santissima, 309, 313,
    349.
Tucames, 444.
Tumbes miracle, 351.

V.

Vaca, Isla de la, 150.
Vacadas, 312.

Vanclein, M., 112.
Van der Graef, 270.
    „ Dongen, 270.
    „ Vin, 103.
Vanero, 432.
Velas, Punta de, 435.
Veraguas, 112.
Veycon, 44.
Vigilias, 86.
Vinosa—*see* Wine Palm.

W.

Wafer, L., xxxix., xlii., 425.
Walrus, 396.
Watling, Capt. John, 399, 405,
    411.
West India Co., French, 1.
William, Mosquito Indian, 400.
Wine palm, 23 ; potato, 43 ;
    banana, 44.
Wood pullets—*see* Pintadas.

X.

Xagoa, 131.
Ximenez, J., 5, 126.

Y.

Yannas, 8.
Ycao, 26.

Z.

Zuera, Rio de, 245.

CATALOGUE OF DOVER BOOKS

Books Explaining Science and Mathematics

WHAT IS SCIENCE?, N. Campbell. The role of experiment and measurement, the function of mathematics, the nature of scientific laws, the difference between laws and theories, the limitations of science, and many similarly provocative topics are treated clearly and without technicalities by an eminent scientist. "Still an excellent introduction to scientific philosophy," H. Margenau in PHYSICS TODAY. "A first-rate primer . . . deserves a wide audience," SCIENTIFIC AMERICAN. 192pp. 5⅜ x 8.　　　　S43 Paperbound **$1.25**

THE NATURE OF PHYSICAL THEORY, P. W. Bridgman. A Nobel Laureate's clear, non-technical lectures on difficulties and paradoxes connected with frontier research on the physical sciences. Concerned with such central concepts as thought, logic, mathematics, relativity, probability, wave mechanics, etc. he analyzes the contributions of such men as Newton, Einstein, Bohr, Heisenberg, and many others. "Lucid and entertaining . . . recommended to anyone who wants to get some insight into current philosophies of science," THE NEW PHILOSOPHY. Index. xi + 138pp. 5⅜ x 8.　　　　S33 Paperbound **$1.25**

EXPERIMENT AND THEORY IN PHYSICS, Max Born. A Nobel Laureate examines the nature of experiment and theory in theoretical physics and analyzes the advances made by the great physicists of our day: Heisenberg, Einstein, Bohr, Planck, Dirac, and others. The actual process of creation is detailed step-by-step by one who participated. A fine examination of the scientific method at work. 44pp. 5⅜ x 8.　　　　S308 Paperbound **75¢**

THE PSYCHOLOGY OF INVENTION IN THE MATHEMATICAL FIELD, J. Hadamard. The reports of such men as Descartes, Pascal, Einstein, Poincaré, and others are considered in this investigation of the method of idea-creation in mathematics and other sciences and the thinking process in general. How do ideas originate? What is the role of the unconscious? What is Poincaré's forgetting hypothesis? are some of the fascinating questions treated. A penetrating analysis of Einstein's thought processes concludes the book. xiii + 145pp. 5⅜ x 8.　　　　T107 Paperbound **$1.25**

THE NATURE OF LIGHT AND COLOUR IN THE OPEN AIR, M. Minnaert. Why are shadows sometimes blue, sometimes green, or other colors depending on the light and surroundings? What causes mirages? Why do multiple suns and moons appear in the sky? Professor Minnaert explains these unusual phenomena and hundreds of others in simple, easy-to-understand terms based on optical laws and the properties of light and color. No mathematics is required but artists, scientists, students, and everyone fascinated by these "tricks" of nature will find thousands of useful and amazing pieces of information. Hundreds of observational experiments are suggested which require no special equipment. 200 illustrations; 42 photos. xvi + 362pp. 5⅜ x 8.　　　　T196 Paperbound **$2.00**

THE UNIVERSE OF LIGHT, W. Bragg. Sir William Bragg, Nobel Laureate and great modern physicist, is also well known for his powers of clear exposition. Here he analyzes all aspects of light for the layman: lenses, reflection, refraction, the optics of vision, x-rays, the photoelectric effect, etc. He tells you what causes the color of spectra, rainbows, and soap bubbles, how magic mirrors work, and much more. Dozens of simple experiments are described. Preface. Index. 199 line drawings and photographs, including 2 full-page color plates. x + 283pp. 5⅜ x 8.　　　　T538 Paperbound **$1.85**

SOAP-BUBBLES: THEIR COLOURS AND THE FORCES THAT MOULD THEM, C. V. Boys. For continuing popularity and validity as scientific primer, few books can match this volume of easily-followed experiments, explanations. Lucid exposition of complexities of liquid films, surface tension and related phenomena, bubbles' reaction to heat, motion, music, magnetic fields. Experiments with capillary attraction, soap bubbles on frames, composite bubbles, liquid cylinders and jets, bubbles other than soap, etc. Wonderful introduction to scientific method, natural laws that have many ramifications in areas of modern physics. Only complete edition in print. New Introduction by S. Z. Lewin, New York University. 83 illustrations; 1 full-page color plate. xii + 190pp. 5⅜ x 8½.　　　　T542 Paperbound **95¢**

CATALOGUE OF DOVER BOOKS

THE STORY OF X-RAYS FROM RONTGEN TO ISOTOPES, A. R. Bleich, M.D. This book, by a member of the American College of Radiology, gives the scientific explanation of x-rays, their applications in medicine, industry and art, and their danger (and that of atmospheric radiation) to the individual and the species. You learn how radiation therapy is applied against cancer, how x-rays diagnose heart disease and other ailments, how they are used to examine mummies for information on diseases of early societies, and industrial materials for hidden weaknesses. 54 illustrations show x-rays of flowers, bones, stomach, gears with flaws, etc. 1st publication. Index. xix + 186pp. 5⅜ x 8. T622 Paperbound **$1.50**

SPINNING TOPS AND GYROSCOPIC MOTION, John Perry. A classic elementary text of the dynamics of rotation — the behavior and use of rotating bodies such as gyroscopes and tops. In simple, everyday English you are shown how quasi-rigidity is induced in discs of paper, smoke rings, chains, etc., by rapid motions; why a gyrostat falls and why a top rises; precession; how the earth's motion affects climate; and many other phenomena. Appendix on practical use of gyroscopes. 62 figures. 128pp. 5⅜ x 8. T416 Paperbound **$1.25**

SNOW CRYSTALS, W. A. Bentley, M. J. Humphreys. For almost 50 years W. A. Bentley photographed snow flakes in his laboratory in Jericho, Vermont; in 1931 the American Meteorological Society gathered together the best of his work, some 2400 photographs of snow flakes, plus a few ice flowers, windowpane frosts, dew, frozen rain, and other ice formations. Pictures were selected for beauty and scientific value. A very valuable work to anyone in meteorology, cryology; most interesting to layman; extremely useful for artist who wants beautiful, crystalline designs. All copyright free. Unabridged reprint of 1931 edition. 2453 illustrations. 227pp. 8 x 10½. T287 Paperbound **$3.00**

A DOVER SCIENCE SAMPLER, edited by George Barkin. A collection of brief, non-technical passages from 44 Dover Books Explaining Science for the enjoyment of the science-minded browser. Includes work of Bertrand Russell, Poincaré, Laplace, Max Born, Galileo, Newton; material on physics, mathematics, metallurgy, anatomy, astronomy, chemistry, etc. You will be fascinated by Martin Gardner's analysis of the sincere pseudo-scientist, Moritz's account of Newton's absentmindedness, Bernard's examples of human vivisection, etc. Illustrations from the Diderot Pictorial Encyclopedia and De Re Metallica. 64 pages. **FREE**

THE STORY OF ATOMIC THEORY AND ATOMIC ENERGY, J. G. Feinberg. A broader approach to subject of nuclear energy and its cultural implications than any other similar source. Very readable, informal, completely non-technical text. Begins with first atomic theory, 600 B.C. and carries you through the work of Mendelejeff, Röntgen, Madame Curie, to Einstein's equation and the A-bomb. New chapter goes through thermonuclear fission, binding energy, other events up to 1959. Radioactive decay and radiation hazards, future benefits, work of Bohr, moderns, hundreds more topics. "Deserves special mention . . . not only authoritative but thoroughly popular in the best sense of the word," Saturday Review. Formerly, "The Atom Story." Expanded with new chapter. Three appendixes. Index. 34 illustrations. vii + 243pp. 5⅜ x 8. T625 Paperbound **$1.60**

THE STRANGE STORY OF THE QUANTUM, AN ACCOUNT FOR THE GENERAL READER OF THE GROWTH OF IDEAS UNDERLYING OUR PRESENT ATOMIC KNOWLEDGE, B. Hoffmann. Presents lucidly and expertly, with barest amount of mathematics, the problems and theories which led to modern quantum physics. Dr. Hoffmann begins with the closing years of the 19th century, when certain trifling discrepancies were noticed, and with illuminating analogies and examples takes you through the brilliant concepts of Planck, Einstein, Pauli, Broglie, Bohr, Schroedinger, Heisenberg, Dirac, Sommerfeld, Feynman, etc. This edition includes a new, long postscript carrying the story through 1958. "Of the books attempting an account of the history and contents of our modern atomic physics which have come to my attention, this is the best," H. Margenau, Yale University, in "American Journal of Physics." 32 tables and line illustrations. Index. 275pp. 5⅜ x 8. T518 Paperbound **$1.50**

SPACE AND TIME, E. Borel. Written by a versatile mathematician of world renown with his customary lucidity and precision, this introduction to relativity for the layman presents scores of examples, analogies, and illustrations that open up new ways of thinking about space and time. It covers abstract geometry and geographical maps, continuity and topology, the propagation of light, the special theory of relativity, the general theory of relativity, theoretical researches, and much more. Mathematical notes. 2 Indexes. 4 Appendices. 15 figures. xvi + 243pp. 5⅜ x 8. T592 Paperbound **$1.75**

FROM EUCLID TO EDDINGTON: A STUDY OF THE CONCEPTIONS OF THE EXTERNAL WORLD, Sir Edmund Whittaker. A foremost British scientist traces the development of theories of natural philosophy from the western rediscovery of Euclid to Eddington, Einstein, Dirac, etc. The inadequacy of classical physics is contrasted with present day attempts to understand the physical world through relativity, non-Euclidean geometry, space curvature, wave mechanics, etc. 5 major divisions of examination: Space; Time and Movement; the Concepts of Classical Physics; the Concepts of Quantum Mechanics; the Eddington Universe. 212pp. 5⅜ x 8. T491 Paperbound **$1.35**

Nature, Biology,

NATURE RECREATION: Group Guidance for the Out-of-doors, William Gould Vinal. Intended for both the uninitiated nature instructor and the education student on the college level, this complete "how-to" program surveys the entire area of nature education for the young. Philosophy of nature recreation; requirements, responsibilities, important information for group leaders; nature games; suggested group projects; conducting meetings and getting discussions started; etc. Scores of immediately applicable teaching aids, plus completely updated sources of information, pamphlets, field guides, recordings, etc. Bibliography. 74 photographs. + 310pp. 5⅜ x 8½.   T1015 Paperbound **$1.75**

HOW TO KNOW THE WILD FLOWERS, Mrs. William Starr Dana. Classic nature book that has introduced thousands to wonders of American wild flowers. Color-season principle of organization is easy to use, even by those with no botanical training, and the genial, refreshing discussions of history, folklore, uses of over 1,000 native and escape flowers, foliage plants are informative as well as fun to read. Over 170 full-page plates, collected from several editions, may be colored in to make permanent records of finds. Revised to conform with 1950 edition of Gray's Manual of Botany. xlii + 438pp. 5⅜ x 8½.   T332 Paperbound **$2.00**

HOW TO KNOW THE FERNS, F. T. Parsons. Ferns, among our most lovely native plants, are all too little known. This classic of nature lore will enable the layman to identify almost any American fern he may come across. After an introduction on the structure and life of ferns, the 57 most important ferns are fully pictured and described (arranged upon a simple identification key). Index of Latin and English names. 61 illustrations and 42 full-page plates. xiv + 215pp. 5⅜ x 8.   T740 Paperbound **$1.35**

MANUAL OF THE TREES OF NORTH AMERICA, Charles Sprague Sargent. Still unsurpassed as most comprehensive, reliable study of North American tree characteristics, precise locations and distribution. By dean of American dendrologists. Every tree native to U.S., Canada, Alaska, 185 genera, 717 species, described in detail—leaves, flowers, fruit, winterbuds, bark, wood, growth habits etc. plus discussion of varieties and local variants, immaturity variations. Over 100 keys, including unusual 11-page analytical key to genera, aid in identification. 783 clear illustrations of flowers, fruit, leaves. An unmatched permanent reference work for all nature lovers. Second enlarged (1926) edition. Synopsis of families. Analytical key to genera. Glossary of technical terms. Index. 783 illustrations, 1 map. Two volumes. Total of 982pp. 5⅜ x 8.   T277 Vol. I Paperbound **$2.25**
T278 Vol. II Paperbound **$2.25**
The set **$4.50**

TREES OF THE EASTERN AND CENTRAL UNITED STATES AND CANADA, W. M. Harlow. A revised edition of a standard middle-level guide to native trees and important escapes. More than 140 trees are described in detail, and illustrated with more than 600 drawings and photographs. Supplementary keys will enable the careful reader to identify almost any tree he might encounter. xiii + 288pp. 5⅜ x 8.   T395 Paperbound **$1.35**

GUIDE TO SOUTHERN TREES, Ellwood S. Harrar and J. George Harrar. All the essential information about trees indigenous to the South, in an extremely handy format. Introductory essay on methods of tree classification and study, nomenclature, chief divisions of Southern trees, etc. Approximately 100 keys and synopses allow for swift, accurate identification of trees. Numerous excellent illustrations, non-technical text make this a useful book for teachers of biology or natural science, nature lovers, amateur naturalists. Revised 1962 edition. Index. Bibliography. Glossary of technical terms. 920 illustrations; 201 full-page plates. ix + 709pp. 4⅝ x 6⅜.   T945 Paperbound **$2.35**

FRUIT KEY AND TWIG KEY TO TREES AND SHRUBS, W. M. Harlow. Bound together in one volume for the first time, these handy and accurate keys to fruit and twig identification are the only guides of their sort with photographs (up to 3 times natural size). "Fruit Key": Key to over 120 different deciduous and evergreen fruits. 139 photographs and 11 line drawings. Synoptic summary of fruit types. Bibliography. 2 Indexes (common and scientific names). "Twig Key": Key to over 160 different twigs and buds. 173 photographs. Glossary of technical terms. Bibliography. 2 Indexes (common and scientific names). Two volumes bound as one. Total of xvii + 126pp. 5⅝ x 8⅜.   T511 Paperbound **$1.25**

INSECT LIFE AND INSECT NATURAL HISTORY, S. W. Frost. A work emphasizing habits, social life, and ecological relations of insects, rather than more academic aspects of classification and morphology. Prof. Frost's enthusiasm and knowledge are everywhere evident as he discusses insect associations and specialized habits like leaf-rolling, leaf-mining, and case-making, the gall insects, the boring insects, aquatic insects, etc. He examines all sorts of matters not usually covered in general works, such as: insects as human food, insect music and musicians, insect response to electric and radio waves, use of insects in art and literature. The admirably executed purpose of this book, which covers the middle ground between elementary treatment and scholarly monographs, is to excite the reader to observe for himself. Over 700 illustrations. Extensive bibliography. x + 524pp. 5⅜ x 8.   T517 Paperbound **$2.50**

CATALOGUE OF DOVER BOOKS

COMMON SPIDERS OF THE UNITED STATES, J. H. Emerton. Here is a nature hobby you can pursue right in your own cellar! Only non-technical, but thorough, reliable guide to spiders for the layman. Over 200 spiders from all parts of the country, arranged by scientific classification, are identified by shape and color, number of eyes, habitat and range, habits, etc. Full text, 501 line drawings and photographs, and valuable introduction explain webs, poisons, threads, capturing and preserving spiders, etc. Index. New synoptic key by S. W. Frost. xxiv + 225pp. 5⅜ x 8. T223 Paperbound **$1.45**

THE LIFE STORY OF THE FISH: HIS MANNERS AND MORALS, Brian Curtis. A comprehensive, non-technical survey of just about everything worth knowing about fish. Written for the aquarist, the angler, and the layman with an inquisitive mind, the text covers such topics as evolution, external covering and protective coloration, physics and physiology of vision, maintenance of equilibrium, function of the lateral line canal for auditory and temperature senses, nervous system, function of the air bladder, reproductive system and methods—courtship, mating, spawning, care of young—and many more. Also sections on game fish, the problems of conservation and a fascinating chapter on fish curiosities. "Clear, simple language . . . excellent judgment in choice of subjects . . . delightful sense of humor," New York Times. Revised (1949) edition. Index. Bibliography of 72 items. 6 full-page photographic plates. xii + 284pp. 5⅜ x 8. T929 Paperbound **$1.65**

BATS, Glover Morrill Allen. The most comprehensive study of bats as a life-form by the world's foremost authority. A thorough summary of just about everything known about this fascinating and mysterious flying mammal, including its unique location sense, hibernation and cycles, its habitats and distribution, its wing structure and flying habits, and its relationship to man in the long history of folklore and superstition. Written on a middle-level, the book can be profitably studied by a trained zoologist and thoroughly enjoyed by the layman. "An absorbing text with excellent illustrations. Bats should have more friends and fewer thoughtless detractors as a result of the publication of this volume," William Beebe, Books. Extensive bibliography. 57 photographs and illustrations. x + 368pp. 5⅜ x 8½. T984 Paperbound **$2.00**

BIRDS AND THEIR ATTRIBUTES, Glover Morrill Allen. A fine general introduction to birds as living organisms, especially valuable because of emphasis on structure, physiology, habits, behavior. Discusses relationship of bird to man, early attempts at scientific ornithology, feathers and coloration, skeletal structure including bills, legs and feet, wings. Also food habits, evolution and present distribution, feeding and nest-building, still unsolved questions of migrations and location sense, many more similar topics. Final chapter on classification, nomenclature. A good popular-level summary for the biologist; a first-rate introduction for the layman. Reprint of 1925 edition. References and index. 51 illustrations. viii + 338pp. 5⅜ x 8½. T957 Paperbound **$1.85**

LIFE HISTORIES OF NORTH AMERICAN BIRDS, Arthur Cleveland Bent. Bent's monumental series of books on North American birds, prepared and published under auspices of Smithsonian Institute, is the definitive coverage of the subject, the most-used single source of information. Now the entire set is to be made available by Dover in inexpensive editions. This encyclopedic collection of detailed, specific observations utilizes reports of hundreds of contemporary observers, writings of such naturalists as Audubon, Burroughs, William Brewster, as well as author's own extensive investigations. Contains literally everything known about life history of each bird considered: nesting, eggs, plumage, distribution and migration, voice, enemies, courtship, etc. These not over-technical works are musts for ornithologists, conservationists, amateur naturalists, anyone seriously interested in American birds.

BIRDS OF PREY. More than 100 subspecies of hawks, falcons, eagles, buzzards, condors and owls, from the common barn owl to the extinct caracara of Guadaloupe Island. 400 photographs. Two volume set. Index for each volume. Bibliographies of 403, 520 items. 197 full-page plates. Total of 907pp. 5⅜ x 8½. Vol. I T931 Paperbound **$2.50** / Vol. II T932 Paperbound **$2.50**

WILD FOWL. Ducks, geese, swans, and tree ducks—73 different subspecies. Two volume set. Index for each volume. Bibliographies of 124, 144 items. 106 full-page plates. Total of 685pp. 5⅜ x 8½. Vol. I T285 Paperbound **$2.50** / Vol. II T286 Paperbound **$2.50**

SHORE BIRDS. 81 varieties (sandpipers, woodcocks, plovers, snipes, phalaropes, curlews, oyster catchers, etc.). More than 200 photographs of eggs, nesting sites, adult and young of important species. Two volume set. Index for each volume. Bibliographies of 261, 188 items. 121 full-page plates. Total of 860pp. 5⅜ x 8½. Vol. I T933 Paperbound **$2.35** / Vol. II T934 Paperbound **$2.35**

THE LIFE OF PASTEUR, R. Vallery-Radot. 13th edition of this definitive biography, cited in Encyclopaedia Britannica. Authoritative, scholarly, well-documented with contemporary quotes, observations; gives complete picture of Pasteur's personal life; especially thorough presentation of scientific activities with silkworms, fermentation, hydrophobia, inoculation, etc. Introduction by Sir William Osler. Index. 505pp. 5⅜ x 8. T632 Paperbound **$2.00**

Puzzles, Mathematical Recreations

SYMBOLIC LOGIC and THE GAME OF LOGIC, Lewis Carroll. "Symbolic Logic" is not concerned with modern symbolic logic, but is instead a collection of over 380 problems posed with charm and imagination, using the syllogism, and a fascinating diagrammatic method of drawing conclusions. In "The Game of Logic" Carroll's whimsical imagination devises a logical game played with 2 diagrams and counters (included) to manipulate hundreds of tricky syllogisms. The final section, "Hit or Miss" is a lagniappe of 101 additional puzzles in the delightful Carroll manner. Until this reprint edition, both of these books were rarities costing up to $15 each. Symbolic Logic: Index. xxxi + 199pp. The Game of Logic: 96pp. 2 vols. bound as one. 5⅜ x 8.   T492 Paperbound **$1.75**

PILLOW PROBLEMS and A TANGLED TALE, Lewis Carroll. One of the rarest of all Carroll's works, "Pillow Problems" contains 72 original math puzzles, all typically ingenious. Particularly fascinating are Carroll's answers which remain exactly as he thought them out, reflecting his actual mental process. The problems in "A Tangled Tale" are in story form, originally appearing as a monthly magazine serial. Carroll not only gives the solutions, but uses answers sent in by readers to discuss wrong approaches and misleading paths, and grades them for insight. Both of these books were rarities until this edition, "Pillow Problems" costing up to $25, and "A Tangled Tale" $15. Pillow Problems: Preface and Introduction by Lewis Carroll. xx + 109pp. A Tangled Tale: 6 illustrations. 152pp. Two vols. bound as one. 5⅜ x 8.   T493 Paperbound **$1.50**

AMUSEMENTS IN MATHEMATICS, Henry Ernest Dudeney. The foremost British originator of mathematical puzzles is always intriguing, witty, and paradoxical in this classic, one of the largest collections of mathematical amusements. More than 430 puzzles, problems, and paradoxes. Mazes and games, problems on number manipulation, unicursal and other route problems, puzzles on measuring, weighing, packing, age, kinship, chessboards, joiners', crossing river, plane figure dissection, and many others. Solutions. More than 450 illustrations. vii +. 258pp. 5⅜ x 8.   T473 Paperbound **$1.25**

THE CANTERBURY PUZZLES, Henry Dudeney. Chaucer's pilgrims set one another problems in story form. Also Adventures of the Puzzle Club, the Strange Escape of the King's Jester, the Monks of Riddlewell, the Squire's Christmas Puzzle Party, and others. All puzzles are original, based on dissecting plane figures, arithmetic, algebra, elementary calculus and other branches of mathematics, and purely logical ingenuity. "The limit of ingenuity and intricacy," The Observer. Over 110 puzzles. Full Solutions. 150 illustrations. vii + 225pp. 5⅜ x 8.
T474 Paperbound **$1.25**

MATHEMATICAL EXCURSIONS, H. A. Merrill. Even if you hardly remember your high school math, you'll enjoy the 90 stimulating problems contained in this book and you will come to understand a great many mathematical principles with surprisingly little effort. Many useful shortcuts and diversions not generally known are included: division by inspection, Russian peasant multiplication, memory systems for pi, building odd and even magic squares, square roots by geometry, dyadic systems, and many more. Solutions to difficult problems. 50 illustrations. 145pp. 5⅜ x 8.   T350 Paperbound **$1.00**

MAGIC SQUARES AND CUBES, W. S. Andrews. Only book-length treatment in English, a thorough non-technical description and analysis. Here are nasik, overlapping, pandiagonal, serrated squares; magic circles, cubes, spheres, rhombuses. Try your hand at 4-dimensional magical figures! Much unusual folklore and tradition included. High school algebra is sufficient. 754 diagrams and illustrations. viii + 419pp. 5⅜ x 8.   T658 Paperbound **$1.85**

CALIBAN'S PROBLEM BOOK: MATHEMATICAL, INFERENTIAL AND CRYPTOGRAPHIC PUZZLES, H. Phillips (Caliban), S. T. Shovelton, G. S. Marshall. 105 ingenious problems by the greatest living creator of puzzles based on logic and inference. Rigorous, modern, piquant; reflecting their author's unusual personality, these intermediate and advanced puzzles all involve the ability to reason clearly through complex situations; some call for mathematical knowledge, ranging from algebra to number theory. Solutions. xi + 180pp. 5⅜ x 8.
T736 Paperbound **$1.25**

MATHEMATICAL PUZZLES FOR BEGINNERS AND ENTHUSIASTS, G. Mott-Smith. 188 mathematical puzzles based on algebra, dissection of plane figures, permutations, and probability, that will test and improve your powers of inference and interpretation. The Odic Force, The Spider's Cousin, Ellipse Drawing, theory and strategy of card and board games like tit-tat-toe, go moku, salvo, and many others. 100 pages of detailed mathematical explanations. Appendix of primes, square roots, etc. 135 illustrations. 2nd revised edition. 248pp. 5⅜ x 8.
T198 Paperbound **$1.00**

MATHEMAGIC, MAGIC PUZZLES, AND GAMES WITH NUMBERS, R. V. Heath. More than 60 new puzzles and stunts based on the properties of numbers. Easy techniques for multiplying large numbers mentally, revealing hidden numbers magically, finding the date of any day in any year, and dozens more. Over 30 pages devoted to magic squares, triangles, cubes, circles, etc. Edited by J. S. Meyer. 76 illustrations. 128pp. 5⅜ x 8.   T110 Paperbound **$1.00**

THE BOOK OF MODERN PUZZLES, G. L. Kaufman. A completely new series of puzzles as fascinating as crossword and deduction puzzles but based upon different principles and techniques. Simple 2-minute teasers, word labyrinths, design and pattern puzzles, logic and observation puzzles — over 150 braincrackers. Answers to all problems. 116 illustrations. 192pp. 5⅜ x 8.
T143 Paperbound **$1.00**

NEW WORD PUZZLES, G. L. Kaufman. 100 ENTIRELY NEW puzzles based on words and their combinations that will delight crossword puzzle, Scrabble and Jotto fans. Chess words, based on the moves of the chess king; design-onyms, symmetrical designs made of synonyms; rhymed double-crostics; syllable sentences; addle letter anagrams; alphagrams; linkograms; and many others all brand new. Full solutions. Space to work problems. 196 figures. vi + 122pp. 5⅜ x 8.
T344 Paperbound **$1.00**

MAZES AND LABYRINTHS: A BOOK OF PUZZLES, W. Shepherd. Mazes, formerly associated with mystery and ritual, are still among the most intriguing of intellectual puzzles. This is a novel and different collection of 50 amusements that embody the principle of the maze: mazes in the classical tradition; 3-dimensional, ribbon, and Möbius-strip mazes; hidden messages; spatial arrangements; etc.—almost all built on amusing story situations. 84 illustrations. Essay on maze psychology. Solutions. xv + 122pp. 5⅜ x 8.
T731 Paperbound **$1.00**

MAGIC TRICKS & CARD TRICKS, W. Jonson. Two books bound as one. 52 tricks with cards, 37 tricks with coins, bills, eggs, smoke, ribbons, slates, etc. Details on presentation, misdirection, and routining will help you master such famous tricks as the Changing Card, Card in the Pocket, Four Aces, Coin Through the Hand, Bill in the Egg, Afghan Bands, and over 75 others. If you follow the lucid exposition and key diagrams carefully, you will finish these two books with an astonishing mastery of magic. 106 figures. 224pp. 5⅜ x 8. T909 Paperbound **$1.00**

PANORAMA OF MAGIC, Milbourne Christopher. A profusely illustrated history of stage magic, a unique selection of prints and engravings from the author's private collection of magic memorabilia, the largest of its kind. Apparatus, stage settings and costumes; ingenious ads distributed by the performers and satiric broadsides passed around in the streets ridiculing pompous showmen; programs; decorative souvenirs. The lively text, by one of America's foremost professional magicians, is full of anecdotes about almost legendary wizards: Dede, the Egyptian; Philadelphia, the wonder-worker; Robert-Houdin, "the father of modern magic;" Harry Houdini; scores more. Altogether a pleasure package for anyone interested in magic, stage setting and design, ethnology, psychology, or simply in unusual people. A Dover original. 295 illustrations; 8 in full color. Index. viii + 216pp. 8⅜ x 11¼.
T774 Paperbound **$2.25**

HOUDINI ON MAGIC, Harry Houdini. One of the greatest magicians of modern times explains his most prized secrets. How locks are picked, with illustrated picks and skeleton keys; how a girl is sawed into twins; how to walk through a brick wall — Houdini's explanations of 44 stage tricks with many diagrams. Also included is a fascinating discussion of great magicians of the past and the story of his fight against fraudulent mediums and spiritualists. Edited by W.B. Gibson and M.N. Young. Bibliography. 155 figures, photos. xv + 280pp. 5⅜ x 8.
T384 Paperbound **$1.35**

MATHEMATICS, MAGIC AND MYSTERY, Martin Gardner. Why do card tricks work? How do magicians perform astonishing mathematical feats? How is stage mind-reading possible? This is the first book length study explaining the application of probability, set theory, theory of numbers, topology, etc., to achieve many startling tricks. Non-technical, accurate, detailed! 115 sections discuss tricks with cards, dice, coins, knots, geometrical vanishing illusions, how a Curry square "demonstrates" that the sum of the parts may be greater than the whole, and dozens of others. No sleight of hand necessary! 135 illustrations. xii + 174pp. 5⅜ x 8.
T335 Paperbound **$1.00**

EASY-TO-DO ENTERTAINMENTS AND DIVERSIONS WITH COINS, CARDS, STRING, PAPER AND MATCHES, R. M. Abraham. Over 300 tricks, games and puzzles will provide young readers with absorbing fun. Sections on card games; paper-folding; tricks with coins, matches and pieces of string; games for the agile; toy-making from common household objects; mathematical recreations; and 50 miscellaneous pastimes. Anyone in charge of groups of youngsters, including hard-pressed parents, and in need of suggestions on how to keep children sensibly amused and quietly content will find this book indispensable. Clear, simple text, copious number of delightful line drawings and illustrative diagrams. Originally titled "Winter Nights Entertainments." Introduction by Lord Baden Powell. 329 illustrations. v + 186pp. 5⅜ x 8½.
T921 Paperbound **$1.00**

STRING FIGURES AND HOW TO MAKE THEM, Caroline Furness Jayne. 107 string figures plus variations selected from the best primitive and modern examples developed by Navajo, Apache, pygmies of Africa, Eskimo, in Europe, Australia, China, etc. The most readily understandable, easy-to-follow book in English on perennially popular recreation. Crystal-clear exposition; step-by-step diagrams. Everyone from kindergarten children to adults looking for unusual diversion will be endlessly amused. Index. Bibliography. Introduction by A. C. Haddon. 17 full-page plates. 960 illustrations. xxiii + 401pp. 5⅜ x 8½.
T152 Paperbound **$2.00**

Entertainments, Humor

ODDITIES AND CURIOSITIES OF WORDS AND LITERATURE, C. Bombaugh, edited by M. Gardner. The largest collection of idiosyncratic prose and poetry techniques in English, a legendary work in the curious and amusing bypaths of literary recreations and the play technique in literature—so important in modern works. Contains alphabetic poetry, acrostics, palindromes, scissors verse, centos, emblematic poetry, famous literary puns, hoaxes, notorious slips of the press, hilarious mistranslations, and much more. Revised and enlarged with modern material by Martin Gardner. 368pp. 5⅜ x 8. T759 Paperbound **$1.75**

A NONSENSE ANTHOLOGY, collected by Carolyn Wells. 245 of the best nonsense verses ever written, including nonsense puns, absurd arguments, mock epics and sagas, nonsense ballads, odes, "sick" verses, dog-Latin verses, French nonsense verses, songs. By Edward Lear, Lewis Carroll, Gelett Burgess, W. S. Gilbert, Hilaire Belloc, Peter Newell, Oliver Herford, etc., 83 writers in all plus over four score anonymous nonsense verses. A special section of limericks, plus famous nonsense such as Carroll's "Jabberwocky" and Lear's "The Jumblies" and much excellent verse virtually impossible to locate elsewhere. For 50 years considered the best anthology available. Index of first lines specially prepared for this edition. Introduction by Carolyn Wells. 3 indexes: Title, Author, First lines. xxxiii + 279pp. T499 Paperbound **$1.35**

THE BAD CHILD'S BOOK OF BEASTS, MORE BEASTS FOR WORSE CHILDREN, and A MORAL ALPHABET, H. Belloc. Hardly an anthology of humorous verse has appeared in the last 50 years without at least a couple of these famous nonsense verses. But one must see the entire volumes—with all the delightful original illustrations by Sir Basil Blackwood—to appreciate fully Belloc's charming and witty verses that play so subacidly on the platitudes of life and morals that beset his day—and ours. A great humor classic. Three books in one. Total of 157pp. 5⅜ x 8. T749 Paperbound **$1.00**

THE DEVIL'S DICTIONARY, Ambrose Bierce. Sardonic and irreverent barbs puncturing the pomposities and absurdities of American politics, business, religion, literature, and arts, by the country's greatest satirist in the classic tradition. Epigrammatic as Shaw, piercing as Swift, American as Mark Twain, Will Rogers, and Fred Allen, Bierce will always remain the favorite of a small coterie of enthusiasts, and of writers and speakers whom he supplies with "some of the most gorgeous witticisms of the English language" (H. L. Mencken). Over 1000 entries in alphabetical order. 144pp. 5⅜ x 8. T487 Paperbound **$1.00**

THE PURPLE COW AND OTHER NONSENSE, Gelett Burgess. The best of Burgess's early nonsense, selected from the first edition of the "Burgess Nonsense Book." Contains many of his most unusual and truly awe-inspiring pieces: 36 nonsense quatrains, the Poems of Patagonia, Alphabet of Famous Goops, and the other hilarious (and rare) adult nonsense that place him in the forefront of American humorists. All pieces are accompanied by the original Burgess illustrations. 123 illustrations. xiii + 113pp. 5⅜ x 8. T772 Paperbound **$1.00**

MY PIOUS FRIENDS AND DRUNKEN COMPANIONS and MORE PIOUS FRIENDS AND DRUNKEN COMPANIONS, Frank Shay. Folksingers, amateur and professional, and everyone who loves singing: here, available for the first time in 30 years, is this valued collection of 132 ballads, blues, vaudeville numbers, drinking songs, sea chanties, comedy songs. Songs of pre-Beatnik Bohemia; songs from all over America, England, France, Australia; the great songs of the Naughty Nineties and early twentieth-century America. Over a third with music. Woodcuts by John Held, Jr. convey perfectly the brash insouciance of an era of rollicking unabashed song. 12 illustrations by John Held, Jr. Two indexes (Titles and First lines and Choruses). Introductions by the author. Two volumes bound as one. Total of xvi + 235pp. 5⅜ x 8½. T946 Paperbound **$1.25**

HOW TO TELL THE BIRDS FROM THE FLOWERS, R. W. Wood. How not to confuse a carrot with a parrot, a grape with an ape, a puffin with nuffin. Delightful drawings, clever puns, absurd little poems point out far-fetched resemblances in nature. The author was a leading physicist. Introduction by Margaret Wood White. 106 illus. 60pp. 5⅜ x 8. T523 Paperbound **75¢**

PECK'S BAD BOY AND HIS PA, George W. Peck. The complete edition, containing both volumes, of one of the most widely read American humor books. The endless ingenious pranks played by bad boy "Hennery" on his pa and the grocery man, the outraged pomposity of Pa, the perpetual ridiculing of middle class institutions, are as entertaining today as they were in 1883. No pale sophistications or subtleties, but rather humor vigorous, raw, earthy, imaginative, and, as folk humor often is, sadistic. This peculiarly fascinating book is also valuable to historians and students of American culture as a portrait of an age. 100 original illustrations by True Williams. Introduction by E. F. Bleiler. 347pp. 5⅜ x 8. T497 Paperbound **$1.50**

THE HUMOROUS VERSE OF LEWIS CARROLL. Almost every poem Carroll ever wrote, the largest collection ever published, including much never published elsewhere: 150 parodies, burlesques, riddles, ballads, acrostics, etc., with 130 original illustrations by Tenniel, Carroll, and others. "Addicts will be grateful . . . there is nothing for the faithful to do but sit down and fall to the banquet," N. Y. Times. Index to first lines. xiv + 446pp. 5⅜ x 8.
T654 Paperbound **$2.00**

DIVERSIONS AND DIGRESSIONS OF LEWIS CARROLL. A major new treasure for Carroll fans! Rare privately published humor, fantasy, puzzles, and games by Carroll at his whimsical best, with a new vein of frank satire. Includes many new mathematical amusements and recreations, among them the fragmentary Part III of "Curiosa Mathematica." Contains "The Rectory Umbrella," "The New Belfry," "The Vision of the Three T's," and much more. New 32-page supplement of rare photographs taken by Carroll. x + 375pp. 5⅜ x 8.
T732 Paperbound **$2.00**

THE COMPLETE NONSENSE OF EDWARD LEAR. This is the only complete edition of this master of gentle madness available at a popular price. A BOOK OF NONSENSE, NONSENSE SONGS, MORE NONSENSE SONGS AND STORIES in their entirety with all the old favorites that have delighted children and adults for years. The Dong With A Luminous Nose, The Jumblies, The Owl and the Pussycat, and hundreds of other bits of wonderful nonsense. 214 limericks, 3 sets of Nonsense Botany, 5 Nonsense Alphabets, 546 drawings by Lear himself, and much more. 320pp. 5⅜ x 8.
T167 Paperbound **$1.00**

THE MELANCHOLY LUTE, The Humorous Verse of Franklin P. Adams ("FPA"). The author's own selection of light verse, drawn from thirty years of FPA's column, "The Conning Tower," syndicated all over the English-speaking world. Witty, perceptive, literate, these ninety-six poems range from parodies of other poets, Millay, Longfellow, Edgar Guest, Kipling, Masefield, etc., and free and hilarious translations of Horace and other Latin poets, to satiric comments on fabled American institutions—the New York Subways, preposterous ads, suburbanites, sensational journalism, etc. They reveal with vigor and clarity the humor, integrity and restraint of a wise and gentle American satirist. Introduction by Robert Hutchinson. vi + 122pp. 5⅜ x 8½.
T108 Paperbound **$1.00**

SINGULAR TRAVELS, CAMPAIGNS, AND ADVENTURES OF BARON MUNCHAUSEN, R. E. Raspe, with 90 illustrations by Gustave Doré. The first edition in over 150 years to reestablish the deeds of the Prince of Liars exactly as Raspe first recorded them in 1785—the genuine Baron Munchausen, one of the most popular personalities in English literature. Included also are the best of the many sequels, written by other hands. Introduction on Raspe by J. Carswell. Bibliography of early editions. xliv + 192pp. 5⅜ x 8.
T698 Paperbound **$1.00**

THE WIT AND HUMOR OF OSCAR WILDE, ed. by Alvin Redman. Wilde at his most brilliant, in 1000 epigrams exposing weaknesses and hypocrisies of "civilized" society. Divided into 49 categories—sin, wealth, women, America, etc.—to aid writers, speakers. Includes excerpts from his trials, books, plays, criticism. Formerly "The Epigrams of Oscar Wilde." Introduction by Vyvyan Holland, Wilde's only living son. Introductory essay by editor. 260pp. 5⅜ x 8.
T602 Paperbound **$1.00**

MAX AND MORITZ, Wilhelm Busch. Busch is one of the great humorists of all time, as well as the father of the modern comic strip. This volume, translated by H. A. Klein and other hands, contains the perennial favorite "Max and Moritz" (translated by C. T. Brooks), Plisch and Plum, Das Rabennest, Eispeter, and seven other whimsical, sardonic, jovial, diabolical cartoon and verse stories. Lively English translations parallel the original German. This work has delighted millions since it first appeared in the 19th century, and is guaranteed to please almost anyone. Edited by H. A. Klein, with an afterword. x + 205pp. 5⅝ x 8½.
T181 Paperbound **$1.15**

HYPOCRITICAL HELENA, Wilhelm Busch. A companion volume to "Max and Moritz," with the title piece (Die Fromme Helena) and 10 other highly amusing cartoon and verse stories, all newly translated by H. A. Klein and M. C. Klein: Adventure on New Year's Eve (Abenteuer in der Neujahrsnacht), Hangover on the Morning after New Year's Eve (Der Katzenjammer am Neujahrsmorgen), etc. English and German in parallel columns. Hours of pleasure, also a fine language aid. x + 205pp. 5⅝ x 8½.
T184 Paperbound **$1.00**

THE BEAR THAT WASN'T, Frank Tashlin. What does it mean? Is it simply delightful wry humor, or a charming story of a bear who wakes up in the midst of a factory, or a satire on Big Business, or an existential cartoon-story of the human condition, or a symbolization of the struggle between conformity and the individual? New York Herald Tribune said of the first edition: ". . . a fable for grownups that will be fun for children. Sit down with the book and get your own bearings." Long an underground favorite with readers of all ages and opinions. v + 51pp. Illustrated. 5⅜ x 8½.
T939 Paperbound **75¢**

RUTHLESS RHYMES FOR HEARTLESS HOMES and MORE RUTHLESS RHYMES FOR HEARTLESS HOMES, Harry Graham ("Col. D. Streamer"). Two volumes of Little Willy and 48 other poetic disasters. A bright, new reprint of oft-quoted, never forgotten, devastating humor by a precursor of today's "sick" joke school. For connoisseurs of wicked, wacky humor and all who delight in the comedy of manners. Original drawings are a perfect complement. 61 illustrations. Index. vi + 69pp. Two vols. bound as one. 5⅜ x 8½.
T930 Paperbound **75¢**

Say It language phrase books

These handy phrase books (128 to 196 pages each) make grammatical drills unnecessary for an elementary knowledge of a spoken foreign language. Covering most matters of travel and everyday life each volume contains:

Over 1000 phrases and sentences in immediately useful forms — foreign language plus English.

Modern usage designed for Americans. Specific phrases like, "Give me small change," and "Please call a taxi."

Simplified phonetic transcription you will be able to read at sight.

The only completely indexed phrase books on the market.

Covers scores of important situations: — Greetings, restaurants, sightseeing, useful expressions, etc.

These books are prepared by native linguists who are professors at Columbia, N.Y.U., Fordham and other great universities. Use them independently or with any other book or record course. They provide a supplementary living element that most other courses lack. Individual volumes in:

Russian 75¢	Italian 75¢	Spanish 75¢	German 75¢
Hebrew 75¢	Danish 75¢	Japanese 75¢	Swedish 75¢
Dutch 75¢	Esperanto 75¢	Modern Greek 75¢	Portuguese 75¢
Norwegian 75¢	Polish 75¢	French 75¢	Yiddish 75¢
Turkish 75¢		English for German-speaking people 75¢	
English for Italian-speaking people 75¢		English for Spanish-speaking people 75¢	

Large clear type. 128-196 pages each. 3½ x 5¼. Sturdy paper binding.

Listen and Learn language records

LISTEN & LEARN is the only language record course designed especially to meet your travel and everyday needs. It is available in separate sets for FRENCH, SPANISH, GERMAN, JAPANESE, RUSSIAN, MODERN GREEK, PORTUGUESE, ITALIAN and HEBREW, and each set contains three 33⅓ rpm long-playing records—1½ hours of recorded speech by eminent native speakers who are professors at Columbia, New York University, Queens College.

Check the following special features found only in LISTEN & LEARN:

- **Dual-language recording.** 812 selected phrases and sentences, over 3200 words, spoken first in English, then in their foreign language equivalents. A suitable pause follows each foreign phrase, allowing you time to repeat the expression. You learn by unconscious assimilation.
- **128 to 206-page manual** contains everything on the records, plus a simple phonetic pronunciation guide.
- **Indexed for convenience. The only set on the market** that is completely indexed. No more puzzling over where to find the phrase you need. Just look in the rear of the manual.
- **Practical.** No time wasted on material you can find in any grammar. LISTEN & LEARN covers central core material with phrase approach. Ideal for the person with limited learning time.
- **Living, modern expressions,** not found in other courses. Hygienic products, modern equipment, shopping—expressions used every day, like "nylon" and "air-conditioned."
- **Limited objective.** Everything you learn, no matter where you stop, is immediately useful. You have to finish other courses, wade through grammar and vocabulary drill, before they help you.
- **High-fidelity recording.** LISTEN & LEARN records equal in clarity and surface-silence any record on the market costing up to $6.

"Excellent . . . the spoken records . . . impress me as being among the very best on the market," **Prof. Mario Pei,** Dept. of Romance Languages, Columbia University. "Inexpensive and well-done . . . it would make an ideal present," CHICAGO SUNDAY TRIBUNE. "More genuinely helpful than anything of its kind which I have previously encountered," **Sidney Clark,** well-known author of "ALL THE BEST" travel books.

UNCONDITIONAL GUARANTEE. Try LISTEN & LEARN, then return it within 10 days for full refund if you are not satisfied.

Each set contains three twelve-inch 33⅓ records, manual, and album.

SPANISH	the set $5.95	GERMAN	the set $5.95
FRENCH	the set $5.95	ITALIAN	the set $5.95
RUSSIAN	the set $5.95	JAPANESE	the set $6.95
PORTUGUESE	the set $5.95	MODERN GREEK	the set $5.95
MODERN HEBREW	the set $5.95		

Americana

THE EYES OF DISCOVERY, J. Bakeless. A vivid reconstruction of how unspoiled America appeared to the first white men. Authentic and enlightening accounts of Hudson's landing in New York, Coronado's trek through the Southwest; scores of explorers, settlers, trappers, soldiers. America's pristine flora, fauna, and Indians in every region and state in fresh and unusual new aspects. "A fascinating view of what the land was like before the first highway went through," Time. 68 contemporary illustrations, 39 newly added in this edition. Index. Bibliography. x + 500pp. 5⅜ x 8.   T761 Paperbound **$2.25**

AUDUBON AND HIS JOURNALS, J. J. Audubon. A collection of fascinating accounts of Europe and America in the early 1800's through Audubon's own eyes. Includes the Missouri River Journals —an eventful trip through America's untouched heartland, the Labrador Journals, the European Journals, the famous "Episodes", and other rare Audubon material, including the descriptive chapters from the original letterpress edition of the "Ornithological Studies", omitted in all later editions. Indispensable for ornithologists, naturalists, and all lovers of Americana and adventure. 70-page biography by Audubon's granddaughter. 38 illustrations. Index. Total of 1106pp. 5⅜ x 8.
T675 Vol I Paperbound **$2.25**
T676 Vol II Paperbound **$2.25**
The set **$4.50**

TRAVELS OF WILLIAM BARTRAM, edited by Mark Van Doren. The first inexpensive illustrated edition of one of the 18th century's most delightful books is an excellent source of first-hand material on American geography, anthropology, and natural history. Many descriptions of early Indian tribes are our only source of information on them prior to the infiltration of the white man. "The mind of a scientist with the soul of a poet," John Livingston Lowes. 13 original illustrations and maps. Edited with an introduction by Mark Van Doren. 448pp. 5⅜ x 8.
T13 Paperbound **$2.00**

GARRETS AND PRETENDERS: A HISTORY OF BOHEMIANISM IN AMERICA, A. Parry. The colorful and fantastic history of American Bohemianism from Poe to Kerouac. This is the only complete record of hoboes, cranks, starving poets, and suicides. Here are Pfaff, Whitman, Crane, Bierce, Pound, and many others. New chapters by the author and by H. T. Moore bring this thorough and well-documented history down to the Beatniks. "An excellent account," N. Y. Times. Scores of cartoons, drawings, and caricatures. Bibliography. Index. xxviii + 421pp. 5⅝ x 8⅜.   T708 Paperbound **$1.95**

THE EXPLORATION OF THE COLORADO RIVER AND ITS CANYONS, J. W. Powell. The thrilling first-hand account of the expedition that filled in the last white space on the map of the United States. Rapids, famine, hostile Indians, and mutiny are among the perils encountered as the unknown Colorado Valley reveals its secrets. This is the only uncut version of Major Powell's classic of exploration that has been printed in the last 60 years. Includes later reflections and subsequent expedition. 250 illustrations, new map. 400pp. 5⅝ x 8⅜.
T94 Paperbound **$2.25**

THE JOURNAL OF HENRY D. THOREAU, Edited by Bradford Torrey and Francis H. Allen. Henry Thoreau is not only one of the most important figures in American literature and social thought; his voluminous journals (from which his books emerged as selections and crystallizations) constitute both the longest, most sensitive record of personal internal development and a most penetrating description of a historical moment in American culture. This present set, which was first issued in fourteen volumes, contains Thoreau's entire journals from 1837 to 1862, with the exception of the lost years which were found only recently. We are reissuing it, complete and unabridged, with a new introduction by Walter Harding, Secretary of the Thoreau Society. Fourteen volumes reissued in two volumes. Foreword by Henry Seidel Canby. Total of 1888pp. 8⅜ x 12¼.   T312-3 Two volume set, Clothbound **$20.00**

GAMES AND SONGS OF AMERICAN CHILDREN, collected by William Wells Newell. A remarkable collection of 190 games with songs that accompany many of them; cross references to show similarities, differences among them; variations; musical notation for 38 songs. Textual discussions show relations with folk-drama and other aspects of folk tradition. Grouped into categories for ready comparative study: Love-games, histories, playing at work, human life, bird and beast, mythology, guessing-games, etc. New introduction covers relations of songs and dances to timeless heritage of folklore, biographical sketch of Newell, other pertinent data. A good source of inspiration for those in charge of groups of children and a valuable reference for anthropologists, sociologists, psychiatrists. Introduction by Carl Withers. New indexes of first lines, games. 5⅜ x 8½. xii + 242pp.   T354 Paperbound **$1.75**

Art, History of Art, Antiques, Graphic Arts, Handcrafts

ART STUDENTS' ANATOMY, E. J. Farris. Outstanding art anatomy that uses chiefly living objects for its illustrations. 71 photos of undraped men, women, children are accompanied by carefully labeled matching sketches to illustrate the skeletal system, articulations and movements, bony landmarks, the muscular system, skin, fasciae, fat, etc. 9 x-ray photos show movement of joints. Undraped models are shown in such actions as serving in tennis, drawing a bow in archery, playing football, dancing, preparing to spring and to dive. Also discussed and illustrated are proportions, age and sex differences, the anatomy of the smile, etc. 8 plates by the great early 18th century anatomic illustrator Siegfried Albinus are also included. Glossary. 158 figures, 7 in color. x + 159pp. 5⅝ x 8⅜.　　　　　T744 Paperbound **$1.50**

AN ATLAS OF ANATOMY FOR ARTISTS, F Schider. A new 3rd edition of this standard text enlarged by 52 new illustrations of hands, anatomical studies by Cloquet, and expressive life studies of the body by Barcsay. 189 clear, detailed plates offer you precise information of impeccable accuracy. 29 plates show all aspects of the skeleton, with closeups of special areas, while 54 full-page plates, mostly in two colors, give human musculature as seen from four different points of view, with cutaways for important portions of the body. 14 full-page plates provide photographs of hand forms, eyelids, female breasts, and indicate the location of muscles upon models. 59 additional plates show how great artists of the past utilized human anatomy. They reproduce sketches and finished work by such artists as Michelangelo, Leonardo da Vinci, Goya, and 15 others. This is a lifetime reference work which will be one of the most important books in any artist's library. "The standard reference tool," AMERICAN LIBRARY ASSOCIATION. "Excellent," AMERICAN ARTIST. Third enlarged edition. 189 plates, 647 illustrations. xxvi + 192pp. 7⅞ x 10⅝.　　　T241 Clothbound **$6.00**

AN ATLAS OF ANIMAL ANATOMY FOR ARTISTS, W. Ellenberger, H. Baum, H. Dittrich. The largest, richest animal anatomy for artists available in English. 99 detailed anatomical plates of such animals as the horse, dog, cat, lion, deer, seal, kangaroo, flying squirrel, cow, bull, goat, monkey, hare, and bat. Surface features are clearly indicated, while progressive beneath-the-skin pictures show musculature, tendons, and bone structure. Rest and action are exhibited in terms of musculature and skeletal structure and detailed cross-sections are given for heads and important features. The animals chosen are representative of specific families so that a study of these anatomies will provide knowledge of hundreds of related species. "Highly recommended as one of the very few books on the subject worthy of being used as an authoritative guide," DESIGN. "Gives a fundamental knowledge," AMERICAN ARTIST. Second revised, enlarged edition with new plates from Cuvier, Stubbs, etc. 288 illustrations. 153pp. 11⅜ x 9.　　　　　　　　　　　　　　T82 Clothbound **$6.00**

THE HUMAN FIGURE IN MOTION, Eadweard Muybridge. The largest selection in print of Muybridge's famous high-speed action photos of the human figure in motion. 4789 photographs illustrate 162 different actions: men, women, children—mostly undraped—are shown walking, running, carrying various objects, sitting, lying down, climbing, throwing, arising, and performing over 150 other actions. Some actions are shown in as many as 150 photographs each. All in all there are more than 500 action strips in this enormous volume, series shots taken at shutter speeds of as high as 1/6000th of a second! These are not posed shots, but true stopped motion. They show bone and muscle in situations that the human eye is not fast enough to capture. Earlier, smaller editions of these prints have brought $40 and more on the out-of-print market. "A must for artists," ART IN FOCUS. "An unparalleled dictionary of action for all artists," AMERICAN ARTIST. 390 full-page plates, with 4789 photographs. Printed on heavy glossy stock. Reinforced binding with headbands. xxi + 390pp. 7⅞ x 10⅝.　　　　　　　　　　　　　　　　　　　　　　　　T204 Clothbound **$10.00**

ANIMALS IN MOTION, Eadweard Muybridge. This is the largest collection of animal action photos in print. 34 different animals (horses, mules, oxen, goats, camels, pigs, cats, guanacos, lions, gnus, deer, monkeys, eagles—and 21 others) in 132 characteristic actions. The horse alone is shown in more than 40 different actions. All 3919 photographs are taken in series at speeds up to 1/6000th of a second. The secrets of leg motion, spinal patterns, head movements, strains and contortions shown nowhere else are captured. You will see exactly how a lion sets his foot down; how an elephant's knees are like a human's—and how they differ; the position of a kangaroo's legs in mid-leap; how an ostrich's head bobs; details of the flight of birds—and thousands of facets of motion only the fastest cameras can catch. Photographed from domestic animals and animals in the Philadelphia zoo, it contains neither semiposed artificial shots nor distorted telephoto shots taken under adverse conditions. Artists, biologists, decorators, cartoonists, will find this book indispensable for understanding animals in motion. "A really marvelous series of plates," NATURE (London). "The dry plate's most spectacular early use was by Eadweard Muybridge," LIFE. 3919 photographs; 380 full pages of plates. 440pp. Printed on heavy glossy paper. Deluxe binding with headbands. 7⅞ x 10⅝.　　　　　　　　　　　　　　　　　　　　　　T203 Clothbound **$10.00**

THE AUTOBIOGRAPHY OF AN IDEA, Louis Sullivan. The pioneer architect whom Frank Lloyd Wright called "the master" reveals an acute sensitivity to social forces and values in this passionately honest account. He records the crystallization of his opinions and theories, the growth of his organic theory of architecture that still influences American designers and architects, contemporary ideas, etc. This volume contains the first appearance of 34 full-page plates of his finest architecture. Unabridged reissue of 1924 edition. New introduction by R. M. Line. Index. xiv + 335pp. 5⅜ x 8. **T281 Paperbound $2.00**

THE DRAWINGS OF HEINRICH KLEY. The first uncut republication of both of Kley's devastating sketchbooks, which first appeared in pre-World War I Germany. One of the greatest cartoonists and social satirists of modern times, his exuberant and iconoclastic fantasy and his extraordinary technique place him in the great tradition of Bosch, Breughel, and Goya, while his subject matter has all the immediacy and tension of our century. 200 drawings. viii + 128pp. 7¾ x 10¾. **T24 Paperbound $1.85**

MORE DRAWINGS BY HEINRICH KLEY. All the sketches from Leut' Und Viecher (1912) and Sammel-Album (1923) not included in the previous Dover edition of Drawings. More of the bizarre, mercilessly iconoclastic sketches that shocked and amused on their original publication. Nothing was too sacred, no one too eminent for satirization by this imaginative, individual and accomplished master cartoonist. A total of 158 illustrations. Iv + 104pp. 7¾ x 10¾. **T41 Paperbound $1.85**

PINE FURNITURE OF EARLY NEW ENGLAND, R. H. Kettell. A rich understanding of one of America's most original folk arts that collectors of antiques, interior decorators, craftsmen, woodworkers, and everyone interested in American history and art will find fascinating and immensely useful. 413 illustrations of more than 300 chairs, benches, racks, beds, cupboards, mirrors, shelves, tables, and other furniture will show all the simple beauty and character of early New England furniture. 55 detailed drawings carefully analyze outstanding pieces. "With its rich store of illustrations, this book emphasizes the individuality and varied design of early American pine furniture. It should be welcomed," ANTIQUES. 413 illustrations and 55 working drawings. 475. 8 x 10¾. **T145 Clothbound $10.00**

THE HUMAN FIGURE, J. H. Vanderpoel. Every important artistic element of the human figure is pointed out in minutely detailed word descriptions in this classic text and illustrated as well in 430 pencil and charcoal drawings. Thus the text of this book directs your attention to all the characteristic features and subtle differences of the male and female (adults, children, and aged persons), as though a master artist were telling you what to look for at each stage. 2nd edition, revised and enlarged by George Bridgman. Foreword. 430 illustrations. 143pp. 6⅛ x 9¼. **T432 Paperbound $1.50**

LETTERING AND ALPHABETS, J. A. Cavanagh. This unabridged reissue of LETTERING offers a full discussion, analysis, illustration of 89 basic hand le..ering styles — styles derived from Caslons, Bodonis, Garamonds, Gothic, Black Letter, Oriental, and many others. Upper and lower cases, numerals and common signs pictured. Hundreds of technical hints on make-up, construction, artistic validity, strokes, pens, brushes, white areas, etc. May be reproduced without permission! 89 complete alphabets; 72 lettered specimens. 121pp. 9⅜ x 8. **T53 Paperbound $1.35**

STICKS AND STONES, Lewis Mumford. A survey of the forces that have conditioned American architecture and altered its forms. The author discusses the medieval tradition in early New England villages; the Renaissance influence which developed with the rise of the merchant class; the classical influence of Jefferson's time; the "Mechanicsvilles" of Poe's generation; the Brown Decades; the philosophy of the Imperial facade; and finally the modern machine age. "A truly remarkable book," SAT. REV. OF LITERATURE. 2nd revised edition. 21 illustrations. xvii + 228pp. 5⅜ x 8. **T202 Paperbound $1.75**

THE STANDARD BOOK OF QUILT MAKING AND COLLECTING, Marguerite Ickis. A complete easy-to-follow guide with all the information you need to make beautiful, useful quilts. How to plan, design, cut, sew, appliqué, avoid sewing problems, use rag bag, make borders, tuft, every other aspect. Over 100 traditional quilts shown, including over 40 full-size patterns. At-home hobby for fun, profit. Index. 483 illus. 1 color plate. 287pp. 6¾ x 9½. **T582 Paperbound $2.00**

THE BOOK OF SIGNS, Rudolf Koch. Formerly $20 to $25 on the out-of-print market, now only $1.00 in this unabridged new edition! 493 symbols from ancient manuscripts, medieval cathedrals, coins, catacombs, pottery, etc. Crosses, monograms of Roman emperors, astrological, chemical, botanical, runes, housemarks, and 7 other categories. Invaluable for handicraft workers, illustrators, scholars, etc., this material may be reproduced without permission. 493 illustrations by Fritz Kredel. 104pp. 6½ x 9¼. **T162 Paperbound $1.00**

PRIMITIVE ART, Franz Boas. This authoritative and exhaustive work by a great American anthropologist covers the entire gamut of primitive art. Pottery, leatherwork, metal work, stone work, wood, basketry, are treated in detail. Theories of primitive art, historical depth in art history, technical virtuosity, unconscious levels of patterning, symbolism, styles, literature, music, dance, etc. A must book for the interested layman, the anthropologist, artist, handicrafter (hundreds of unusual motifs), and the historian. Over 900 illustrations (50 ceramic vessels, 12 totem poles, etc.). 376pp. 5⅜ x 8. **T25 Paperbound $2.25**

Fiction

FLATLAND, E. A. Abbott. A science-fiction classic of life in a 2-dimensional world that is also a first-rate introduction to such aspects of modern science as relativity and hyperspace. Political, moral, satirical, and humorous overtones have made FLATLAND fascinating reading for thousands. 7th edition. New introduction by Banesh Hoffmann. 16 illustrations. 128pp. 5⅜ x 8. T1 Paperbound **$1.00**

THE WONDERFUL WIZARD OF OZ, L. F. Baum. Only edition in print with all the original W. W. Denslow illustrations in full color—as much a part of "The Wizard" as Tenniel's drawings are of "Alice in Wonderland." "The Wizard" is still America's best-loved fairy tale, in which, as the author expresses it, "The wonderment and joy are retained and the heartaches and nightmares left out." Now today's young readers can enjoy every word and wonderful picture of the original book. New introduction by Martin Gardner. A Baum bibliography. 23 full-page color plates. viii + 268pp. 5⅜ x 8. T691 Paperbound **$1.50**

THE MARVELOUS LAND OF OZ, L. F. Baum. This is the equally enchanting sequel to the "Wizard," continuing the adventures of the Scarecrow and the Tin Woodman. The hero this time is a little boy named Tip, and all the delightful Oz magic is still present. This is the Oz book with the Animated Saw-Horse, the Woggle-Bug, and Jack Pumpkinhead. All the original John R. Neill illustrations, 10 in full color. 287 pp. 5⅜ x 8. T692 Paperbound **$1.50**

28 SCIENCE FICTION STORIES OF H. G. WELLS. Two full unabridged novels, MEN LIKE GODS and STAR BEGOTTEN, plus 26 short stories by the master science-fiction writer of all time! Stories of space, time, invention, exploration, future adventure—an indispensable part of the library of everyone interested in science and adventure. PARTIAL CONTENTS: Men Like Gods, The Country of the Blind, In the Abyss, The Crystal Egg, The Man Who Could Work Miracles, A Story of the Days to Come, The Valley of Spiders, and 21 more! 928pp. 5⅜ x 8. T265 Clothbound **$4.50**

THREE MARTIAN NOVELS, Edgar Rice Burroughs. Contains: Thuvia, Maid of Mars; The Chessmen of Mars; and The Master Mind of Mars. High adventure set in an imaginative and intricate conception of the Red Planet. Mars is peopled with an intelligent, heroic human race which lives in densely populated cities and with fierce barbarians who inhabit dead sea bottoms. Other exciting creatures abound amidst an inventive framework of Martian history and geography. Complete unabridged reprintings of the first edition. 16 illustrations by J. Allen St. John. vi + 499pp. 5⅜ x 8½. T39 Paperbound **$1.85**

SEVEN SCIENCE FICTION NOVELS, H. G. Wells. Full unabridged texts of 7 science-fiction novels of the master. Ranging from biology, physics, chemistry, astronomy to sociology and other studies, Mr. Wells extrapolates whole worlds of strange and intriguing character. "One will have to go far to match this for entertainment, excitement, and sheer pleasure . . . ," NEW YORK TIMES. Contents: The Time Machine, The Island of Dr. Moreau, First Men in the Moon, The Invisible Man, The War of the Worlds, The Food of the Gods, In the Days of the Comet. 1015pp. 5⅜ x 8. T264 Clothbound **$4.50**

THE LAND THAT TIME FORGOT and THE MOON MAID, Edgar Rice Burroughs. In the opinion of many, Burroughs' best work. The first concerns a strange island where evolution is individual rather than phylogenetic. Speechless anthropoids develop into intelligent human beings within a single generation. The second projects the reader far into the future and describes the first voyage to the Moon (in the year 2025), the conquest of the Earth by the Moon, and years of violence and adventure as the enslaved Earthmen try to regain possession of their planet. "An imaginative tour de force that keeps the reader keyed up and expectant," NEW YORK TIMES. Complete, unabridged text of the original two novels (three parts in each). 5 illustrations by J. Allen St. John. vi + 552pp. 5⅜ x 8½. T1020 Clothbound **$3.75** / T358 Paperbound **$2.00**

3 ADVENTURE NOVELS by H. Rider Haggard. Complete texts of "She," "King Solomon's Mines," "Allan Quatermain." Qualities of discovery; desire for immortality; search for primitive, for what is unadorned by civilization, have kept these novels of African adventure exciting, alive to readers from R. L. Stevenson to George Orwell. 636pp. 5⅜ x 8. T584 Paperbound **$2.00**

A PRINCESS OF MARS and A FIGHTING MAN OF MARS: TWO MARTIAN NOVELS BY EDGAR RICE BURROUGHS. "Princess of Mars" is the very first of the great Martian novels written by Burroughs, and it is probably the best of them all; it set the pattern for all of his later fantasy novels and contains a thrilling cast of strange peoples and creatures and the formula of Olympian heroism amidst ever-fluctuating fortunes which Burroughs carries off so successfully. "Fighting Man" returns to the same scenes and cities—many years later. A mad scientist, a degenerate dictator, and an indomitable defender of the right clash—with the fate of the Red Planet at stake! Complete, unabridged reprinting of original editions. Illustrations by F. E. Schoonover and Hugh Hutton. v + 356pp. 5⅜ x 8½. T1140 Paperbound **$1.75**

Music

A GENERAL HISTORY OF MUSIC, Charles Burney. A detailed coverage of music from the Greeks up to 1789, with full information on all types of music: sacred and secular, vocal and instrumental, operatic and symphonic. Theory, notation, forms, instruments, innovators, composers, performers, typical and important works, and much more in an easy, entertaining style. Burney covered much of Europe and spoke with hundreds of authorities and composers so that this work is more than a compilation of records . . . it is a living work of careful and first-hand scholarship. Its account of thoroughbass (18th century) Italian music is probably still the best introduction on the subject. A recent NEW YORK TIMES review said, "Surprisingly few of Burney's statements have been invalidated by modern research . . . still of great value." Edited and corrected by Frank Mercer. 35 figures. Indices. 1915pp. 5⅜ x 8. 2 volumes.   T36 The Set, Clothbound **$12.50**

A DICTIONARY OF HYMNOLOGY, John Julian. This exhaustive and scholarly work has become known as an invaluable source of hundreds of thousands of important and often difficult to obtain facts on the history and use of hymns in the western world. Everyone interested in hymns will be fascinated by the accounts of famous hymns and hymn writers and amazed by the amount of practical information he will find. More than 30,000 entries on individual hymns, giving authorship, date and circumstances of composition, publication, textual variations, translations, denominational and ritual usage, etc. Biographies of more than 9,000 hymn writers, and essays on important topics such as Christmas carols and children's hymns, and much other unusual and valuable information. A 200 page double-columned index of first lines — the largest in print. Total of 1786 pages in two reinforced clothbound volumes. 6¼ x 9¼.
The set, T333 Clothbound **$17.50**

MUSIC IN MEDIEVAL BRITAIN, F. Ll. Harrison. The most thorough, up-to-date, and accurate treatment of the subject ever published, beautifully illustrated. Complete account of institutions and choirs; carols, masses, and motets; liturgy and plainsong; and polyphonic music from the Norman Conquest to the Reformation. Discusses the various schools of music and their reciprocal influences; the origin and development of new ritual forms; development and use of instruments; and new evidence on many problems of the period. Reproductions of scores, over 200 excerpts from medieval melodies. Rules of harmony and dissonance; influence of Continental styles; great composers (Dunstable, Cornysh, Fairfax, etc.); and much more. Register and index of more than 400 musicians. Index of titles. General Index. 225-item bibliography. 6 Appendices. xix + 491pp. 5⅝ x 8¾.   T705 Clothbound **$10.00**

THE MUSIC OF SPAIN, Gilbert Chase. Only book in English to give concise, comprehensive account of Iberian music; new Chapter covers music since 1941. Victoria, Albéniz, Cabezón, Pedrell, Turina, hundreds of other composers; popular and folk music; the Gypsies; the guitar; dance, theatre, opera, with only extensive discussion in English of the Zarzuela; virtuosi such as Casals; much more. "Distinguished . . . readable," Saturday Review. 400-item bibliography. Index. 27 photos. 383pp. 5⅜ x 8.   T549 Paperbound **$2.25**

ON STUDYING SINGING, Sergius Kagen. An intelligent method of voice-training, which leads you around pitfalls that waste your time, money, and effort. Exposes rigid, mechanical systems, baseless theories, deleterious exercises. "Logical, clear, convincing . . . dead right," Virgil Thomson, N.Y. Herald Tribune. "I recommend this volume highly," Maggie Teyte, Saturday Review. 119pp. 5⅜ x 8.   T622 Paperbound **$1.35**

Prices subject to change without notice.

Dover publishes books on art, music, philosophy, literature, languages, history, social sciences, psychology, handcrafts, orientalia, puzzles and entertainments, chess, pets and gardens, books explaining science, intermediate and higher mathematics, mathematical physics, engineering, biological sciences, earth sciences, classics of science, etc. Write to:

> *Dept. catrr.*
> *Dover Publications, Inc.*
> *180 Varick Street, N.Y. 14, N.Y.*